D1726454

In and Out of the City

Contexts of Ancient and Medieval Anthropology

Editors

Anna Usacheva, Jörg Ulrich, Siam Bhayro

Advisory Board

Vol. 4

Mattia C. Chiriatti, Carmen Trillo San José (Eds.)

In and Out of the City

Female Environments, Relations and Dynamics of Space (400–1500)

BRILL | SCHÖNINGH

Cover image: Giovanni Boccaccio, illuminated manuscript (BL Royal 20 C V, f. 5). First image: a messenger presenting a letter to Semiramis. Second image: a queen with four female musicians. Source: europeana.eu

This book has been published with the kind support of the research project "El área periurbana de una ciudad islámica: Granada (XIV–XVI)[(P18.RT.3588)]", funded by the Ministry of Economy, Knowledge, Business, and University (Junta de Andalucía, PAIDI 2020–2023) and FEDER funds, within the framework of the R&D call (Retos de la sociedad).

Bibliographic information published by the Deutsche Nationalbibliothek

The Deutsche Nationalbibliothek lists this publication in the Deutsche Nationalbibliografie; detailed bibliographic data available online: http://dnb.d-nb.de

© 2024 by Brill Schöningh, Wollmarktstraße 115, 33098 Paderborn, Germany, an imprint of the Brill-Group (Koninklijke Brill NV, Leiden, The Netherlands; Brill USA Inc., Boston MA, USA; Brill Asia Pte Ltd, Singapore; Brill Deutschland GmbH, Paderborn, Germany; Brill Österreich GmbH, Vienna, Austria) Koninklijke Brill NV incorporates the imprints Brill, Brill Nijhoff, Brill Hotei, Brill Schöningh, Brill Fink, Brill mentis, Brill Wageningen Academic, Vandenhoeck & Ruprecht, Böhlau and V&R unipress.

www.brill.com

Cover design: Evelyn Ziegler, Munich
Production: Brill Deutschland GmbH, Paderborn

ISSN 2698-3079
ISBN 978-3-506-79147-4 (hardback)
ISBN 978-3-657-79147-7 (e-book)

†Edu (1977–2023)

Id agamus ut iucunda nobis amissorum fiat recordatio. Nemo libenter ad id redit quod non sine tormento cogitaturus est, sicut illud fieri necesse est, ut cum aliquo nobis morsu amissorum quos amavimus nomen occurrat; sed hic quoque morsus habet suam voluptatem.

(Sen., *Ep.* 63.4–5)

Table of Contents

PART IV
Islam in the West

Introduction

Mattia C. Chiriatti, Carmen Trillo San José

The work that the reader holds in their hands concludes a series of projects that its editors, Mattia C. Chiriatti and Carmen Trillo San José, have dedicated to the female figure, her role, and her prominence in historical developments, particularly within urban and peri-urban contexts.[1]

Indeed, the choice of the spatial criterion that connects the studies collected herein is derived from research on women throughout various historical periods, carried out by the various researchers and authors who have participated in the project *El área periurbana de una ciudad islámica: la Vega de Granada (siglos XIV–XVI)* (P18.RT.3588), funded by the Ministry of Economy, Knowledge, Business, and University (Junta de Andalucía, PAIDI 2020–2023) and FEDER funds, within the framework of the R&D call (*Retos de la sociedad*).

It was not in vain as, when putting together this edition we believed that examining the theme of women's evolution during these crucial centuries – based on the call's outlined premises – represented a social, university and scientific challenge that could not be ignored. This is why we held the international conference titled *The City and Its Environment: Queenship, Power, and Dynamics of Space* in November 2022 at the University of Granada. The initiative, funded by various entities, including the Ministry of Science and Innovation, the Ministry of Economy, Knowledge, Business, and University of the Junta de Andalucía, University of Granada, and the *Historia: de Europa a*

---

1 M.C. Chiriatti, *Female Power and its Propaganda*, in: M. Vinzent / M.C. Chiriatti / D. Olkinuora (eds.), *Studia Patristica. Vol. CXXX – Papers presented at the Eighteenth International Conference on Patristic Studies held in Oxford 2019, volume 27: From the Fifth Century Onwards (Latin Writers); Female Power and its Propaganda; Theologizing Performance in the Byzantine Tradition; Nachleben*, Leuven / Paris / Bristol (CT) 2021; M.C. Chiriatti / R. Villegas Marín (eds.), *Mujeres imperiales, mujeres reales. Representaciones públicas y representaciones del poder en la Antigüedad tardía y Bizancio*, Paderborn 2021; C. Trillo, *El patrimonio de las reinas moras: Datos para su estudio*, in: *Estudios sobre patrimonio, cultura y ciencia medievales*, 24 (2022), 491–520; Ead., *Fátima, hija del alcaide Avengarrón: sus propiedades en Cubillas y Granada, según documentos árabes romanceados inéditos (1465–1466)*, in: *Espacio, Tiempo y Forma* 3/35 (2022), 651–678; M.C. Chiriatti / M. Vallejo Girvés (eds.), *Riflessi di porpora. Declinazioni di potere femminile tra Roma, Bisanzio e l'Occidente Medievale*, Spoleto 2023; C. Trillo, *The Naṣrid princesses, sisters of King Sa'd: their economic influence and function in the dynasty's power network according to translated Arabic documents (1460 and 1469)*, in: M.C. Chiriatti / M. Vallejo Girvés (eds.), *Riflessi di porpora. Declinazioni di potere femminile tra Roma, Bisanzio e l'Occidente Medievale*, Spoleto 2023, 397–415.

América. Sociedades, Poderes, Culturas EURAME Master's programme, is the genesis of this work, where contributions from authors who took part in the aforementioned workshop gathered together. Similarly, in a broader chronological and thematic scope, we conducted the training workshop *Mujeres en la Historia* in March 2022 as a programme for the Doctoral School at the University of Granada, under its History and Arts programme.

Our intention when planning this book was to build upon those research endeavours by offering a more comprehensive perspective on the female role in the governance of urban and peri-urban areas during Late Antiquity and the Middle Ages. Our main objective, from assembling the volume to selecting the themes presented in it, has been to move away from widely discussed topics concerning the segregation of sexes, such as female invisibility, their limited prominence in the public sphere, and their lack of social leadership roles. Therefore, we embarked on an exploration for new aspects that aim to present a more authentic portrayal of women across a diverse historical spectrum and in various settings, including courts, monastic communities, and civil contexts, encompassing different social classes and cultural environments. While bearing in mind that this is a challenging issue, precisely due to their historical marginalisation it has been subjected to, and often driven by social, ideological, political, and economic considerations. Drawing from recent research in this field, we thus aimed to explore the activities undertaken by these women; their domestic and public spaces both within and outside urban areas; the contexts of their political, social, and economic engagement; what image they projected in society through iconography and public representations, and their potential for social mobility, autonomy, and leadership.

Within this overarching framework, as mentioned earlier, our focus has been specifically on the topic of female figures within urban and peri-urban settings. This choice arises from the complexity of urban and peri-urban areas, which significantly differ from the generally more traditional and static rural environment. In both urban and suburban settings, the new ideas that accompany economic, cultural, religious, and social exchanges are projected more easily.

Because this occurs within a wide spatial and chronological framework, the study's chapters encompass as historically and culturally diverse areas as Western Europe, Byzantium, and the Mediterranean, and thematically cover the Islamic and Christian spheres. The chronological limits established in the volume are also extensive, fitting for a diachronic overview of society and women from Late Antiquity to the conclusion of the Middle Ages, spanning from 400 to 1500.

The contributions encompass many of these facets, addressing a wide array of issues and sectors, in which the female prominence in both urban and rural spheres becomes evident. Religious aspects related to women in this initial period are explored by Marta Sancho and Jordina Sales (University of Barcelona) in *Seclusion Spaces During the First Centuries of Female Asceticism*, and by Clelia Martínez (University of Málaga) in *Networking, Power and Gender in Anglo-Saxon Religious Life: Abbess Æthelthryth of Ely in Bede's Work*. In the first contribution, the analysed forms of asceticism range from isolated to collective practices, united by seclusion as a type of spirituality, and it examines various strategies to evade male authority. The second contribution discusses the role of women from royal families as abbesses and how the expansion of monasticism also served as a power strategy. The Early Middle Ages section concludes with Pablo Poveda's study (University of Valladolid), focusing on *Luchas de Poder en la Galia Merovingia: Oposición y Confrontación entre Reinas y Obispos*, where the author presents the challenges in the relationships between Merovingian queens and bishops during a period of consolidating royal and ecclesiastical authority.

The portrayal of women in the Byzantine context, both within and beyond the court, particularly within and outside Constantinople, is exemplified by emblematic yet lesser-known imperial female figures such as Augustas Verina and Ariadne (explored by Elena Tinas and Mattia C. Chiriatti, University of Granada) and Empress Theodora II, also known as Theodora the Armenian (analysed by Álvaro Ibañez, University of Granada). In the first study, *Dentro y Fuera de Constantinopla: Elia Verina y Elia Ariadna en la Corte Leónida (457–518)*, which reconstructs the life stories of Verina and her daughter Ariadne in a tumultuous historical setting characterised by power struggles, usurpations and ecclesiastical conflicts, it becomes evident that both empresses succeeded in asserting their authority within the Leonid court, discernible in their public expressions and depictions in art. The second study, *L'Elezione del Patriarca Ignazio (847): l'Imperatrice Teodora II nella Politica Ecclesiastica Bizantina* explores the influence that Empress Theodora II might have had in the selection of Ignatius as the Patriarch of Constantinople. These studies contemplate this comprehensive analysis of female imperial agency in Byzantium in matters related to both the courtly and, by extension, political and ecclesiastical spheres.

Shifting to the Western context, focusing on the Late Middle Ages, Sylvie Duval (University of Bologna) discusses the history of a female abbey established in Lyon during the sixth century. The study traces her history, marked by periods of prosperity and crisis, until the 16th century, in *Les Très Puissantes*

Dames de Saint-Pierre. Premiers Jalons pour Une Histoire de l'Abbaye Saint-Pierre de Lyon (VIᵉ–XVIᵉ s.). The article by Diana Pelaz (University of Santiago de Compostela): *The King Away from Court, the Queen in His Place. Castile, 12th–15th Centuries*, details the functions that the queen consorts exercised at different times in the history of the Kingdom of Castile. It was an institutional role but also a personal one, and were roles that influential groups in society acknowledged. Within the 13th-century Kingdoms of Castile and Aragon, Antonella Liuzzo (University of Lincoln) examines the impact of women on a network of political, diplomatic, cultural, and social relations in *Women, Trust and The Politics of Space in Thirteenth-Century Iberia*.

Continuing in the Late Middle Ages, in the border of the Kingdom of Murcia adjoining the Nasrid emirate, María Martínez (University of Murcia) delves into the case of an elite woman acting in this political domain. *María de Quesada's Leadership during the Castilian Crisis and the Different Factions of the Fajardo Clan (Kingdom of Murcia, mid-15th Century)*, shows us a woman who led the defence of an advanced position, representing the king in the Kingdom of Murcia, on behalf of her minor son, Pedro Fajardo. Indeed, she effectively commanded a faction in the war between the Fajardo clan, which was aligned with the political crisis in Castile between John II and his court favourite, against Aragonese infantry, and the conflicts with the Nasrid emirate.

Lastly, Islam, particularly the end of al-Andalus during the Nasrid emirate in the 13th to 15th centuries, is covered by two contributions. Mercedes Delgado (University of Seville) analyses the political influence of women in the Alhambra in *El poder en la sombra. Las sultanas y el harén en la corte nazarí de Granada (siglos XIII–XV)*, through three contemporary chronicles. To conclude, Carmen Trillo San José (University of Granada) closes the volume with *Naṣrid women inside and outside Madīna Garnāṭa: wealth and influence*, a study on Nasrid women at the end of the 15th century. In it she explores their roles within the court and upper social classes, establishing a connection between their power and autonomy with the ownership and management of economic assets, particularly real estate, as well as with certain social strategies in marriage.

To end this brief presentation of the work, a heartfelt thank you, on behalf of the authors and editors, is owed to Professor Jörg Ulrich of the *Martin-Luther-Universität Halle-Wittenberg* and to the editors of the CAMA (Contexts of Ancient and Medieval Anthropology) collection (Anna Usacheva, Jörg Ulrich, Siam Bhayro) for their interest in this volume and their generous support. Likewise, we would like to acknowledge the assistance provided by students of the University of Halle (Kai Klemm-Lorenz, Janna Rieke Lüttmann and Hannah Felicitas Simmat) for their collaboration in streamlining the editorial task. Last but not least, many thanks to Daniel Montiel (PhD student, University of Granada), to Martina Kayser and the entire Brill-Schöningh team for their invaluable assistance.

Granada, 11 September 2023

PART I

Byzantium

Dentro y Fuera de Constantinopla

Elia Verina y Elia Ariadna en la Corte Leónida (457–518)

Mattia C. Chiriatti, Elena Tinas Uceda

Abstract

This work explores the lives, roles, impacts and legacy of Elia Verina and Elia Ariadne, Leonid dynasty augustas (457 and 518), and their agency within the imperial court. Both empresses existed within a historical and religious context that redefined the role for imperial women, elevating them beyond traditional motherly roles and highlighting their increased prominence and active engagement, evident in public expressions and iconography.

Introducción

El advenimiento del Imperio romano significó un antes y un después para el papel de las mujeres en el ámbito público y cortesano, desempeñando éstas un nuevo rol, más activo y visible dentro de la corte. La relevancia de estos cambios se manifestó visiblemente en la institucionalización de la sucesión al poder dentro de la estructura de una *domus*, lo que convirtió el acceso al trono imperial en un derecho de familia. En este contexto, las emperatrices ejercieron un papel crucial, convirtiéndose en figuras clave dentro de la sucesión dinástica como madres y esposas. Así, a medida que el poder se centralizaba en el emperador y su familia, las mujeres imperiales adquirieron un estatus más prominente y una mayor influencia en la vida política y social del imperio. Dicho estatus iba asociado, en las representaciones iconográficas de las emperatrices del Alto Imperio, a la asimilación simbólica a deidades del panteón romano y a sus virtudes, de modo que los súbditos del imperio entendieran que tanto el *princeps* como su *domus* –teniendo la emperatriz un papel predominante dentro de esta– ocupaban un lugar sagrado con respecto al resto de la población.[1]

---

[1] M.J. Hidalgo de la Vega, *Las emperatrices romanas: sueños de púrpura y poder oculto*, Salamanca 2012, 299; R.M. Cid López, *Las Augustae en la dinastía Julio-Claudia. Marginalidad política, propaganda religiosa y reconocimiento social*, en: P. Pavón (ed.), *Marginación y mujer en el Imperio Romano*, Roma 2018, 136–140.

© BRILL SCHÖNINGH, 2024 | DOI:10.30965/9783657791477_002

Asimismo, la progresiva expansión del cristianismo en el Imperio tuvo grandes consecuencias para las funciones cortesanas de emperatriz. Constantino mostró una clara voluntad de otorgar tanto a su madre como a su esposa, Helena y Fausta respectivamente, un rango oficial preeminente, mostrando al pueblo romano la configuración de una *domus* estable que hiciera factible la consecución de la *aeternitas* romana. Así se refleja este aspecto en las representaciones numismáticas y en los discursos áulicos, que demuestran la intención de Constantino de establecer un linaje sólido.[2] Del mismo modo, consciente de la importancia a nivel simbólico que podían tener dichas representaciones y dichos discursos en el reforzamiento de su recién fundada dinastía, Teodosio confirió a las mujeres de su familia una mayor visibilización pública, como ya hizo Constantino en su día. Utilizando como modelo a Helena, las Augustas teodosianas fueron adquiriendo nuevas funciones más allá de su papel como aseguradoras de la estabilidad dinástica. En concreto, estas mujeres se convirtieron en un ejemplo a seguir por su devoción y munificencia, siendo representadas como defensoras de la ortodoxia católica y alabadas por su actividad evergética. Así, por primera vez, en los retratos de las Augustas no se enfatizaba únicamente su imagen como madres,[3] sino que, tras la consolidación de la ortodoxia cristiana, las emperatrices cristianas fueron asumiendo paulatinamente mayores cotas de poder político, asumiendo un papel determinante en la gestión del Imperio y, en especial modo, en los asuntos de carácter eclesiástico. Y es que, aunque tradicionalmente la definición de poder ha tendido a realizarse en términos masculinos, ellas, como evergetas y defensoras de la ortodoxia nicena, adquirieron verdaderamente un nuevo rol en la gestión del imperio como correinantes (κοινωνία). No obstante, pese a que no adquirieronadquirieron realmente los poderes magisteriales ejecutivos propios de un Augusto,[4] se estableció entre los súbditos del imperio la idea de que estas

---

2 J.M. Rodríguez Gervás, *Mujeres imperiales en la domus constantiniana*, en: Studia historica. Historia antigua 22 (2004), 126–127.

3 D. Angelova, *The Ivories of Ariadne and Ideas about Female Imperial Authority in Rome and Early Byzantium*, Gesta 43 (2004), 8; C. Buenacasa Pérez, *Poder y legitimación de las emperatrices teodosianas y su reflejo en la iconografía numismática*, en M.C. Chiriatti / R. Villegas Marín (eds.), *Mujeres imperiales, mujeres reales. Representaciones públicas y representaciones de poder en la Antigüedad Tardía*, CAMA 2, Leiden 2021, 117.

4 El jurista Ulpiano, a este propósito, recordaba que: *Princeps legibus solutus est: Augusta autem licet soluta non est. Principes tamen eadem illi privilegia tribuunt, quae ipsi haberent* (I, 3, 31). Como bien subraya la profesora Marcos Sánchez acerca de este aspecto en su estudio, "desde el punto de vista legal, las emperatrices romanas carecían de cualquier autoridad. La ley y la costumbre en Roma no autorizaban a las mujeres a desempeñar funciones públicas y la esposa del emperador –él mismo durante mucho tiempo considerado un ciudadano más–

estaban en pie de igualdad con su consorte imperial.[5] Por consiguiente, la pro-
liferación de imágenes públicas de las Augustas con las insignias imperiales y
el entendimiento por parte de la sociedad bizantina tardoantigua de que estas
verdaderamente ocupaban una posición de poder era una clara evidencia de
ello.[6] Al igual que sus antecesoras, Elia Verina y Elia Ariadna adoptaron este
nuevo linaje y se sirvieron de la nueva ideología imperial femenina creada por
las *Kaiserinnen* teodosianas para asentarse en el poder y consolidar las bases
de una nueva dinastía, comenzada por el tracio León I. Si bien el periodo que
comprendió su reinado se caracterizó por su contexto político volátil e ines-
table, su papel predominante en la corte imperial, junto con la toma de decisiones en acontecimientos cruciales para el Imperio, sentó las bases para una
nueva ideología imperial femenina.[7]

1   Los Comienzos Turbulentos de la Dinastía Tracia y la Primacía de Verina

La llegada de la dinastía tracia al trono del Imperio romano de Oriente fue
marcada por un clima político extremadamente convulso y agitada por múltiples conflictos religiosos, por usurpaciones protagonizadas por los miembros de la propia familia y, como colofón, por la debacle del Imperio romano
occidental tras la deposición del último emperador Rómulo Augústulo por el
rey hérulo Flavio Odoacro en el 476 d.C. El emperador León I, fundador de la
dinastía y *curator* de la familia del todopoderoso Aspar y de su esposa Verina,
pasó a ocupar, tras la muerte del emperador de Oriente Marciano, el trono que
venía siendo auspiciado por el mismo Aspar. Claramente, este patricio de origen alano era consciente del hecho de que los súbditos del imperio no habrían
aceptado de buen grado a un bárbaro como soberano, de forma que la elección
a emperador recayó sobre León, un tracio romanizado cuya función habría

---

no era una excepción" (M. Marcos Sánchez, *Representaciones visuales del poder en época tardoantigua: la imagen de la emperatriz*, en: HispSac 98 [1996], 514).

5   En este sentido y en palabras de Gregorio de Nisa, Flaccila, primera esposa de Teodosio, en
calidad de Augusta compartió plenamente con Teodosio I la dignidad imperial (la βασιλεία y
la ἀρχή). Gr. Nyss., Placill. 478,20–479,1. Véase: Buenacasa Pérez, 2021, 120. La traducción del
texto del mismo discurso en castellano se halla en M.C. Chiriatti, *La representación literaria
de la emperatriz Elia Flavia Flaccila en el βασιλικὸς λόγος de Gregorio de Nisa*, en: M.C. Chiriatti /
R. Villegas Marín (eds.), 2021, 46–63.

6   Angelova, 2004, 1–15.

7   A. Busch, *Die Frauen der theodosianischen Dynastie. Macht und Repräsentation kaiserlicher
Frauen im 5. Jahrhundert*, Stuttgart 2015, 21–26.

sido en un principio ser la cabeza de un régimen títere, pero que sin embargo conseguiría deshacerse del *magister militum praesentialis* Aspar.[8]

Del matrimonio de León y Verina sobrevivieron dos hijas: Ariadna, la primogénita y futura emperatriz, nacida antes del ascenso de sus padres al trono imperial (450), y Leoncia, ya porfirogéneta. Al fallecer poco después de nacer el descendiente varón que la pareja imperial tuvo, León emprendió una política de búsqueda activa de legítimos sucesores a la casa imperial y válidos consortes para las princesas reales, los cuales pudieran garantizar un heredero y, de este modo, mantener la dinastía en el trono. Aspar esperaba que León casase a Ariadna con uno de sus hijos, Patricio, de modo que el futuro descendiente de este matrimonio se convirtiera *de iure* en emperador. León I, sin embargo, no seguiría en un principio las directrices del alano romanizado, pero era consciente de que necesitaba su apoyo ya que parte del ejército, también de origen bárbaro, le obedecía. Aspar dirigía de hecho uno de los dos *comitatus praesentales*, su hijo Ardaburo estaba al mando del ejército oriental y Teodorico Estrabón, su aliado, lideraba a los ostrogodos federados en Tracia.[9] Así, la política matrimonial de la pareja imperial estuvo marcada por el objetivo de minar la autoridad de Aspar. Para ello, el emperador optó por apoyarse en una serie de individuos que, si bien también eran considerados como bárbaros por la población constantinopolitana, igualmente pertenecían al ejército romano y esta les consideraba como bárbaros romanizados, ya que procedían de la región de Isauria, dentro del *limes* del propio Imperio. Uno de estos hombres isaurios que poco a poco fue medrando en el ejército romano sería Zenón, de nombre original *Trascalasios* o *Tarasicoidisa*. León I se apoyó en el isaurio para librarse de Aspar, llegando incluso a tomar la decisión de que su hija mayor Ariadna contrajera matrimonio con él. Del mismo modo y para contentar a Aspar, acordó el compromiso matrimonial de su hija Leoncia, nacida en la púrpura, con Patricio, de manera que el alano tuviera la convicción de que sería el hijo de ambos y el futuro sucesor de León. No obstante, este casamiento nunca se llegó a producir, quedando más bien en un mero compromiso matrimonial. Zenón sí que llegó a convertirse en el yerno de León e incluso en su hombre de confianza, confabulando ambos para que Aspar y sus hijos cayeran en desgracia. Argumentando que la familia entera estaba al servicio de los persas, Aspar y sus hijos fueron llevados a palacio para ser asesinados (471).[10]

---

8   M. Vallejo Girvés, *¿Quién mató a Zenón? La enigmática muerte de un emperador de Bizancio*, en: E. Fernandez de Mier / J. Cortés Martín (eds.), *¿Pero quién mató a ...? Muertes enigmáticas en el mundo Antiguo*, Madrid 2016, 197.

9   W. Treadgold, *Breve historia de Bizancio*, Barcelona 2001, 69.

10   Ibid., 199.

Los últimos cuatro años del reinado de León I fueron suficientes para que este buscara un nuevo marido con el que casar a su hija menor, Leoncia. El elegido fue Marciano, hijo del emperador de Occidente Antemio y nieto de Marciano, antecesor de León en la *pars Orientis*. Pese a que seguramente la intención de León fuese que el hijo de esta pareja le sucediera, murió en 474 antes de que lograra tener descendencia. Por el contrario, Zenón y Ariadna sí que tuvieron un hijo, deliberadamente llamado con el mismo nombre que su abuelo el emperador. En el último año de reinado de León, el menor fue asociado al trono, comenzando a reinar bajo el nombre de León II a su muerte. El nuevo emperador contaba solamente con seis o siete años de edad, de modo que tanto sus padres como su abuela Verina hicieron que en la propia ceremonia de coronación Zenón quedara, mediante la *adfinitas*, como emperador asociado.[11] El protagonismo con el que contó el isaurio durante los años finales del reinado de León I legitimó esta decisión, y, por consiguiente, le permitió convertirse en el emperador del Imperio Romano de Oriente junto con su esposa, Ariadna, tras la prematura muerte de su hijo después de solo unos pocos meses de reinado.

A lo largo del gobierno de León I, miembros de la familia de Verina desempeñaron altos cargos estatales, lo que implica una cierta influencia de esta en su marido. El propio Basilisco llegó a ser cónsul y a ocupar otros puestos como el de *magister militum praesentalis* o el de senador. Sería él el elegido para comandar la desafortunada campaña contra el reino vándalo en 468 y, según las fuentes, la intercesión de Verina ante León fue decisiva para que este no tomara represalias contra su cuñado.[12] Ciertamente, autores como Teófanes narran el fracaso de esta expedición, que contó con costosos preparativos e implicó grandes pérdidas para el ejército y la quiebra del tesoro imperial, como un primitivo intento de Basilisco junto con Aspar de zozobrar la posición del emperador. El éxito de la expedición habría mejorado ciertamente la situación del Imperio Romano de Occidente y, con ello, también la reputación del emperador. Basilisco fue igualmente comandante de los ejércitos en Tracia y su cargo lo ocuparía luego Armato, supuesto sobrino de Verina y Basilisco, aunque no

---

11   M. Vallejo Girvés, Ad ecclesiam confugere: *tonsuras y exilios en la familia de León y Verina*, en: M. Vallejo Girvés / J.A. Bueno Delgado / C. Sánchez-Moreno Ellart (eds.), *Movilidad forzada entre la Antigüedad Clásica y Tardía*, Alcalá de Henares 2015, 144.

12   Teófanes el Confesor (Thphn., chron. a.m 5961) sostiene que Aspar y su hijo acordaron dar el Imperio a Basilisco, hermano de la Augusta Verina, si hubiese entregado a traición a Geiserico la flota y la armada del emperador. Malalas (Jo. Mal., chron. 14.44) también menciona la traición de Basilisco, que aceptó ser sobornado por Geiserico, aunque sin dar motivo alguno. Ambos se basan en la versión del historiador bizantino Prisco de Panio, contemporáneo a los hechos.

podemos recabar de las fuentes qué tipo de relación familiar mantenían.[13] De grandes habilidades militares, era una persona de gran influencia en la corte y, especialmente, durante el reinado de Basilisco. Igualmente, algunas fuentes señalan que la única razón por la que él contó con tanto poder fue por la relación sentimental extramatrimonial que mantuvo con Zenonis, esposa de Basilisco. Precisamente Armato, junto con el cuñado de Verina Zuzus, habían sido los encargados de acabar con la vida de Aspar y de sus hijos. Marciano, su otro yerno y, además, esposo de Leoncia, ocupaba igualmente un lugar destacado en palacio. Asimismo, parece ser que Julio Nepote, emperador de la *pars Occidentalis*, mantenía lazos familiares con la emperatriz.[14]

A raíz de lo argumentado anteriormente, Verina debió ser una mujer fuerte y defensora del poder que su grupo familiar había logrado alcanzar. A la muerte de su esposo, esta siguió viviendo en palacio con la intención de reforzar su posición a través de su hija y sobre todo de su nieto. Sin embargo, la prematura muerte de León II en enero del 474 desató un enfrentamiento abierto entre Verina y su grupo familiar contra el nuevo emperador y marido de su hija, Zenón. Esta situación dejaba a Ariadna en un punto ambiguo dentro de los dos bandos.[15] De hecho, la hostilidad entre ambas facciones se agudizó tras la confabulación liderada por Basilisco contra Zenón, quien acabó depuesto refugiándose en su región natal. Junto con él viajó Ariadna, pese a que quienes conspiraron contra su marido eran miembros de su propio grupo familiar. Efectivamente, ella era emperatriz gracias a su matrimonio con Zenón, posición que perdería enteramente en caso de apoyar a su madre y que podría recuperar si Zenón reorganizaba su vuelta al trono desde Isauria, como así sucedió.[16] En cuanto al protagonismo de Verina en este complot, sigue abierta una gran controversia historiográfica tanto en las fuentes como en las investigaciones llevadas a cabo sobre el tema.[17] A partir del análisis de las fuentes, que

---

13   En el artículo de Lezska sobre Armato (M.J. Leska, *Armatus: A Story of a Byzantine General From the 5th Century*, in: Eos 87 [2000], 335), el historiador precisa que Teófanes (Thphn. chron. a.m 5969) emplea el vocablo griego ἀνεψιός, que significa a la vez hijo de hermano o de hermana.

14   M.J. Leszka, *Empress-widow Verina's political activity during the reign of emperor Zeno*, en: W. Ceran (ed.), *Mélanges Oktawiusz Jurewicz, Mélanges d'histoire byzantine offerts à Oktawiusz Jurewicz à l'occasion de son soixante-dixième anniversaire* (Byzantina Lodziensia 3), Łódź 1998, 129; id., *The role of Empress Verina in the Events of 475/476 – Revisited*, in: Byzantinoslavica 75 (2017), 30; Vallejo Girvés, 2016, 201.

15   Vallejo Girvés, 2016, 201–202.

16   Ibid., 202.

17   Leszka, 2000, 30–34.

retraen negativamente a Verina por su directa relación con la usurpación,[18] la hipótesis más valorada por los estudiosos reconoce que Verina no fue la líder de la conjura, sino que simplemente se unió a ella a cambio de que Patricio, su aliado político y candidato potencial a esposo, fuera elevado para cogobernar con Basilisco.[19] Por otro lado, Verina informó sobre el complot a su yerno con la esperanza de que este abandonara cualquier propósito de resistir o principalmente para proteger a Ariadna del peligro que resultaría del enfrentamiento directo de ambos bandos, logrando la pareja imperial, por tanto, refugiarse en Isauria junto con el tesoro imperial.[20]

La deposición de Zenón parecía por tanto estar previamente planeada, puesto que, además de aquellos emparentados con Basilisco, otros grandes hombres del ejército apoyaron el levantamiento contra él, como Teodorico Estrabón, Illos y su hermano Trocundes, líderes isaurios que también contaban con el apoyo de hombres leales en las filas del ejército y que poco a poco fueron disfrutando cada vez más de un gran peso en el panorama político del Imperio.[21] Basilisco, por el contrario, no gozaba del apoyo popular después del desastre del año 468, y su política en favor del monofisismo incrementó aún más su impopularidad en Constantinopla.

Por si fuera poco, en menos de dos años, los protagonistas de la confabulación acabaron enfrentándose y con ello, debilitando su posición. En el caso concreto de Verina, parece ser que una vez elevado Basilisco a la silla imperial, este se negó a atender sus peticiones con respecto a Patricio o incluso llegó a asesinarlo, según Cándido Isaurio.[22] Ante esto, la relación entre Verina y su hermano llegó muy probablemente a tensarse, de manera que su posición en palacio se debilitó considerablemente. Algunos autores, como Daniel el Estilita

---

18 Candidus 52–59; 89–94 (R.C. Blockley, *The fragmentary classicising historians of the later Roman Empire: Eunapius, Olympiodorus, Priscus and* Malchus, Arca 6, Liverpool 1983, 466–469); Jo. Mal., chron. 15. 1–3.

19 Podemos dividir en tres dictámenes diferentes los autores que hablan de la agencia de Verina de cara a la usurpación: el primer grupo, formado por Cándido, Malalas y Jordanes, presenta a Verina como la precursora de la trama. La segunda versión defiende que tanto Verina como Basilisco estuvieron involucrados por igual en los orígenes de la misma, y la encontramos en la Vida de Daniel Estilita, la obra de Teodoro Lector, El Conde Marcelino, Juan de Antioquía y Teófanes. Finalmente, en el tercero solo se menciona a Basilisco como protagonista, perteneciendo a este grupo los autores Josué Estilista, Procopio, Evagrio y los *Excerpta Valesiana* (véase Leszka, 2000, 35).

20 Malalas relata acerca del complot de Verina para asesinar a su hijastro (Jo. Mal., chron.15. 2); Leszka, 2000, 32–34; S. Williams / G. Friell, *The Rome that did not fall: the Survival of the East in the Fifth Century*, London 1999, 182.

21 Vallejo Girvés, 2016, 206; R. Kosiński, *The Emperor Zeno. Religion and Politics*, Cracow 2010, 80.

22 Candidus, 60–65 (R.C. Blockley, 1983, 466–469; véase también Vallejo Girvés, 2015, 143).

o Cándido Isaurio mencionan incluso el propósito de Basilisco de eliminar físicamente a Verina.[23] La única manera de cambiar esta situación habría sido mediante el regreso de su yerno, de forma que Verina, junto con el resto de confabulados, apoyaran desde dentro del palacio la vuelta de Ariadna y Zenón. Estos mismos, durante su estancia en Isauria, habían logrado organizar un ejército considerable y se encontraban a las puertas de la ciudad para recuperar el trono.[24] Ciertamente, el regreso de la pareja no fue de forma gratuita: Verina demandó vivir en palacio con las mismas prerrogativas que antaño; Armato se convertiría en *magister militum praesentalis* perpetuo y su hijo, llamado también Basilisco, sería nombrado César o coemperador con Zenón, puesto que las fuentes divergen en cuanto a la categoría otorgada al menor.[25]

2   Dentro y Fuera de Palacio: el Regreso de Zenón, el Aislamiento de Verina y la Usurpación de Leoncia y de Marciano en Oriente

Suprimida la usurpación de Basilisco, Zenón trató de recuperar el orden mediante la búsqueda de un equilibrio entre Constantinopla, el núcleo de poder en Isauria y los ostrogodos federados en Iliria y Tracia, fundamentales para proteger las fronteras de potenciales invasores. En la capital oriental la situación política para Zenón seguía siendo difícil. Las mismas personas que previamente lo habían traicionado al apoyar a Basilisco y en cuya lealtad no podía confiar, ahora ocupaban los cargos de máxima responsabilidad del imperio. Consciente de ello, el retorno de Zenón tuvo consecuencias nefastas para la familia de Verina y Ariadna, pues la mayoría de ellos fueron paulatinamente eliminados por el emperador. Basilisco, Zenonis y el hijo de ambos consiguieron refugiarse en la Iglesia de Santa Sofía. Zenón accedió a sus peticiones de asilo y decretó su destierro. Sin embargo, una vez llegaron a su destino, Cucusa, fue ordenado su encierro en una cisterna, donde murieron de hambre y de frío.[26]

En cuanto a Armato, su nueva posición le otorgó un poder demasiado incómodo para Zenón. Este ya había dejado claras sus ambiciones al exigir no solo el cargo más alto del ejército, sino también que su hijo fuera asociado al trono.

---

23   Candidus, 60–65; Vita Sancti Danielis Stylitae 69 (J.S. Palmer [ed.], *La vida sobre una columna: Vida de Simeón Estilita, Vida de Daniel Estilita*, Madrid 2014, 106–107). Véase también Vallejo Girvés, 2015, 143.

24   Vallejo Girvés, 2016, 202–203.

25   Ibid., 202; B. Croke, *Basiliscus the boy-emperor*, in: *Greek, Roman and Byzantine studies* 24–1 (1983), 81–91.

26   Vallejo Girvés, 2016, 203–204.

Pero Armato tenía también otros enemigos en la corte, siendo probablemente uno de ellos Illos. El general isaurio había cambiado de bando mucho antes de que lo hiciera Armato y, especialmente, a razón de la sangrienta masacre emprendida por Basilisco contra los isaurios que se habían quedado en Constantinopla después de la huida de Zenón[27]. Illos fue precisamente quien convenció a Armato para que hiciera lo mismo, y seguramente no estaría contento de que fuera él el que ocupara el cargo de *magister militum praesentalis*. No obstante, el general isaurio era aparentemente igual de peligroso para Zenón, pero este, con el fin de protegerse contra el emperador, mantenía como rehén a Longino, su hermano. Por si fuera poco, el hermano de Illos, Trocundes, era *magister militum per Orientem* y mantenía el control sobre Siria, de manera que, por el momento, era mucho mejor para Zenón mantener a este poderoso comandante como aliado político.[28] Armato fue asesinado cuando iba en dirección al Hipódromo de Constantinopla, si no por la orden directa de Zenón, al menos bajo su consentimiento.[29] El destino de Basilisco, su hijo, bien podría haber sido el mismo que el de su padre.

Sin hijos y sin herederos, el pequeño asociado al trono era sobrino nieto de Ariadna y, en consecuencia, el candidato más factible para suceder a Zenón. De este modo, el grupo familiar de Ariadna y Verina conseguiría su propósito de acceder al trono legítimamente sin necesidad de una nueva usurpación.[30] Las fuentes coevas afirman a la postre que, puesto que Ariadna tenía conocimiento de la intención del emperador, esta pudo salvar al joven llevándolo a la Iglesia de las Blaquernas, donde lo tonsurarían y le ordenarían lector. La tonsura eclesiástica imposibilitaba por consiguiente su acceso al trono, si bien le salvó la vida.[31] Este hecho demuestra por tanto que, pese a que Ariadna marchara junto a Zenón a Isauria tras la usurpación de Basilisco, todavía su principal preocupación era el destino de su grupo familiar. La actitud que tomó Zenón contra sus familiares debió enfurecer a Verina, pues una vez reinsertada en la corte continuó confabulando contra él.

Asimismo, el asesinato de Armato incrementó aún más si cabe la autoridad de Illos en Constantinopla, convirtiéndose este último en el actor más importante de la escena política del momento, pasando a ocupar el cargo de *magister officiorum*, y recibiendo el título de cónsul en el año 478.[32] Verina, que seguía viviendo en palacio, no veía con buenos ojos la influencia que el

---

27   Williams / Friell, 1999, 182.
28   Kosiński, 2010, 100.
29   Ibid., 204; Leszka, 2000, 342.
30   Vallejo Girvés, 2015, 148.
31   Vallejo Girvés, 2016, 205.
32   Kosiński, 2010, 100–101.

general tenía en Zenón, pues mermaba la que pudiera tener su hija Ariadna. En ese mismo año, Illos sufrió un intento de asesinato por parte de Epinikos, prefecto del pretorio durante el reinado de Basilisco, que continuó ejerciendo una considerable influencia en la corte una vez regresado Zenón gracias a la protección de Verina. El intento fue un fracaso y Epinikos cayó en manos de Illos, quien lo llevó como prisionero a Isauria. Allí confesó al cónsul que era la suegra del emperador quien había orquestado el fallido atentado.[33] Zenón requirió la presencia de Illos en Constantinopla, quien se negó a entrar en la ciudad a menos que se le entregara como rehén a Verina. El emperador accedió a esta petición, puesto que de esta manera conseguía librarse de las intrigas de palacio y a su vez contentaba al poderoso general. Tras ser entregada a Illos, Verina fue trasladada a Tarso y encerrada en una fortaleza de Cilicia, donde permaneció aislada hasta el año 488.[34]

Por otro lado, la situación de Zenón en el poder continuó siendo tensa. Al terremoto que afligió Constantinopla, en agosto del 478, se le debe sumar la prolongada guerra contra Teodorico Estrabón. Después de la usurpación de Basilisco, las negociaciones entre Zenón y Estrabón sobre la posición que debía ocupar este último en el Imperio no llegaron a buen puerto, dando lugar a una nueva guerra en Tracia. Zenón entonces decidió elevar la posición de Teodorico el Amalo, líder de los ostrogodos en Iliria, reconociendo la existencia de su estado tribal en Moesia y prometiéndole el pago de subsidios anuales a su pueblo. La rápida promoción de Teodorico el Amalo era una estrategia de Zenón para que ambos grupos de ostrogodos lucharan entre sí.[35]

Esta situación de inestabilidad política fue aprovechada por Leoncia, hermana de Ariadna y su esposo Marciano, hijo del emperador Antemio, para intentar derrocar a Zenón hacia finales del 479. La pareja se rebeló contra el emperador invocando la ilegalidad del trato a Verina y alegando que Marciano tenía más derechos al trono que Zenón, al ser Leoncia porfirogéneta. Los conspiradores estuvieron a punto de arrebatarle el poder al isaurio, pues contaban con el apoyo de los habitantes de Constantinopla tanto por su gobierno como por su condición de bárbaro. Acorralado Zenón en el palacio imperial, finalmente las tropas de Illos lograron cruzar el estrecho del Bósforo y sorprender a los rebeldes, liberando al emperador.[36]

---

33   Ibid., 101.
34   E.W. Brooks, *The Emperor Zenon and the Isaurians*, in: EHR 30 (1893), 218; Vallejo Girvés, 2016, 206.
35   Kosiński, 2010, 101–103.
36   Ibid., 104–106; Vallejo Girvés, 2016, 207.

En Constantinopla las intrigas continuaron, pese al aislamiento de Verina. Según el relato de Jordanes, Illos convenció a Zenón de que Ariadna estaba maquinando en su contra para arrebatarle el trono. Ante tal denuncia, parece ser que Zenón trató de acabar con la vida de la emperatriz sin éxito.[37] Después de que ella misma fuera víctima de Zenón, Ariadna entendió que su madre Verina le era de mayor utilidad en la corte que encerrada en Cilicia. Fue así como la emperatriz reclamó a Zenón la vuelta de su madre a palacio, petición que rotundamente Illos nunca aprobaría. Ariadna entonces, con el apoyo del emperador, ordenó a un sicario que se deshiciera de Illos.[38] El sicario solo logró amputarle una oreja e Illos, como represalia, liberó a Verina de su encierro y le obligó a proclamar a un emperador títere, Leoncio (484).[39]

Tras esta enfrenta, la coalición de Zenón con Teodorico el Amalo, *magister militum praesentalis* y cónsul en el año 484,[40] consiguió derrotar a Illos, que huyó junto con Verina a Isauria. Nueve días después de llegar, Verina fallecería de cansancio. Illos consiguió resistir cuatro años más hasta que finalmente, en el año 488, las tropas imperiales acabaran con él y con Leoncio, el emperador títere. Ariadna pidió a Zenón que el cuerpo de su madre fuera llevado a Constantinopla, donde fue enterrado con los honores imperiales en el mismo sarcófago que el de León I.[41]

---

37   Según relata Jordanes (Iordan., rom. 349–351), Zenón encargó a un cubiculario que asesinara a Ariadne. Sin embargo, este comunicó el plan a la emperatriz, quien huyó al Palacio Episcopal. Allí le contó los planes de Illos y Zenón al Patriarca Acacio, quien le ofreció refugio. Zenón tuvo que pedir perdón al Patriarca y ordenar el regreso de Ariadna a palacio (Iordan., rom. 350–351: *Qui, deliberans eam perimere, uni suorum rem tacite demandavit. Quod dum ille agere nititur, cuidam cubiculariae prodit scelus eadem nocte facturum. Regina scelus cognovit, suoque in lectulo eadem quae rem suggesserat collocata, in episcopium ad Acacium nemine sciente subterfugit. Posteraque die Zeno, rem aestimans perpetratam, dum, luctum quendam quasi gerens, neminem suscipit, Acacius episcopus ingressus et facti arguit impietatem, veniaeque fidem exposcit, Augustamque suspicionis innoxiam compromittit; acceptaque fide, veniae pactione, Augusta revertitur*). No obstante, el resto de fuentes no hacen mención a esta historia (Vallejo Girvés, 2016, 208).

38   Thphn., chron. a. m. 5972; Jo. Mal., chron. 15.13.

39   Jo. Mal., chron. 15.13; Vallejo Girvés, 2016, 208–210.

40   Era la primera vez que un bárbaro no ciudadano del Imperio alcanzaba tan alta distinción, véase S. Mitchell, *A history of the Later Roman Empire. AD 284–641* (2nd ed.), Hoboken 2014, 125–126.

41   Vallejo Girvés, 2016, 210.

3   El Auge de Ariadna y su Actuación Política en el Advenimiento de Anastasio I

El fallecimiento del emperador Zenón, el 9 de abril del año 491, produjo un hecho tan insólito como singular: Ariadna quedaba como única sucesora en el trono imperial. Como emperatriz viuda no podía gobernar *per se*. Sin embargo, el Senado y el pueblo de Constantinopla reconocieron su poder en la elección del nuevo emperador, ya que era portadora de la legitimidad imperial. Uno de los pasajes del *De Caeremoniis aulae Byzantinae*, tradicionalmente atribuido al emperador Constantino VII Porfirogénito (913–959), reproduce el desarrollo del ritual mediante el cual Ariadna convirtió a Anastasio en legítimo emperador, gracias al matrimonio de ambos. La descripción del proceso pertenece a un fragmento del Περὶ πολιτικῆς καταστάσεως del funcionario bizantino Pedro Patricio, *magister officiorum* ya en la corte de Justiniano, y posteriormente recogido en el tratado del siglo X.[42]

El pasaje relata que, durante la noche del 10 de abril, la Augusta convocó a los dignatarios de palacio, a los senadores y al patriarca Eufemio para designar de forma indemorable al nuevo emperador. Mientras, los soldados y la muchedumbre de Constantinopla se habían dirigido al hipódromo a la espera de noticias sobre los acontecimientos venideros.[43] Las súplicas de la multitud y el furor popular hicieron que los funcionarios palatinos consideraran oportuno que Ariadna se dirigiera al pueblo. Vestida con las insignias imperiales y escoltada por el cortejo imperial, la emperatriz se encaminó hacia el hipódromo para calmar la multitud constantinopolitana enfurecida.[44] En esta *adlocutio* se percibe la intención de Ariadna de revocar el Edicto del *Henotikón* (Ἑνωτικόν) del fallecido consorte y poner fin, por consiguiente, al cisma con la Iglesia de Occidente, distanciándose de las medidas emprendidas por su primer esposo en materia religiosa. No olvidemos, de hecho, que la política de Zenón orientada a la reconciliación del Estado con la parte monofisita del Imperio le había propiciado una gran impopularidad en la capital. Siendo consciente de ello, la emperatriz entendía que los constantinopolitanos y los sectores monásticos

---

42   M.C. Chiriatti, *La elección de Anastasio I según el* De caeremoniis aulae byzantinae: *un análisis histórico-literario*, en: QRiBi(S) 18 (2017), 179.

43   Ibid., 181; B. Croke, *Ariadne Augusta. Shaping the identity of the early Byzantine Empress*, en: G. Dunn / W. Mayer (eds.), *Christians shaping identity from the Roman Empire to Byzantium*, Leiden–Boston 2015, 306.

44   Chiriatti, 2017, 182–183.

de la ciudad jamás aceptarían la elevación a la púrpura de un emperador que no fuera calcedonense.[45]

Una vez tranquilizado el pueblo, Ariadna se retiró en el *Augusteion* mientras que Eufemio y los dignatarios palatinos continuaron discutiendo en el *Delphax* sobre quién debía ser el candidato elegido para futuro emperador. Las negociaciones no parecían llegar a buen puerto, hasta tal punto que el *praepositus sacri cubiculi* Urbicio aconsejó que fuera precisamente Ariadna la única persona válida para escoger al pretendiente que estimara más adecuado.[46] Sin vacilación alguna, la Augusta escogió a uno de los decuriones de los silenciarios, Anastasio. Este veterano funcionario, con más de sesenta años de edad en el momento de su elección, era una figura conocida en la corte. Pese a ser oriundo de *Dyrrachium* y no contar con el cargo de senador, seguramente sus méritos y su estrecha vinculación con palacio justificaban su elección.[47] Sabemos también que a la muerte del Patriarca de Antioquía Pedro Fulo (488), en plena disputa entre calcedonianos y anticalcedonianos, Anastasio fue uno de los candidatos para posible sucesor, aunque su candidatura fue posteriormente rechazada. Esto nos hace pensar que Anastasio estuviera anteriormente inmiscuido en ambientes cercanos a lo eclesiástico.[48] Empero, el patriarca Eufemio, junto con la emperatriz y el Senado, obligaron a Anastasio a firmar un documento en el que se declaraba la vigencia del Concilio de Calcedonia con el fin de que la población de Constantinopla aceptara su ascenso al trono.[49]

El matrimonio de ambos pues, cuarenta y cinco días después de la muerte de Zenón, sirvió para conservar la línea dinástica tracia y establecer un gobernante masculino competente. Obviando el *cursus honorum* de Anastasio, el aspirante esperado para suceder a Zenón era el hermano de este, Longino. Tras la revuelta de Illos y una vez recuperada su libertad, Longino había iniciado su carrera militar alentada por el apoyo del emperador. Así, ascendió a *magister militum praesentialis* en el año 485 y fue nombrado cónsul en el 486 y en el 490.[50] El ascenso de Longino al poder se hubiese visto como la continuación del reinado de Zenón y con ello, de su política religiosa e inestabilidad gubernamental. Mediante su matrimonio con Anastasio, Ariadna regularizó el

---

45   M. Vallejo Girvés, *El patriarca Macedonio II y la aristocracia femenina de Constantinopla*, en: G. Vespignani (ed.), *Polidoro. Studi offerti ad Antonio Carile*, Spoleto 2013, 85.

46   Chiriatti, 2017, 184–185.

47   Ibid., 185.

48   L. Magliaro, *Arianna. La garante della porpora*, Milano 2013, 126–127.

49   Vallejo Girvés, 2013, 85.

50   Marcellin. Com., chron. a. 485.1; Jo. Mal., chron. 386; Thphn., chron., a.m. 5975; F.K. Haarer, *Anastasius I. Politics and Empire in the Late Roman World*, Cambridge 2006, 20–21.

encumbramiento, puesto que era ella la receptora de la dignidad imperial. La condición de esposo y, por tanto, también la de emperador eran inseparables.

La actuación de Ariadna en este acontecimiento ha dado lugar a una disparidad de versiones contradictorias en las distintas fuentes. Por una parte, algunas de ellas se limitan simplemente a afirmar que el emperador murió de epilepsia o de disentería[51] sin sucesor y, por tanto, Ariadna entregó la corona a Anastasio[52] otras recogen el odio que la soberana profesaba hacia el emperador. Según las mismas, Ariadna había aprovechado el estado de embriaguez del emperador para enterrarlo todavía con vida: una vez sepultado el emperador, los guardias que custodiaban el *Heroon* (ἡρῷον) de Constantino y las tumbas imperiales de la Iglesia de los Santos Apóstoles escucharon gritos y sollozos de la tumba del isaurio suplicando que le dejaran salir. Los guardias avisaron a sus superiores, que llevaron la información hasta la emperatriz Ariadna. Una vez advertida, esta dio expresamente la orden de que no se abriera el sarcófago ni se hiciera caso a sus lamentaciones.[53]

Ciertamente, las fuentes literarias que nos transmiten esta interpretación de los hechos se corresponden con autores muy posteriores a los acontecimientos.[54] Existe también la hipótesis, y no necesariamente exclusiva, de que la elección de Anastasio como emperador –y también por tanto la razón de la impiedad de Ariadna– se debía a la relación amorosa de la emperatriz con Anastasio.[55] Por otro lado, tampoco sabemos si los motivos por los cuales eligió al silenciario eran de tipo religioso. Lamentablemente, no se conservan testimonios que nos puedan dilucidar la postura de la Augusta ante el *Henotikón* de su primer marido antes de la entronización de Anastasio. Del mismo modo, ninguna de las fuentes que nos hablan sobre la emperatriz, sean éstas difisitas o monofisitas, muestra una clara animadversión hacia la misma, siendo eso sí mucho más elogiada por estas últimas.[56]

Lo que sí que queda evidente es que la ascensión de Anastasio fue otro ejemplo más de cómo las viudas imperiales, al igual que ya hizo Verina en su día, seguían manteniendo su influencia dentro de la corte y podían ejercerla, por ejemplo, mediante la legitimación de un nuevo soberano. Así, aunque las emperatrices en sí tuviesen un papel secundario dentro de la vida pública, su

---

51 Jo. Mal., chron., 15.16.

52 Evagr., h.e, 3.29; M. Whitby, *The ecclesiastical history of Evagrius Scholasticus*, TTH 33, Liverpool 2000, 164.

53 Autores como Jorge Cedreno o Juan Zonaras. Véase Vallejo Girvés, 2016, 191–193.

54 En concreto se trataría de Miguel Psello, Cedreno, Zonaras y Nicéforo Calixto Xantopulo. Véase: Vallejo Girvés, 2016, 193.

55 Chiriatti, 2017, 186.

56 Vallejo Girvés, 2013, 85.

implicación y participación en la gestión del imperio no era meramente simbólica.[57] A pesar de las revueltas acontecidas durante su reinado, lo cierto es que Anastasio demostró ser un emperador competente dispuesto a acometer las reformas que el Imperio necesitaba para su supervivencia. Ariadna había convivido en palacio con el silenciario durante décadas, siendo conocedora de las habilidades de gestión del ilirio. De este modo, tanto su elección como la obligación de acatar el Concilio de Calcedonia fueron movimientos hábiles y astutos por parte de nuestra emperatriz, dispuesta a acabar con la inestabilidad que marcó el mandato de su primer esposo.

Durante esta primera década de reinado, las fuentes no hacen alusión a Ariadna. Claramente, la emperatriz debió permanecer ocupada ejerciendo unas funciones meramente cortesanas. Sin embargo, estos aspectos pasan más desapercibidos y no suelen contar con la suficiente atención como para su registro, siendo mayoritariamente documentadas en las fuentes las campañas militares o las revueltas internas.[58] No obstante, sabemos que la opinión favorable de la pareja imperial no pareció durar mucho, puesto que autores como el Conde Marcelino y Juan de Antioquía nos hablan de una rebelión surgida en el hipódromo para el año 492–493, en la cual se derribaron las estatuas de bronce de los emperadores.[59]

Asimismo, tenemos constancia de que Ariadna trató de continuar ejerciendo su agencia en Anastasio más allá de su protagonismo en el ascenso al trono del silenciario. También en torno a estas fechas, el *De Magistratibus* del contemporáneo Juan de Lido menciona la presión ejercida por parte de la Augusta para que su marido nombrara a miembros de familia en importantes cargos en la corte.[60] Después de la revuelta de su hermana Leoncia y su cuñado Marciano, no quedaba en palacio ningún integrante del grupo familiar de Ariadna. Pese a las continuas usurpaciones, el hecho de que Ariadna tratara de revertir esta situación significa que verdaderamente su posición contaba con autoridad y dominio en la corte, y que la participación de miembros de su familia en la gestión del imperio le era de utilidad en el juego de influencias políticas de la misma.

En este sentido, Ariadna propuso a Anastasio como ὕπαρχος τῶν πραιτωρίων (*praefectus praetorio*) a Antemio, hermano de Marciano e hijo del emperador de la *pars Occidentalis* del mismo nombre. Antemio había formado parte de

57   Chiriatti, 2017, 190.

58   Croke, 2015, 308.

59   M. Vallejo Girvés, *Crisis de transición y la exhibición de la majestad imperial de la emperatriz Ariadne (474–518)*, en: P. Pavón Torrejón (coord.), Conditio feminae: *imágenes de la realidad femenina en el mundo romano*, Roma 2021, 681.

60   Vallejo Girvés, 2013, 89.

la infructuosa revuelta protagonizada por el cuñado de Ariadna en el año 479 contra Zenón, después de la cual huyó a Roma. A pesar de que la oferta fue rechazada por Anastasio, Antemio permaneció leal a ambos llegando a convertirse en cónsul el año de la muerte de Ariadna (515).[61] De la misma manera parece ser que nuestra emperatriz, este también intercedió para que el hijo de Antemio adquiriera algún tipo de cargo en la corte.[62]

Sin lugar a duda, el asunto en el que Ariadna aparece mayormente involucrada y cuya agencia, según las fuentes, queda patentemente de manifiesto, es en la política religiosa del emperador. Pese a ser obligado a firmar el documento por el cual se comprometía a respetar lo dictado en Calcedonia, poco a poco Anastasio le fue mostrando mayores simpatías al credo surgido a raíz del Edicto de Unión.[63] Durante su reinado, Anastasio tuvo que acometer grandes reformas económicas que mejoraran la maltrecha situación por la que pasaba la hacienda pública. Como ya hicieron Basilisco y Zenón en su día, Anastasio era consciente de la importancia que tenían las provincias más proclives al monofisismo para el fisco del Imperio. La actitud del emperador, que fue acogida con alegría por las provincias de Egipto y Siria, fue duramente criticada por el patriarca Eufemio, quien constantemente le recordaba al emperador lo pactado.[64] La tensión entre el patriarca y el emperador culminó con el exilio de Eufemio (496), bajo la falsa acusación de que este estaba confabulado con los rebeldes isaurios.[65] Con mucha probabilidad Ariadna se vio perjudicada por esta deposición, contando con un aliado político menos. Parece ser que la Augusta entonces le recomendó a Anastasio que la sede patriarcal de la capital fuera ocupada por Macedonio, un clérigo de Santa Sofía de avanzada edad. Esta propuesta fue aceptada por el emperador, pero Macedonio poco pudo hacer para que Anastasio frenara su paulatino acercamiento a las posturas monofisitas. Macedonio entonces apoyó la deriva del emperador, quien llegó incluso a intentar que los monasterios de Constantinopla acataran el *Henotikón* con el consiguiente desafecto de los eclesiásticos de la ciudad.[66]

Aun así, la relación entre el Patriarca y el emperador comenzó a enrarecerse en el momento en el que su tendencia hacia el monofisismo se hizo cada vez más patente. En este sentido, la llegada a Constantinopla a finales de la primera década del siglo VI de Severo, futuro obispo de Antioquía y Filoxeno de

---

61   Croke, 2015, 309.
62   Vallejo Girvés, 2013, 89.
63   C. Capizzi, *L'Imperatore Anastasio I. (491–518). Studio sulla sua vita, la sua opera e la sua personalità*, Roma 1969, 101–105; 112–115.
64   Ibid., 83–86; Croke, 2015, 310.
65   Ibid., 310.
66   Vallejo Girvés, 2013, 86.

Mabbog, dos grandes líderes del monofisismo, fue decisiva. Tras la estancia de estos en la capital y sobre todo durante la de Severo de Antioquía el emperador cambió su actitud y se desvió completamente hacia la opción monofisita. Es entonces cuando Macedonio comenzó a alejarse de Anastasio y acercarse a la posición de los monasterios y de la población de la capital, partidarios del Concilio de Calcedonia. Al igual que su antecesor, Macedonio fue finalmente depuesto.[67]

Ciertamente, las fuentes mencionan a Ariadna en el relato de estos acontecimientos y, sin embargo, se nos hace muy difícil saber cuál fue la actitud de la emperatriz ante los mismos. Como ya hemos explicado, los monofisitas elogian profusamente a la emperatriz mientras que los autores vinculados al calcedonismo no escriben nada abiertamente en su contra, que sí reprueban al emperador. Los calcedonenses concretamente hacen mención a la tristeza de la Augusta en el momento en el que Anastasio destituyó a Macedonio, entendemos que por esta misma razón.[68] En el caso de los monofisitas, las versiones son diferentes, pero todas alaban a la emperatriz en general. Precisamente Severo de Antioquía, ya asentado como obispo en la ciudad siria, pronunció según Pseudo Zacarías de Mitilene, una homilía en la que alababa a los emperadores y especialmente a Ariadna. Severo atribuía a la Augusta las mismas virtudes masculinas que su esposo pese a su sexo: su humildad y su paciencia de espíritu.[69] Destaca también una carta del presbítero monofisita Simeón de Amida, testigo de los acontecimientos y contrario a Macedonio, que transmite que la pareja imperial se negó a recibir la comunión de Macedonio en la consagración de un *martyrium* en el *Hebdomon* (Ἕβδομον) de Constantinopla.[70] Asimismo, algunos han entendido que esta actuación de Ariadna mostraría más bien el rechazo a los problemas ocasionados ante la negativa de Macedonio de acatar lo dictado por el emperador, más que por ella seguir verdaderamente la doctrina monofisita.[71]

Teniendo en cuenta que la influencia que Ariadna mantenía en el emperador y su alta conciencia política, probablemente la emperatriz también modificó su convencimiento religioso o/y que esta llegó a la misma conclusión que Anastasio, entendiendo que al Imperio le era más ventajosa la unión de

---

67   Ibid., 87.
68   Ibid., 87–88.
69   Sev. Ant., *hom.* 21, 1, 34–35 (M. Brière / F. Graffin [eds.], *Les Homiliae Cathedrales de Sévère d'Antioche. Traducction syriaque de Jacques d'Edesse. Homélies I à XVII*, en: Patrologia Orientalis, 37,1, Turnhout, 1975); Vallejo Girvés, 2013, 90–91.
70   Ps. Zach., h.e. 7. 18; Vallejo Girvés, 2013, 88.
71   Ibid., 88.

la Iglesia oriental pese a que significara alejarse del ámbito occidental.[72] En definitiva, aunque no podamos pronunciarnos con firmeza sobre la fe de la emperatriz, parece ser que esta varió de planteamiento doctrinal durante el reinado de Anastasio.[73]

4   Verina, Ariadna y la Consolidación de una Nueva Doctrina Imperial Femenina Cristiana

La afinidad ideológica entre la dinastía teodosiana y la leónida iba más allá de la doctrina imperial que promovía una mayor presencia de las emperatrices en el poder, especialmente durante el reinado de León I. El emperador, que había ascendido al poder gracias Aspar –*magister militum* siempre fiel a los teodosianos[74]– ofreció diversos tributos a Marciano y Pulqueria, últimos miembros del linaje teodosiano, de manera que a los ojos de los constantinopolitanos, su gobierno fuera comprendido como una continuación de su proyecto político. En uno de los breves comentarios de las *Parastaseis Syntomoi Chronikai*[75] se hace mención al traslado por parte de León I de las estatuas de Marciano y Pulqueria a la Puerta Teodosiana, en la entrada del palacio situado en el *Hebdomon*, mediante una exhibición pública. No obstante, el nuevo emperador enalteció en mayor medida a la figura de Pulqueria, evergeta y última emperatriz teodosiana en Oriente.[76] Según las *Parastaseis Syntomoi Chronikai*, León I colocó una imagen de la Augusta en palacio para su veneración, siendo seguramente esta una representación de la emperatriz en sí misma o que retrataba algún episodio de su vida.[77] Estas iniciativas por parte de León dejaban constancia de la importancia que tenía lo visual en esta época y su repercusión pública, especialmente de cara a la propaganda de la figura de la emperatriz. Teniendo en cuenta las bajas tasas de alfabetización, las imágenes cobraban

---

72   Ibid., 89.

73   Ibid., 91.

74   M. Vallejo Girvés, *Portraits of a Dinasty: Graphic Representations of the Families of the Empress Verina and Ariadne (457–491)*, en: M.C. Chiriatti / R. Villegas Marín (eds.), *Mujeres imperiales, mujeres reales. Representaciones públicas y representaciones de poder en la Antigüedad Tardía*, CAMA 2, Leiden 2021, 136–137.

75   Paras. Synt. Chron. 45 (Cameron / Herrin, 1984, 122).

76   Pulqueria fue buenamente valorada por sus decisiones políticas, siendo considerada por el pueblo como "la custodia del emperador" (Soz., h.e. 9.1.2–3; Thphn., chron. a. m. 5905) Además, esta sería incluso aclamada por los obispos dentro del contexto del Concilio de Calcedonia (451) como la "Nueva Helena" (K. Holum, *Theodosian Empresses: Women and Imperial Dominion in late Antiquity*, Berkeley 1982, 214–216).

77   Cameron / Herrin, 1984, 235.

un mayor sentido y significado que el de hoy en día, tanto en ambientes mundanos y cotidianos como sobre todo en los palaciegos y eclesiásticos.[78] De este modo evocando a la difunta Pulqueria, última teodosiana en Oriente, mediante representaciones de la emperatriz *post mortem*, León lograba vincular su recién instituida dinastía con la anterior.[79]

Por otro lado, siguiendo el ejemplo de Helena,[80] soberana y evergeta, las emperatrices teodosianas destacaron por impulsar grandes proyectos de construcción. Estas iniciativas contribuyeron a mejorar su reputación, distinguiéndose del resto de la población por su *pietas*. Además, ofrecían a la emperatriz una mayor autoridad y prestigio más allá de la ciudad de Constantinopla. No obstante, en el caso de Pulqueria, la mayoría de sus construcciones se ubicaron en la capital,[81] siendo muchas terminadas ya durante el reinado de León I.[82] De hecho, tradicionalmente se ha aceptado que la fundación de las Iglesias de la Virgen *Chalkoprateia* (Χαλκοπρατεῖα) y de la Virgen *Blachernitissa* (Βλαχερνίτισσα) corrieron a cargo de Pulqueria y, sin embargo, estudios recientes han apuntado a que seguramente ambas iglesias fueran fundadas por Verina, siguiendo el modelo de emperatrices constructoras.[83] Del mismo modo ocurriría con la Iglesia de *Haghia Irene* (Ἁγία Εἰρήνη), en Perama.[84]

---

78 L.A. Wainwright, *Portraits of Power: The Representations of Imperial Women in the Byzantine Empire* (PhD thesis), Birmingham 2018, 1–25.

79 Vallejo Girvés, 2021, 136–137.

80 Helena más que ser recordada por su historia personal y su papel político dentro de la corte de Constantino, lo es por la historia que le atribuye el hallazgo de la Vera Cruz (*lignum crucis*), hazaña que le valió el reconocimiento de Santa. La leyenda sobre el descubrimiento de la Cruz y los clavos por Helena se originó en Jerusalén en la segunda mitad del siglo IV, después de su muerte. Ya en sus primeras versiones, se presentaba a Helena como devota y munificente, basadas en la descripción de la emperatriz dada por Eusebio de Cesarea en su *Vita Constantini*. En concreto, el obispo alaba la piedad de la Augusta durante su peregrinación a las provincias orientales (Eus., h.e. 3.41.2), su amor hacia los indefensos y sus diferentes actos de fe, como serían la construcción de dos iglesias en Belén y en el Monte de los Olivos respectivamente (J. Hillner, *Helena Augusta: Mother of the Empire*, Oxford 2022, 10–12; I. Lasala Navarro, *Helena Augusta: una biografía histórica*, Tesis Doctoral, Universidad de Zaragoza, Zaragoza, 2013: 38–41; 269; J.W. Drijvers, *Helena Augusta: The Mother of Constantine the Great and the Legend of Her Finding of the True Cross*, Leiden 1993, 85).

81 L. James, *Making a Name: Reputation and Imperial Founding and Refounding in Constantinople*, in: *Wiener Jahrbuch für Kunstgeschichte* 60 (2012), 63–72. Para conocer los proyectos de construcción concretos de Pulqueria, véase Ibid., 65–68.

82 Vallejo Girvés, 2021, 136.

83 James, 2012, 68.

84 M. Vallejo Girvés, *Empress Verina among the Pagans*, en: M. Sághy / E.M. Schoolman (eds.), *Pagans and Christians in the Late Roman Empire. New Evidence, New Approaches (4th–8th*

Además de los motivos políticos e ideológicos evidentes que llevaron a
Verina a continuar las iniciativas constructivas de las emperatrices teodosianas y, por tanto, a fundar las iglesias mencionadas anteriormente, existe otra
razón para datar su construcción en los inicios de la dinastía leónida. Marciano
y Pulqueria fueron de hecho los primeros gobernantes en promover activamente el culto a la Virgen María después del Concilio de Éfeso (431).[85] Tras la
asimilación de Helena a la Virgen María en el *De obitu Theodosii* de Ambrosio
de Milán, el obispo creó un prototipo divino para las emperatrices, puesto que
María, virgen y humana, había concebido al hijo de Dios (Θεοτόκος).[86] Al mostrar especial devoción a la *Theotokos* por primera vez, éstos contribuyeron a
robustecer la nueva ideología imperial femenina, reforzando por tanto la analogía entre la emperatriz y la Virgen. A su vez, al reverenciar explícitamente a la
Madre de Dios, trataron de convertirla en la protectora de la pareja imperial.[87]

Si bien, en primer lugar, el culto que León y Verina tributaron a la Virgen
tenía la finalidad de mostrar a los súbditos del imperio la relación armoniosa
entre ambos y su capacidad para gobernar, en última instancia el mensaje que
subyacía detrás de esta imagen estaba directamente relacionado con la legitimación divina de toda una dinastía. En este sentido, y según transmitido por
un manuscrito del siglo X, conocemos la existencia de un mosaico en la capilla
relicaria *Hagia Soros* (Ἁγία Σορός) –mandada construir por León I– de la Iglesia
de las Blaquernas (Ἡ Παναγία τῶν Βλαχερνῶν), en el que aparecía representado

---

        centuries), Budapest 2017, 46; D. Bogdantsalis, Οἰκεῖοι: *The Network of Empress Verina*, en:
        Diogenes 13 (2022), 15.

85   Bogdantsalis, 2022, 5–22.

86   El panegírico fúnebre *De obitu Theodosii* de Ambrosio de Milán y, en concreto, el famoso
        pasaje sobre el descubrimiento de las reliquias del *lignum crucis* por Helena (Ambros.,
        Theod. 40–46), madre de Constantino, supone la plasmación teórica de esta nueva ideo-
        logía imperial femenina. En la oración, Ambrosio trata de vincular las reliquias con el
        poder imperial mediante el simbolismo de la diadema y la brida, argumentando de forma
        gráfica el poder moderador y legitimador de la fe cristiana. Al ser Helena la protagonista
        de los hechos y al asociar a la Augusta con la Virgen María, el obispo resaltó a las empera-
        trices como agentes activos dentro del nuevo estado cristiano y equiparó su autoridad a la
        del emperador. No obstante, la trayectoria de Elia Flaccila, cronológicamente anterior a la
        muerte de Teodosio y, por tanto, también a la redacción de esta oración fúnebre, vendría
        a demostrar que lo expuesto en el texto por Ambrosio de Milán sería más bien el reflejo
        de una realidad ya aceptada dentro de la nueva dinastía reinante. Las emperatrices teo-
        dosianas vinieron a retomar en su propio beneficio una doctrina ya articulada en tiempos
        de Constantino con Helena, manteniendo con ello en alta posición su imagen dinástica.
        Véase Angelova, 2014, 236–237; D. Natal Villazala, Sed non totus recessit. *Legitimidad,
        Incertidumbre, y cambio político en el* De Obitu Theodosii, en: Gerión 28 (2010), 321; Lazala
        Navarro, 2013, 273; Buenacasa Pérez, 2021, 115.

87   James, 2014, 69.

el grupo familiar ante la Virgen.[88] La capilla de la Iglesia había sido ricamente ornamentada para albergar, en concreto, las reliquias de las vestiduras de la Virgen, traídas desde Galilea a Constantinopla. Verina entregaba a la Virgen a su nieto, León II, rogándole por el amparo de su recién fundada dinastía. Cualquier súbdito que entrara a la Iglesia y observara la imagen, entendería el mensaje de que el gobierno de la pareja imperial y el de toda la dinastía estaba amparado por la Madre de Dios (Θεοτόκος).

Finalmente, tanto Ariadna como Verina siguieron el modelo flacciliano y eudoxiano y antepusieron *Aelia* a su nombre personal en clara analogía a estas.[89] Aunque no se tiene muy claro cuál era el significado de este título honorífico, parece tener relación con la intención de estas a remontarse a las emperatrices anteriores en su afán por mostrar continuidad dinástica.[90] A este respecto, prosiguiendo con la tradición y con los mismos fines políticos, tanto Verina como Ariadna añadieron Elia a su nombre, como se puede observar en las leyendas de sus respectivas emisiones monetales.

5   Verina y Ariadna dentro y fuera de la Corte: Estrategias de Poder y *Networking* político

En cuanto al protagonismo político de Verina, recordemos la influencia que debió tener la emperatriz en su marido y en la toma de decisiones imperiales, como demuestra el hecho de que muchos de los miembros de su familia desempeñaran altos cargos estatales a lo largo del reinado de León I. Del

---

88   Desafortunadamente, el mosaico fue destruido en algún momento durante la Querella Iconoclasta, pero sabemos de su existencia gracias al testimonio del *Codex Parisinus Graecus* (fol. 257–258), un manuscrito del siglo X. Según este relato, dentro del rico ornamento de esta capilla se encontraba un gran mosaico, en el cual aparecían representados los miembros más importantes de la dinastía tracia – León I y Verina junto con Ariadne y su hijo, el futuro León II – y la Virgen entronizada junto al niño Jesús. En concreto, en la imagen el infante León era ofrecido a la Virgen por su abuela, Verina, en vez de por su madre Ariadna. Así, Verina aparecía representada como matriarca de la dinastía, siendo la encargada de suplicar a la Virgen que protegiera al futuro heredero y gobernador del Imperio. Por otro lado, destacaba también la ausencia de Zenón, padre de León II y marido de Ariadna, mientras que esta sí que aparecía representada. La pareja imperial quería por tanto dejar un registro gráfico y espiritual señalando los miembros de la dinastía que iban a gobernar el Imperio en el futuro, a través de su hija y nieto. Véase M. Vallejo Girvés, *Augusta Verina's Symbols of Power in the Context of Leontius's Usurpation of Zeno*, en: B. Girotti / G. Marsili / M.E. Pomero (eds.), *Il potere dell'immagine e della parola. Elementi distintivi dell'aristocrazia femminile da Roma a Bisanzio*, Spoleto 2022, 75–94.

89   L. James, *Empresses and power in early Byzantium*, London 2001, 130.

90   Ibid., 128.

mismo modo, pese a las catastróficas consecuencias que tuvo la derrota en la campaña militar contra el Reino Vándalo (468), Basilisco no fue apartado de la corte gracias a la intercesión de Verina, pudiendo protagonizar posteriormente la revuelta contra Zenón. La prematura muerte de León II, por tanto, ponía en peligro la posición que la emperatriz había logrado alcanzar en palacio, así como el poder de su grupo familiar. Por ello y demostrando su ambición, independientemente de cuál fuera su grado de participación en el complot, decidió actuar para recuperar el estatus del que disfrutó tanto ella como su familia durante el reinado de León I.

Asimismo, como bien apunta la profesora Vallejo Girvés, las maniobras políticas de Verina denotaban que esta estaba firmemente convencida de que ella misma era portadora de la legitimidad de la dinastía iniciada por León I, una convicción claramente percibida también por los rivales de Zenón, que deseaban explotar los atributos del poder de Verina para su acceso al dominio del Imperio.[91] De este modo, Verina, como Augusta, fue el principal agente de legitimidad de tres usurpadores distintos: Basilisco, Marciano y Leoncio. La simbología imperial, ahora compartida por la pareja en su conjunto, jugó un papel primordial en estos momentos de levantamientos y gran inestabilidad política. Por ejemplo, sabemos que durante la sublevación de Illos, Verina fue obligada a vestir la túnica imperial –o por lo menos, una lo suficientemente ostentosa– a la hora de coronar al usurpador Leoncio.[92] Investido fuera de la corte de Constantinopla y con una rebelión en marcha, la importancia del ritual era clave para que el pueblo entendiera la legitimidad y la solemnidad de la coronación, cualidades transmitidas a Leoncio a partir de Verina.[93] Los súbditos del imperio habían visualizado durante los años del reinado de León I la imagen de la emperatriz ataviada con la clámide imperial, símbolo indispensable de su poder y magnificencia. Así, este elemento resultaba esencial en la proyección de su poder, autoridad y estatus de la emperatriz y, por tanto, otorgaba mayor licitud al levantamiento.

Por otro lado, para sumar al resto de provincias del imperio a su causa, los rebeldes obligaron a Verina a firmar una serie de documentos como *Perpetua Augusta*. Tanto Juan Malalas como Teófanes nos hablan de que la emperatriz mandó un rescripto imperial a los gobernadores de Antioquía, Egipto, Libia y Oriente para que aceptaran a Leoncio como emperador y no se opusieran a él.[94] Este título, que aparece en la leyenda de muchas monedas de emperadores

---

91   Vallejo Girvés, 2021, 76.
92   Thphn., chron. a. m. 5973.
93   Vallejo Girvés, 2022, 78–79.
94   Thphn., chron. a. m. 5974; Jo. Mal., chron. 15.14.

tardoantiguos –incluidos León I y el mismo Zenón–.[95] indicaba en el caso de Verina que la emperatriz no había perdido ni el título ni por tanto su estatus pese al fallecimiento de su marido el emperador. Al ser *Perpetua Augusta*, tenía la legitimidad de levantarse.[96] Asimismo, en el texto Verina haría mención expresa a que fue ella junto con León I quien eligió emperador a Zenón,[97] y que, debido a la mala gestión del Imperio y la política religiosa emprendida por este, se había visto obligada a buscar un emperador sustituto que pusiera remedio a la situación –Leoncio–.[98] Claramente, siendo la emperatriz obligada a participar en esta usurpación, realmente no sería ella quien escribiría el documento o lo hizo de forma obligada. Sin embargo, como se ha podido inferir a partir de los testimonios de las fuentes, esta nueva percepción de la emperatriz como agente político activo en la toma de decisiones que concernían al gobierno de este ya existía en la mentalidad de los súbditos del Imperio.

En el caso de la rebelión de Illos, asimismo, Verina sería una pieza clave para su legitimación mediante su título de Augusta y el simbolismo detrás del mismo. Tal es así que Zenón, consciente de ello, retiró esta denominación a Verina y la convirtió en una traidora del Imperio por sus delitos de *laesa maiestas*. Habiéndole sido revocado su título de Augusta, el nombramiento de Leoncio pasaba a ser ilegítimo.[99] Pese a su fallecimiento nueve días después de que Illos se viese obligado a refugiarse en Isauria, por razones obvias el cuerpo de Verina fue embalsamado y conservado por los rebeldes durante los cuatro años que duró el levantamiento. Igualmente, tampoco beneficiaba a Zenón dar un entierro imperial a la Augusta que había sido la fuente de poder legítimo de una usurpación que todavía no había sido sofocada.[100] No obstante, y pese a la multitud de problemas que causó Verina para el gobierno de Zenón, sus restos mortales fueron finalmente devueltos a Constantinopla y enterrados con honores y distinciones. Al fin y al cabo, a Zenón también interesaba que la pareja imperial de Verina y León, quienes lo habían elegido a él como emperador, estuvieran enterrados y consagrados juntamente con el fin de fortalecer la legitimidad imperial de su reinado.[101] Es por eso que Zenón, seguramente

---

95   Jo. Mal., chron. 15.12.
96   Vallejo Girvés, 2022, 80–82.
97   Este hecho también queda relatado en Evag., h.e. 2.17 y Thphn., chron. a. m. 5966, quedando reflejado entonces el poder político que sus contemporáneos asimilaban a la emperatriz.
98   Thphn. chron. a. m. 5973–5974.
99   Vallejo Girvés, 2021, 88.
100 Ibid., 84–85.
101 Ibid., 85–90.

influenciado por Ariadna,[102] decidiera devolverle el título de Augusta a su suegra, traer su cuerpo a Constantinopla y enterrarla en el *heroon* de Constantino de la Iglesia de los Santos Apóstoles junto a su marido, León I.[103] De este modo, la figura de Verina fue rehabilitada *post mortem*.

Más allá de su poder e influencia política como Augusta, Verina demostró a lo largo de su vida ser carismática, determinada y audaz, dispuesta a tomar riesgos para alcanzar sus objetivos políticos. Mientras que en la rebelión de Illos su figura fue utilizada como herramienta ideológica para legitimar el levantamiento, en el caso de las usurpaciones de su hermano Basilisco Verina tuvo un protagonismo clave.[104] En este sentido, la emperatriz demostró su habilidad política creando durante el reinado de su marido una camarilla de asociados que le serían de gran utilidad para el triunfo de este levantamiento. Y es que, junto a sus familiares, Verina consiguió crear una gran red de partidarios.[105] Por un lado, estaría un determinado grupo de funcionarios civiles y militares (οἰκεῖοι) que en su día se asociaron con la Augusta y que debían el comienzo de sus carreras a la misma. A esta facción pertenecería Patricio, *magister officiorum* jubilado y supuesto amante de la emperatriz; Epinikos, enviado por Verina para asesinar a Illos y Urbicio, *praepositus sacri cubiculi* en diferentes periodos durante los años 430–500 y quien apoyó a la misma durante la usurpación de su hermano.[106] Además de sus destrezas en las estrategias de la arena política, Verina logró contar con el apoyo de estas figuras gracias a la reforma del tesoro imperial realizada por León I, que le permitió ser la primera emperatriz económicamente independiente.[107] Durante el último periodo de su reinado, la *res privata* del emperador fue dividida en dos partes, pasando una de ellas a manos de la Augusta.[108] Este hecho demuestra la estima que León profesaba a su esposa y a su vez la influencia que Verina tenía en él, permitiéndole acumular una autoridad y una independencia sin precedentes.

Por otro lado, Verina participó activamente en el nuevo papel en asuntos religiosos que paulatinamente iban recubriendo las emperatrices cristianas, consiguiendo gracias al mismo rodearse de hombres y mujeres destacables por su devoción y, al mismo tiempo, quienes constituyeron también parte de su

---

102   Thphn., chron. a. m. 5975.
103   Vallejo Girvés, 2021, 90–93.
104   Como afirmado por Leszka, 1998, 135, en nuestra opinión también Marciano utilizó como pretexto la situación de Verina para proclamarse como emperador. Además, estando ella en Isauria encerrada, su influencia en Constantinopla sería cuestionable.
105   Bogdantsalis, 2022, 6.
106   Ibid., 11–14.
107   Croke, 2015, 299.
108   Ibid.; Bogdantsalis, 2022, 11.

círculo cercano de aliados. Estas compañías aumentaron la reputación devota de la emperatriz, llevando a ser considerada, al igual que Pulqueria en su día, como una *nueva Helena*.[109]

A este propósito, podemos hacer referencia a la visita que realizó la emperatriz durante el reinado de su marido León I a Matrona de Perge, una figura destacada del monacato femenino en aquellos entonces. Tras su visita, muchas mujeres nobles de la capital comenzaron a seguir el ejemplo de Verina.[110] Por la misma época, Verina también visitó a Daniel el Estilita, con quien la pareja real mantuvo buenas relaciones. La *Vita S. Danielis Stylitae* menciona que, gracias a las oraciones y bendiciones del santo, Verina dio a luz a un hijo, aunque fallecería poco después.[111] También relata que la emperatriz, junto con León I, fue a pedirle al santo la interferencia divina después del gran incendio que azotó Constantinopla en el año 465. Así, de forma general, el escritor anónimo de la obra nos muestra una imagen muy favorable de la soberana, llegando incluso a justificar su participación en la trama de Basilisco, de quien el santo no era partidario por su política monofisita.[112]

Si el protagonismo político de Verina es innegable, no debemos subestimar la influencia, el patrocinio y la autoridad con las que contó Ariadna durante los reinados de Zenón y Anastasio. De hecho, las abundantes imágenes conservadas apuntan a su elevado estatus y autoridad como emperatriz.[113]

En cuanto a sus acciones políticas, sería precisamente su deseo de guardar su posición social como Augusta –título que recibió seguramente al a muerte de su padre tras la entronización de su hijo, León II (474)– lo que le haría apoyar, en las sucesivas revueltas protagonizadas por sus familiares, a su marido Zenón. Efectivamente, ella era emperatriz gracias a su matrimonio con el isaurio, quien en primera instancia había sido elegido por su padre y la misma Verina para gobernar el imperio. Así, Ariadna hubiese perdido su estatus en caso de apoyar a sus familiares en la usurpación de Basilisco (474–476) y en el intento de su cuñado Marciano (479). De hecho, tanto Malalas[114] como Evagrio Escolástico[115] nos narran que Ariadna huyó en secreto de su madre, como decimos, prefiriendo mantener su condición y privilegios asociados al título de Augusta en caso de que Zenón recuperara el trono, antes que perder su rango en un Imperio gobernado por alguno de sus familiares. Miroslaw J. Leszka

---

109 Croke, 2015, 301.
110 Bogdantsalis, 2022, 16; Vallejo Girvés, 2017, 47.
111 Bogdantsalis, 2022, 16.
112 Vallejo Girvés, 2017, 45; Bogdantsalis, 2022, 16–17.
113 Croke, 2015, 294.
114 Jo. Mal., chron. 14.2.
115 Evagr., h.e. 3.28.

afirma que Verina habría informado sobre el complot a su yerno principalmente para proteger a Ariadna,[116] pero existe también la opción, más acorde
con la versión de Malalas y Evagrio, de que la emperatriz considerase que su
hija iba a permanecer en Constantinopla junto con su familia. No obstante,
esto no significa que Ariadna no se preocupara por el destino de sus parientes,
encontrándose en un punto ambiguo dentro de los dos bandos.[117] Así quedó
demostrado cuando logró salvar al hijo de Armato, Basilisco, llevándolo a la
Iglesia de las Blaquernas para que lo tonsuraran.[118] Al hacerlo, este quedaba
imposibilitado de acceder al trono y, por tanto, ya no resultaba un problema
para Zenón, salvándole de este modo la vida.

Aparentemente, la relación entre Ariadna y Verina osciló siempre entre el
vínculo maternofilial y los deseos de ambas de mantener su posición como
Augustae. Una vez recuperado el trono Zenón (476), la influencia en palacio
de Verina dejó de ser la ostentada durante el reinado de su marido. Aun así,
conservó algunos resquicios como progenitora de Ariadna. La posición prominente de Illos en la corte chocaba con los intereses de madre e hija, mermando
el crédito que Ariadna pudiese tener en Zenón gracias a que permaneció a su
lado durante la usurpación de su tío. Sin embargo, una vez encerrada Verina
en Cilicia, hasta que Ariadna no fue víctima por sí misma de la influencia que
ejercía Illos en Zenón, no trató de devolver a su madre a la corte.

Pese a que las relaciones entre Ariadna y Zenón no fuesen seguramente
buenas, incluso si como afirma Jordanes el emperador había autorizado el asesinato de su esposa, el caso es que la emperatriz conservó la independencia de
sus propios recursos financieros, pudiendo al igual que Verina en su día mantener a un séquito de leales. En este sentido, durante el exilio de Verina muchos
de sus confidentes presumiblemente entraron en el círculo de partidarios de
Ariadna. Este sería el caso, por ejemplo, del *praepositus sacri cubiculi* de Urbicio. Después de que Ariadna le diera un ultimátum a Zenón para que este eligiera entre Illos o ella,[119] Urbicio sería el encargado de contratar al sicario que
solo consiguió arrancarle una oreja al militar.[120] Del mismo modo, fue Urbicio
quien sugirió que debía ser Ariadna quien eligiera al sucesor de Zenón.[121] Con
ello, el prepósito del cubículo estaba tratando de asegurar la influencia y el
poder de Ariadna en el reinado del nuevo emperador, al ser este de su elección.

---

116   Leszka, 2017, 34.
117   Vallejo Girvés, 2016, 201–202.
118   Thphn., chron. a.m. 5969.
119   Thphn., chron. a.m. 5972; Jo. Mal., chron. 15.13.
120   Bogdantsalis, 2022, 14.
121   Chiriatti, 2021, 185.

Al igual que Verina durante la coronación de Leoncio, Ariadna apareció en el hipódromo tras la muerte de Zenón ataviada con las insignias imperiales, símbolos de su poder como Augusta y, en esta ocasión, de su legitimidad a la hora de escoger al sucesor de Zenón. En la *adlocutio* de Ariadna y en su intención de revocar el Edicto del *Henotikón*, como así deseaban los constantinopolitanos, la emperatriz demostró su astucia política, consciente de que los sectores monásticos de la ciudad jamás aceptarían la elevación a la púrpura de Longino o de otro emperador que no fuera calcedonense. Este episodio serviría a Ariadna para mostrarse, siguiendo la ideología imperial creada por sus antecesoras, como garante de la ortodoxia católica. Así, la emperatriz se casaría con Anastasio solo después de que este firmara la declaración en la cual se comprometía a seguir lo dictado en el Concilio de Calcedonia.[122] Gracias a este matrimonio, siendo su unión con Ariadna lo que legitimaba la posición de Anastasio como emperador, ambos comenzaron a gobernar el Imperio.[123]

Más allá de su protagonismo en el ascenso al trono del silenciario, Ariadna trató de continuar participando en la toma de decisiones políticas. En este sentido, la emperatriz ejerció su influencia política para que su marido nombrarse a Antemio y a su hijo, parientes suyos, en importantes cargos en la corte.[124] Siendo ella la única que quedaba de su grupo familiar en palacio tras la revuelta de Leoncia y Marciano, si Ariadna quería revertir esta situación, esto venía a significar que la participación de miembros de su familia en la gestión del imperio le era de utilidad en el juego de influencias políticas de la misma. A este respecto, sabemos que, dentro de las medidas económicas de Anastasio, una de ellas fue la de revertir la reforma de León I por la cual el tesoro personal del emperador pasaba a estar compartido con la emperatriz.[125] Por tanto, sin los medios económicos para sufragar su círculo de influencias, la vuelta de sus familiares a puestos significativos en la corte sería la estrategia elegida por la emperatriz para mantenerse influyente dentro de esta.

En lo relativo a lo religioso, al igual que sus antecesores, a Anastasio y a Ariadna se le asocia la construcción o reconstrucción de una iglesia de Santa Eufemia en Petra, la de los Cuarenta Mártires situada cerca de las Termas de Constantino y la de San Miguel Arcángel en la Nea Moudania. A estas habría que añadirle la Iglesia de Elías atribuida a Zenón y Ariadna.[126] Para Ariadna, tal y como para su madre y las teodosianas antes que ella, la construcción de

---

122 Thphn., chron. a.m. 5983; Evagr., h.e. 3.32.
123 Jo. Mal., chron. 16.1.
124 Vallejo Girvés, 2013, 89.
125 Bogdantsalis, 2022, 11.
126 Croke, 2015, 309.

iglesias simbolizaba tanto su piedad como su poder político, siendo capaces de erigir semejantes construcciones. Del mismo modo, la fundación y refundación de edificios sagrados mejoraba la reputación de la pareja imperial.[127] Siguiendo con los asuntos en materia religiosa, es precisamente sobre estos la mayor parte de información que las fuentes nos transmiten sobre Ariadna. Poco a poco y pese a lo pactado, Anastasio fue mostrando mayores simpatías al credo surgido a raíz del Edicto de Unión de Zenón. Ariadna perdió como aliado político al patriarca Eufemio (496) y, pese a que logró bajo su recomendación que la sede patriarcal de la capital fuera ocupada por Macedonio, finalmente este también fue depuesto.[128] La opinión favorable que tanto las fuentes calcedonenses como monofisitas expresan sobre nuestra emperatriz además de su alto sentido político, hacen pensar que esta también pudo modificar su convencimiento religioso o/y que esta llegara a la misma conclusión que Anastasio, consciente de los beneficios que acarrearía la comunión de la Iglesia Oriental.[129]

Ariadna murió en el año 515, tres años antes que su consorte. Su obra política, al igual que su posición social dentro de la corte le otorgó un grado significativo de influencia política pese a su rol secundario dentro del gobierno del Imperio y las limitaciones impuestas a su género. Así, ambas tuvieron acceso directo a la toma de decisiones y participaron directamente en la política imperial, incluso en los momentos más cruciales para el Estado cuando, en su caso concreto, el vacío de poder dejado por el monarca fallecido la convirtió en *la garante della porpora*.[130]

6   Algunas Conclusiones

El legado de Verina y Ariadna nos demuestra que el nuevo papel de las emperatrices cristianas no fue solo simbólico ni tuvo fines meramente propagandísticos. Ciertamente, en ocasiones los rivales de Zenón usaron los atributos de Verina como Augusta para legitimar sus acciones, dando fe igualmente de la autoridad que revestía este título. No obstante, ella misma participó en el juego político de la corte según sus intereses sobre la proyección de su poder, tratando de mantener o mejorar su autoridad y estatus dentro y fuera de ella. Del mismo modo ocurrió con Ariadna, quien además fue la elegida por los

---

127   Ibid., 309; James, 2012, 72.
128   Vallejo Girvés, 2013, 86–90.
129   Vallejo Girvés, 2013, 89.
130   Magliaro, 2013.

funcionarios de palacio y senadores para designar al nuevo emperador ante la muerte de Zenón, logrando tranquilizar a los habitantes de Constantinopla.

En cuanto a los aspectos religiosos, la asimilación de la emperatriz a la Virgen María realizada durante el reinado de Verina y León, ya formulada en el panegírico sobre la muerte de Teodosio (*De obitu Theodosii*), marcaría un importante precedente, ya que posteriores emperatrices y reinas comenzarán a tener como ejemplo seguir a la Virgen,[131] frente al modelo creado por las teodosianas basado en la figura de Helena. En este sentido, la propaganda imperial de la emperatriz como garante de la ortodoxia fue sumamente eficaz en el caso de Ariadna, siendo llamativo que la opinión de los autores sobre la misma sea positiva independientemente de que éstas sean de extracción calcedonense o monofisita. Los súbditos del imperio, influidos también por la iconografía de las imágenes públicas de la emperatriz, mantuvieron la concepción de la misma como valedora de la verdadera fe.

En definitiva, amparadas por esta nueva identidad de las emperatrices cristianas y sus insólitas posibilidades financieras, sumadas a la personalidad, carisma y las habilidades políticas de madre e hija, nuestras emperatrices lograron acaparar mayores cotas de poder de las asociadas en primera instancia al rango de Augusta. Su historia nos ofrece una visión renovada sobre el protagonismo histórico del cual las mujeres gozaron en un pasado, participando activamente en el transcurso de la dinastía y sirviéndose de estrategias típicamente femeninas para consolidar su poder.

---

131   Angelova, 2014, 234.

L'Elezione del Patriarca Ignazio (847)

l'Imperatrice Teodora II nella Politica Ecclesiastica Bizantina

Álvaro Ibáñez Chacón

Abstract

Byzantine sources do not detail why Empress Theodora favored the election of Ignatius as patriarch of Constantinople; in fact, it was considered a non-canonical choice, but Ignatius descended from the Imperial family, was an iconodule and had created his own clerical brotherhood, so that the election could be part of the policy of reconciliation carried out by Theodora after the dissolution of Iconoclasm.

1   Teodora, imperatrice iconodula

Come accadde anche per altre imperatrici bizantine, Teodora II (*ca.* 805–858, PMBZ 7286) fu un personaggio di grande importanza nella politica del suo tempo[1], al punto da essere onorata con un'agiografia (BHG 1731) che la descrive più come βασίλισσα che ἁγία[2].

Figlia di Marino (PMBZ 4812) e di Teoctiste (PMBZ 8025), sorella di Petrona (PMBZ 5929), Barda (PMBZ 791), Sofia (PMBZ 6842), Maria (PMBZ 4738) e Irene (PMBZ 1448), proveniva – come d'altronde tutta la sua famiglia – da Ebissa, in Paflagonia, e aveva quindi origini armene, come sembrano dimostrare le fonti e il suo rapporto di parentela con lo zio paterno Manuele Magistro

---

*   Desidero ringraziare il collega, Dott. Lorenzo Ciolfi (*École des hautes études en sciences sociales*, Parigi), per l'attenta lettura del mio contributo, la revisione accurata della traduzione in lingua italiana e per aver arricchito il mio testo con i suoi preziosissimi suggerimenti.

1   Sono già classici gli studi di L. Garland, *Byzantine Empress, Women and Power in Byzantium, AD 527–1204*, London 1999 e di J. Herrin, *Women in Purple. Rulers of Medieval Byzantium*, London 2001.

2   Il testo è stato curato da A. Markopoulos, *Βίος τῆς αὐτοκρατείρας Θεοδώρας (BHG 1731)*, in: Συμμείκτα 5 (1983), 249–285, tradotto da M.P. Vinson, *Life of St. Theodora the Empress*, in: A.-M. Talbot (ed.), *Byzantine defenders of images. Eight Saint's Lives in English Translation*, Washington 1998, 353–382 e da L. Franco, *Cinque sante bizantine. Storie di cortigiane, transvestite, eremite, imperatrici*, Milano 2017, 115–142; cf. Á. Narro, *El culto a las santas y a los santos en la Antigüedad Tardía y la época bizantina*, Madrid 2019, 167–168. Si dice che il corpo di Teodora sia conservato nella Chiesa di Santa Teodora a Corfù: O.F.A. Meinardus, *A Study of the Relics of Saints of the Greek Orthodox Church*, in: OrChr 54 (1970), 130–278 (253).

l'Armeno (PMBZ 4707)[3]. Se si dà credito alla tradizione, Teodora fu scelta sposa da Teofilo (PMBZ 8167; reg. 829–842), l'ultimo imperatore iconoclasta[4], mediante un *bride show*, ma non c'è consenso tra i bizantinisti sulla veracità di questo singolare concorso[5]. Dal matrimonio fra Teodora e Teofilo nacquero poi Costantino (PMBZ 3931), Tecla (PMBZ 7261), Anna (PMBZ 460), Anastasia (PMBZ 231), Pulcheria (PMBZ 6384), Maria (PMBZ 4735) e il futuro imperatore Michele III (PMBZ 4991; reg. 842–867)[6].

Quando Teofilo morì nell'842, Teodora assunse il potere in vece di Michele, allora minore, restaurando il culto alle immagini e ottenendo il perdono *post mortem* per lo sposo iconoclasta attraverso un sotterfugio onirico-profetico. Secondo la cosiddetta *Narratio de Theophili imperatoris absolutione*[7], Teodora avrebbe avuto un sogno ammonitore mentre il marito era ancora sul letto di

---

3 Theoph. cont. 4.1, ed. M. Featherstone / J. Signes Codoñer, *Chronographiae quae Theophanis continuati nomine fertur libri I–IV*, CFHB 53, Boston / Berlin, 2015, 148; Gen. 3.2, ed. A. Lesmueller-Werner / J. Turn, *Iosephi Genesii regum libri quattuor*, CFHB 14, Berlin / New York 1978, 36; BHG 1731 §2, ed. Markopoulos, 1983, 257.

4 Sulla politica di Teofilo si veda J. Signes Codoñer, *The Emperor Theophilos and the East, 829–842: Court and Frontier in Byzantium during the Last Phase of Iconoclasm*, London / New York ²2016.

5 Ci sono alcuni che, come W. Treadgold, *The Bride-Shows of the Byzantine Emperors*, in: Byz 49 (1979), 395–413, danno per certo il concorso matrimoniale; altri invece credono che si tratti soltanto di un *topos* folcloristico aggiunto dalle fonti letterarie, come afferma L. Rydén, *The Bride-Shows in the Byzantine Court. History of Fiction?*, in: Eranos 83 (1985), 175–191, anche se tali episodi introducono qualche precisione nel dettaglio. Per la scelta di Teodora si veda M.P. Vinson, *The Life of Theodora and the Rhetoric of the Byzantine Bride Show*, in: JÖB 49 (1999), 31–60; Garland, 1999, 96–98; Herrin, 2001, 190–191. La tradizione racconta che la poetessa Cassia (PMBZ 3637) prese parte allo stesso concorso, ma non fu selezionata: I. Rochow, *Studien zu der Person, den Werken und dem Nachleben der Dichterin Kassia*, BBA 38, Berlin 1967, 20–26; Ó. Prieto Domínguez, *Casia de Constantinopla, Poemas*, Madrid 2019, 10–14; L.M. Ciolfi, *Cassia, Sentenze*, in: E. Lelli (ed.), *Proverbi, sentenze e massime di saggezza in Grecia e a Roma. Tutte le raccolte da Pitagora all'Umanesimo*, Milano 2021, 940–955, 1808–1811 (1809).

6 Per il suo regno si veda P. Varona Codeso, *Miguel III (842–867). Construcción histórica y literaria de un reinado*, BGAP 33, Madrid 2009.

7 Di questo racconto ci sono diverse redazioni: BHG 1732–1734k, ed. W. Regel, *Analecta Byzantino–Russica*, Petropoli / Lipsiae 1891, 19–39. Per le altre versioni si vedano M. Vinson, *The Terms ἐγκόλπιον and τενάντιον and the Conversion of Theophilus in the Life of Theodora (BHG 1731)*, in: GRBS 36 (1995), 89–99; A. Markopoulos, *The Rehabilitation of the Emperor Theophilos*, in: L. Brubaker (ed.), *Byzantium in the Ninth Century: Dead or Alive?*, London / New York 1998, 37–49; Herrin, 2001, 205–206; P. Karli-Hayter, *Restoration of Orthodoxy, the Pardon of Theophilos and the Acta Davidis, Symeonis et Georgii*, in: E.M. Jeffreys (ed.), *Byzantine Style, Religion, and Civilization. In Honour of Sir Steven Runciman*, Cambridge / New York 2006, 361–373; Varona Codeso, *Miguel III*, 2009, 77–80; A. Timotin, *Visions, prophéties et pouvoir à Byzance*, Dossiers byzantins 10, Paris 2010, 143–149; L. Brubaker, *Inventing Byzantine Iconoclasm*, Bristol 2012, 107–114.

morte: l'imperatrice vide Teofilo, nudo e ammanettato, mentre veniva tortu-
rato sulla piazza pubblica e, al momento del verdetto finale – sentenziato da
un uomo imponente e terribile seduto davanti a un'immagine di Gesù Cristo –,
ella pregò per lui e ne ottenne il perdono celeste. Quanto accadde nei sogni,
fu poi confermato dalle autorità ecclesiastiche quando anche il patriarca
Metodio (PMBZ 4977)[8] ricevette un sogno rivelatore che confermava la riabilitazione dell'imperatore. L'immagine di Teofilo non solo fu redenta, bensì la
tradizione successiva considerò il sovrano un re giusto, come si può vedere nel
dialogo anonimo *Timarion* (XII sec.), nel quale egli è incluso, insieme ad Eaco
e Minosse, come terzo giudice dell'Ade, retto e virtuoso:

Ὅ γε μὴν Θεόφιλος οὐδέν τι λαμπρὸν ἢ ἀνθηρὸν ἐνεδέδυτο· λιτότητι δὲ καὶ αὐχμηρίᾳ
συνεσκεύαστο καὶ μελανειμονίᾳ. Ἐλέγετο δὲ κἀν τῇ βασιλείᾳ τοιοῦτος εἶναι, ἄκομ-
ψος πάνυ τῷ φαινομένῳ καὶ ἀπέριττος· τῇ γε μὴν εὐθυδικίᾳ καὶ τῇ ἄλλῃ ἀρετῇ πάνυ
λαμπρὸς καὶ φιλότιμος. Ἀλλὰ καὶ οὕτως ἔχων αὐχμοῦ, χάριν τῶν ὀφθαλμῶν ἀπεδίδου
καὶ λαμπρὸς ἦν τὸ πρόσωπον καὶ τεθαρρηκώς.

"Teofilo invece non indossava nulla di splendido e fiorito: era abbigliato con
gretta semplicità e di nero. Così dicevano che fosse stato anche da imperatore,
disadorno nell'aspetto e semplice, ma splendido e venerando per l'equilibrio e le
altre virtù. Ora, pur così disadorno, spirava tuttavia grazia dagli occhi, splendido
e sereno nell'espressione".[9]

Accanto alla riabilitazione del marito, il governo di Teodora maturò notevoli
meriti dal punto di vista del ripristino dell'iconodulia, fino a farle raggiungere
una speciale reputazione in seno all'ortodossia. Come si può leggere nell'agiografia a lei dedicata (la summenzionata BHG 1731), la santità dell'imperatrice
fu più politica che religiosa. Anche se i *miracula* non fossero imprescindi-
bili per diventare santo nel periodo mesobizantino[10], Teodora non ne operò

---

8   Sulla vita e sull'opera di Metodio si rimanda a G. da Costa-Louillet, *Saints de Constantino-
    ple aux VIIIᵉ, IXᵉ, Xᵉ siècles*, in: Byz 24 (1954), 453–511 (453–461); B. Zielke, *Methodios I.*, in:
    R.-J. Lilie (ed.), *Die Patriarchen der ikonoklastischen Zeit: Germanos I. – Methodios I. (715–
    847)*, BBySt 5, Frankfurt 1999, 183–260; J. Cotsonis, *The Imagery of Patriarch Methodios I's
    Lead Seals and the New World Order of Ninth-Century Byzantium*, in: G. Dragas (ed.), *Legacy
    of Achievement: Metropolitan Methodios of Boston. Festal Volume on the 25th Anniversary
    of His Consecration to the Episcopate*, Boston 2008, 366–387; G.P. Bithos, *Saint Methodios
    of Constantinople. A Study of His Life and Works*, Rollinsford 2009; Ó. Prieto Domínguez,
    Literary Circles in Byzantine Iconoclasm, Cambridge 2020, 99–118.

9   Timar. 33, ed. e trad. di R. Romano, *Pseudo-Luciano: Timarione*, Napoli 1974. Non deve
    essere dimenticata la natura satirica dell'opera.

10 M. Kaplan, *Le miracle est-il nécessaire au saint byzantin?*, in: D. Aigle (ed.), *Miracle et
    Karāma. Hagiographies médiévales comparées*, BEHE.R 109, Turnhout 2000, 167–196.

personalmente alcuno[11]. Ciononostante, si raccontavano diverse storie in merito alla sua devozione verso la Vergine. I *Patria*, ad esempio, riferiscono che Teodora ricevette la notizia della sua gravidanza mentre si recava al famoso santuario della *Theotokos* τῶν Βλαχερνῶν[12] e, lì dove aveva ricevuto tale annuncio prodigioso, fondò la Chiesa di Sant'Anna[13]. Inoltre, nella collezione di miracoli della Vergine del Convento della Fontana (Μονὴ τῆς Πηγῆς)[14] si narra che sua figlia Tecla soffrì di terribili febbri ma, grazie alle supliche della madre, ella fu guarita dalle acque miracolose; per questo motivo, il convento ricevette numerosi beni e privilegi come segno della gratitudine imperiale[15]. Teodora, in realtà, ottenne la santità in merito alla restaurazione del culto alle icone (fig. 2.1) che, secondo il *Sinaxarium Constantinopolitanum*, venerava segretamente[16]:

Αὕτη δέ εἰ καὶ φανερῶς οὐκ ἐτόλμα προσκυνεῖν τὰς ἁγίας εἰκόνας, ὅμως εἶχεν αὐτὰς κεκρυμμένας ἐν τῷ κοιτῶνι αὐτῆς, καὶ τῇ νυκτὶ ἵστατο προσευχομένη καὶ παρακαλοῦσα τὸν Θεὸν ἵνα ποήσει ἔλεος μετὰ τῶν ὀρθοδόξων.[17]

---

11   Così sostiene Franco, 2017, 110.

12   Uno dei santuari mariani più frequentati dai bizantini: R. Janin, *La géographie ecclésiastique de l'Empire byzantine. Les églises et les monastères*, Paris ²1969, 161–171.

13   *Patria* III.41, ed. T. Preger, *Scriptores originum Constantinopolitanarum*, II, Lipsiae 1907, 232–233. Esiste anche una traduzione inglese in A. Berger, *Accounts of Medieval Constantinople: The Patria*, Dumbarton Oaks Medieval Library 24, Harvard 2013, 165; cf. anche Janin, ²1969, 37 e Ruggieri, 1991, 188.

14   Il convento era situato fuori città e fu fondato da Leone I o Giustiniano: S. Bénay, *Le monastère de la Source à Constantinople*, in: EOr 3 (1900), 223–228, 295–300; J. Ebersolt, *Sanctuaires de Byzance. Recherches sur les anciens trésors des églises de Constantinople*, Paris 1921, 61–65; Janin, ²1969, 232–237.

15   Si veda la collezione di *miracula* in BHG 1072, con la traduzione inglese di A.-M. Talbot, *The Anonymous Miracles of the Shrine of the Pege*, in: S. Johnson / A.-M. Talbot (eds.), *Miracle Tales from Byzantium*, Dumbarton Oaks Medieval Library 12, Cambridge 2012, 203–297 (224–225); sulla collezione si faccia riferimento a S. Efthymiadis, *Le monastère de la Source à Constantinople et ses deux recueils de miracles. Entre hagiographie et patrographie*, in: REByz 64–65 (2006–2007), 283–309.

16   Miniatura del cosiddetto *Menologio di Basilio II*, Vaticano, Biblioteca Apostolica Vaticana, Vat. gr. 1613, f. 392, opera di Jorge, uno degli otto artisti che l'hanno decorato: I. Ševčenko, *The Illuminators of the Menologium of Basil II*, in: DOP 16 (1962), 243–276; A. Zacharova, *Los ocho artistas del Menologio de Basilio II*, in: F. D'Aiuto (dir.), *El Menologio de Basilio II (Città del Vaticano, Biblioteca Apostolica Vaticana, Vat. gr. 1613). Libro de Estudios con ocasión de la edición del facsímil*, versione spagnola a cura di I. Pérez Martín, Madrid 2009, 131–195; E. Boeck, *Un-Orthodox imagery: voids and visual narrative in the Madrid Skylitzes manuscript*, in: BMGS 33 (2009), 17–41 (28–29).

17   H. Delehaye, *Synaxarium Ecclesiae Constantinopolitanae*, Bruxellis 1902, 459–460, sebbene la notizia non sia comunemente accettata, cf. L.M. Ciolfi, *La porpora nel Sinassario di Costantinopoli. Imperatori ed imperatrici in odore di santità?*, in: M.C. Chiriatti /

"Sebbene non osasse venerare apertamente le sacre immagini, ella le aveva nascoste nella sua stanza e durante la notte pregava davanti a loro e chiedeva a Dio di avere compassione degli Ortodossi".[18]

Fig. 2.1

2 Sovrana e regina madre

Dal punto di vista politico, alla stregua di altre imperatrici dell'era bizantina, Teodora fu molto attiva durante la reggenza[19], così come aveva già mostrato il

R. Villegas Marín (eds.), *Mujeres imperiales, mujeres reales. Representaciones públicas y representaciones del poder en la Antigüedad tardía y Bizancio*, CAMA 2, Paderborn 2021, 409–437 (422).

18   La *Vita* racconta che aveva anche segretamente (κρυφίως) aiutato gli ortodossi perseguitati: BHG 1731 §6 ed. Markopoulos, 1983, 262.

19   Tra gli studi dedicati alle diverse vicende della sua vita si rimanda a P.A. Hollingsworth, *Theodora*, in: ODB 3 (1991), 2037–2038; Garland, 1999, 95–108; Herrin, 2001, 185–239; K. Kotsis, *Empress Theodora: A Holy Mother*, in: C. Fleiner / E. Woodacre (eds.), *Virtuous or Villainess? The Image of the Royal Mother from the Early Medieval to the Early Modern Era*, New York 2016, 11–36.

Fig. 2.2

valore della sua importante azione quando Teofilo era ancora vivo[20]. Oltre che sul fronte interno, il governo di Teodora fu anche coinvolto nei conflitti contro i Bulgari (fig. 2.2)[21], che segnarono la storia delle relazioni internazionali bizantine durante il IX secolo[22]. La sua posizione, variabile secondo le fonti[23], si riflette bene nella versione di Teofane Continuato:

---

20   Ad esempio, durante l'ambasciata dal Califfato di Cordoba nel 839/840: É. Lévi-Provençal, *Un échange d'ambassades entre Cordoue et Byzance au IXe siècle*, in: Byz 12 (1937), 1–24; J. Signes Codoñer, *Diplomatie und Propaganda im 9. Jahrhundert: die Gesandtschaft des al-Ghazal nach Konstantinopel*, in: C. Sode / S. Takács (eds), *Novum Millennium. Studies on Byzantine history and culture dedicated to Paul Speck*, Aldershot 2001, 379–392; E. Cardoso, *The Poetics of the Scenography of Power: The Embassy of Yahya al-Ghazāl to Constantinople*, in: Hamsa 2 (2015), 54–64; J. Sypianski, *Comprendre les Sarrasins à Byzance dans la premièr moitié du IXe siècle*, in: N.S.M. Matheou / Th. Kampianaki / L.M. Bondioli (eds.), *From Constantinople to the Frontier. The City and the Cities*, Leiden / Boston 2016, 277–293.

21   Didascalia sull'immagine di sinistra: "Bogoris, il sovrano dei Bulgari, mentre scambia messaggi con l'imperatrice Teodora" (Βόγορις ὁ ἄρχων Βουλγάρων μηνύων τῇ βασιλίδι Θεοδώρᾳ) / Didascalia sull'immagine di destra: "L'imperatrice Teodora, mentre accoglie gli inviati di Bogoris" (ἡ βασιλὶς Θεογώρα δεχομένη τοὺς παρὰ τοῦ Βογορίσει πεμφθέντες). Come sottolinea V. Tsamakda, *The Illustrated Chronicle of Iohannes Skylitzes*, Leiden 2002, 112, la *inscriptio* è stata spostata. Sull'iconografia di Teodora e Metodio in questo manoscritto si veda Boeck, 2009, 27–38.

22   Si vedano, tra l'altro, I. Dujčev, *Medioevo bizantino-slavo*, I–III, SeL 102, 113, 119, Roma 1965–1971; A. Vlasto, *The Entry of the Slavs into Christendom*, Cambridge 1970; F. Dvornik, *Byzantine Missions among the Slavs*, New Jersey 1979; L. Simeonova, *Diplomacy of the Letter and the Cross. Photios, Bulgaria and the Papacy, 860s–880s*, Amsterdam 1998; P. Sophoulis, *Byzantium and Bulgaria, 775–831*, Leiden / Boston 2012, 173–245; Signes Codoñer [2]2016, 349–366. Inoltre, si consideri l'antologia di testi commentati e annotati in M. Casas Olea, *Fuentes griegas sobre los eslavos II*, Granada 2020.

23   Un'analisi dettagliata è in P. Varona, *Teodora y los búlgaros. Una nueva lectura de las fuentes griegas*, in: Erytheia 30 (2009), 9–34.

Ὅ γε μὴν ἄρχων Βουλγαρίας – Βώγωρις οὗτος ἦν – θρασύτερον ἐξεφέρετο γυναῖκα τῆς βασιλείας κρατεῖν διακηκοώς· ὅθεν καί τινας ἀγγέλους ἀπέστελλεν πρὸς αὐτήν, τὰς συνθήκας λέγων καταλύειν καὶ κατὰ τῆς τῶν Ῥωμαίων ἐκστρατεύειν γῆς. Ἀλλ᾿ αὐτὴ μηδὲν θῆλυ ἐννοοῦσα καὶ ἄνανδρον "καὶ ἐμέ", αὐτῷ κατεμήνυεν, "κατὰ σοῦ εὑρήσεις ἀντιστρατεύουσαν. καὶ ἐλπίζω μὲν κυριεῦσαί σου· εἰ δ᾿ – ὃ μὴ γένηται – ἐκνικήσεις με, καὶ οὕτω σου περιέσομαι, τὴν νίκην ἀρίδηλον ἔχουσα· γυναῖκα γάρ, ἀλλ᾿ οὐκ ἄνδρα ἕξεις τὸν ἡττηθέντα σοι". Διὰ τοῦτο μὲν οὖν καὶ ἐφ᾿ ἡσυχίας ἔμεινεν, μηδὲν τολμήσας νεανιεύεσθαι, καὶ τὰς τῆς ἀγάπης αὖθις ἀνενέου σπονδάς.[24]

"Poi il capo dei Bulgari – si trattava di Bogoris (*i.e.* Bori)– si comportò in modo più insolente quando seppe che una donna governava l'Impero e pertanto le inviò dei messaggeri per informarla che si accingeva a sciogliere i trattati e muovere contro i Romei. Tuttavia, ella non reagì in modo femminile e codardo, ma gli rispose: "Mi troverai a contrattaccarti e spero anche di soggiogarti; ma – volesse il Cielo che ciò non accada! – ove tu mi sconfigga, anche così io ti avrò sconfitto con una vittoria evidente, perché avrai avuto come sconfitto una donna e non un uomo". Per questo motivo, non solo è rimasto calmo senza osare fare sciocchezze, ma ha rinnovato i patti di pace".

L'atteggiamento virile di un'imperatrice è un *topos* retorico spesso legato alla celebrazione di una sovrana potente e coraggiosa, modellato sulla particolare figura di Irene (PMBZ 1439; reg. 797–802)[25], ma anche pregno di risonanze classiche, come si intravede nella risposta della regina delle Amazzoni ad Alessandro Magno secondo il racconto dello Ps.-Callistene[26].

Gli aspetti del potere di Teodora sono esemplificati anche nella coniazione dei solidi con due programmi iconografici specifici: alcuni con l'immagine del Cristo sul dritto e sul rovescio la propria effigie accanto a quella di Michele; altri con la sua figura esaltata da tutti i segni del potere e la leggenda ΔΕϹΠΥΝΑ (vale a dire δέσποινα) nel dritto e le immagini dei suoi figli Michele e Tecla sul rovescio (fig. 2.3), a voler sottolineare la propria figura di regina madre[27]. Ma Teodora fu soprattutto protagonista di uno degli eventi più conflittuali del IX

---

24   Theoph. cont. 4.13, ed. Featherstone / Signes Codoñer, 2015, 230; cf. anche Gen. 4.7.

25   Si vedano, tra l'altro, D. Barbe, *Irène de Byzance. La femme empereur*, Paris 1990; Garland, 1999, 73–94; Herrin, 2001, 51–129; N. Bergamo, *Irene, Imperatore dei Romani?*, in: Chiriatti / Villegas Marín (eds.), 2021, 325–353.

26   Ps.-Callisth. 3.25, ed. W, Kroll, *Historia Alexandri Magni*, III, Berlin 1926, 35. Si faccia riferimento anche a I. Dujčev, *Légendes byzantines sur la conversión des Bulgares*, in: *Medioevo bizantino-slavo*, III, Roma 1971, 63–75 (65); Varona, *Teodora*, 2009, 18; Casas Olea, 2020, 77 n. 13. Un aneddoto simile è raccontato dal cronografo siriano Bar Hebraeus (XIII sec.) in riferimento ad una certa ambasciata araba: Herrin, 2001, 235–236.

27   Garland, 1999, 102–103; Herrin, 2001, 202; Kotsis, 2016, 13–20. Gli stessi elementi sono rappresentati sui sigilli: G. Zacos / Veglery, *Byzantine Lead Seals*, I.1, Basel 1972, 48–49, nn. 54–55.

secolo dentro e fuori i confini di Bisanzio: l'elezione di Ignazio (PMBZ 2666) a patriarca di Costantinopoli[28].

Fig. 2.3

3 La sfortunata nomina di Ignazio

Figlio di Michele I Rangabe (PMBZ 4989, reg. 811–813) e di Procopia (PMBZ 6351), figlia a sua volta dell'imperatore Niceforo I (PMBZ 5252, reg. 802–811), Ignazio appartenne alla famiglia imperiale fino all'abdicazione di Michele I il 11 luglio 813. Allora, ottenendo l'impero Leone V (PMBZ 4244, reg. 813–820), tutti i membri della sua famiglia furono esiliati, mentre Ignazio, appena quattordicenne, venne castrato e ordinato monaco[29]. Malgrado queste sventure,

---

28 Gli studi già citati di Garland o Herrin non si occupano di ciò. La monografia su Ignazio, ormai datata, di G.-N. Maultrot, *Histoire de Saint Ignace et de Photios, usurpateur de son siège*, Paris 1791 offre una visione assolutamente parziale; si vedano, tra gli altri, R. Janin, *Ignace*, in: DTC 7 (1903), 713–722; Costa-Louillet, 1954, 461–478; D. Stiernon, *Ignazio*, in: BSS 7 (1966), 665–672; A. Kazhdan, *Ignatios*, in: ODB 2 (1991), 983–984; R. Aubert, *Ignace, patriarche de Constantinople*, in: DHGE 25 (1995), 699–700; F. Dvornik, *Ignatius*, in: NCE 7 (2003), 351–352; M. Mormino, *Modello di Santità e Modelli di Empietà. Il patriarca Ignazio di Costantinopoli prima di Fozio: dalla fine della dinastia isauriana allo 'scisma' di Gregorio Absestas (790–858)*, Università degli Studi di Messina 2017/2018 (Tesi di Dottorato).

29 Attraverso la mutilazione di Michele I e dei suoi figli il nuovo imperatore faceva sì che nessuno tra quelli legittimati potesse pretendere il trono nel futuro: J.B. Bury, *A History of the Eastern Roman Empire: From the Fall of Irene to the Accession of Basil I, A.D. 802–867*, London 1912, 29; K.M. Ringrose, *The Perfect Servant. Eunuchs and the Social Construction of Gender in Byzantium*, Chicago / London 2003, 62; H. Chadwick, *East and West. The Making of a Rift in the Church*, Oxford 2003, 121; Mormino, 2017/2018, 106–107. Sulla fortuna di

egli conservò certi privilegi grazie alla sua egregia stirpe e, benché eunuco[30], non solo passò per i diversi gradi della carriera ecclesiastica e fondò numerosi monasteri, ma ne diventò addirittura ἡγούμενος[31], andando a costituire una propria rete di contatti a imitazione di quanto accadeva nella cerchia degli Studiti[32] (fig. 2.4)[33].

Dopo la morte di Metodio, il 3 luglio 847, Ignazio fu scelto come nuovo patriarca di Costantinopoli[34]. Nonostante su tale circostanza le fonti siano parche, criptiche e talvolta anche discordanti, si possono individuare due chiare tipologie di testimonianza. Da una parte, si trovano i testi propriamente pro-ignaziani, in particolare l'agiografia di Niceta David Paflagone[35] e l'enco-

---

	Procopia si veda Á. Ibáñez Chacón, *Rumores (in)fundados en torno a la emperatriz Procopia*, in: M.C. Chiriatti / M. Vallejo Girvés (eds.), *Riflessi di porpora. Declinazioni di potere femminile tra Roma, Bisanzio e l'Occidente Medievale*, Spoleto 2023, 205–213.
30	La maggior parte dei monasteri bizantini non consentiva che gli eunuchi rivestissero ruoli importanti: R. Janin, *Le monachisme byzantin au Moyen Âge. Commende et typica (X^e–XIVe siècle)*, in: REByz 22 (1964), 5–44 (22). Tuttavia, la cattiva reputazione sugli eunuchi che aveva radici nell'epoca tardoantica si trasformò in una nuova giustificazione di santità: Ringrose, 2003, 111–127. Anche il suo predecessore, Metodio, era stato castrato, ma si pensa che, in realtà, si trattasse di un'automutilazione ascetica oppure alla risoluzione di una qualche patologia genitale: Varona Codeso, *Miguel III*, 2009, 90–92, con la bibliografia relativa.
31	J. Pargoire, *Les Monastères de S. Ignace et les cinq plus petits îlots de l'Archipel des Princes*, in: BIARC 7 (1901), 56–91; R. Janin, *Les églises et les monastères des grands centres byzantins*, Paris 1975, 62–67; Mormino, 2017/2018, 158–174.
32	P. Hatlie, *The Monks and Monasteries of Constantinople, ca. 350–850*, Cambridge 2007, 328–330; Mormino, 2017/2018, 158–174; Prieto Domínguez, 2020, 285–287.
33	In questa immagine, Ignazio è rappresentato come un eunuco anziano. In seguito, è apparso un altro tipo iconografico in cui egli era raffigurato barbuto e con i capelli neri, cf. A. Grabar, *Un calice byzantin aux images des patriarches de Constantinople*, in: DCAH 4 (1964/1965), 45–51; M. Sacopoulo, *A Saint-Nicolas du Toit deux effigies inedites de patriarches constantinopolitains*, in: CAr 17 (1967), 193–202 (195–199); C. Mango / E.J. Hawkins, *The Mosaics of St. Sophia at Istanbul. The Church Fathers in the North Tympanum*, in: DOP 26 (1985), 1–41 (9–11, 28–30); L. Milanovic, *Beards that matter. Visual representations of Patriarch Ignatios in Byzantine art*, in: Zograf 41 (2017), 25–36. Per l'iconografia dei suoi sigilli si veda J.A. Cotsonis, *The Imagery of Patriarch Ignatios's Lead Seals and the rota Fortunae of Ninth-Century Byzantine Ecclesio-political Policies*, in: T. Fitzgerald (ed.), *Servant of the Gospel. Studies in Honor of His-All Holiness Ecumenical Patriarch Bartholomew*, Brookline 2011, 52–98.
34	PMBZ 2666 offre questa data esatta sulla base del *Synodicon vetus*, 159.
35	Edizione e traduzione inglese curate da A. Smithies / J.M. Duffy, *Nicetas David. The Life of Patriarch Ignatius*, CFHB 51, Washington 2013; traduzione italiana in L. Lapenna, *La vita di Ignazio di Niceta di Paflagonia. Il testo e le sue interpretazioni*, in: Nicolaus 36 (2009), 7–80. Si vedano K. Krumbacher, *Geschichte der byzantinischen Litteratur*, II, München 1897, 167–168; H.-G. Beck, *Kirche und theologische Literatur im byzantinischen Rech*, München 1959, 548–549, 565–566; R.H. Jenkins, *A Note on Nicetas David Paphlago and the Vita Ignatii*, in:

Fig. 2.4

DOP 19 (1965), 241–247; I. Tamarkina, *The Date of the Life of Patriarch Ignatius Reconsidered*, in: ByZ 99 (2006), 615–630; M. Mormino, *Duceque et adiutore Deo, spiritu veritatis. La ricerca della verità, l'aiuto divino: alcune note sulla Vita Ignatii (BHG 817) di Niceta David Paflagone*, in: Porphyra 11 (2014), 4–39; C. Crimi, *Emozioni e rappresentazione nei bioi dei patriarchi costantinopolitani Ignazio (BHG 817) ed Eutimio (BHG 651)*, in: P.B. Cipolla *et al.* (eds.), *Spazi e tempi delle emozioni. Dai primi secoli all'eta bizantina*, Roma 2018, 81–100;

mio composto da un tale Michele Sincello[36], il *libellus* portato a Roma da Teognosto[37] e il cosiddetto *Synodicon vetus*[38]. Per tutte queste fonti, infatti, Ignazio sarebbe stato eletto in modo canonico, cioè mediante un sinodo locale e con il sostegno del clero e dell'imperatrice:

> Τοῦ γὰρ τρισμακαρίου Μεθοδίου τὸν πατριαρχικὸν θρόνον θανάτῳ ἀπολιπόντος, ἡ χριστόφρων Θεοδώρα σύνοδον πατέρων ποιησαμένη μετά γε τῶν ἐν συγκλήτῳ βουλῆς καὶ τοῦ κλήρου παντὸς τὸν Ἰγνάτιον πατριάρχην καθίστησι.[39]

"Infatti, quando alla sua morte il tre volte beato Metodio lasciò vacante la sede patriarcale, Teodora, ispirata da Cristo, convocò il sinodo dei padri e nominò Ignazio patriarca con l'approvazione del Senato e di tutto il clero" (fig. 2.5).

In questo caso, è frequente porre le virtù di Ignazio e del suo lignaggio a motivo per la sua intronizzazione a scapito degli altri possibili candidati, ai quali fa allusione Niceta (*Vita Ignatii* 10); solo il cronografo Genesio ne riferisce il nome, Basilio (PMBZ 927) e Gregorio (PMBZ 2474), figli di Leone V e per questo scartati dalla selezione a causa dell'eresia paterna (κἂν τῇ τοῦ πατρὸς ἐπιψόγῳ αἱρέσει σμικρυνομένων)[40]. Dall'altra parte, troviamo la documentazione filo-foziana, che insiste sull'elezione irregolare di Ignazio: il necessario

---

A. Luzzi, *Osservazioni su una recente edizione della Vita Ignatii attribuita a Niceta David Paflagone*, in: TMCB 23 (2019), 465–480.

36   Siccome ci sono diversi personaggi omonimi (cf. Beck, 1959, 503–505; A. Kolia-Dermitzaki, *Michael the Synkellos*, in: D. Thomas *et al.* [eds.], *Christian-Muslim Relations. A Bibliographical History*, I, Leiden 2009, 627–630; Prieto Domínguez, 2020, 302–319), non è possibile stabilire in modo preciso chi sia l'autore dell'encomio. Rimandiamo per ogni approfondimento alla nuova edizione curata da Á. Ibáñez Chacón, *El Encomio a Ignacio de Miguel Sincelo (BHG 818): introducción, edición y traducción anotada*, in: Talia Dixit 16 (2021), 29–58.

37   Su questo fedele ignaziano si veda M. Jugie, *Théognoste*, in: DTC 15 (1946), 337–338. Il testo del *libellus*, curato da M. Rader, *Acta Sacrosancti et Oecumenici concilii octavi, Constantinopolitani quarti*, Ingolstadii 1604, 203–211, deve essere riveduto e analizzato con precisione in considerazione del suo decisivo ruolo nel cambio di atteggiamento che Roma ebbe nei confronti della controversia bizantina: F. Dvornik, *The Patriarch Photius in the Light of Recent Research*, in: IX *Internationalen Byzantinisten-Kongress*, III.2, München 1958, 1–56 (25–26); F. Ronconi, *Le 'schisme photien': la contribution de Francis Dvornik*, in: BySl 76 (2018), 49–64 (62–63).

38   Edizione e traduzione inglese curate da J. Duffy / J. Parker, *The Synodicon vetus*, CFHB 15, Washington 1979, 134–137 per i *capitula* su Ignazio e Fozio.

39   Mich. Sync. *Laud. Ign.* (BHG 818) §7.

40   Gen. 4.18, ed. Lesmueller-Werner / Turn, 1978, 70–71. Secondo il cerimoniale tradizionale, erano infatti tre i candidati proposti dai metropoliti: cf. L. Bréhier, *L'investiture des patriarches de Constantinople au Moyen Âge*, in: *Miscellanea Giovanni Mercati*, III, StT 123, Città del Vaticano 1946, 368–372.

Fig. 2.5

sinodo locale non si era infatti mai tenuto e la nomina non era stata ratificata dalla Sede Apostolica[41]. A questo fatto vanno aggiunti i dissidi di Ignazio con l'imperatore Michele III e il cesare Barda: quando Ignazio apprese che Barda manteneva rapporti illeciti con la nuora, si rifiutò pubblicamente di darle la comunione il giorno dell'Epifania (siamo verosimilmente nell'anno 858), guadagnandosi da allora la sua inimicizia[42]. Inoltre, Barda convinse l'imperatore a tonsurare e chiudere in clausura le sue sorelle e Teodora, che era già stata espulsa dal palazzo e imprigionata nella Μονὴ τῶν Γαστρίων, fondazione della famiglia imperiale[43], dove rimase fino alla sua morte[44]. Poiché Ignazio rifiutò,

41 F. Dvornik, *Photius, Nicholas I and Hardian II*, in: BySl 34 (1973), 33–50 (36) insiste sul fatto che Roma non aveva confermato ufficialmente l'elezione di Ignazio; D. Stiernon, *Constantinople IV*, Paris 1967, 15 pensa invece che l'illegittimità della nomina fosse parte delle calunnie anti-ignaziane.

42 Si vedano J. Hergenröther, *Photius, Patriarch von Konstantinopel: sein Leben, seine Schriften und das griechische Schisma*, I, Regensburg 1867, 357; Bury, 1912, 188; F. Dvornik, *Patriarch Ignatius and Caesar Bardas*, in: BySl 27 (1966), 7–22; Simeonova, 1998, 48–49; Varona Codeso, *Miguel III*, 2009, 152–155. Da parte sua, M.P. Vinson, *Gender and Politics in the Post-Iconoclastic Period: The Lives of Antony the Younger, the Empress Theodora, and the Patriarch Ignatios*, in: Byz. 68 (1998), 469–515 presenta un'interessante analisi dei caratteri dei protagonisti (Ignazio, Fozio, Teodora e Barda) nelle fonti agiografiche.

43 Janin, ²1969, 67–68; Ruggieri, 1991, 191.

44 P. Karlin-Hayter, *La mort de Théodora*, in: JÖB 40 (1990), 205–208; Herrin, 2001, 226–229; Varona Codeso, *Miguel III*, 2009, 123–128.

rimasto senza il sostegno della sua protettrice, fu quindi accusato di tradimento e deposto dalla sede patriarcale il 23 novembre 858.

L'ex-patriarca iniziò quindi un lungo itinerario di reclusione e tortura attraverso diversi monasteri e prigioni, che i suoi avversari avevano pensato con l'intenzione di farlo abdicare formalmente. Non ebbero successo[45]. Nel frattempo, Fozio (PMBZ 6253), nominato patriarca nel Natale dell'858, presiedette diversi sinodi locali per sancire ufficialmente la deposizione di Ignazio, pur *in absentia*, ma di tutti questi tentativi rimangono solo riferimenti isolati e ambigui nelle fonti[46]. Quanto alla sorte di Ignazio, l'agiografia di Niceta David riporta una lunga serie di tormenti[47]: egli fu prima trasferito sull'isola di Terebinto, dove c'era un monastero fondato da lui[48]; da lì passò a Hierea, προάστειον dall'altra parte del Bosforo (oggi Fenerbahçe) usato come prigione di passaggio[49], dove Ignazio fu rinchiuso in un recinto di capre (cf. Nic. Dav. *Vit. Ign.* 25: εἰς μάνδραν αἰγῶν); fu quindi trasferito in un luogo chiamato τὰ Προμότου[50], dove un certo Leone Lalacone (PMBZ 4508) colpì Ignazio così forte da strappargli ben due molari (cf. Nic. Dav. *Vit. Ign.* 25, 8–14). Da lì poi fu tradotto nella famosa prigione τὰ Νούμερα, situata nei vecchi bagni di Zeusippo a Costantinopoli[51], quindi a Mitilene, dove rimase per sei mesi. Alla fine, fu riportato a Terebinto e imprigionato nel palazzo τὰ Πόσεως, proprietà della sua famiglia[52], dove attese fino alla celebrazione del sinodo dell'861.

Conosciamo un po' meglio quel sinodo, chiamato σύνοδος πρωτοδευτέρα, perché combinava decisioni disciplinari già prese in un sinodo locale dell'858. Anche se gli *atti* di tale concilio furono poi distrutti durante l'Ottavo Concilio Ecumenico[53], da una copia dei verbali inviata a Roma il cardinale Deusdedit

---

45   Bury, 1912, 189–192; Stiernon, 1967, 31; Ó. Prieto Domínguez, *Recounting Suffering: Patriarchal Tortures in Greek Medieval Literature*, in: Á. Martínez Fernández *et al.* (eds.), *Ágalma. Homenaje a Manuel García Teijeiro*, Valladolid 2014, 581–586.

46   F. Dvornik, *The Photian Schism. History and Legend*, Cambridge 1948, 53–63; Stiernon, 1967, 29–35; V. Grumel / J. Darrouzès, *Les regestes des actes du patriarcat de Constantinople*, I.2, PatByz 1, Paris ²1989, 98–99; R. Price / F. Montinaro, *The Acts of the Council of Constantinople of 869–70*, Liverpool 2022, 9–13.

47   Con meno dettagli, gli episodi sono in Theoph. cont. 4.31, Gen. 4.18, Scylit. 17, Ps.-Sym. 28.

48   Pargoire, 1901, 64–65; Janin, 1975, 61–63.

49   Cf. R. Janin, *La banlieue asiatique de Constantinople, III*, in: EOr 22 (1923), 50–58.

50   Non è specificato se ci si riferisca alla località lungo la costa europea del Bosforo ovvero alla regione costantinopolitana: Janin, ²1969, 444–445.

51   R. Janin, *Constantinople byzantine*, AOC 4A, Paris ²1964, 222–224; R. Guilland, *Études de topographie de Constantinople byzantine*, BBA 37, Berlin / Amsterdam 1959, 41–55.

52   Situato nell'omonimo quartiere della Capitale: Janin, ²1964, 415.

53   Hergenröther, 1867, 419–438; C.-J. Hefele / H. Leclercq, *Histoire des Conciles*, 4.1, Paris 1911, 275–280; G. Every, *The Byzantine Patriarchate, 451–1204*, London 1947, 118–121; Dvornik,

fece un estratto in latino (XI sec.)[54]. Sappiamo così che, il 6 aprile dell'861, Domenica di Pasqua, si tenne il sinodo anti-ignaziano nella Chiesa dei Santi Apostoli, presieduto dall'imperatore Barda e i due apocrisiari di Roma, Radoaldo di Porto (PMBZ 6404) e Zaccaria d'Anagni (PMBZ 8638)[55]. Durante le varie sessioni, il caso contro Ignazio fu riesaminato e il patriarca "deposto" fu più volte esortato, ma senza successo, ad abdicare definitivamente[56]. A questo momento Niceta (*Vit. Ign.* 35) riferisce l'umiliante punizione cui fu sottoposto Ignazio: rinchiuso nella bara dell'imperatore iconoclasta Costantino V (fig. 2.6), detto il Copronimo (PMBZ 3703, reg. 743–775)[57], uno dei suoi carcerieri, Teodoro il Pazzo (Μωροθεόδωρος, PMBZ 7725)[58] lo costrinse a firmare un foglio bianco; su questo Fozio stesso avrebbe poi scritto la presunta confessione di Ignazio nella quale egli asseriva di non essere stato eletto regolarmente (ἀψηφίστως) e di aver esercitato una sorta di tirannia nel corso del suo patriarcato (ἐτυράννουν)[59].

1948, 70–90; Stiernon, 1967, 35–45; Chadwick, 2003, 139–146; Price / Montinaro, 2022, 15–19.

54 Edizione curata da V. Wolf von Glanvell, *Die Kanonessammlung des Kardinals Deusdedit*, Paderborn 1905, 603–610. I canoni, invece, si sono conservati completi; forse aggiunti dallo stesso Fozio alla raccolta che era stata iniziata nel VI secolo da Giovanni Scolastico, questi possono ora essere letti nell'edizione curata da F. Lauritzen, *Concilium Constantinopolitanum – 861*, in: A. Melloni (ed.), *The Great Councils of the Orthodox Churches. Decisions and Synodika from Constantinople 681 to Constantinople 1872*, COGD 4.1, Turnhout 2016, 1–22.

55 I rappresentanti di papa Nicola I furono inviati a Costantinopoli per esaminare il processo, non per confermare la destituzione di Ignazio: per questo motivo, entrambi furono scomunicati nel sinodo romano dell'863: M.V. Anastos, *The Papal Legates at the Council of 861 and Thier Compliance with the Wishes of the Emperor Michael III*, in: Ἁρμός. Τιμητικός τόμος στον Καθηγητήν Ν.Κ. Μουτσόπουλο για τα 25 χρόνια πνευματικής του προσφοράς στο Πανεπιστήμιο, Thessaloniki 1990, 185–200; M. Mormino, *Memoria, esegesi, ruolo delle legazioni romane a Costantinopoli (861–866): spunti dalle missive ad res Orientales pertinentes di papa Nicola I (858–867)*, in: Humanities 8 (2015), 161–181.

56 L'abdicazione è menzionata solo in due documenti: Grumel / Darrouzès, ²1989, 92–93.

57 Sebbene i resti dell'imperatore fossero già stati riesumati per ordine della stessa Teodora, la reclusione nel suo feretro era una punizione umiliante e degradante: Ph. Grierson, *The Tombs and Obits of the Byzantine Emperors (337–1042), with an additional note by C. Mango and I. Ševčenko*, in: DOP 16 (1962), 1–63 (53–54); I. Rochow, *Kaiser Konstantin V. (741–775). Materialen zu seinem Leben und Nachleben*, BBySt 1, Frankfurt 1994, 138–139; Herrin, 2001, 213; Varona Codeso, *Miguel III*, 2009, 156–157; Prieto Domínguez, 2014, 583–584.

58 Insieme a Giovanni Gorgonites (PMBZ 3306) e Nicola (PMBZ 7991), costui era uno dei μαγγλαβιταί di Barda, la guardia del corpo incaricata di catturare, torturare ed uccidere i nemici dell'imperatore: A. Kazhdan, *Manglabites*, in: ODB 2 (1991), 1284.

59 Dvornik, 1948, 87 invita ad una necessaria cautela nella lettura del racconto agiografico: infatti, Niceta si riferisce al sinodo come συνέδριον, con tutte le connotazioni negative che il termine porta con sé: M. Mormino, *Alcune osservazioni sul ruolo e il significato del*

Fig. 2.6

4   Legittimazione agiografica

Per l'argomento che qui ci interessa, si deve notare come nel sinodo dell'861 si insistesse non solo sull'elezione anticanonica di Ignazio, ma anche sul fatto che egli fosse stato nominato da una donna. Da questo capo di imputazione, lo stesso accusato si difese ricordando che lo stesso Tarasio era già stato scelto da una donna (*dominus Tharasius pater a femina promotus est*)[60], cioè da Irene[61]. Però, Ignazio non era stato il solo beneficiario dei favori di Teodora, in quanto l'imperatrice aveva precedentemente favorito anche la nomina di Metodio, ma attraverso una procedura più regolare e con una serie di incontri di consultazione con il potere politico ed ecclesiastico[62].

La controversia ecclesiastica e politica suscitata attorno alla figura di Ignazio e Fozio sfruttò quindi la partecipazione diretta di Teodora alla dinamica dell'elezione secondo gli interessi dell'una o dell'altra parte in gioco e questo spiega – crediamo – l'invenzione di certi aneddoti da parte dei circoli ignaziani.

Tale è dunque il significato della finzione introdotta nell'*Encomio a Ignazio* (BHG 818, §6), secondo la quale i famosi monaci profeti Gioannicio (PMBZ 3389) e Teofane il Confessore (PMBZ 8197) avrebbero predetto l'ascesa al

---

         sacerdozio nella Vita Ignatii (BHG 817) *di Niceta David il Paflagone*, in: Peloro 1 (2016),
         39–75 (54, n. 50).
60   Wolf von Glanvell, 1905, 605.
61   Every, 1947, 106–108; C. Ludwig / T. Pratsch, *Tarasios (784–806)*, in: Lilie (ed.), 1999, 57–108.
62   Zielke, 1999, 223–230; Varona Codeso, *Miguel III*, 2009, 75–77.

trono di Ignazio[63]. L'aneddoto si rivela essere un *topos* dell'agiografia[64], forse tratto dalla tradizione popolare su Metodio[65] ed in seguito incorporato nella proto-biografia di Ignazio, a sua volta fonte dell'encomio e della *Vita Ignatii* di Niceta David[66]. In questa opera, si aggiungono inoltre i seguenti elementi (§16):

Πρὸ πάντων δὲ τῶν ἀρχιερέων καὶ τῶν λαῶν τῆς βασιλίδος ἀποστειλάσης καὶ ἀξιωσάσης διὰ Κυρίου γνωρίσαι τὸν ἄξιον, προφητικῶς ὁ μέγας τούτον Ἰωαννίκιος ψηφίζεται.

"Quando l'imperatrice ebbe ritenuto opportuno conoscere chi fosse meritevole attraverso il Signore e lo consultò prima di tutti i vescovi e del popolo, il grande Gioannicio lo ratificò profeticamente".

Tale fatto è insolito, anacronistico e impossibile. Non solo questo è omesso nelle biografie dei santi profeti[67] e dell'imperatrice stessa che sono giunte fino a noi; poi Gioannicio era morto nell'846, quindi prima della morte di Metodio e della nomina di Ignazio[68]. Il *topos* della predizione e della consultazione con i profeti è stato volutamente introdotto per dare autorità all'intronizzazione e legittimare la libera scelta presa da Teodora, episodio tanto problematico da essere totalmente ignorato nella *Vita* della santa imperatrice, nella quale si passa dalla morte di Teoctisto (§10)[69] all'espulsione dal palazzo (§11).

Il salto cronologico è troppo brusco e denota un chiaro interesse ad eliminare dalla biografia di Teodora un fatto che avrebbe potuto offuscare il suo buon lavoro in materia religiosa. Nonostante ciò, che sia avvenuta secondo le leggi canoniche o in maniera irregolare, l'elezione di Ignazio a patriarca di Costantinopoli potrebbe far parte della politica di riconciliazione portata avanti da Teodora nel tentativo di calmare gli animi dopo i conflitti di Metodio con gli

---

63   Si tratterebbe del solo Teofane nella *Vita Ignatii* 14; sulle profezie di Gioannicio: Timotin, 2010, 182–194; Narro, 2019, 242–244.

64   T. Pratsch, *Der hagiographische Topos*, Berlin / New York 2005, 290–297.

65   Si diceva che Metodio, anch'egli profeta (cf. W. Treadgold, *The Prophecies of the Patriarch Methodius*, in: REByz 62 [2004], 229–237), avesse anche ricevuto presagi dai monaci stessi: *Vita Michaelis Syncelli* (BHG 1296, §26), ed. M.B. Cunningham, *The Life of Michael the Synkellos*, Belfast 1991.

66   Ibáñez Chacón, 2021, 39.

67   Il dettaglio non appare né nella *Vita Theophanis* composta dallo stesso Metodio (BHG 1787z), ed. V. Latyšev, *Methodii patriarchae Constantinopolitani Vita S. Theophanis confessoris e codice Mosquensi n° 159*, in: *Mémoires de L'Académie des Sciences de Russie* 13 (1918), 1–40, né nelle diverse versioni della *Vita Ioannicii*: AASS Nov. II.1, 332–384 y 384–435; ne esiste una traduzione inglese: D. Sullivan, *Life of St. Ioannikios*, in: Talbot (ed.), 1998, 243–351.

68   Dvornik, 1948, 18; Da Costa-Louillet, 1954, 463; Mormino, 2017/2018, 172–173.

69   Varona Codeso, *Miguel III*, 2009, 114–117.

Studiti e gli iconoclasti[70]. Tuttavia, Ignazio non era affatto un patriarca docile e moderato, come dimostrano i suoi rapporti con Roma, che lo portarono presto alla scomunica per la sua opposizione all'evangelizzazione degli Slavi[71].

Comunque sia, per la tradizione ortodossa Teodora ha continuato a far parte a pieno titolo degli eroi iconoduli, come riassume l'autore della sua *Vita*:

> Παρθενίαν ἐτίμησε, γάμον ἐδόξασε, τὸν ἄνδρα διεσώσατο, ἀνθρώπων πλήθη εἰς φῶς καθωδήγησεν, ἐπέβη πρὸς οὐρανούς, ἀπέλαβε διὰ τῆς ἐλπίδος τὰ ἐλπιζόμενα, περι-ελάμφθη τῷ φωτὶ τῆς ἄνω λαμπρότητος.

> "Onorò la verginità, glorificò il matrimonio, condusse alla salvezza il marito, guidò verso la luce una moltitudine di uomini, ascese al cielo, ricevette, grazie alla speranza, ciò che aveva sperato, fu illuminata dalla luce dello splendore celeste".[72]

Figure

Fig. 2.1 L'imperatrice Teodora con un'icona di Cristo (Miniatura del cosiddetto *Menologio di Basilio II*, Vaticano, BAV, Vat. gr. 1613, p. 392).

Fig. 2.2 Rappresentazione di Bogoris e Teodora nel cosiddetto *Scilitze* di Madrid (Madrid, BNE, Vitr. 26–2, f. 67v).

Fig. 2.3 Solido di Teodora (Auction Bank Leu 77 Zürich, 5/12/2000, lot. 868): dritto † ΘΕΟΔΟΡΑ (*sic*) ΔΕΣΠΥΝΑ (*sic*) / rovescio ΜΙΧΑΗΛ ΚΑΙ ΘΕΚΛΑ.

---

70 P. Karlin-Hayter, *Gregory of Siracusa, Ignatios and Photios*, in: A. Bryer / J. Herrin (eds.), *Iconoclasm*, Birmingham 1977, 141–145 (141–142). Sull'atteggiamento di Metodio verso gli iconoclasti e i dissidenti Studiti si vedano le considerazioni di Hergenröther, 1867, 351–355; J. Pargoire, *S. Méthode et la persécution*, in: EOr 6 (1903), 183–191; E. von Dobschütz, *Methodius und die Studiten. Strömungen und Gegenströmungen in der Hagiographie des 9. Jahrhunderts*, in: ByZ 18 (1909), 41–105; Bury, 1912, 181–182; V. Grumel, *La politique religieuse du patriarche saint Méthode*, in: EOr 34 (1935), 385–401; Stiernon, 1967, 11–13; J. Darrouzès, *Le patriarche Méthode contre les Iconoclastes et les Stoudites*, in: REByz 45 (1987), 15–57; D.E. Afinogenov, *Κωνσταντινούπολις ἐπίσκοπον ἔχει. Part II: From the Second Outbreak of Iconoclasm to the Death of Methodios*, in: Erytheia 17 (1996), 47–71; Zielke, 1999, 230–256; K. Maksimovič, *Patriarch Methodios I. (843–847) und das studitische Schisma: Quellenkritische Bemerkungen*, in: Byz 72 (2000), 422–446; Chadwick, 2003, 119–120; P. Karlin-Hayter, *Methodios and his Synod*, in: A. Louth / A. Casiday (eds.), *Byzantine Orthodoxies*, Aldershot 2006, 55–74; Mormino, 2017/2018, 174–200.

71 Hergenröther, 1867, 594–617; Every, 1947, 122–138; F. Dvornik, *The Slavs. Their Early History and Civilization*, Boston 1956, 119–120; Simeonova, 1998, 298–317.

72 Ed. Markopoulos, 1983, 271; trad. Franco, 2017, 141–142.

Fig. 2.4 "Ignazio il Giovane" (ΙΓΝΑΤΙΟC Ο ΝΕΟC). Particolare del mosaico del timpano di Santa Sofia (Istanbul).

Fig. 2.5 "Il patriarca Ignazio è eletto" (χειροτονεῖται πατριάρχης Ἰγνάτιος). Rappresentazione dello *Scilitze* di Madrid (Madrid, BNE, Vitr. 26–2, f. 76r).

Fig. 2.6 Ignazio è rinchiuso nella tomba di Costantino V. Rappresentazione dello *Scilitze* di Madrid (Madrid, BNE, Vitr. 26–2, f. 76v).

PART II

Northern and Central Europe

Seclusion Spaces during the First Centuries of Female Asceticism

Jordina Sales-Carbonell, Marta Sancho i Planas

Abstract

From the beginning of Christian monasticism, ascetic women assumed the traditional role they had been playing in the Greco-Roman world: to be relegated to a certain physical-domestic seclusion to guarantee their protection from the 'dangers of the world'. However, these "mischievous" women developed extreme but also ingenious strategies to delimit borders (both physical and symbolic) that would protect them from the outside world but also from the control of ecclesiastical hierarchies.

Introduction

From the earliest stages of Christian monasticism,[1] ascetic woman[2] accepted traditional Greco-Roman social roles, in which Christianity developed, without question. These included patterns of domestic seclusion which, in varying degrees throughout time, location and specific cultural settings, ensured their isolation in order to protect them from the 'perils of the world' – essentially men outside their closest family or social circles.

Since the arrival of a Christian monastic movement was initially characterised by anchorite or eremitical features, pioneering women who practiced solitary ascetism remained largely secluded.[3] There was, however, a key development: these women chose to do so on their own terms, free from the patriarchal control of their families and away from the traditional social pressures

---

1   This paper falls within the framework of the project: *Monastic Landscapes: Representations and Virtualisations of Medieval Spiritual and Material Realities in the Western Mediterranean (6th–16th Centuries)*, PGC2018-095350-B-I00, Universitat de Barcelona.

2   For the semantics of term 'asceticism' in Late Antiquity, see A. Diem, *The Limitations of Ascetism*, in: W. Pohl / A. Gingrich (eds.), *Monasteries and Sacred Landscapes: Byzantine Connections*, Medieval Worlds 9 (2019), 112–138.

3   This essay will not address the material aspects of these ascetics, with the obvious challenge of finding and identifying archaeological sites from such a long time ago, when there were still no defined architectural models for monasteries (a fact that did not consolidate itself until the Middle Ages). See R. Gilchrist, *Gender and Material Culture: The Archaeology of Religious Women*, London 1994, 188–191.

that had hitherto kept them enclosed in their own homes. The early desert hermits were empowered by the idea that their spiritual quest was fuelled by personal freedom and a mysterious power that had allowed them to break countless social barriers.[4] Knowingly or not, the ideas held so dearly by these monks must have also inspired female ascetics in the desert.

This initial power-vacuum over female hermits was gradually filled by Christian hierarchies who set themselves up as their guardians and these women were to be ruled over and controlled under the pretence of protecting them from the time-tested narratives of a 'dangerous world'. Some women, however, slipped through the net.

Their story begins in the desert and continues in the city,[5] crossing every conceivable micro-geographical location in which the ideals of seclusion and recognition were made possible. Following a chronological line through the use of written sources, this chapter will outline the main aspects of a unique movement in which female anchorites brimmed with life and energy, refusing to relegate themselves to social mores and determined to live an ascetic life of solitude, even if this meant they had to physically close themselves in so as to become isolated from the world. This conscious separation from earthly affairs was characterised by a certain amount of religious decoration, which in some cases was meant to legitimise what might otherwise be a personal lifestyle choice rather than a spiritual quest. However, it should be noted that this movement was shaped by a rebellious streak that traditional – male – historiography has often labelled as the work of deranged female zealots,[6] which is an unfortunate and severely limiting interpretation of events.

Despite its predominance, not all secluded ascetics chose a life of enclosure. What is beyond doubt is that the greater part of the 'self-enclosing' anchorite movement was spearheaded by women right up until its pinnacle in the Medieval period of Western Christianity.[7] This high point, however, cannot be understood without taking into consideration the early female pioneers of Late Antiquity, particularly during the final centuries of the Roman Empire.

---

4   P. Brown, *The World of Late Antiquity*, London 1971, 102–104.

5   A. Jensen, *God's Self-Confident Daughters: Early Christianity and the Liberation of Women*, Louisville 1996; S. Carrasquer Pedrós, *Madres Orientales (ss. I–VII)*, Burgos 2008; S. Carrasquer Pedrós, *Las Madres Occidentales (ss. I–VII)*, Burgos 2008.

6   Although perfectly sane women could become deranged after years left unchecked. This was the case of a nun at the monastery of Poitiers. See Greg. -T., Hist. 11.11.

7   In the furthest Western parts of Europe, for example, the apogee took place between the 10th and 11th centuries: G. Cavero Domínguez, Inclusa intra parietes, in: *La reclusión voluntaria en la España medieval*, Toulouse 2010, 87–120.

1   The Desert Mothers

With regard to the earliest ascetic manifestations, one must analyse the role of the desert mothers, even if the information about them is both scarce and chronologically later than that of their male counterparts. Not at all alien to the symbolism of the desert in biblical tradition, these women also wandered the Eastern deserts, probably from as far back as the third century, although they do not feature in written sources until the fourth century (when Christianity is tolerated by Constantine I and later becomes the official and only acceptable faith under Theodosius I). Some of these written sources illustrate the range of strategies employed by these women from the earliest days of the monastic movement.

Considering how Christian spirituality flourished in the Eastern deserts, is it fair talk about seclusion in the context of such vast emptiness? The answer is obviously yes, all the more so when we consider the hardship and physical dangers that these spiritual seekers endured. The act of seclusion is especially telling in the case of early anchorite women, whose legacy both inspired and established the template for generations to come.

These women secluded themselves willingly, determined to leave the world behind them in an act of penance. This much is evident from the fourth century life of Syncletica, whose hermitic asceticism was marked by her enclosure inside a crypt near Alexandria. "In this world, those who have broken a rule are sent to prison against their will; whereas we imprison ourselves because of our sins, that such willing sentence may free us from future punishment".[8] Although seclusion may first appear as a way of ensuring physical protection, it is above all a voluntary act of self-punishment that is part of a set of specific choices meant to leave the world behind, feel closer to God and receive some of His love and forgiveness.

For these anchorite women, their body represented the biggest prison of all and consequently the one they were most determined to escape. The female body was a burden that had to be fought day and night, relentlessly, so that men may not be distracted by earthly pleasures from the true purpose of seeking God's grace. For women, the battle against carnal instincts went beyond *topos*: Christianity held women as the worst version of Eve, which meant that those seeking a true anchorite path should strive to acquire a male soul, even if it remained trapped inside the body – the 'prison' – of a woman. "I am a woman by sex, but not so my soul".[9] Renouncing womanhood – the root of the

---

8   Apophth. Patr. 7.18.
9   Apophth. Patr. 10.73.

original sin – was understood to be an indispensable step in the pursuit of a spiritual life that was worthy of receiving the love of God.[10]

For an ascetic man, the worst possible enclosure was being locked inside the body of a woman. A female ascetic may have seemed to be the embodiment of virtue, but only in as much as her soul, as a metaphor, was that of a man.[11] That was the case of a *vir*, which etymologically evolved into *virgo:* a male soul trapped by female body. "For the difference is one of bodies not of souls: 'in Christ Jesus,' according to the divine Apostle, 'there is neither male nor female',"[12] said Theodoret of Cyrus in what may come across as a foresighted act of sex parity – hailing the virtues of the few anchorite women whose lives he addresses, even if the bulk of his work makes his male-centred views entirely clear, such as his insistence on seeing female acts of courage as the manifestation of a male essence, despite the fact that some scholars identify certain traces of resistance to the male textualisation of their flesh.[13]

Obviously, places of seclusion could just as much be mental constructions, shown in a person's disregard for what surrounds them, as if a thick wall stood between them and the world at large. A case in hand is that of *ammâ* Sara, who spent sixty years next to a river without ever venturing out to see it.[14]

Furthermore, there were known cases of women whose seclusion strategies consisted of transvestism, perhaps to stress their rejection of womanhood and what it represented, or perhaps to ensure a certain amount of peace and freedom of movement that kept neighbouring hermits at bay. We cannot reject the idea that some may even have been transgender and have willingly set out to live freely on their own terms. The case of two monks in the monastery of Samson, near Jerusalem, is worth mentioning. They lost their bearings while returning from a pilgrimage in the Sinai and wandered aimlessly until they came across a small hermitage whose resident had just passed away. As the two monks set about burying the body, they realised that the dead hermit was in

---

10   G. Cloke, *This Female Man of God: Women and Spiritual Power in the Patristic Age, 350–450,* London 1995, 19–23. K. Aspegren, *The Male Woman: A Feminine Ideal in the Early Church,* Uppsala 1990.

11   K. Vogt, 'Becoming Male': A Gnostic, Christian and Islamic Metaphor, in: K.E. Børrensen / K. Vogt (eds.), *Women's Studies of the Christian and Islamic Traditions: Ancient, Medieval and Renaissance Foremothers,* Dordrecht 1993, 217–242.

12   Theod. Cyr., Hist. mon. Syr. 30.5 (transl. R.M. Price, *A History of the Monks of Syria by Theodoret of Cyrrhus,* Kentucky 1985, 187).

13   V. Burrus, *Word and Flesh: The Bodies and Sexuality of Ascetic Women in Christian Antiquity,* in: Journal of Feminist Studies in Religion 10 (1994), 27–51.

14   Apophth. Patr. 7.19.

fact a woman.[15] This story may seem like an isolated incident – and it is treated as such by ancient written sources – but it might just as well be the tip of the iceberg of a reality we barely acknowledge, in large part because these acts of pretending to be a man in the middle of the desert were so successful.

Other instances of extreme seclusion, such as living at the top of a tree ('Dendrites') or perched on top of a column ('Stylites'), almost certainly had female representation.[16] As we know, however, the popularity of both traditions eventually stirred the opposite kind of effect to what was intended: gatherings of devotees instead of acts of solitude. Although we have male tales, such as Simon the Stylite, there are no known accounts that mention female cases.

Even though Christian monasticism arose in the desert, the movement soon spread to urban centres, even if these were initially towns located in the middle of the desert. It should come as no surprise, therefore, that the earliest Patristics, which mention consecrated virgins, have an African / Eastern origin. Long before he proclaimed the Peace of the Church, Tertullian wrote about how female Christians ought to behave, with particular attention to those who chose to lead a life in the full service of God. His treatise, *De virginibus velandis*, gives specific instructions regarding a classic element of female seclusion: the garments they wore, that is to say, the need for a veil. Patriarchal society had a clear idea of what sort of clothes and outward appearance a female ascetic was required to wear, especially if she moved around town, even if some managed to sidestep these requirements by pretending to be men or, in some cases, by vocally rejecting them.[17] In fact, as far as the Church Fathers were concerned, the only garments an ascetic woman should refuse were ostentatious clothes and unnecessary decorations.[18]

2   Ascetic and Seclusion Practices in the midst of Christian Aristocracies (4th–5th Centuries)

It is known that the earliest acts of ascetism in the Late Roman era were practiced spontaneously by certain aristocrats towards the end of the fourth

---

15   Johannes Moschus, *Pratum spirituale – Historias bizantinas de locura y santidad*, J.S. Palmer (ed.), Barcelona 1999, 177–178.

16   H. Delehaye, *Les femmes stylites*, in: AnBoll 27 (1908), 391–392.

17   E.g. Pall., h. Laus. 125 (transl. J. Wortley, *Palladius of Aspuna. The Lausiac History*, Collegeville 2015).

18   For example, in the middle of the third century Cyprian of Carthage developed a full thesis about 'the outward ways of virgins' in his treatise *De habitu virginum*.

century, inspired as they were by the monastic movement in the Egyptian desert. Nevertheless, the ascetism of these early 'converted' aristocrats – usually marriages – for the first time offered Christian women an orderly and legitimate monastic practice: the 'protection' afforded by the walls of their private properties and homesteads allowed them to enjoy their spiritual pursuit without constraints, surrounded by family members.[19]

In the context of such aristocratic spirituality, and within a second variation of 'patrician ascetism', widows and virgins became a coveted object of spiritual desire,[20] to be haggled over by a wide range of charismatic leaders such as Priscillian and Jerome, who gathered a following of widows and consecrated virgins dedicated to an ascetic lifestyle, often in a state of seclusion with a strong domestic character.

This ascetic movement driven by Western aristocracies is best exemplified in the lives of consecrated virgins in Rome, with its resulting urban character, whereas other areas such as the Iberian Peninsula illustrate the pattern of married seclusions within their *villae*, as well as ascetic circles of widows and virgins living in rural homesteads. We should, however, consider that Hispania in the last quarter of the fourth century and early fifth century was a land renowned for its proliferation of different heterodoxies,[21] as was the case in the East and other corners of the Roman Empire. In fact, we know that Church Fathers such as Jerome – who is, in addition, the great driving force behind Western monasticism – actively fought against numerous heresies.[22] In the case of Hispania, the main heresies were Arianism, Priscillianism, Gnosticism, Manichaeism, and Novatianism, despite the fact that the prefecture of Gaul (and consequently the vicarate of Hispania) suffered the most extreme

---

19   S.A. Harvey, *Housekeeping: An Ascetic Theme in Late Antiquity*, in: R.D. Young / M.J. Blanchard (eds.), *To Train His Soul in Books: Syriac Asceticism in Early Christianity*, Washington 2011, 134–154. For specific female asceticism, see E. Magnani / L. Brouillard, *Female House Ascetics from the Fourth to the Twelfth Century*, in: A. Beach / I. Cochelin (eds.), *The Cambridge History of Medieval Monasticism in the Latin West*, Cambridge 2020, 213–231.

20   Despite sharing a common purpose, in early female asceticism both virgins and widows gathered in separate orders which were not fully institutionalised until the rise of coenobitic monasticism (H. Lebourdellès, *Les ministères feminins dans le Haut Moyen Âge en Occident*, in: M. Roucher / J. Heuclin [eds.], *La femme au Moyen Âge*, Paris 1990, 15–17).

21   M.V. Escribano Paño, *Herejía y poder en el s. IV*, in: J.M. Candau / F. Gascó / A. Ramírez de Verger (eds.), *La conversión de Roma. Cristianismo y paganismo*, Madrid 1990, 151–189.

22   B. Jeanjean, *Saint Jérôme et l'hérésie*, Paris 1999.

measures of religious totalitarianism applied by Emperor Maximus after the year 383.[23]

Amidst the religious turmoil portrayed by written sources, Christians from Hispania who were devoting themselves to an ascetic life[24] required clear and concise spiritual guidance, which local or diocesan hierarchies did not always provide (often due to their own doctrinal conflicts). This is why monasticism, rebellious by nature against structures, was often organised away from priestly hierarchies, which in turn led to all manner of theological disputes.

Different sources make it clear that a certain amount of confusion and heterodoxy existed among Hispanic Christians, who were torn between conflicting currents. At the end of the day, one could be either orthodox or heterodox depending on who was interpreting such matters, or indeed according to the powers that be at the time. It is therefore unsurprising that ascetics, desperate as they were to ensure a proper orthodox practice, ended up seeking the counsel of higher, exogenous and unbiased authorities in order to receive instructions[25]–from the likes of Jerome in his later life, for instance. Furthermore, the fear of falling into heterodoxy and ending up like Priscillian (who was executed in 385) probably influenced the decision to seek approval from higher authorities, a process that had already been clearly established in canonical documents such as the decretal letter (*litterae decretales*) that Pope Siricius sent to Bishop Himerius of Tarraco (Tarragona) in 385.[26] Despite not providing further details, this letter mentioned – for the first time in Hispania – that consecrated virgins and those pursuing any other form of asceticism had to submit themselves to the diocesan authority: a lifetime of seclusion in a punishment cell, *in suis ergastulis*,[27] was mandated for any ascetic man or woman unable to restrain their sexual desires.

---

23 M.J. Crespo Losada, 'Introducción general', in: M.J. Crespo Losada (ed.), *Prisciliano de Ávila. Tratados*, Madrid 2017, 22.

24 J. Fontaine, *L'aristocratie occidentale devant le monachisme aux IVe et Ve siècles*, in: RSLR 15 (1979), 28–53 already analysed the Western ascetic model that established itself in *villae* and Christian aristocratic urban properties in the fourth century.

25 As confirmed by Jerome himself in ep. 75, addressed to an ascetic from Hispania–vid. *infra*.

26 Siric., ep. 1.7 (PL 13, 1131–1147).

27 See J. Torres Prieto, *El término ergastulum en la primera literatura monástica*, in: A. González Blanco / J.M. Blázquez Martínez (eds.), *Cristianismo y aculturación en tiempos del Imperio Romano* (=Antigüedad y Cristianismo VII, 1990), 287–290; ead., *La pena de reclusión en las reglas monásticas hispanas. Algunas cuestiones terminológicas*, in: M. Vallejo Girvés / J.A. Bueno Delgado (eds.), *Confinamiento y Exilio en la Antigüedad Tardía*, Madrid 2018, 181–193.

Within the Christian world, the fact that Jerome was based in the Holy Land – next to the Church of the Nativity in Bethlehem, no less – increased his reputation and authority. Such influence stretched back to his days as 'secretary of Latin letters' for Pope Damasus I in the later decades of the fourth century, a time in which he surrounded himself with notable Roman matrons who were keen to devote themselves to asceticism under the guidance of a spiritual master. They usually bestowed their properties in order to establish monasteries and other acts of charity. Jerome's animosity towards Origenism[28] and his committed struggle against a wide range of heterodoxies helped him rise to the position of undisputed reference within the Catholic orthodoxy, a spiritual father for many Roman aristocrats.

Of all the documented heterodoxies in Hispania, the most influential was arguably Priscillianism, not only because of its intrinsic importance but also due to the apparent similarities it shared with Jerome's organisational outline and the way he secluded female disciples. Both figures largely surrounded themselves with women – aristocratic matrons, widows, and virgins – who sought a charismatic leader to organise them along domestic lines and provide a measure of ascetic status. As far as documented sources are concerned, women were the absolute protagonists of early asceticism in Hispania: they are mentioned as 'consecrated virgins' in the Synod of Elvira, which took place in the early fourth century, whereas male devotees are not mentioned until later in the century. These female ascetics acquired a formal religious commitment under the tutelage of ecclesiastical ministers, underlined by a requirement of sexual containment.[29]

As for Jerome, we should remember that the first person he convinced to take a vow of chastity was his own sister, a fact that is known to have led to considerable family tensions along with his refusal to pursue a profitable career in the court of Valentinian I, prompting him to travel eastwards.[30] His second journey to the East was also motivated by the disastrous consequences that followed the conversion to asceticism of another woman; in this case, the young

---

28   J. Bautista Valero, 'Introducción', *San Jerónimo. Obras completas, Xa. Epistolario, I* (*cartas 1–85***), Madrid 2013, 45–65.

29   See M. Marcos Sánchez, *El ascetismo y los orígenes de la vida monástica*, in: R. Teja (ed.), *La Hispania del siglo IV. Administración, economía, sociedad, cristianización*, Bari 2002, 231–266. On the other hand, we know that Jerome wrote various treatises that dealt with female virginity, a popular topic in ancient Christianity–see N. Adkin, *Jerome on Virginity: A Commentary on the Libellus* de virginitate servanda (*Letter 22*), Cambridge 2003.

30   Hier., ep. 45.

widow Blaesilla, whose health deteriorated to such an extent that she passed away in a matter of months.[31]

Priscillian and Jerome shared a similar age and a strong charisma that was able to attract female Roman aristocrats to their ranks.[32] Written sources, however, suggest that Priscillian distinguished himself by treating male and female devotees equally, a fact that set him apart from Jerome and which led to all sorts of accusations from his earnest enemies. As some authors have pointed out, "Jerome's rhetoric against heretics who surrounded themselves with women is somewhat artificial, his invective statements outright hypocritical [...]"[33] when we consider his own well-known circle of ascetic Roman matrons. It is surprising, therefore, to learn that Jerome berates his enemies in faith exclaiming, "The chatty old woman, the doting old man, and the wordy sophist, one and all take in hand the Scriptures, rend them in pieces and teach them before they have learned them. Some with brows knit and bombastic words, balanced one against the other philosophize concerning the sacred writings among weak women. Others-I blush to say it-learn of women what they are to teach men; and as if even this were not enough, they boldly explain to others what they themselves by no means understand. I say nothing of persons who, like myself have been familiar with secular literature before they have come to the study of the holy scriptures".[34] Other works from Jerome warn against heretics who have fallen prey to the seduction of wealthy females by allowing them to join their ranks.[35]

Nonetheless, Jerome prevailed in all theological disputes and used his base in the Holy Land to consolidate his authority. He corresponded with the Christian aristocracy of the time, including three figures from Hispania: a married couple who had devoted themselves to asceticism, and a blind hermit.[36] These characters appear in three surviving letters (num. 71, 75 and 76), which were written between 398 and 399. The information contained in

---

31   See Jerome's justification in his ep. 39.

32   In the case of Priscillian, there are numerous accounts of aristocrats who rose in his defence and who were executed for doing so–see Marcos Sánchez, 2002, 244–245.

33   Crespo Losada, 2017, 14–15: "A este respecto, resultan artificialmente retóricas, y algo hipócritas, las invectivas de Jerónimo contra los herejes por aparecer acompañados de mujeres [...]".

34   Hier., ep. 53.7 (transl. https://www.tertullian.org/fathers2/NPNF2-06/Npnf2-06-03.htm# P1993_495856).

35   See, for example, Comm. in Is. 17.64.

36   The Christianisation of Western rural gentry from the fourth century onwards has been extensively discussed. A noteworthy account is Chapter 8 of the monograph of Brogiolo and Chavarria Arnau (G.P. Brogiolo / A. Chavarria Arnau, *Aristocrazie e campagne nell'Occidente da Costantino a Carlo Magno*, Firenze 2005, 127–150).

them is scarce, but it does provide an outline of the essential character of early Western monasticism and the role women played in it.

Letters 71 (*Ad Lucinum baeticum*, year 398) and 75 (*Ad Theodoram spanam de morte Lucini*, year 399) from Jerome's epistles were sent to Lucinius and his wife Theodora, wealthy landowners from *Hispania Baetica*[37] and generous euergetists of the Christian cause who, having detached themselves from worldly life in their rural homestead, devoted themselves to asceticism thanks to the epistolary influence of Jerome. Lucinius had sent Jerome vast sums of money for churches in Jerusalem and Alexandria, as well as simple but highly symbolic gifts of woollen clothes and two capes worn by him as proof of his rejection of earthly matters and his conversion to the 'perfect life'.[38] Jerome blessed their choice and sent them sackcloth, mentioning the orthodoxy of their practice in writing and inviting them to live in the Holy Land.[39]

Letter 75, on the other hand, was sent a few months later on occasion of Lucinius' death. Jerome lauded his disciple and encouraged his widow Theodora to pursue 'the perfect life', having already succeeded in restraining her sexual urges in the final years of their marriage.[40] This letter lays bare the widespread heresies that were part of Hispania at the time, which seem to have made headway in large part thanks to female aristocratic devotees.

> "And now that I have once mentioned the word 'heresy', where can I find a trumpet loud enough to proclaim the eloquence of our dear Lucinius, who, when the filthy heresy of Basilides raged in Spain and like a pestilence ravaged the provinces between the Pyrenees and the ocean, upheld in all its purity the faith of the church and altogether refused to embrace Armagil, Barbelon, Abraxas, Balsamum, and the absurd Leusibora. Such are the portentous names which, to excite the minds of unlearned men and weak women, they pretend to draw from Hebrew sources, terrifying the simple by barbarous combinations which they admire the more the less they understand them."[41]

In the same paragraph, Jerome echoes the idea that these heterodox currents sought "the houses of the wealthy, and in these especially the women, concerning whom we are told that they are led away with divers lusts, ever learning and

---

37   Ep. 71.3–4. Marcos Sánchez, 2002, 254 claims that this Hispanic marriage was not part of the senatorial aristocracy, but instead belonged to the wealthy urban elite.

38   Ep. 75.4. The better part of this money was used to fund Jerome' extensive monastic works in the Holy Land.

39   Ep. 71.7; 75.3.

40   P. Laurence, *Jérôme et le nouveau modèle féminin. La conversion à la 'vie parfaite'*, Paris 1997, 274–276.

41   Ep. 75.3 (transl. https://www.tertullian.org/fathers2/NPNF2-06/Npnf2-06-03.htm#P3131_819038).

never able to come to the knowledge of the truth". Being on the 'wrong side' of orthodoxy, in short, made these women lustful, a curious fact on Jerome's part when we consider how he is criticising the very same strategies he himself employed: seeking wealthy matrons to sustain his projects.

Due to their content, Letters 71 and 75 are considered a defence of monasticism, a tradition that was spreading in Hispania by means of married couples who secluded themselves in their homesteads and continued to embrace a family lifestyle, albeit under strict rules of chastity and moderation. Their plentiful financial resources were the cornerstone of veritable monasteries, often within the premises of their own households.[42] The cases of the Paulinus nobles (from Gaul) and Therasia (of Hispanic origin) are particularly interesting because in the later stages of their ascetic lives they founded the monasteries of Nola, in southern Italy. Paulinus of Nola was actually from Bordeaux and had initiated his ascetic life alongside his wife while living in Hispania, a choice that was influenced by the death of their newborn son Celsus around the years 390 to 393.[43] The asceticism of this marriage, therefore, was no different from Lucinius' and Theodora's. A further step was taken by husband and wife Melania the Younger and Pinianus, who chose to part ways in their own ascetic pursuits following the death of their two children: Melania gathered around her servants and mother while Pinianus joined the ranks of some thirty monks.[44]

Jerome's Letter 76 is short, plain and simple. It presents the blind Abigaus, who devoted himself to asceticism under the epistolary influence of Jerome. Abigaus appears surrounded by *sancti* and is therefore associated with an unnamed community of proto-monastic traits. Some authors have mentioned that Lucinius and Theodora may have been part of it, an interesting proposition if we are to further understand the coenobitic organisation in the far Western corners of the Roman Empire. It is striking that Jerome asks Abigaus to take care of the widowed Theodora,[45] as this would suggest that hierarchies

42   J. Sales-Carbonell, *Jerome and the Western Monasticism: Asceticism, Evergetism and Orthodoxy within the Late Fourth Century Hispania*, in: BoVe 81 (2021), 425–436.

43   Paulinus would have met Therasia thanks to the divine intervention of Saint Felix: Paul., Carm. 21, 398–402; see J. Martínez Gázquez, *Paulino de Nola e Hispania*, in: Boletín del Instituto de Estudios Helénicos 7 (1973), 27–33.

44   Pall., h. Laus. 61, 129–131 (transl. J. Wortley, *Palladius of Aspuna, The Lausiac History*, Collegeville 2015). Melania was buried dressed in the different garments of holy men that she had collected as relics, and that gave her the appearance of a male monk. See R. Krawiec, *Garments of Salvation: Representations of Monastic Clothing in Late Antiquity*, in: JECS 17 (2009), 137–139; I.S. Gilhus, *Clothes and Monasticism in Ancient Christian Egypt: New Perspectives on Religious Garments*, Oxford 2021.

45   Ep. 76.3.

were determined that ascetic women who became widows did not end up pursuing their spiritual quest without undue supervision. Equally significant is the final part of the letter, in which Theodora's voyage to the Holy Land is mentioned – a popular choice among ascetics of the time, as evidenced by the journeys of Melania the Elder and the famous Egeria of Galicia, who left a written account of her visits to holy places between 381 and 384.

Married couples tended to enclose themselves in *villae* – 'moving to the countryside' was popular among the aristocracy of Late Imperial Rome – whereas the case of devoted widows and virgins is documented mainly in urban centres. As previously mentioned, whether in rural or urban locations, private estates where early asceticism was practiced eventually became monasteries. During these early stages of monasticism, however, not all female devotees did so next to their husbands or any sort of male authority. Many of these women went about their spiritual quest freely, on their own, and resorted to more extreme cases of enclosure. The choice, nonetheless, did not always pay off. Such is the case of Marana and Kyra of Syria, whose seclusion is vividly reported by Theodoret of Cyrus in his *Historia monachorum Syriae*, written as a sequence of biographies around the year 444. Theodoret mentions meeting both women in person and, despite some hyperbolic statements, his words should be considered a reliable first-hand account of the highest order. It is not until the penultimate chapter of *Historia monachorum Syriae* (num. 29)[46] that he finally concerns himself with women, stating that:

> "After recording the way of life of the heroic men, I think it useful to treat also of women who have contended no less if not more; for they are worthy of still greater praise, when, despite having a weaker nature, they display the same zeal as the men and free their sex from its ancestral disgrace."[47]

Marana and Kyra were high noblewomen from *Beroea* – current Aleppo – and it is unclear if they were related given how loosely the term 'family' could be interpreted (some have speculated that they were sisters). In any event, both enclosed themselves in a small building on the outskirts of town, leaving their servants to live in a nearby cabin. The doors to their rooms were darkened with clay and stone, although it seems there was no roof. Their penance included

---

46   The following chapter, num. 30, is partially concerned with another solitary ascetic – Domnina – although her life of penance took place in a small hut located in the vegetable garden of her mother's house. The second part of the article, however, is interesting because it mentions 'many women who have chosen a solitary life' not only in Syria but across the Roman Empire, including 'the entirety of Europe'.

47   Thdt., h. Syr. 29.1 (transl. R.M. Price, *A History of the Monks of Syria by Theodoret of Cyrrhus*, Kentucky 1985, 183).

fasting, rough clothes that covered the entirety of their body (including their face and hands), heavy weights attached to themselves and a vow of silence that only Marana broke during the Pentecost and if she was receiving a female visitor. In such instances, the conversation took place through a small window, which also served to deliver food. Their accounts were written by the time they had spent forty-two years in their enclosure, a period that was only interrupted twice: for a pilgrimage to Jerusalem and for a pilgrimage to the tomb of Saint Thecla in Isauria.[48] An exception was made for Theodoret, Bishop of Cyrus as well as their biographer, who admits that "I have often been inside the door in order to see them; for out of respect for the episcopal office they have bidden me dig through the door".[49] Once again, we can see how episcopal hierarchies were keenly aware of the absolute control they held over these women, even if this meant interrupting their self-imposed routines.

Not long before Theodoret, Palladius had written his *Historia Lausiaca* (419/420), a work full of biographies of both male and female ascetics, whether anchorite or coenobite, who still inhabited the deserts of Egypt. Indeed, Palladius himself had spent time there and his work bears witness to the presence of women, albeit in smaller numbers than men. Some of the female ascetics he mentions followed 'classic' practices, but there is mention of a singular woman who 'feigned madness' in order to humiliate herself in front of the congregation.[50] Especially notable is the fact that Palladius' writings reinforced the idea that a woman who achieved spiritual perfection had, by extension, ceased to be a woman. Such is the case of Melania the Elder, an aristocrat from Hispania who devoted herself to asceticism and eventually travelled to meet the desert fathers and mothers: she is described by Palladius as "the woman, a man of God".[51]

---

48   Thdt., h. Syr. 29.7: "Conceiving a desire to behold as well the shrine of the triumphant Thecla in Isauria, in order from all sources to kindle the firebrand of their love for God, they journeyed both there and back without food- to such a degree has divine yearning driven them to frenzy, so much has divine love for the Bridegroom driven them mad. Since by such a way of life they have adorned the female sex, becoming as models for other women, they will be crowned by the Master with the wreaths of victory. I myself, having displayed the benefit therefrom and culled their blessing, shall pass on to another account" (transl. Price, 1985, 185).

49   Thdt., h. Syr. 29.5 (transl. Price, 1985, 184).

50   Pall., h. Laus. 34.79–81 (transl. J. Wortley, Palladius of Aspuna. The Lausiac History, Collegeville 2015).

51   Pall., h. Laus, 46.109 (transl. J. Wortley, 2015).

3   Consolidation of the Monastic Movement (5th–6th centuries):
       Solitary Ascetics by means of Coenobitic Enclosure

The consolidation of an organised monastic movement under coenobitic guidelines was meant to ensure definitive control over female asceticism. Improvised hermitages and private homes converted into ascetic centres gave way to more formal spaces in which to organise a proper religious community. Women were no longer secluded, but enclosed. Individual acts of seclusion required a strong sense of self-discipline, whereas coenobitic enclosure was driven by strict obedience to an authority –"obedience breeds humility".[52]

This transition from *domus* to *monasterium* largely developed throughout the fifth century and can also be followed by looking at the various disputes between ecclesiastical authorities: debates on how to eliminate, or at least curtail, female asceticism, or else how to bring solitary hermits into the fold, especially those who happened to be women. Ecclesiastical authorities strove to bring women who devoted themselves to asceticism in the privacy of their own homes into carefully managed monasteries, both as a way of consolidating these institutions and tightening their grip over devotees who evaded their control.

Monastic rules were an integral part of this campaign to control, and those who wrote them – mostly bishops – made it clear that asceticism was infinitely better within an organised community rather than practiced as solitary devotion. A case in hand concerned Leander, Bishop of Seville, who penned a normative text for his sister – and aspiring coenobite – Florentina: Chapter XXVI begs her:

> "Avoid private life, I beg you; do not try to imitate those nuns who live in cells in the cities, who are bothered by many kinds of care; first, they have to please the world and not go forth in unseemly clothing; and they are troubled by worries at home and are busy obtaining a livelihood, and less involved in the things that pertain to God."[53]

On the other hand, there are frequent mentions in ecumenical decrees of 'false monasteries', that is to say, places in which a basilica was consecrated "under the pretext that they are monasteries" but actually served a religious

---

52   Apophth. Patr., 14.9,205.
53   Leand. Hisp., De instit. uirg. 26 (transl. C.W. Barlow, *The Fathers of the Church. Iberian Fathers* 1: *Martin of Braga, Paschasius of Dumium, Leander of Seville*, Washington 1969, 221).

community that did not live "under the approved rule of a bishop", according to one such case.[54]

4   Women who Remained at Large

Despite the evolution of monasticism towards a coenobitic template, both in Eastern and Western Christendom, it is nevertheless a fact that many women continued to devote themselves to a solitary pursuit, often in defiance of family and ecclesiastical pressures. In other words, they continued the tradition of self-seclusion, as opposed to imposed enclosure, and therefore enjoyed a certain degree of freedom. Nevertheless, whether by choice or under pressure, they often transitioned to a coenobitic lifestyle. Such is the case of Monegundis, from Gaul, who in the sixth century devoted herself to solitary asceticism after losing her two daughters. With time, she became the abbess of a monastery she founded, even though she asked to be buried in her cell located near the tomb of Martin of Tours.[55] Burial in one's own cell was understood as an act of permanent monastic seclusion, practiced by both men and women[56] who awaited Judgement Day in such manner.[57]

Whether at the beginning or at the end of their lives, these 'unruly' devotees who chose to endure their asceticism individually and domestically were forced to take extreme – and often ingenious – measures to establish boundaries, both physical and symbolic, which could thus ensure their protection and separation from the world. As we have seen, this was done against a backdrop of increasingly assertive hierarchies bent on regulating, promoting and, we might add, strong-arming devotees into a communal monastic life.

It was precisely at such a time that a sort of 'golden age' of extreme seclusion took place, especially among female ascetics, who in many ways were forced into a double struggle to secure their individual pursuit of solitary penance. Although these 'rebels' were systematically silenced by the Church, written

---

54   Conc. Ilerd. (a. 546), can. III, in: F. Rodríguez / G. Martínez (eds.), *La Colección Canónica Hispana* 4, Madrid 1984, 297–311.

55   Greg. - T., Vit. Patr. 19 (*Gregory of Tours: Life of the Fathers*, E. James [ed.], Liverpool 1991, 118–125).

56   For example, a monk from the monastery of Cauliana, not far from Emerita Augusta, who in the sixth century was buried in his cell–Vit. Patr. Emer. 2. Another example is the aforementioned case of the desert female hermit who had pretended to be a man and was buried in her own cave.

57   Vit. Patr. Emer. 2.21 (A. Maya Sánchez [ed.], *Vitas sanctorum patrum Emeretensium*, CChr. SL 116, Turnhout 1992).

sources, often in uncodified texts, bear witness to the unease felt by religious authorities towards such practices, sparing no effort in denouncing them, much in the same way as they had struggled against secular paganism.

5   Conclusions

The role of women in early Christianity is varied and complex. Committing themselves wholeheartedly to the new religion allowed some to amass considerable power and status within their communities.[58] The anchoritic tradition allowed others to shine in their own quests for solitary seclusion, which in many ways went beyond a merely contemplative life and further strengthened the idea of a penitential life.

The three main stages follow a consecutive chronological order: early ascetics in the desert with a strong eremitic character, followed by urban-domestic ascetics and finally coenobitic nuns. The early tradition of desert anchorites who endured the most diverse and peculiar forms of seclusion did not actually fade away and coexisted with the tradition of virgins and widows living in seclusion, both in towns and on aristocratic rural estates. Once monasteries for nuns had been established, there remained solitary hermits, both in urban and rural settings, who nonetheless drew increasingly disapproving looks from priestly hierarchies.

On the other hand, there were also those who opposed monastic life and all its eccentricities, including seclusion. This much is made clear in *Contra Vigilantium*, a treatise written by Jerome, a priest from *Barcino*[59] that dealt with monasticism and other core issues of Christianity such as worshipping saints and relics. His frontal opposition to monasticism stemmed from his rejection of celibacy, a key element in asceticism according to both the Church and early Christendom during the Late Roman Empire, especially when it concerned women.[60] Vigilantius did not accept asceticism in all its forms, considering it a ploy to evade society that was further reinforced by seclusion.[61]

---

58   G. Clark, *Women in Late Antiquity: Pagan and Christian Lifestyles*, Oxford 1993, 40–57; M.D. Martín Trutet, *El fet monàstic femení*, in: I. Brugués / C. Boada / X. Costa (eds.), *El monestir de Sant Joan. Primer cenobi femení dels comtats catalans (887–1017)*, Barcelona 2019, 25–26.

59   Vigilantius was originally from Aquitania–Hier., Adv. Vigil., cols. 355 et sq.

60   J.A. McNamara, *A New Song: Celibate Women in the First Three Christian Centuries*, New York 1983.

61   Hier., Adv. Vigil., cols. 356–357.

In conclusion, and despite sharing social criticism, asceticism afforded Christian women a degree of freedom that had hitherto been denied by civil society, which established clear guidelines on marriage and procreation. It was the problem of resistance to male control that most concerned ascetic women, and once they had escaped the social and sexual domination of men, they even constructed an alternative ascetic culture.[62]

For some it was about rejecting these social expectations – 'evading society' in Vigilantius' words – while others sought a spiritual path, but in any event the consequence was a life of seclusion and the rejection of their female essence and soul. Such endurance was especially noted among aristocratic women, who played a key role in early female monasticism.

---

62   V. Burrus, *Word and Flesh: The Bodies and Sexuality of Ascetic Women in Christian Antiquity*, in: JFSR 10 (1994), 32.

Luchas de Poder en la Galia Merovingia

Oposición y Confrontación entre Reinas y Obispos

Pablo Poveda Arias

Abstract

The Merovingian queens, particularly the most powerful ones, were often involved in situations of collaboration and confrontation with bishops from their respective kingdoms. In this contribution we will analyse the latter, examining the different forms of confrontation that arose and how they were resolved. We will also explore the extent to which these episodes strengthened or weakened the power of the Merovingian female rulers.

Introducción

Uno de los propósitos del presente estudio es reivindicar el papel de las reinas merovingias como agentes activos de poder, en particular el de algunas de ellas.[1] Incluimos así a casos concretos de soberanas en el esquema del *queenship*, esto es, concediéndoles la capacidad de "establecer una serie de relaciones de poder no institucionales, pudiendo disfrutar de una posición desde la cual era posible influir en otros y así alcanzar unos objetivos que engrandecieran su propio prestigio".[2] El concepto en cuestión se centra especialmente en los mecanismos informales en el ejercicio del poder. Recientemente hemos

* Este trabajo se ha desarrollado en el marco de los proyectos de investigación PID2020-112506GB-C42 y PID2021.123986NB.I00, financiados por MCIN/AEI/10.13039/501100011033 y, en el caso del segundo proyecto, también por "FEDER Una manera de hacer Europa".

1 Para una perspectiva teórica de la agencia femenina, véase: M.C. Eler / M. Kowaleski, *Introduction. A New Economy of Power Relations: Female Agency in the Middle Ages*, en: M.C. Eler / M. Kowaleski (eds.), *Gendering the Master Narrative: Women and Power in the Middle Ages*, Ithaca 2003, 1–16.

2 A. Pagès Poyatos, *El Queenship como modelo teórico de poder formal e informal aplicado a la nobleza: apuntes para una propuesta metodológica*, en: Journal of Feminist, Gender and Women Studies 5 (2017), 48. Sobre este concepto, véase también: J.C. Parsons, *Family, Sex, and Power: The Rhythms of Medieval Queenship*, en: J.C. Parsons (ed.), *Medieval Queenship*, New York 1998, 1–11; J.N. Nelson, *Medieval Queenship*, en: L.E. Mitchell (ed.), *Women in Medieval Western European Culture*, New York 1998, 179–207; T. Earenfight, *Queenship in Medieval Europe*, New York 2013; E. Woodacre (ed.), *A Companion to Global Queenship*, Leeds 2018.

destacado el papel que desempeñó entre estos la construcción de unas redes de influencia sobre el episcopado de sus respectivos reinos.[3] No abordamos entonces la contra vertiente de ese mismo proceso, esto es, el estudio de los episodios de rivalidad e, incluso, de enfrentamiento entre reinas y obispos. Estos existieron, sin duda. De hecho, algunos de los episodios más detallados ofrecidos por Gregorio de Tours en su obra histórica están dedicados a los enfrentamientos que algunos de sus homólogos episcopales mantuvieron con las reinas merovingias de su tiempo.[4]

Las soberanas del período merovingio no ejercieron una agencia política estructural, sino que esta adquirió un carácter más episódico, encarnado en reinas de una personalidad excepcional o derivado de circunstancias particulares –o por la concurrencia de ambos factores–.[5] Se entiende que en estos contextos surgiesen algunas figuras, tanto laicas como eclesiásticas, reacias a aceptar su autoridad. No debemos sin embargo generalizar estas situaciones de enfrentamiento. La cooperación con ciertos sectores del episcopado era perfectamente compatible con la confrontación con otros, o incluso la coexistencia de ambas situaciones.[6] Por ejemplo, a la hora de estudiar las relaciones entre reyes y obispos en el siglo VI, se ha advertido una situación de competencia entre ambas instancias de poder coexistiendo o intercalándose con un panorama general de cooperación entre ellas.[7] En un sentido similar se puede entender la relación del episcopado con las reinas. Debemos, por

---

3   P. Poveda Arias, *Tras las bamblinas del poder: la inclusión del episcopado galo en las redes políticas de las reinas merovingias*, en: M.C. Chiriatti / M. Vallejo Girvés (eds.), *Riflessi di porpora: declinazioni di potere femminile tra Rome, Bisanzio e l'Occidente Medievale*, QRiBi(S), Spoleto 2023, 313–339.

4   Con todo, las mujeres reciben una atención muy escasa en la obra del autor turonense. D. Harrison, *The Age of Abbesses and Queens: Gender and Political Culture in Early Medieval Europe*, Lund 1998, 75–76.

5   S. Lebecq, *Sur les femmes et leurs éventuels pouvoirs au premier Moyen Âge*, en: S. Lebecq / A. Dierkens / R. Le Jan / J.-M. Sansterre (eds.), *Femmes et pouvoirs des femmes à Byzance et en Occident (VIe–XIe siècles)*, IRHiS 19, Lille 1999, 251–256. Véase: A. Livingstone, *Recalculating the Equation: Powerful Woman = Extraordinary*, en: Medieval Feminist Forum. A Journal of Gender and Sexuality 51 (2015), 17–29. No descartamos, sin embargo, que otras reinas hubiesen alcanzado una extraordinaria influencia política, pero su escasa visibilidad en las fuentes sigue apuntando a la excepcionalidad de este fenómeno.

6   Cabe reseñar el potencial del concepto de "coopetición" a la hora de valorar la coexistencia entre situaciones de cooperación y competición. Véanse: R. Le Jan / G. Bührer-Thierry / S. Gasparri (eds.), *Coopétition. Rivaliser, coopérer dans les sociétés du haut Moyen Âge (500–1000)*, HaMA 31, Turnhout 2018; P. Poveda Arias, *Coexisting Leaderships in the Visigothic Cities: A 'Coopetitive' Model*, en: D. Castro / F. Ruchesi (eds.), *Leadership, Social Cohesion, and Identity in Late Antique Spain and Gaul (500–700)*, LAEMI 11, Amsterdam 2023, 159–183.

7   Y. Hen, *The Church in Sixth-Century Gaul*, en: A.C. Murray (ed.), *A Companion to Gregory of Tours*, BCCT 63, Leiden 2016, 237.

tanto, rechazar el condicionante de género como el principal factor explicativo detrás de tales episodios. Al mismo tiempo que contamos con casos de enfrentamientos, disponemos también de numerosos testimonios que reflejan una aceptación de la autoridad femenina. No podemos descartar, por consiguiente, buscar un origen a estos enfrentamientos en los recelos que podía generar toda acción política.[8] Ello no implica que rechacemos toda incidencia del factor de género. Su propia condición de mujeres reinantes las obligaba a actuar en muchas ocasiones de forma diferente a sus homólogos masculinos o al menos a recurrir a las mismas estrategias que estos, pero de forma más sistemática o contundente, en aras de reivindicarse como soberanas y perpetuarse en el poder.[9] En este esquema, el modelo de *queenship* nos permite analizar en mejores condiciones tales episodios de confrontación, en particular las estrategias desplegadas por las reinas en tales contextos. Se hace particularmente necesario preguntarse "sur la marge de manœuvre dont disposent les femmes et sur ce qui les distingue sur ce plan de leurs homologues masculins, et donc de s'intéresser aux ressources et aux forces sur lesquels elles peuvent compter ainsi qu'aux stratégies qu'elles sont en mesure d'élaborer".[10] A lo largo de las siguientes páginas analizaremos y pondremos en común los distintos casos de enfrentamientos entre reinas merovingias y obispos, focalizando nuestra atención especialmente en las estrategias desplegadas por las soberanas,[11] lo que nos permitirá entender en mejores condiciones su trasfondo, pero también el funcionamiento de las dinámicas de poder en la Galia merovingia, en particular cuando se introduce en ellas la variable de género.

---

8   "on ne constate nulle réticence de la part des hommes à ce qu'une femme exerce l'autorité, y compris royale, et si la reine doit faire face à des oppositions, ce n'est pas parce qu'elle est femme, mais parce que, comme tout souverain, son autorité suscite des oppositions". E. Santinelli-Foltz, *Brunehilde, Bathilde, Hildegarde, Richilde, Gerberge étaient-elles considérées comme des femmes de pouvoir ? La perception masculine du pouvoir royal féminin et son évolution du VIe au Xe siècle*, en: A. Nayt-Dubois / E. Santinelli-Foltz (eds.), *Femmes de pouvoir et pouvoir des femmes dans l'Occident médiéval et moderne*, Valenciennes 2009, 81.

9   Introduciendo una perspectiva de género en el estudio de la política de estas sociedades, ibid. Una visión diferente en: N. Gradowicz-Pancer, *De-gendering Female Violence: Merovingian Female Honour as an 'Exchange of Violence'*, en: EMEu 11 (2002), 1–18.

10   A. Nayt-Dubois / E. Santinelli-Foltz, *Femmes de pouvoir et pouvoir des femmes: concepts, bilan et perspectives*, en: A. Nayt-Dubois / E. Emmanuelle Santinelli-Foltz (eds.), *Femmes de pouvoir et pouvoir des femmes dans l'Occident médiéval et moderne*, Valenciennes 2009, 28.

11   Un análisis más amplio sobre las estrategias de poder que podían desplegar las reinas merovingias en: Harrison, 1998, 347–380.

1   Un Conflicto de Escala Local: Radegunda y Maroveo de Poitiers

El primer enfrentamiento protagonizado por una reina y un obispo al que las fuentes dedican cierta atención es al mantenido entre la reina-monja Radegunda y el obispo Maroveo de Poitiers.[12] Tal confrontación hunde sus raíces en la fundación de un cenobio femenino en Poitiers por iniciativa de la propia Radegunda, que decidió recluirse en él cuando optó por abandonar a su marido, el rey Clotario, y adoptar una vida religiosa.[13] En este proceso fundacional, contó con la colaboración del propio Clotario, del *dux* Austrapius y del entonces obispo Piencio de Poitiers. En calidad de fundadora y principal benefactora (*mater et domna*), nombró a la primera abadesa del lugar, Agnes, aunque sin duda la propia Radegunda se reservó para ella altas cotas de control y autoridad sobre el convento.[14] Aunque durante los años inmediatamente posteriores, y según el testimonio de Gregorio y de Baudonivia, la nueva comunidad monástica vivió en comunión con el episcopado de Poitiers, el nombramiento episcopal de Maroveo en el 568 supuso un cambio en las relaciones.[15] Es posible que las desavenencias tuviesen origen en el celo de Maroveo de imponer la ascendencia que la normativa canónica otorgaba a los obispos sobre los monasterios radicados en sus respectivas diócesis.[16] Poco le

---

12   Sobre este: B. Brennan, *St. Radegund and the Early Development of her Cult at Poitiers*, en: JRH 13 (1985), 343–346; R. Van Dam, *Saints and Their Miracles in Late Antique Gaul*, Princeton 1993, 30–36; B.H. Rosenwein, *Negotiating Space: Power, Restraint, and Privileges of Immunity in Early Medieval Europe*, Ithaca 1999, 52–58; E.T. Dailey, *Queens, Consorts, Concubines: Gregory of Tours and Women of the Merovingian Elite*, MnS 381, Leiden 2015, 68–79.

13   Baudonivia, v. Rad. 7.

14   Greg.-T., Hist. 3.7; 9.42; Venant., v. Rad.; Baudonivia, v. Rad. Sobre el convento fundado por Radegunda, G. Scheibelreiter, *Königstöchter im Kloster. Radegund († 587) und der Nonnenaufstand von Poitiers (589)*, en: MIÖG 87 (1979), 1–37; E. T. Dailey, *Misremembering Radegund's Foundation of Sainte-Croix*, en: H. Brandt / B. Pohl / W.M. Sprague / L.K. Hörl (eds.), *Erfahren, Erzählen, Erinnern: Narrative Konstruktionen von Gedächtnis und Generation in Antike und Mittelalter*, BamHS 9, Bamberg 2012, 117–140; J.C. Edwards, *Superior Women: Medieval Female Authority in Poitiers' Abbey of Sainte-Croix*, Oxford 2019. Sobre la posición y el papel de liderazgo de Radegunda en el seno de su comunidad, S. Gäbe, *Radegundis, Sancta, regina ancilla: Zum Heiligkeitsideal der Radegundisviten von Fortunat und Baudonivia*, en: Francia 16 (1989), 14–15.

15   Greg.-T., Hist. 9.40–42; Baudonivia, v. Rad. 5. Sobre la figura de Maroveo, R. Mineau, *Un évêque de Poitiers au VIe siècle: Marovée*, en: Bulletin de la Société des Antiquaires de l'Ouest et des musées de Poitiers 11 (1971/1972), 361–383.

16   Concilio de Agde (506), cc. 27–28; Concilio de Orleans (511), cc. 7; 19; Concilio de Epaón (517), cc. 8–10; Concilio de Orleans (533), c. 21; Concilio de Orleans (538), c. 26 (23); Concilio de Orleans (541), c. 11; Concilio de Arlés (554), cc. 2–3; 5. Es más, el propio Gregorio de Tours reconoce la teórica jurisdicción de Maroveo sobre el monasterio de Radegunda.

importó que la principal perjudicada fuese una reina, un factor que sin duda
pesó en la actitud complaciente de sus predecesores. El consiguiente cambio
en el *status quo* vigente hasta entonces trajo consigo la lógica resistencia de
Radegunda y Agnes de ver limitada su libertad de acción. Con todo, tal hipótesis no deja de entrar en el campo especulativo, puesto que no sabemos en realidad el orden concreto de los acontecimientos. Tal y como pone en evidencia
Jennifer C. Edwards, "it is nuclear from the available sources, however, whether
Radegund took efforts to sidestep Maroveus' authority and protect her abbey
from his influence as a result of his hostility, or if those very efforts provoked
his resentment".[17]

Sin saber exactamente si funcionó como causa o como consecuencia, aunque por nuestra parte nos inclinamos más por esta segunda opción,[18] lo cierto
es que las relaciones entre Radegunda y Maroveo se enrarecieron sobre todo
a raíz de la obtención por parte de la propia reina-monja de una reliquia de
la Cruz para su convento. Ello lo logró gracias, aparte de su tesón y habilidad política, a la intercesión de Sigiberto, que intercambió embajadas con el
Imperio oriental solicitándole la partícula de la Cruz.[19] Pero sobre todo fue
su emérita, y aún efectiva, posición como reina lo que le otorgó tal capacidad
de influencia política.[20] Su regia condición no era vista, al menos a ojos de

---

Greg.-T., Hist. 9.40. En una línea no muy alejada, Brennan, 1985, 344. Sobre esta normativa
canónica y el celo de Maroveo en aplicarla, Scheibelreiter, 1979, 9–11, 20–22.

17   Edwards, 2019, 51.

18   No creemos casual que sea en el episcopado de Maroveo y no antes cuando Radegunda se
dispuso a obtener la reliquia de la Cruz.

19   Greg.-T., Hist. 9.40; 9.42; Baudon. v. Rad. 16. Sobre tal embajada, véanse: I. Moreira,
'Provisatrix optima': *St. Radegund of Poitiers' Relic Petitions to the East*, en: JMedHist 19
(1993), 285–305; Edwards, 2019, 60–66. Sobre la importancia de las reliquias en la sociedad merovingia del momento, P. Brown, *Relics and Social Status in the Age of Gregory of
Tours*, en: P. Brown, *Society and the Holy in Late Antiquity*, Berkeley 1982, 222–250. Es de
suponer que tal apoyo hacia el monasterio de Radegunda habría degradado sus relaciones con Maroveo. G.I. Halfond, *Bishops and the Politics of Patronage in Merovingian Gaul*,
Ithaca 2019, 59.

20   Así lo pone en evidencia el propio Venancio Fortunato en el poema que dedicó a los emperadores Justino y Sofía. En él se defiende que la entrega de la reliquia se hace a una reina y
no a una monja. Venant., carm. app. 7. Véanse también: Scheibelreiter, 1979, 21; Gäbe, 1989,
1–30; Harrison, 1998, 94. Se tornan bastante elocuentes las palabras de Edwards, 2019, 50:
"Although she gave up her royal titles, she embraced the power and authority her former
networks could ensure for her new family". Haciéndonos eco también de las palabras de
Scheibelreiter, 1979, 23: "Radegund kannt keine Ambivalenz von demütiger Nonne und
ehemaliger Königin was ihre Persönlichkeit betraf". Fue igualmente su regia posición la
que determinó, más allá de su papel en la obtención de la reliquia de la Cruz, la asimilación que se hizo de su figura con la de Santa Elena. Sobre tal asimilación, S. Joye, *Basine,
Radegonde et la Thuringe chez Grégoire de Tours*, en: Francia 32 (2005), 13.

la propia Radegunda, en contradicción con su vida religiosa, sino que la instrumentalizó a su favor, en este caso para reforzar la posición religiosa de su figura y su monasterio en un contexto de competencia con Maroveo. La obtención de la reliquia de la Cruz funcionó, por tanto, como una estrategia –bastante innovadora por otra parte– desplegada por Radegunda en aras de hacer frente a una amenaza a la autonomía que había venido imperando hasta entonces en su fundación monástica.

Maroveo, por su parte, al reclamar una jurisdicción efectiva sobre el monasterio de Radegunda, buscó contrarrestar la pujanza de un centro religioso que, bajo su episcopado, y más allá de los movimientos dirigidos a obtener la reliquia de la Cruz, buscó desvincularse de su obispo, también en los aspectos eminentemente religiosos. De hecho, en una provocación clara a Maroveo, el monasterio impulsó el culto a santos propios de otras ciudades, como San Martín de Tours, mientras minimizó el del patrón de la propia Poitiers, San Hilario.[21] A esta provocación se le sumó la adopción por parte del monasterio de Radegunda de la *regula ad virgines* de Cesáreo de Arlés, la cual sustraía a esta comunidad monástica del control del obispo en cuya diócesis se radicase el cenobio.[22] La obtención de la reliquia se entiende como un movimiento más dirigido a minar la autoridad episcopal de Maroveo, pero en este caso ya no

---

21   Van Dam, 1993, 31. Sobre las implicaciones de este hecho: "The decision to patronize a specific cult and its related institutions was indicative not only of the royal patron's faith in the spiritual power of the saint, but also of the patron's relationship with the episcopal guardian of that saint's cult as well as the *civitas* with which the cult was linked". G.I. Halfond, 'Sis Quoque Catholicis Religionis Apex': The Ecclesiastical Patronage of Chilperic I and Fredegund, en: ChH 81 (2012), 71. Véanse también: C.M.M. Casias, *Rebel Nuns and the Bishop Historian: The Competing Voices of Radegund and Gregory*, en: *Studies in Late Antiquity* 6 (2022), 18; Dailey, 2015, 70–71; Edwards, 2019, 67–70.

22   Greg.-T., Hist. 9.39. W.E. Klingshirn, *Caesarius's Monastery for Women in Arles and the Composition and Function of the* Vita Caesarii, en: RBen 100 (1990), 456–464; A. Diem, *Gregory's Chess Board: Monastic Conflict and Competition in Early Medieval Gaul*, en: P. Depreux / F. Bougard / R. Le Jan (eds.), *Compétition et sacré au haut Moyen* Âge: entre médiation et exclusion, HaMA 21, Turnhout 2015, 184. Sobre esta regla y sus implicaciones en la comunidad monástica de Radegunda, C. Thiellet, *La Règle de saint Césaire d'Arles et les fondations monastiques féminines*, en: R.-H. Bautier / P. Racinet (eds.), *Pratique et sacré dans les espaces monastiques au Moyen Âge et à l'époque moderne*, vol. 2, Amiens 1998, 23–33; A. Diem, *Inventing the Holy Rule: Some Observations on the History of Monastic Normative Observance in the Early Medieval West*, en: H. Dey / E. Fentress (eds.), *Western Monasticism* ante litteram: The Spaces of Monastic Observance in Late Antiquity and Early Middle Ages, DiMo 7, Turnhout 2011, 58–64; Edwards, 2019, 38–45. Recientemente se ha planteado la posibilidad de que la recepción y adopción de esta regla se produjeron antes del conflicto entre Radegunda y Maroveo, incluso en el momento de la fundación del cenobio de la Santa Cruz. Sin embargo, como el propio autor de la propuesta reconoce, se trata de una hipótesis difícil de confirmar. Dailey, 2015, 77.

solo con implicaciones únicamente en lo que al monasterio se refiere, sino en el conjunto de su diócesis, puesto que ahora, y gracias al enorme capital religioso que traía consigo la partícula de la Cruz, el cenobio de Radegunda se convertía en el principal centro de culto de Poitiers y su territorio.[23]

Maroveo exteriorizó claramente su oposición a la llegada de la nueva reliquia al negarse a oficiar su *adventus* y deposición en el centro religioso de Radegunda.[24] Actuando de esta manera, y haciéndonos eco de las palabras de Raymond Van Dam, "Maroveus was simply defending his prerogatives as bishop and the influence of the patron saint of the city".[25] Tal hostilidad forzó a que la ceremonia fuese oficiada por otro obispo, Eufronio de Tours, una intervención que obedeció ante todo, y más allá de la mediación de nuevo de Sigiberto, a los vínculos personales entre Radegunda y el propio prelado turonense.[26]

La actitud de Maroveo puso en guardia a Radegunda, quien se centró los años restantes de su vida en proteger su cenobio y asegurar su seguridad aún cuando ella no estuviese. Para ello, la reina-monja se dirigió por carta a los obispos galos, con excepción de Maroveo, pidiéndoles garantías de que protegerían su monasterio frente a cualquier amenaza que se cerniese sobre él, con independencia de que su causante tuviese condición laica o episcopal. Igualmente, solicitó la intervención de estos obispos ante cualquier incumplimiento de la regla monástica, ya fuera por parte de cualquiera de las propias monjas o por cualquier agente externo.[27] No resulta descabellado pensar que las inquietudes transmitidas por Radegunda a los obispos tenían en Maroveo un nombre propio.[28] Siete obispos respondieron de forma afirmativa a tales demandas, entre los que destacaban los metropolitanos de Tours y Rouen.[29] No estamos sin embargo ante un acto de altruismo y solidaridad por parte de los obispos, sino que seguramente tal fue el resultado de una negociación que se saldó con cesiones por parte de la propia Radegunda. En particular, en su carta la reina-monja cedió y reconoció la autoridad episcopal sobre su monasterio y por tanto sobre su propia persona, pero solo a los obispos a los que se dirigió y, por tanto, nunca a Maroveo.[30] Para Radegunda era preferible reconocer una

---

23   S.J. Coates, *Regendering Radegund? Fortunatus, Baudonivia and the Problem of Female Sanctity in Merovingian Gaul*, en: SCH(L) 34 (1998), 44; Van Dam, 1993, 31–36; Moreira, 1993, 299.

24   Venant., carm. 2.6; Greg.-T., Hist. 9.40.

25   Van Dam, 1993, 32.

26   Venant., carm. 2.6. Edwards, 2019, 47–48, 70.

27   Greg.-T., Hist. 9.42.

28   Edwards, 2019, 49.

29   Greg.-T., Hist. 9.39.

30   Greg.-T., Hist. 9.42. Véase: Casias, 2022, 5–34.

teórica y, sin duda, retórica subordinación a obispos foráneos, los cuales únicamente habrían intervenido en su monasterio de forma excepcional, que ofre-
cerle su sumisión a Maroveo y que este tuviese el control directo de su cenobio.
Haciéndonos eco de las palabras de Cassandra M. M. Casias, "Radegund formed alliances and even friendships with various bishops, but ultimately she
was a player in a game for influence against the episcopacy as well".[31] En resu-
men, Radegunda vio en el recurso a otros poderes episcopales, pero lejanos,
una vía para inclinar la balanza a su favor.

No hay motivos para cuestionar el éxito de Radegunda en su obstinación
por proteger su monasterio, al menos hasta su muerte. Sus ambiciones fueron,
por tanto, bastante modestas, pero es cierto que, en el camino de preservación
de los intereses y la autonomía de su cenobio, la propia Radegunda se situó en
una posición de liderazgo espiritual sobre Poitiers y su entorno. En definitiva,
su acción se enmarca en el contexto de una rivalidad local entre la institución
monástica de la que ella funcionaba como patrona y la autoridad episcopal de
Poitiers que encarnaba Maroveo. Cierto es que se trató de un enfrentamiento
con un fuerte componente personal, con un enconamiento muy pronunciado
de las hostilidades entre sus dos protagonistas, que trascendió incluso la vida
de estos.[32] Para imponerse en el juego de poder, diseñó y desplegó diversas
estrategias, algunas más tradicionales, como el establecimiento de redes de
poder con el episcopado, pero también otras más innovadoras, como la obtención, en este caso gracias a la mediación de los poderes seculares, de la reliquia
de la Cruz para su cenobio. El tiempo, sin embargo, acabaría dándole la razón a
Maroveo, puesto que años después, ya fallecida Radegunda, el rey Childeberto
II sancionó la autoridad del obispo de Poitiers sobre todos los monasterios de
su diócesis, incluido el fundado por su difunta enemiga.[33]

2 Hacia el Control del *Regnum*: los Procesos Judiciales contra Obispos

El resto de casos disponibles de enfrentamientos entre reinas y obispos
adquiere un cariz más político y, aunque tienen unas claras repercusiones en
la escala local, se insertan en un panorama más general, con unas ambiciones que iban mucho más allá del control de una única ciudad y su territorio.

---

31   Casias, 2022, 25.
32   Maroveo de hecho se negó incluso a oficiar el funeral de Radegunda y, por extensión, del
      personaje más ilustre de Poitiers. Venant., carm. 8.12; Greg.-T., l.i.g.c. 104.
33   Greg.-T., Hist. 9.40. Scheibelreiter, 1979, 13–14.

Emmanuelle Santinelli puso hace unos años de manifiesto el diseño por parte de algunas reinas merovingias de una política de control territorial claramente definida, en la que reservaron a los obispos un papel bastante destacado.[34] En particular, habrían impulsado el nombramiento de prelados afines en las sedes episcopales de su interés en aras de lograr proyectar su influencia en estos territorios, pero también de nutrir su base de apoyos políticos frente a facciones opositoras. En otros casos, y con los mismos fines, habrían intentado atraerse el apoyo de obispos ya en el cargo, por ejemplo, a través de preben-das.[35] Tales iniciativas se llevaron a cabo especialmente en su condición de regentes de un monarca en minoría de edad, pero en algunos casos también en vida de sus maridos. En ocasiones, sin embargo, las reinas se toparon con dificultades para lograr atraerse el apoyo y las simpatías de determinados obis-pos de sus respectivos reinos, ya fuera porque las lealtades de estos se encon-traban depositadas en otro rey o simplemente por falta de afinidad. Ante estas situaciones, podían adoptarse actitudes muy distintas, esto es, bien podían simplemente tolerar la coexistencia con estos prelados –tónica más habitual–, bien podían optar directamente por desbancarlos de su cátedra episcopal. Esto último ocurrió quizás en el plano de la excepcionalidad, pero cuando se dio abría las puertas al conflicto entre las reinas y estos obispos. En estas situacio-nes, las soberanas desplegarían estrategias de diverso tipo que solo es posible explicar analizando cada caso y cada contexto. Con todo, un elemento común a la mayoría de estos enfrentamientos es el recurso en primera instancia a la vía judicial como forma de desplazar a los obispos de sus cátedras episcopales y, por ende, del poder.

Una de las reinas que destacó por sus enfrentamientos con los obispos fue Fredegunda. Gregorio de Tours es especialmente duro a la hora de juzgar a esta figura, acusándola de un trato sistemáticamente vejatorio hacia el epis-copado.[36] Con todo, no debemos ofrecer completa verosimilitud al panorama que dibuja el autor turonense. A fin de cuentas, él mismo mantuvo un enfren-tamiento con Fredegunda, lo cual sin duda condicionó el juicio negativo que

---

34   E. Santinelli, *Les reines mérovingiennes ont-elles une politique territoriale?*, en: RNord 85 (2003), 631–653.

35   Véase: J.L. Nelson, *Queens as Jezebels: The Careers of Brunhild and Balthild in Merovingian History*, en: D. Baker (ed.), *Medieval Women: Dedicated and Presented to Prof. Rosalind M. T. Hill on the Occasion of her Seventieth Birthday*, SCH(L).S 1, Oxford 1978, 31–77; Poveda Arias, 2023, 323–325.

36   Sobre la imagen construida por Gregorio en torno a la figura de Fredegunda, Harrison, 1998, 123–126; Dailey, 2015, 152–156.

hace de ella a lo largo de su obra.[37] Antes de analizar este caso, se torna pertinente analizar uno anterior, que sin duda influirá en el proceso impulsado años después contra Gregorio. Nos referimos al primer enfrentamiento que mantuvo con Pretextato de Rouen. Se sabe que tanto su marido Chilperico I, pero especialmente ella, o al menos es lo que trasluce del testimonio de Gregorio, instigaron y consumaron en el 577 un plan para deponerle y colocar en su lugar a un tal Melanio.[38] El pretexto fue la acusación de alta traición que se vertió sobre él por su apoyo al usurpador Meroveo, pero también por guardar supuestamente la intención de asesinar a Chilperico. Lo cierto es que las acciones del propio Pretextato no hablaban a su favor. Él mismo ofició el matrimonio entre Meroveo y la tía de este, la reina Brunequilda, en lo que constituía una clara amenaza para Chilperico y Fredegunda.[39] Haciéndonos eco de las palabras de Nira Gradowicz-Pancer, "du point de vue de la reine, Prétextat n'est autre qu'un pernicieux et dangereux conspirateur".[40] Se torna lógico el deseo de los reyes por castigar a los apoyos del príncipe rebelde y así desbancar del poder a todos sus enemigos internos.[41] A Fredegunda no le importó recurrir a todos los medios a su alcance, en este caso a mecanismos informales y subrepticios, para lograr que el juicio se saldase según sus intereses. El testimonio de Gregorio pone en evidencia la intimidación a la que se veían sometidos los obispos por parte de la reina, pero también al pago por esta misma de sobornos a los prelados para que condenasen a Pretextato o, al menos, lograsen convencerle de que asumiese la acusación de traición a cambio de la clemencia regia. Los movimientos de Fredegunda, pero también de Chilperico, dieron sus frutos, puesto que el obispo de Rouen se inculpó y, en consecuencia, lejos de

---

37 Véanse I.N. Wood, *The Secret Histories of Gregory of Tours*, en: RBPH 71 (1993), 253–270; Halfond, *Sis Quoque*, 2012, 51. Sobre las precauciones a tomar a la hora de usar el testimonio de Gregorio de Tours para analizar el trato de Fredegunda a los obispos, véanse también: N. Gradowicz-Pancer, *Femmes royales et violences anti-*épiscopales *à l'époque mérovingienne: Frédégonde et le meurtre de l'évêque Prétextat*, en: N. Fryde / D. Reitz (eds.), *Bischofsmord in Mittelalter = Murder of Bishops*, VMPIG 191, Göttingen 2003, 39–42. Confía, sin embargo, en el testimonio de Gregorio: Dailey, 2015, 121.

38 Greg.-T., Hist. 5.18. Sobre la participación de Fredegunda en el proceso, T. Stüber, *Der inkriminierte Bischof. Könige im Konflikt mit Kirchenleitern in westgotischen und fränkischen Gallien (466–614)*, Berlin 2020, 224–225.

39 Greg.-T., Hist. 5.2. Dailey, 2015, 121. Sobre este juicio, véanse también: Halfond, *Sis Quoque*, 2012, 60–61; Stüber, 2020, 218–243.

40 Gradowicz-Pancer, 2003, 141–142.

41 En una línea similar, Stüber, 2020, 241.

recibir el perdón, fue condenado según las prescripciones canónicas esgrimi-
das por el propio monarca. En virtud de estas, fue destituido y condenado al
exilio.[42]

Llama la atención la contención del propio rey que, tal y como ha defendido
Éric Fournier recientemente, "as a ruler, Chilperic could simply have ordered
Pratextatus' execution for *maiestas*".[43] En su lugar, y más allá de las acusaciones
de Gregorio de injusticia y arbitrariedad regias en el proceso, se cumplieron de
forma escrupulosa los procedimientos legales y los obispos participaron activamente en su resolución.[44] Ciertamente se ejercieron ciertas dosis de presión
e intimidación a los prelados presentes en el concilio, pero ello mismo evidencia la importancia que daban tanto Chilperico como Fredegunda a la legitimidad que podía otorgar el colectivo episcopal a un proceso impulsado desde la
corte. Quizás tal exhibición de escrupulosidad procesal hubiese sido innecesa-
ria si Pretextato no hubiese contado con apoyos entre el episcopado, como el
propio Gregorio de Tours. Estos habrían sido sin duda minoritarios o, en caso
contrario, el juicio se habría podido resolver de una forma distinta. Por otro
lado, el restringir la causa a la exclusiva justicia del rey habría podido generar
tensiones innecesarias entre un episcopado colaborativo y sumiso, que se evi-
taban transmitiendo una formalidad procesal que, aunque aparente, resultaba
bastante efectiva a la hora de impedir resistencias al veredicto.

En el año 580, Gregorio de Tours también debió hacer frente a un proceso
judicial que tuvo lugar en Berny-Rivière y que estuvo protagonizado por los
mismos monarcas, aunque por razones distintas.[45] En su caso, fue acusado
de difundir el rumor de que la reina Fredegunda mantenía una relación adúl-
tera con el obispo Bertrán de Burdeos.[46] No se trataba de una cuestión baladí,
puesto que tal acusación implicaba al mismo tiempo poner en cuestión la propia filiación regia de la descendencia de Fredegunda y, por ende, también su
legitimidad, y la de la propia reina, de alcanzar el poder después de la muerte

---

42   Greg.-T., Hist. 5.18.
43   É. Fournier, *Everyone but the Kings: The Rhetoric of (Non-)persecution in Gregory of Tours'
      Histories*, en: É. Fournier / W. Mayer (eds.), *Heirs of Roman Persecution: Studies on a Chris-
      tian and Para-Christian Discourse in Late Antiquity*, London 2019, 192. En una línea similar,
      J.M. Wallace-Hadrill, *The Frankish Church*, OHCC 3, Oxford 1983, 44, quien explica la acti-
      tud de Chilperico en el respeto que le infundía el poder corporativo del episcopado.
44   Stüber, 2020, 233–241.
45   Greg.-T., Hist. 5.49. Sobre este juicio, Van Dam, 1993, 69–73; I.N. Wood, *The Individuality
      of Gregory of Tours*, en: K. Mitchell / I. Wood (eds.), *The World of Gregory of Tours*, CBT 8,
      Leiden 2002, 44; G. Halsall, *Nero and Herod? The Death of Chilperic and Gregory's Wri-
      tings of History*, en: K. Mitchell / I. Wood (eds.), *The World of Gregory of Tours*, CBT 8,
      Leiden 2002, 340–341; Dailey, 2015, 152–156; Stüber, 2020, 243–265.
46   Wood, 1993, 257.

de Chilperico.[47] El propio Gregorio defendió su inocencia culpabilizando a sus enemigos en Tours de las acusaciones vertidas contra él, entre los que destacaba el *comes* Leudasto.[48] Por lo tanto, debemos entender parcialmente este caso como consecuencia de las rivalidades faccionales que se dieron en el seno de la sede turonense.[49]

Curiosamente, el proceso se saldó con la exculpación de Gregorio y con la inculpación de sus acusadores por injuria. Únicamente se le exigió prestar juramento como vía de purificación y exoneración de culpas.[50] Cabe preguntarse por qué se libró de una condena a sabiendas de la mutua animadversión entre Fredegunda y su propia persona.[51] Quizás los monarcas, especialmente Chilperico, habrían valorado que una sentencia desfavorable para el obispo de Tours habría traído más problemas que beneficios,[52] especialmente ante un proceso que no demostraba de forma irrefutable su culpabilidad.[53] A este respecto, se tornan bastante elocuentes las palabras de Gregory I. Halfond: "the king was aware that episcopal, and perhaps even popular, sentiment lay with the accused".[54] Por lo tanto, a diferencia del caso anterior, Gregorio habría contado con un apoyo más o menos unánime entre sus homólogos. A esto se le sumó una intensa tarea de persuasión al rey en la que participaron, aparte de los propios obispos, otros agentes como una de sus hijas o Venancio Fortunato.[55] Además, con tal comportamiento, y más allá de las verdaderas simpatías de Gregorio hacia ambos gobernantes, lo cierto es que, tal y como su obra demuestra, la absolución regia implicó la sumisión del propio obispo de Tours que, salvo insinuaciones veladas, no se lanzó a manifestarse contra ninguno de los gobernantes hasta después de la muerte de Chilperico. Únicamente se atrevió a cuestionar de forma muy sutil la paternidad oficial de Clotario II, insinuando así que Chilperico no era su padre, pero nunca manifestó tales opiniones de forma directa. De hecho, en ningún momento de su obra

---

47 E.T. Dailey, *Gregory of Tours and the Paternity of Chlothar II: Strategies of Legitimation in the Merovingian Kingdoms*, en: Journal of Late Antiquity 7 (2014), 16–17.

48 Greg.-T., Hist. 5.49.

49 Stüber, 2019, 259–260.

50 Greg.-T., Hist. 5.49.

51 Más allá de la causa del juicio contra él, tengamos en cuenta que el propio Gregorio actuó en defensa de Pretextato y, por tanto, en contra de los intereses de la reina.

52 A este respecto, se tornan bastante elocuentes las palabras de Éric Fournier (2019, 194): "[...] there was a limit to the power that kings exercised over bishops, over whom God kept and everlasting watch, and who could destroy the unity of the Church over perceived mistreatment of one of their colleagues".

53 Stüber, 2020, 243–265.

54 Halfond, *Sis Quoque*, 2012, 61.

55 Van Dam, 1993, 71; Wood, 2002, 44.

acusa explícitamente a Fredegunda de adulterio, en lo que ha sido interpretado como una consecuencia del proceso judicial que sufrió.[56] Obtenemos por tanto la impresión de que la causa contra Gregorio, con independencia de su absolución, le sometió a Chilperico, pero también a Fredegunda, asegurando su sumisa colaboración.[57]

La propia participación de buena parte de los obispos del reino en estos juicios habría otorgado legitimidad a tales procesos y, ante el alineamiento episcopal a la voluntad regia, habría servido como mecanismo de disuasión para todo aquel prelado que pretendiese actuar contra cualquiera de los dos monarcas.[58] De hecho, fueron bastante excepcionales las causas judiciales contra obispos durante el reinado de Chilperico, a pesar del juicio negativo que se difundió sobre su figura.[59] Todo cambiaría, sin embargo, a la muerte de este monarca y con el ascenso de Fredegunda a la regencia del reino.[60]

En contraposición a Fredegunda, la imagen que recibe Brunequilda de la pluma de Gregorio de Tours es mucho más positiva, quizás por el respeto que mostraba a esta figura, pero quizás también por miedo a ella.[61] Por extensión, retrata unas relaciones con el episcopado mucho más amistosas que las mantenidas en el caso de su eterna rival. Se trata, sin embargo, de una imagen alejada de la realidad. Podemos asumir que, en líneas generales, la pauta más habitual habría venido marcada por la colaboración entre Brunequilda y los obispos, pero ello no implica que todos los prelados hubiesen guardado simpatías hacia ella, ni tampoco que no surgiesen hostilidades también contra ella, como bien reflejan las fuentes.[62] El primer caso de enfrentamiento evidente entre

---

56 Greg.-T., Hist. 7.7; 8.31. Véanse: Dailey, 2014, 7–11; Dailey, 2015, 153–156.

57 Una prueba de ello la obtenemos en: Greg.-T., Hist. 6.32. Harrison, 1998, 124–125.

58 Sobre la utilidad de este recurso a los obispos, Halfond, *Sis Quoque*, 2012, 61. En lo que respecta a la jurisdicción episcopal en materia de justicia en estos momentos, véase: S. Esders / H. Reimitz, *After Gundovald, before Pseudo-Isidore: Episcopal Jurisdiction, Clerical Privilege and the Uses of Roman Law in the Frankish Kingdoms*, en: EMEu 27 (2019), 85–111.

59 Sobre la imagen de Chilperico en la obra de Gregorio, Wood, 1993, 254–256. Véase también: Halsall, 2002, 337–350.

60 Véase *infra*.

61 Véase, por ejemplo: Greg.-T., Hist. 4.27. Harrison, 1998, 142–143; Dailey, 2015, 142.

62 Dailey, 2015, 126. Sin embargo, es cierto que, a diferencia del caso de Fredegunda, estos enfrentamientos tuvieron lugar a partir del período de regencia que se abrió a la muerte de Sigiberto I. Tampoco es necesario asumir el panorama completamente opuesto que dibuja Fredegario, quien le atribuye los odios del conjunto del episcopado burgundio después de que la región cayese bajo su control. Fredegarius, 4.41. A fin de cuentas, el cronista mostró una clara preferencia política por Clotario II, enemigo de Brunequilda y

Brunequilda y un obispo data del año 590, aunque como veremos este se venía fraguando desde tiempo atrás. Nos referimos al juicio contra Egidio de Reims.[63] La causa contra él se inició a raíz de las serias acusaciones que se vertieron sobre su persona, entre las que se encontraba la de prevaricación, la de alta traición a Brunequilda y Childeberto II por sus contactos con Chilperico y, sobre todo, por conjurar contra la vida de ambos reyes. El propio Egidio acabó confesando parte de los delitos que se le imputaron.[64] Curiosamente, el metropolitano de Reims no fue ni mucho menos un opositor de primera hora de Brunequilda. Sabemos de hecho que disfrutó de su favor, pero también del de su marido Sigiberto I cuando este aún vivía, que le encomendaron distintas misiones diplomáticas.[65] Muerto Sigiberto I, Egidio volvería a dar servicio a Brunequilda, también en una misión diplomática, aunque el contexto había cambiado.[66] Más allá de su servicio a la corte austrasiana, lo cierto es que Egidio se manifestó como un contrapoder de Brunequilda desde el mismo momento de la muerte de Sigiberto I. Por ejemplo, siempre estuvo más inclinado a un acercamiento a Chilperico, por lo que no veía con buenos ojos la revuelta de Meroveo ni por extensión tampoco la política de alineamiento de Brunequilda con el príncipe rebelde. A esto se le suma la competencia que se dio entre ambos por controlar la regencia de Childeberto II hasta que la reina-madre logró apoderarse de ella en el 583.[67] Es en este contexto de concurrencia entre ambos en el que enmarcamos el proceso judicial contra él. De este modo, y haciéndonos eco de las ideas de Bruno Dumézil, posiblemente la causa contra Egidio fue una iniciativa de la propia Brunequilda dirigida a

---

su descendencia, siendo así como se entiende la imagen que imprime sobre ella. Véanse: Harrison, 1999, 222–227; G.I. Halfond, *The Endorsement of Royal-Episcopal Collaboration in the Fredegar Chronica*, en: Tr 70 (2015), 15–16.

63   Sobre el proceso contra Egidio, B. Dumézil, *La reine Brunehaut*, París 2008, 250–251; M.-C. Isaïa, *Egidius de Reims, le traître trahi? En relisant Grégoire de Tours*, en: M. Billoré / M. Soria (eds.), *La Trahison au Moyen Âge. De la monstruosité au crime politique (Vᵉ–XVᵉ siècle)*, Rennes 2009, 89–10; Dailey, 2015, 150–152; Fournier, 2019, 195–196; Stüber, 2020, 312–326.

64   Greg.-T., Hist. 10.19. Sobre los delitos imputados, Stüber, 2020, 317–318.

65   Greg.-T., Hist. 3.3; 6.31; 7.14.

66   Con todo, es cierto que dicho servicio lo desempeñó de forma coyuntural, por un interés instrumental y puntual de la reina. Véase: Dumézil, 2008, 221–222.

67   Dumézil, 2008, 191, 202–211. Véase también: B. Dumézil, *La compétition pour la régence en Austrasie entre 575 et 587*, en: R. Le Jan / G. Bührer-Thierry / S. Gasparri (eds.), *Coopétition: Rivaliser, coopérer dans les sociétés du haut Moyen Âge (500–1100)*, HaMA 31, Turnhout 2018, 77–62.

desactivar de forma definitiva las facciones internas rivales, aprovechándose
para ello de un contexto de indudable fortaleza interna.[68]

La causa contra Egidio se dirimió en un concilio judicial que reunió a buena
parte del episcopado del reino. Es más, los propios obispos austrasianos mostraron mucho celo en que el proceso se llevase a cabo con garantías, hasta el
punto de reprender al rey por haber apresado a Egidio sin un juicio previo y de
forzarle a restituirlo en la sede de Reims hasta que este tuviese lugar.[69] Ciertamente, como en los casos anteriormente expuestos, Childeberto y Brunequilda
podían haber concluido el asunto elevando el proceso a un tribunal secular y
sentenciando a muerte al propio Egidio. Sin embargo, prefirieron ajustarse al
procedimiento canónico, que exigía que los obispos fuesen juzgados por sus
propios pares.[70] De hecho, la propia confesión de Egidio habría sido pretexto
suficiente para su ejecución,[71] pero tampoco en este caso los reyes optaron
por recurrir a la violencia, sino que les bastó con su deposición y posterior
exilio. Es más, Egidio fue uno de los pocos implicados en esta conspiración
que no sufrió la pena de muerte, aunque es cierto que se trataba del único
obispo encausado. Creemos por tanto que la actitud de Brunequilda y Childeberto II buscó de nuevo no tensionar las relaciones con los obispos, quienes,
según el propio Gregorio de Tours, habrían rogado al monarca por la vida de
Egidio.[72] Asimismo, tampoco podemos descartar la aplicación de cierta dosis
de pragmatismo, puesto que, tal y como afirma Bruno Dumézil, "les Grands
qui avouaient leurs fautes furent toujours épargnés, car ils pouvaient un jour
devenir utiles".[73] El episodio se saldó con la deposición y el exilio de Egidio.
En su lugar fue nombrado Romulfo, hijo del *dux* Lupo,[74] quien a su vez había
mantenido años atrás un conflicto con el depuesto obispo de Reims.[75] Más allá
de que los obispos evitasen la ejecución de Egidio, lo cierto es que el proceso
cumplió con los objetivos perseguidos: expulsar a un rival de la reina de los

---

68   Dumézil, 2008, 249–250. Para lecturas alternativas: Wood, 1993, 268–270; Isaïa, 2009,
      89–101; Dailey, 2015, 151; Stüber, 2020, 312–326, 387–388.
69   Greg.-T., Hist. 10.19.
70   Dumézil, 2008, 251; Fournier, 2019, 195–196.
71   De hecho, según el testimonio de Gregorio de Tours, el acusado era plenamente cons-
      ciente de que sus delitos eran suficientes para sufrir la pena de muerte. Greg.-T., Hist. 10.19.
72   Ibid.
73   Dumézil, 2008, 251.
74   Greg.-T., Hist. 10.19.
75   En concreto, Egidio habría conspirado para destituir a Lupo como *dux* en la región.
      Greg.-T., Hist. 9.14. No consideramos casual que fuera su hijo el que acabase sustituyendo
      a Egidio en la cátedra remense. Sobre Lupo, Greg.-T., Hist. 4.46; 6.4.

círculos de poder, desactivar su facción y situar en su lugar a una figura de la presumible confianza de la corte.

Más célebre es el enconado enfrentamiento entre Brunequilda y Desiderio de Vienne.[76] En una primera fase, este obispo metropolitano fue acusado de abusar de una aristócrata de nombre Justa. Ello sirvió como pretexto para iniciar, por iniciativa de la propia Brunequilda, un proceso judicial contra él. Las fuentes disponibles, todas ellas hostiles a la figura de la reina, califican tales acusaciones como calumnias, y no es descartable que en realidad estas solo hubiesen funcionado como excusa para procesarlo.[77] Cabe por tanto plantear la posibilidad de que ante todo hubiese influido aquí un factor más personal, como la falta de confianza y de afinidad política entre Brunequilda y el obispo de Vienne.[78] Las fuentes de hecho son claras a la hora de integrar a Desiderio de Vienne en el círculo de opositores burgundios a la reina y a la nueva regencia que se abrió a la muerte de su hijo Childeberto II († 596).[79] Tengamos en cuenta que en estos momentos Brunequilda estaba inmersa en el proceso de consolidación de su poder en Burgundia –recordemos que hasta el 592 este territorio integraba el núcleo del reino de Gontran–, promocionando a sus afines y, por consiguiente, generando recelos entre los círculos aristocráticos excluidos.[80] Las posiciones se habrían enconado aún más después de que Brunequilda se negase a avalar las aspiraciones de Desiderio al *pallium*.[81] En un nuevo juicio conciliar, celebrado en esta ocasión en Chalon-sur-Saône en el año 603, los obispos concordaron destituir a Desiderio y enviarlo al exilio.[82] Se trató por tanto de una decisión que recibió la aquiescencia episcopal. Otra cuestión es que el temor a la reina y la intimidación ejercida por esta misma hubiesen pesado en cierta manera a la hora de fallar en contra de Desiderio, pero ni mucho menos ello implica una oposición episcopal al resultado del juicio. Es más, poderosos exponentes del episcopado, como Aridio de Lyon,

---

76 Sobre este y su instrumentalización por la literatura posterior, Y. Fox, *The Bishop and the Monk: Desiderius of Vienne and the Columbanian Movement*, en: EMEu 20 (2012), 176–194. Véanse también: Dumézil, 2008, 336–338; Stüber, 2020, 326–346.

77 Sisebutus, v. Desid. 1.4; 1.9; [Anon.], v. Desid. 2.2–3.

78 Para otras lecturas, no necesariamente excluyentes: Nelson, 1978, 57–59; Dumézil, 2008, 337; Fox, 2012, 193.

79 [Anon.], v. Desid. 2.2. No solo Brunequilda, sino también su nieto Teuderico II habría sido objeto de críticas por parte de Desiderio. Sisebutus, v. Desid. 1.15–16. La *Vita Columbani* pone en evidencia la hostilidad regia hacia Desiderio y acusan directamente a Teuderico y a su abuela de su posterior muerte. Ionas Bobbiensis, v. Columb. 1.27.

80 Poniendo en evidencia este contexto, Harrison, 1998, 223–224, quien pone en evidencia la persecución contra algunos de sus opositores.

81 Dumézil, 2008, 340.

82 Sisebutus, v. Desid. 1.4; [Anon.], v. Desid. 2.3; Fredegarius, 4.24.

apoyaron gustosamente el proceso contra Desiderio. La crónica de Fredegario atribuye en primera instancia al propio metropolitano de Lyon la persecución contra el obispo de Vienne y le implicará también en su posterior asesinato.[83] Cabe por tanto plantear la posibilidad de que, a las tensiones con la corte de Brunequilda, debamos sumar la competencia episcopal como factor explicativo complementario de la causa contra Desiderio.[84] Quizás Aridio no veía con buenos ojos las aspiraciones de Desiderio respecto al *pallium*, lo cual le habría colocado en una posición moral superior a cualquier otro obispo de la Galia. Aceptando esta posibilidad, Aridio habría visto en Brunequilda y en los odios de esta hacia Desiderio una oportunidad para lograr acabar con un rival, pero también, por qué no, como una forma de lograr una mayor ascendencia sobre Vienne y su territorio. De hecho, no es descartable que el sustituto de Desiderio en la cátedra de Vienne, Domnulo, hubiese sido escogido como nuevo obispo a instancias de Aridio, por supuesto con la connivencia de Brunequilda.[85]

Un hecho evidente del proceso contra Desiderio es el enorme poder de la reina, que tuvo la capacidad de iniciar por sí misma la causa judicial contra Desiderio.[86] Muy segura tenía que sentirse de su control sobre el episcopado del reino como para elevar la causa a un concilio judicial. Tal estrategia solo tiene sentido a sabiendas de antemano de una resolución favorable del juicio. La iniciativa judicial de Brunequilda y, por tanto, su ascendencia sobre la Iglesia del reino se observan a través de la correspondencia mantenida con Gregorio Magno en relación a otros procesos judiciales contra obispos.[87] Por ejemplo, sabemos que Brunequilda impulsó una causa contra el obispo Menan, de sede desconocida, por crímenes no especificados. A diferencia del caso de Egidio, en este caso la entonces reina-abuela elevó el asunto a Roma al papa Gregorio Magno, que lo declarará inocente.[88] Cabe preguntarse por el recurso a la vía papal para resolver este juicio cuando ella misma tenía capacidad de determinar los resultados de las causas contra obispos. Lamentablemente, la

---

83   Fredegarius, 4.24; 4.27. Véase: Fox, 2012, 191–193. Respecto a las posibles causas detrás de tal hostilidad por parte del obispo de Lyon, Fredegario no ofrece más explicación.

84   Stüber, 2020, 338–340, 346.

85   Sisebutus, v. Desid. 1.4. Fox, 2012, 191.

86   [Anon.], v. Desid. 2.7. S. Savoye, *Le pouvoir des reines mérovingiennes dans l'hagiographie mérovingienne*, en: A. Nayt-Dubois / E. Santinelli-Foltz (eds.), *Femmes de pouvoir et pouvoir des femmes dans l'Occident médiéval et moderne*, Valenciennes 2009, 47.

87   Esta es reconocida por el propio Gregorio Magno, que verá en ella su principal interlocutora para tratar los asuntos eclesiásticos del reino. Véanse: Dumézil, 2008, 329–365; Santinelli-Foltz, 2009, 62–63. Sobre la ascendencia de Brunequilda sobre la Iglesia de su reino, Poveda Arias, 2023, 329–331.

88   Gregorius Magnus, reg. epist. 13.7.

falta de datos únicamente nos permite lanzar especulaciones, pero es posible que, con su recurso a Roma, la reina regente hubiese buscado resolver una causa cuestionable que, en caso de haberse dirimido en concilio por parte del episcopado del reino, habría tensionado en exceso las relaciones con y entre los obispos.

Adolecemos igualmente de falta de información a la hora de analizar las circunstancias que llevaron a la deposición temporal de Bertrán como obispo de Le Mans mientras Brunequilda ejercía su influencia política. Solamente sabemos que fue desplazado de su cátedra episcopal y sufrió la confiscación de bienes en el tiempo en el que Childeberto II y Brunequilda se apoderaron de la ciudad de Le Mans y que fue posteriormente restituido, concretamente cuando Clotario II recuperó este territorio en el 596. También sabemos que en este tiempo Fredegunda y Clotario le regalaron al mismo Bertrán la villa de Bonnelles en Étampes, en lo que se entiende como un reconocimiento a la lealtad mostrada hacia ambos aun cuando su ciudad había caído en manos de Brunequilda. En el 600, Le Mans volvió a manos de Brunequilda y sus nietos, Teuderico II y Teudeberto II, siendo Bertrán depuesto de nuevo. Finalmente, en el 604, Clotario volvió a recuperar la ciudad restituyendo definitivamente a Bertrán como obispo del lugar hasta su muerte en el 616.[89] No sabemos, sin embargo, si en su doble destitución medió un proceso judicial, pero a tenor de los casos anteriores, no es descartable que así fuera. La confiscación de bienes y la posterior restitución que hace personalmente Clotario II de parte de los mismos años después,[90] en lo que por otra parte constituye un *unicum* entre toda la casuística analizada hasta ahora, puede deberse quizás a que el proceso se resolvió en el ámbito secular. En caso de estar en lo cierto, Brunequilda y sus descendientes habrían sido conscientes de que el episcopado del reino no mostraría solidaridad corporativa alguna hacia un obispo enemigo del reino y, por tanto, se habría mostrado indiferente al destino del propio Bertrán.[91] Ello le habría otorgado a los monarcas más margen de maniobra para actuar de forma contundente, pero también más rápida, contra un obispo de su reino leal a Fredegunda y Clotario II.

---

89   Sobre este caso, véanse: I.N. Wood, *The Merovingian Kingdoms, 470–751*, Londres 1994, 207–210; Halfond, 2019, 89.

90   Wood, 1994, 208–209.

91   Sobre la solidaridad corporativa del episcopado, G.I. Halfond, *Corporate Solidarity and Its Limits within the Gallo-Frankish Episcopate*, en: B. Effros / I. Moreira (eds.), *The Oxford Handbook of the Merovingian World*, Oxford 2020, 278–298.

3   El Recurso al Asesinato como Máxima (y Excepcional) Expresión
     de la Oposición entre Reinas y Obispos

Hemos observado hasta ahora el protagonismo que adquirieron algunas reinas, en particular Fredegunda y Brunequilda, a la hora de impulsar procesos judiciales contra determinados obispos. No consideramos que sea casual que las fuentes pongan el foco sobre estas mismas al tratar la manifestación más radical del enfrentamiento con estos, como es el recurso a la violencia, al asesinato de obispos.[92] No consideramos tampoco fortuito que aquellos que sufrieron este destino, Pretextato de Rouen y Desiderio de Vienne, hubiesen protagonizado previamente procesos judiciales dirigidos desde la corte de estas mismas reinas. El asesinato de ambas figuras recibe una especial resonancia en las fuentes, que juzgan con mucha más dureza tales episodios supuestamente instigados por mujeres que aquellos casos homólogos pergeñados por los soberanos masculinos.[93] Curiosamente, como ha puesto recientemente de manifiesto Éric Fournier, Gregorio de Tours nunca atribuye tales acciones violentas contra obispos a los reyes, sino a otros agentes, como en este caso son las reinas.[94] Pero en realidad el recurso a la violencia funcionó tanto para los reyes como para las soberanas como una estrategia de poder más dirigida a proteger sus intereses y preservar su posición.[95] Con todo, con independencia de sus promotores, el uso de la violencia contra los obispos fue bastante excepcional en la Galia merovingia, especialmente si se compara por ejemplo con la realidad carolingia posterior.[96] Debemos sin embargo preguntarnos por los motivos que pudieron llevar a las reinas a recurrir a tan radical estrategia.

---

92   Más allá de la violencia emanada de las reinas, no podemos obviar el hecho de que ellas mismas fueron receptoras frecuentes de la violencia marital. Véase: H. Gallego Franco, *Política y violencia de género en Hispania y el occidente tardoantiguo. Los matrimonios regios visigodos*, en: M. García Sánchez / R.S. Garraffoni (eds.), *Mujeres, género y estudios clásicos: un diálogo entre España y Brasil = Mulheres, gênero e estudos classicos: um diálogo entre Espanha e Brasil*, Barcelona 2019, 335–349.

93   Dailey, 2015, 157–158.

94   Fournier, 2019, 192, 197–201. Intenta buscar una explicación a ello: Harrison, 1998, 361–362; Gradowicz-Pancer, 2002, 16.

95   No había por consiguiente un condicionante de género en su uso. Así lo ha planteado: Gradowicz-Pancer, 2002, 1–18; Gradowicz-Pancer, 2003, 37–50; P. Fouracre, *Why Were so Many Bishops Killed in Merovingian Francia?* en: N. Fryde / D. Reitz (eds.), *Bischofsmord in Mittelalter = Murder of Bishops*, VMPIG 191, Göttingen 2003, 21–22. Sobre el uso de estrategias de poder comunes: "they [las reinas] are always ready to grasp and opportunity, to dispose of their enemies and to create ties of dependence and alliance with whoever happens to be available. There is nothing gender-specific about this. What we see is early medieval politics in action: everyone, man or woman, who wanted to emerge victorious in the dangerous political game had to behave aggressively". Harrison, 1998, 354.

96   Fouracre, 2003, 13–35; Dailey, 2015, 159.

El primer caso a analizar es el del asesinato de Pretextato de Rouen y la posible implicación de Fredegunda en el mismo.[97] Pongámonos en antecedentes. A la muerte de Chilperico, el otrora obispo de Rouen fue restituido en la cátedra de esta misma sede por el rey Gontran, a pesar de las objeciones de la propia Fredegunda, que en ese tiempo posterior a la muerte de su esposo residía precisamente en esta ciudad.[98] Al año siguiente, consolidada en la regencia, iniciaría el envite final contra el restituido obispo. El Domingo de Resurrección del año 585 Pretextato fue apuñalado mientras oficiaba misa, muriendo como consecuencia del ataque.[99] Gregorio de Tours es bastante prudente a la hora de culpar a Fredegunda de este asesinato, lo que contrasta con otros episodios, fueran en grado de tentativa o directamente consumados, en los que la acusa directamente.[100] Con todo, no es descartable su implicación. No en vano, Gregorio atribuye la autoría del asesinato a un esclavo de la propia reina, más allá de que esta intentase enmascarar su participación con la tortura y ejecución de su siervo.[101] Pero, ¿por qué recurrir al asesinato? Se ha propuesto que este obedeció al deseo de Fredegunda de exhibir fuerza y poder para reivindicarse.[102] Tomando esta posibilidad como la más plausible, lo cierto es que en este momento se conjugaron dos situaciones: por un lado, una coyuntura política favorable para Fredegunda, que había logrado liberarse de la amenazante presencia de los otros hijos de Chilperico, Meroveo y Clodoveo, asesinados en 578 y 584 respectivamente, al tiempo que ella y su hijo gozaban del apoyo de buena parte de la aristocracia neustriana.[103] Pero por otro lado debemos atender a la persistencia de unas minorías aristocráticas y eclesiásticas que aún se oponían a ella. La existencia de tales sectores y su posición de fortaleza interna quizás le infundieron la suficiente seguridad para instigar una solución tan radical que disuadiese a sus rivales de actuar contra ella o su hijo. Ciertamente, el problema de Pretextato no tenía que saldarse necesariamente con su asesinato, pero sin duda esta fue la vía más eficaz para infundir miedo a sus enemigos y generar así un clima de intimidación. Fredegunda solo recurrió al asesinato de un obispo en este caso, quizás por tratarse de la figura episcopal con la que mantenía el enfrentamiento más dilatado, pero también

---

97   Sobre este asesinato, véase: Gradowicz-Pancer, 2003, 37–50.

98   Greg.-T., Hist. 7.16; 7.19.

99   Greg.-T., Hist. 8.31.

100   Greg.-T., Hist. 8.31; 8.41. Wood, 1993, 258–259.

101   Greg.-T., Hist. 8.41.

102   Gradowicz-Pancer, 2002, 16.

103   Poniendo en evidencia dicho contexto, Harrison, 1998, 118–120; Gradowicz-Pancer, 2003, 47.

el más enconado.[104] Al mismo tiempo, ya fuera como efecto colateral o como motivación subyacente, la desaparición de Pretextato le permitió restituir al leal Melanio como obispo de Rouen y así recuperar el control de esta ciudad.

Menos información contamos para el enfrentamiento que se dio, ya muerto Chilperico, entre la regente Fredegunda y Leudovaldo de Bayeux al hilo del asesinato de Pretextato. Leudovaldo, quien años antes sirvió como legado del propio Chilperico, elevó quejas por el asesinato del obispo de Rouen, llegando incluso a cerrar las iglesias de Bayeux a modo de protesta. Según el testimonio de Gregorio de Tours, Fredegunda habría respondido planeando su asesinato.[105] La siguiente información de la que disponemos apunta, sin embargo, a una bajada de las tensiones entre ambos, e incluso a una colaboración. De este modo, nos encontramos a Leudovaldo retomando sus pretéritas funciones diplomáticas para la corte neustriana y, por ende, al servicio de la propia Fredegunda.[106] Es posible que el mero hecho de la difusión del plan de asesinato hubiese movido al propio Leudovaldo a retractarse de sus acusaciones a Fredegunda y a someterse fielmente a su regia persona. Se trataría sin duda de una sumisión obligada, en este caso por la vía intimidatoria. Lo cierto es que, con el precedente reciente de Pretextato, Leudovaldo no podía dudar de la determinación de la reina cuando se proponía castigar a sus enemigos. Solo bastó un asesinato para que Fredegunda lograse acallar todo rastro de oposición episcopal a su figura.

En lo referente a Brunequilda, su actitud hacia los obispos menos afines en el tiempo posterior a la muerte de Sigiberto vino marcada por la prudencia, ajustándose a la normativa eclesiástica, como vimos en el caso del proceso contra Egidio de Reims.[107] Sin embargo, pocos años antes de su muerte, las fuentes concuerdan a la hora de culparla del asesinato de su antiguo rival: Desiderio de Vienne.[108] Si nos hacemos caso de los relatos hagiográficos disponibles, curiosamente, pocos años después del concilio de Chalon en el que se depuso a Desiderio, este fue restituido en su sede episcopal, destituyendo en consecuencia a Domnulo como obispo de Vienne.[109] Se ha visto en ello una estrategia de la reina dirigida a aumentar su popularidad entre los grupos

---

104 No descartamos la incidencia de un cierto deseo de venganza contra su figura. Gradowicz-Pancer, 2003, 37–50.

105 Greg.-T., Hist. 6.3; 8.31.

106 Greg.-T., Hist. 9.13. Véase: Halfond, *Sis Quoque*, 2012, 59.

107 Dumézil, 2008, 335.

108 Sisebutus, v. Desid. 1.16; [Anon.], v. Desid. 2.2; 2.7; 2.9; Ionas Bobbiensis, v. Columb. 1.27; Fredegarius, 4.32.

109 No obstante, las fuentes discrepan a la hora de atribuirle la decisión a un sínodo o directamente a los propios monarcas. Sisebutus, v. Desid. 1.10–11; [Anon.], v. Desid. 2.7.

aristocráticos del reino.[110] Sin embargo, entre los años 607 y 611, el restituido obispo de Vienne es de nuevo apresado, en este caso por causar desórdenes públicos en la ciudad, que requirieron el envío de tres *comites* por parte de Brunequilda. En el trascurso de su traslado lejos de Vienne, será asesinado por uno de sus captores.[111]

Frente al consenso que manifiestan las fuentes, no toda la historiografía moderna asume la implicación de Brunequilda en el asesinato de Desiderio. Bruno Dumézil, por ejemplo, la cuestiona esgrimiendo como argumento el trato más benévolo que dispensó a Egidio, que no se saldó en ningún momento con su muerte a pesar de tratarse de un rival directo de la reina.[112] Sin embargo, como hemos observado en el caso de Fredegunda, no son necesariamente contradictorias o excluyentes ambas actitudes, siendo perfectamente asumible la participación intelectual de la reina en este episodio. La pregunta que surge a continuación es: ¿por qué asesinar a Desiderio?[113] Resulta difícil buscar una causa particular, pero sí cabe relacionar su asesinato con una participación renovada del propio Desiderio en la lucha faccional que se daba en Burgundia. Dentro de este esquema, el obispo de Vienne habría integrado la facción que se oponía al poder de Brunequilda y a la influencia austrasiana en el reino burgundio.[114] Cabe incluso plantear la posibilidad de que, en contra de lo que recogen los testimonios hagiográficos, Desiderio hubiera retornado a su sede episcopal de forma unilateral, intensificando así los odios regios hacia su figura.[115] Dentro de este marco, y siguiendo el ejemplo de Fredegunda, el asesinato de Desiderio pudo funcionar como un golpe de efecto, enmarcado en un contexto cada vez menos favorable a la anciana reina y dirigido a castigar a sus círculos opositores y a disuadirles de posibles actuaciones contra ella y su nieto. Es posible sin embargo que en este caso la muerte del obispo de Vienne hubiese generado el efecto contrario. No es quizás casual que la muerte de Desiderio marcase en cierta manera un punto de inflexión en los equilibrios de

---

110　Dumézil, 2008, 337.

111　[Anon.], v. Desid. 2.8–9; 2.11.

112　Dumézil, 2008, 338.

113　Algunos consideran que, en realidad, la muerte de Desiderio no fue el objetivo perseguido, sino únicamente su exilio. Nelson, 1978, 58. De hecho, este fue el destino sufrido por Columbano.

114　Planteando una explicación en clave faccional, Fox, 2012, 188–189: "We must reinterpret Desiderius' entanglement and subsequent assassination as a by-product of his own involvement in the power struggles of the Burgundian kingdom".

115　La crónica de Fredegario, por ejemplo, no atribuye el regreso de Desiderio de su exilio a ninguna decisión sinodal o regia. Fredegarius, 4.32. Harrison, 1998, 225. Esta posibilidad cobra fuerza si atendemos a la impopularidad del propio Desiderio en su propia sede episcopal. [Anon.], v. Desid. 2.8. Sobre tal impopularidad, Stüber, 2020, 344–345.

poder internos y que este hubiese funcionado como acicate en la reactivación
de los movimientos políticos internos contra Brunequilda que, pocos años después, provocaron su caída y su dramática muerte.[116]

El carácter excepcional de los asesinatos de Pretextato de Rouen y Desiderio de Vienne pone de manifiesto la escasa inclinación de Fredegunda y
Brunequilda por recurrir a la violencia como vía de resolución de sus enfrentamientos con los obispos. Ello contrasta, sin embargo, con la recurrencia reite-
rada al asesinato en el caso de su confrontación con agentes laicos. Las fuentes
recogen numerosísimos casos.[117] Tal contraste puede entenderse en un sentido similar al percibido en los juicios contra obispos. Esto es, ante todo habría
imperado una actitud pragmática dirigida a evitar tensionar las relaciones
con el episcopado como ente corporativo. El recurso sistemático a la violencia
contra los prelados opositores habría podido generar el efecto –contrario al
perseguido– de reproducir los odios episcopales contra las reinas.

Más problemático se torna el caso más tardío de Baltilda, regente de su hijo
Clotario III. La *Vita Wilfridi*, escrita en el entorno anglosajón por Eddius Esté-
fano, la acusa de instigar el asesinato de hasta nueve obispos y de perseguir a la
Iglesia del reino.[118] Inmediatamente surge la problemática de valorar la histo-
ricidad de este testimonio. Ya en su día, Eugen Ewig la puso en cuestión, aceptando únicamente la implicación de la reina en el único asesinato atestiguado
en otras fuentes, el de Aunemundo de Lyon,[119] pero no todos los sectores historiográficos avalan esta visión.[120] Con todo, lo cierto es que solamente contamos
con información referida al asesinato del obispo de Lyon. Ninguna otra fuente
franca o extranjera más allá de la *Vita Wilfridi* incrimina a Baltilda en otros
asesinatos, así que lo más prudente es valorar únicamente el caso contrasta-
ble. Aunemundo de Lyon fue acusado de traición por invitar supuestamente

---

116   Sobre las circunstancias que llevaron a la caída de Brunequilda, véanse: Harrison, 1998,
        226–227; Dumézil, 2008, 367–387.
117   Recogiendo la casuística: Harrison, 1998, 105–148, 222–227.
118   Eddius, v. Wilfr. 6. Nelson, 1978, 64–65.
119   E. Ewig, *Die Klosterprivilegien des Metropoliten Emmo von Sens, das Reichskonzil von
        Mâlay-le-Roi (660) und der Sturz des Metropoliten Aunemund von Lyon (661/62)*, en: id., *Spä-
        tantikes und fränkisches Gallien: Gesammelte Schriften (1974–2007)*, vol. 3, Ostfildern 2009,
        591–594. Poniéndolo también en cuestión, R. Folz, *Tradition hagiographique et culte de
        sainte Bathilde, reine des Francs*, en: Comptes rendus des séances de l'Académie des Ins-
        criptions et Belles-Lettres 119 (1975), 370; J.-P. Laporte, *La reine Bathilde ou l'ascension
        sociale d'une esclave*, en: M. Rouche / J. Heuclin (eds.), *La femme au Moyen-Âge. Congrès
        de Maubeuge (1988)*, Maubeuge 1990, 166–167.
120   Véase: Y. Fox, *Power and Religion in Merovingian Gaul: Columbanian Monasticisim and the
        Frankish Elites*, CSMLT 98, Cambridge 2014, 41.

al reino a gentes extranjeras.[121] Ciertos sectores historiográficos asumen que
el factor determinante fueron las luchas faccionales internas en el seno de
la comunidad de Lyon,[122] pero no es contradictorio con la existencia de un
enfrentamiento entre Aunemundo y los reyes Clotario III y Baltilda.[123] Como
consecuencia de su acusación, el obispo de Lyon fue convocado ante ambos
monarcas en una asamblea que tendría lugar en Mareauil, enclave situado
en las cercanías de Orleans. El acusado sin embargo no asistió, lo que forzó a
la regente a ordenar su arresto. En confusas circunstancias, acabó siendo asesinado por dos individuos armados.[124] El *Acta s. Aunemundi* evita atribuir la
iniciativa de la acusación y del ulterior asesinato de Aunemundo a Baltilda,
pero ciertamente resulta cuestionable que no se viese implicada de una u otra
forma.[125] No consideramos casual que fuese la propia Baltilda la que interviniese en el nombramiento del sustituto de Aunemundo, el obispo Ginés, y que
este último fuese uno de sus más leales servidores.[126]

4   Una Oposición Silenciosa: Consecuencias de la *Klosterpolitik* de
      Batilda

El caso aislado del asesinato de Aunemundo no es indicio suficiente para
hablar de una oposición estructural entre Baltilda y los obispos. De hecho, son
mucho más numerosos los casos de colaboración e, incluso, de férrea lealtad
a la reina. Con todo, hay un factor a valorar, difícil de distinguir en las fuentes,
pero no por ello imperceptible, como es la existencia de una oposición silenciosa hacia Baltilda. Esta última fue sin duda la reina que más preocupación e
implicación mostró en los asuntos religiosos, con una intencionalidad clara de
controlar la Iglesia de su reino a través de un programa religioso y eclesiástico
cuidadosamente diseñado, al que la historiografía ha venido denominando

121   [Anon.] a. Aunem. 3–11.
122   P. Fouracre / R.A. Gerberding, *Late Merovingian France: History and Hagiography* (640–
      720), Manchester 1996, 166–179; Nelson, 1978, 63–64. Para otras lecturas, E. Ewig, *Milo
      et eiusmodi similes*, en: *Sankt Bonifatius: Gedenkgaben zum zweölfhundertsten Todestag*,
      Fulda 1954, 432–433; Laporte, 1990, 164–166; Ewig, 2009, 493–494.
123   Fouracre / Gerberding, 1996, 178; Fouracre, 2003, 20–21.
124   [Anon.] a. Aunem.
125   Cuestiona sin embargo este supuesto: S. Tatum, Auctoritas *as* sanctitas: *Balthild's Depic-
      tion as 'Queen-saint' in the* Vita Balthildis, en: European Review of History 16 (2009), 814.
126   B. Krusch, *Die Urkunden von Corbie und Levillains letztes Wort*, en: NA 31 (1906), 337–375.
      Sobre la estrecha relación entre Baltilda y Ginés, [Anon.] v. Balth. 4.

Klosterpolitik.[127] El eje central de este programa fue la fundación o refundación de numerosos monasterios, entre los que destacan Chelles, Corbie o Jumièges, entre otros,[128] pero también la concesión a instancias de la reina de privilegios de inmunidad a diversas instituciones monásticas, tanto de nueva creación como ya existentes.[129] Igualmente, se introdujo un nuevo *sanctus regularis ordo*, dirigido a estandarizar las reglas de las comunidades monásticas del reino.[130]

Se ha propuesto, a mi modo de ver de forma acertada, que la fundación de monasterios y la concesión de privilegios de inmunidad por Baltilda, pero también por otras soberanas, habría desempeñado, aparte de una función piadosa, otra paralela como complemento del control territorial que estas ejercían por otras vías,[131] contribuyendo en consecuencia a reforzar su posición de poder.[132] A fin de cuentas, eran instituciones que, tanto a través de su fundación como de la propia concesión de privilegios, reflejan el propio control de las soberanas sobre estos centros.[133] En algún caso particular, y sin entrar en contradicción con lo que acabamos de plantear, también habrían servido para contrarrestar la influencia de otras instituciones monásticas, siendo quizás esta la razón que motivó, al menos en parte, la fundación de Corbie, en este caso en detrimento del cercano monasterio de Péronne.[134] Sin embargo, no se suele poner el acento en el papel de tales movimientos como

---

127   Sobre esta *Klosterpolitik*, E. Ewig, *Das Privileg des Bischofs Berthefrid von Amiens für Corbie von 664 und die Klosterpolitik der Königin Balthild*, en: Francia 1 (1973), 106–114; Wood, 1994, 197–202; Poveda Arias, 2023.

128   [Anon.] v. Balth. 7–9.

129   Véanse: E. Ewig, *Beobachtungen zu den Klosterpivilegien des 7. und frühen 8. Jahrhunderts*, en: id., *Spätantikes und fränkisches Gallien: Gesammelte Schriften (1952–1973)*, vol. 2, München 1979, 411–426; Ewig, 2009, 575–594; Rosenwein, 1999, 74–81; A. Dierkens, *Prolégomènes à une histoire des relations culturelles entre les Îles Britanniques et le continent pendant le haut Moyen Âge*, en: H. Atsma (ed.), *La Neustrie. Les pays au nord de la Loire de 650 à 850*, vol. 2, Sigmaringen 1989, 371–394.

130   [Anon.] v. Balth. 9.

131   Santinelli, 2003, 642–643. En relación con esto último, recientemente se ha incidido en el papel de estos monasterios como canales de comunicación intermediarios entre la monarquía y los horizontes locales. Fox, 2014, 49.

132   Nelson, 1978, 60.

133   Tatum, 2009, 823. Haciéndonos eco de las ideas de Régine Le Jan, los monasterios funcionaron en época merovingia como centros de poder y, por tanto, su fundación constituyó tanto un acto político como religioso. R. Le Jan, *Convents, Violence, and Competition for Power in Seventh-Century Francia*, en: M. de Jong / F. Theuws (eds.), *Topographies of Power in the Early Middle Ages*, TTRW 6, Leiden 2001, 243. La introducción del *sanctus regularis ordo* habría tenido también la pretensión de reforzar el control regio sobre las instituciones monásticas. Fox, 2014, 49.

134   Esta es la hipótesis planteada por: Dierkens, 1989, 387.

contrapoder al episcopado, una posibilidad que cobra más sentido si atendemos a la situación de competencia que imperó entre los obispos y las instituciones monásticas, los primeros por afirmar su poder sobre los cenobios y las
segundas por liberarse del control episcopal; todo ello además en un contexto
en el que los monasterios empezaban a eclipsar el capital espiritual que los
obispos habían venido disfrutando hasta entonces.[135] No consideramos por
tanto casual que Baltilda hubiese impulsado la concesión de inmunidades y
privilegios a los monasterios de algunos de los principales centros eclesiásticos
del reino como San Simforiano en Autun, San Benigno en Dijon, San Marcel
en Chalon-sur-Saône, San Hilario de Poitiers, San Sulpicio de Bourges o San
Lupo de Troyes.[136] Algunos autores sí que han puesto en evidencia el carácter
perjudicial para los obispos de la concesión de privilegios de inmunidad, que
sin duda contribuyeron a aumentar las prerrogativas de los abades y la influencia regia sobre las instituciones monásticas.[137] En la línea planteada por Ian
Wood, tales medidas no tienen que apuntar necesariamente a una generali-
zada política anti-episcopal,[138] puesto que tenemos bien atestiguada el trato
de favor de Baltilda hacia renombrados obispos de su época.[139] Tampoco es
necesario plantear el extremo contrario, defendido por Gregory I. Halfond,
quien considera que en realidad fueron los obispos los que cedieron de buen
grado tales privilegios a los monasterios como consecuencia de un proceso de

---

135 Véanse: Diem, 2015, 165–191; Halfond, 2019, 165.

136 A estos se suman: San Medardo de Soissons, Saint-Denis, Saint-Pierre-le-Vif de Sens,
     Sithiu, Saint-Omer y Corbie, entre otros. Véanse: Ewig, 1973, 108–109; Nelson, 1978, 40;
     Dierkens, 1989, 389–390; J. Barbier, *Les actes royaux mérovingiens pour Saint-Médard de
     Soissons: une révision*, en: *Saint-Médard. Trésors d'une abbaye royale*, París 1997, 220–221;
     Fox, 2014, 39.

137 Nelson, 1978, 38–39; Wood, 1994, 200. Sobre las implicaciones de tal privilegio de inmu-
     nidad, Janet L. Nelson (1978, 69) se muestra muy elocuente al respecto: "But when at
     the same time the monastery became an immunist, the King while reallocating the
     burdens of royal administration could also hope to gain in terms of close, permanent,
     mutually-beneficial relations with the monastery and more effective control through,
     for example, royal intervention in abbatial appointments". Simbolizando el control regio
     sobre tales acciones, los distintos privilegios episcopales, salvo excepciones muy puntua-
     les, se hacían acompañar de una oración en favor del rey y del reino. E. Ewig, *La prière pour
     le roi et le royaume dans les privilèges épiscopaux de l'époque mérovingienne*, en: *Mélanges
     offerts à jean Dauvillier, professeur honoraire à l'Université des Sciences sociales de Toulouse*,
     Toulouse 1979, 255–267, esp. 263. Por otro lado, no creemos casual que la mayor concen-
     tración cronológica de concesiones de privilegios de este tipo se dé precisamente en el
     tiempo de la regencia de Baltilda.

138 Wood, 1994, 201.

139 Poveda Arias, 2023.

negociación que redundó en su favor.[140] Lo que quizás no valoran estos autores es la compatibilidad de situaciones, esto es, el beneficiar a unos obispos, en particular a los más afines, al tiempo que se perjudica a otros menos proclives a aceptar a la figura reinante de Baltilda y/o sus políticas.

El episcopado apoyó siempre, al menos en apariencia, la agenda política de Baltilda,[141] en muchos casos, como hemos apuntado, por sincera simpatía hacia ella y por su habilidad para tejer redes entre los obispos,[142] pero en otros debemos valorar el factor intimidatorio como móvil detrás de la sanción episcopal a las medidas eclesiásticas de la reina regente. Lo cierto es que su control indiscutido sobre las estructuras eclesiásticas le permitió gobernar la Iglesia a su antojo, incluso en contra de los intereses del episcopado.[143] Los privilegios episcopales concedidos a las instituciones monásticas y que, como hemos señado, sustraían buena parte de las competencias de los obispos sobre los monasterios son la mejor evidencia de ello. En un primer vistazo, da la impresión de que los obispos suscribieron tales privilegios de buen grado, pero hay elementos que permiten obtener conclusiones diferentes. En la concesión de la exención episcopal del obispo Bertefredo de Amiens a la fundación regia de Corbie, queda en evidencia la insistencia que Clotario y Baltilda aplicaron a la hora de solicitar al prelado tales beneficios y, por tanto, la resistencia de este último a ceder.[144] Da la impresión de que incluso se aplicaron ciertas dosis de coacción sobre Bertefredo, y quizás sobre otros obispos, con tal de que dieran su brazo a torcer. En el proceso de persuasión habrían intervenido los más leales a Baltilda, como es el caso de Ginés de Lyon, que figura suscribiendo el diploma de Bertefredo a Corbie.[145] El alto número de suscripciones episcopales ha permitido a Gregory I. Halfond ver tales concesiones en términos mucho más positivos y beneficiosos para los obispos, atribuyéndoles incluso la iniciativa en muchos casos.[146] Sin embargo, no podemos descartar que tales

---

140   G.I. Halfond, *Monastic Exemption and Episcopal Collaboration in Later Merovingian Gaul*, en: RBen 130 (2020), 197–228. En una línea similar se han manifestado también: Dierkens, 1989, 191–393; Rosenwein, 1999, 80–81.

141   Wood, 1994, 201; Halfond, 2019, 165.

142   Poveda Arias, 2023.

143   Haciéndonos eco de las palabras de Tatum, 2009, 814: "Balthild was both autocratic and sometimes even inflexible in her dealings with the Church".

144   Tatum, 2009, 813. Recogiendo el texto, Krusch, 1906, 367–375. Sobre este privilegio, véanse también: Ewig, 1973, 62–114; Rosenwein, 1999, 79–80.

145   No consideramos casual que los obispos que más veces participaron en la suscripción de privilegios, como Burgundofaro de Meaux, Bertefredo de Amiens, Audoino de Rouen, Audomar de Thérouanne, Drauscio de Soissons o Emmo de París, tuviesen sus sedes cerca de la corte.

146   Halfond, *Monastic*, 2020, 197–228.

suscripciones se hubiesen realizado con escaso convencimiento por parte de los obispos, subyaciendo así un falso apoyo a tales privilegios. Así podemos entender, por ejemplo, el escaso margen temporal que se produjo entre la suscripción por Aunemundo del privilegio episcopal de Emmo de Sens a Saint-Pierre-le-Vif y su asesinato.[147]

Ciertamente, una política eclesiástica tan agresiva le habría granjeado los recelos, cuando no la oposición, de determinados sectores eclesiásticos.[148] Aceptando este supuesto, el asesinato de Aunemundo habría sido únicamente la punta del iceberg de una oposición más numerosa hacia Baltilda, aunque no por ello mayoritaria en el sentir episcopal. Es precisamente su carácter minoritario lo que habría permitido que la reina interviniese en los asuntos eclesiásticos sin limitación alguna y que esos mismos obispos poco afines a ella se hubiesen visto forzados a suscribir unas medidas que iban directamente en contra de sus intereses. Ante esta situación, estos prelados solo podían esperar a que los vientos políticos cambiasen de dirección.

5 Instrumentalización de las Reinas

En otros casos, la hostilidad episcopal a las reinas desempeñó un carácter más instrumental, particularmente en sus enfrentamientos con los reyes consortes o con otros actores políticos. Así se advierte, por ejemplo, en las numerosas denuncias de ilegitimidad vertidas por algunos obispos contra ciertos matrimonios regios. La primera denuncia de este tipo data del reinado de Clotario I, quien al anexionarse el reino de su sobrino-nieto Teudebaldo en el año 555 se casó –o al menos guardaba intención de hacerlo– con la viuda de este, Wuldetrada. Los obispos de este territorio mostraron su oposición frontal ante esta unión, catalogándola de incestuosa, lo que forzó a Clotario a repudiarla.[149] Lo curioso es que años atrás, en el año 524, este mismo había tomado en matrimonio a la viuda de su hermano Clodomero, Gunteuca, pero no tenemos

---

147 Poniendo en evidencia este hecho, aunque ofreciendo una lectura diferente, ibid. 223–224.
148 Tatum, 2009, 813–814.
149 Greg.-T., Hist. 4.9; 4.14. Sobre este caso particular, véanse: Dailey, 2015, 90–91; P. Poveda Arias, *Patrones de relación entre los reyes merovingios y el episcopado galo (511–561)*, en: Ant. Tard. 29 (2021), 219. Sobre la problemática del incesto en la legislación de este contexto, M. de Jong, *An Unsolved Riddle: Early Medieval Incest Legislation*, en: I. Wood (ed.), *Franks and Alamanni in the Merovingian Period: An Ethnographic Perspective*, San Marino 1998, 107–140; I.N. Wood, *Incest, Law and the Bible in Sixth-century Gaul*, en: EMEu 7 (1998), 291–304. La acusación de incesto tiene su base legal en: Concilio de Epaón (517), c. 30.

constancia de que se hubiese elevado entonces queja episcopal alguna.[150] El matrimonio con Wuldetrada fue usado así por los obispos del reino de Reims, y particularmente por su líder, Niceto de Tréveris, como mecanismo de resistencia a una dominación – la de Clotario – no deseada. No en vano, y a pesar de los intentos del rey de congraciarse con Niceto, este último le excomulgó en numerosas ocasiones.[151] Uno de los hijos de Clotario, Cariberto, fue también objeto de los ataques episcopales. Concretamente, repudió a Ingoberga para tomar en su lugar como esposa a la esclava Merofleda. Poco después se desposó también con la hermana de esta última, Marcoveva, que además había adoptado la vida religiosa. Su matrimonio fue calificado de incestuoso, siendo en consecuencia excomulgado, junto a su nueva esposa, por Germano de París.[152] A diferencia del caso anterior, Cariberto se negó a romper su matrimonio, desafiando así al obispo de París, con quien curiosamente había mantenido hasta entonces una relación de estrecha colaboración.[153] No es descartable por tanto que en este caso en particular la oposición de Germano hubiese obedecido a una cuestión eminentemente jurídica, en defensa de la rectitud canónica.[154]

En otros casos las denuncias no iban contra el matrimonio en sí, quizás por falta de argumentos, sino contra su descendencia. Así ocurrió con la progenie de Gontran y Austrechilda. El monarca había repudiado a su anterior esposa, Marcatruda, en favor de Austrechilda, de origen servil. Es precisamente la naturaleza de su origen la que fue esgrimida por Sagitario de Gap para deslegitimar el derecho de la descendencia de Gontran y Austrechilda. Se trataba de una visión un poco personal del propio Sagitario, puesto que Gregorio de Tours no muestra su acuerdo con ella. Gontran reaccionó recluyendo al obispo de Gap en un monasterio y confiscándole sus propiedades.[155] En este caso, el ataque contra Austrechilda y su descendencia tampoco tenía un componente personal contra ellos, sino que su explicación radica en el apoyo que granjeaba Sagitario a la anterior reina, Marcatruda, y a su descendencia como legítima heredera al trono,[156] así como al enfrentamiento que mantuvo con el propio Gontran.[157] Prueba de ello es la escasa coherencia mostrada por

---

150   Greg.-T., Hist. 3.6.
151   Greg.-T., Vit. patr. 17.2–3. Poveda Arias, 2021, 219–220.
152   Greg.-T., Hist. 4.26. Sobre este caso, véanse: Wood, 1998, 302–303; G.I. Halfond, *Charibert I and the Episcopal Leadership of the Kingdom of Paris (561–567)*, en: Viator 43 (2012), 1–2, 25–26; Dailey, 2015, 93–94. Respecto a la base legal de tal acusación, Wood, 1998, 295–297.
153   Véase: Halfond, *Charibert I*, 2012, 1–28.
154   En una línea similar, ibid. 27.
155   Greg.-T., Hist. 5.20. Sobre el proceso contra Sagitario, Stüber, 2020, 208–210.
156   Dailey, 2015, 91–93, 98–99.
157   Sobre los pormenores del mismo: Stüber, 2020, 198–212, quien observa un período de tiempo en el que Gontran y Sagitario mantuvieron unas buenas relaciones.

Sagitario al apoyar la revuelta de Gundovaldo, quien paradójicamente reivindicaba sus aspiraciones al trono en calidad de supuesto hijo de Clotario y una concubina.[158]

En todos estos casos, las reinas únicamente desempeñaron un papel instrumental en su confrontación con determinados monarcas. Las acusaciones de ilegitimidad, fuera del matrimonio o de su descendencia, funcionaron para los obispos como un mecanismo de presión contra los reyes. Haciéndonos eco de las palabras de Paul J. Fouracre, "the declaration of illegitimacy was a very powerful weapon in the bishop's armory, and made him a dangerous opponent".[159] La normativa canónica se esgrimía a conveniencia, siendo generalmente obviada cuando las relaciones entre reyes/reinas y obispos eran fluidas. Ya hemos puesto en evidencia el caso del matrimonio de Clotario I con Gunteuca, pero también podemos mencionar el del matrimonio de Brunequilda con su sobrino Meroveo.

6   Reflexiones Finales

Más allá de los casos tratados de confrontación entre reinas y obispos, lo cierto es que no podemos hacer una distinción de situaciones de colaboración o confrontación en función del reinado. Una misma soberana, como es el caso de Brunequilda, Fredegunda o Baltilda, podía aunar ambas. En consecuencia, no podemos atribuir a ninguna reina en particular una actitud anti-episcopal, a pesar de la impresión que nos transmiten algunas fuentes, siendo quizás un caso paradigmático el retrato que dibuja Gregorio de Tours de Fredegunda. Tal y como afirma Gregory I. Halfond aplicado a la política de esta y su marido, Chilperico I, aunque igualmente aplicable a todos los reinados, "to have singled out bishops as a group for attack would have been to undermine one of the major pillars of their *regnum*".[160] Con todo, y como hemos podido analizar, los episodios de confrontación entre reinas y obispos se dieron, ciertamente de forma aislada, pero no por ello eran menos determinantes a la hora de apuntalar el poder de las soberanas.

Cabe preguntarse qué factores condicionaron la dispensa de un trato u otro a los obispos opositores. Ciertamente, en el caso del enfrentamiento de Radegunda y Maroveo de Poitiers, de carácter más local y protagonizado por una reina apartada voluntariamente de la corte y del poder que esta ofrecía,

158   Greg.-T., Hist. 7.29.
159   Fouracre, 2003, 21–22.
160   Halfond, *Sis Quoque*, 2012, 57.

observamos que esta veía en cierta manera más restringido su margen de
actuación. Con todo, su propia reclusión y el capital religioso que su figura, su
monasterio y la reliquia de la Cruz podían infundir se tornaron en instrumentos enormemente efectivos a la hora de imponerse sobre su rival, al menos
hasta su muerte. Sus estrategias fueron sin duda mucho más originales que
en el caso de sus homólogas reinantes. Aprovechándose de los recursos que
ofrecía el trono, aunque el titular del mismo fuera su marido o uno de sus descendientes, la tónica más habitual y preferente en estas últimas fue intentar
desplazar o, al menos, desactivar a estos obispos opositores por la vía judicial. Los juicios tenían generalmente una naturaleza eclesiástica, siendo más
excepcional la vía secular, con el fin de dar una apariencia de transparencia
y legitimidad a los procesos de cara al episcopado, con cuya participación se
contaba. En general, sus regias impulsoras habrían buscado la deposición y el
exilio de estos obispos, pero a veces, como en el caso de Gregorio de Tours, una
sentencia favorable al encausado resultaba igualmente efectiva para lograr la
sumisión episcopal. Aquí se percibe una actitud pragmática por parte de la
corte, que impulsa estos juicios, pero cuidando de no tensionar sus relaciones
con el resto del episcopado. Igualmente, los procesos judiciales contra obispos,
con independencia de su resolución, habrían tenido una función disuasoria
e intimidatoria de cara al resto del episcopado, puesto que la propia existencia de esta amenaza les habría cohibido de actuar contra las reinas. Un papel
similar habrían desempeñado los excepcionales asesinatos de obispos, como
golpes de efecto dirigidos, con mayor o menos éxito, a disuadir a sus opositores
de conspirar contra ellas y su regia descendencia. ¿Pueden ser interpretados
estos episodios como un síntoma de debilidad de sus instigadoras? No necesariamente. Fredegunda y Baltilda maquinaron los asesinatos de Pretextato de
Rouen y Aunemundo de Lyon, respectivamente, en un contexto claramente
favorable a ambas regentes; no así Brunequilda, que conspiró contra la vida de
Desiderio cuando las amenazas se empezaban a cernir sobre su figura. Otros
factores, como la persistencia de tal oposición contra las reinas o la implicación colateral de los faccionalismos locales, habrían tenido un carácter más
determinante a la hora de condicionar la muerte de los obispos tratados.[161]

Con todo, la dosificación de la violencia contra los obispos se tornaba fundamental para evitar reproducir la oposición episcopal contra las reinas que,
recordemos, fue sobre todo un fenómeno excepcional. Es cierto que en ello

---

161   Dos casos de incidencia de estos faccionalismos locales y su imbricación con la alta polí-
      tica se observan en los asesinatos de Desiderio de Vienne y Aunemundo de Lyon. Foura-
      cre, 2003, 23–25. "Every bishop thus had rivals and enemies waiting in the winks, and such
      people were only too ready to team up with outsides to get rid of their shepherds".

desempeñó un papel importante la intimidación ejercida contra los propios prelados, temerosos de sufrir el mismo destino que sus homólogos encausados o asesinados. Usada inteligentemente y en dosis adecuadas, tal intimidación tuvo una eficacia indudable a la hora de mantener a los obispos sometidos a la voluntad de las reinas. Este fue por ejemplo el factor que determinó la sumisión episcopal hacia la *Klosterpolitik* de Baltilda que minó directamente la autoridad del episcopado sobre los monasterios.

Por último, no podemos terminar este texto sin llamar la atención sobre otros muchos otros enfrentamientos entre reinas y obispos que desconocemos o que, con suerte, solamente se pueden intuir a través de las fuentes sin contar con mayores detalles. Es el caso de Gregorio de Tours y Austrechilda, a la que le atribuye un espíritu malvado y compara con Herodes.[162] Brunequilda también se granjeó los odios de Leudemundo de Sion, quien colaboró abiertamente con Clotario para favorecer la caída de la poderosa reina.[163] Igualmente, uno de los antiguos fieles de Brunequilda, Arnulfo de Metz, también participó junto a otros grupos aristocráticos austrasianos del plan que llevó a la caída y a la dramática ejecución de la reina.[164] Fredegario afirma que otros tantos obispos, en este caso de Burgundia, también actuaron en contra de ella.[165] Baltilda también fue objeto de traiciones de sus propios prelados. Sigobrando de París, por ejemplo, quien fue promocionado a la cátedra episcopal con el presumible apoyo de la reina, en un momento dado pasó a integrar las filas de los opositores a Baltilda, quizás porque su relación con ella dejó de dar sus frutos.[166] Más difícil resulta saber si, como ocurrió en el caso de Brunequilda, parte del episcopado tuvo un mínimo grado de implicación en su caída. Lo cierto es que la otrora poderosa reina Baltilda se vio forzada a retirarse a su fundación monástica de Chelles en el 664 o 665 como consecuencia de la lucha faccional en el seno de la corte.[167] Igualmente cierto es que, si conservó un importante apoyo entre el episcopado, este no fue suficiente para mantenerse en el poder. Ello abrió la puerta a un traspaso de lealtades, como ocurrió en el caso de Emmo de Sens o Burgundofaro de Meaux,[168] quizás exponentes, pero

---

162   Greg.-T., Hist. 5.35. Véanse: Wood, 1993, 262–263; Dailey, 2015, 97.

163   Fox, 2014, 45; Stüber, 2020, 352.

164   Fredegarius, 4.40. Sobre la muerte de Brunequilda, Sisebutus, v. Desid. 1.1; Fredegarius, 4.42.

165   Fredegarius, 4.41.

166   Nelson, 1978, 70–71: "Personal bonds held only so long as they were reinforced by real or prospective benefits".

167   [Anon.] v. Balth. 10.

168   Halfond, 2020, 222–223. Es posible que Ouen de Rouen también hubiese protagonizado un cambio de lealtades similar. Véase: Laporte, 1990, 158.

también otros, de esos sectores episcopales que no sentían unas verdaderas simpatías hacia Baltilda, pero que se veían sometidos a la intimidación de la reina. Observamos una realidad de lealtades fluctuantes que se hace evidente en un contexto claro de debilidad o desplazamiento del poder de las reinas, pero no así cuando disfrutaban de una clara superioridad, lo que prueba la eficacia de las estrategias que estas desplegaron contra los aislados conatos de resistencia episcopal hacia sus figuras.

Networking, Power and Gender in Anglo-Saxon Religious Life

Abbess Æthelthryth of Ely in Bede's Work

Clelia Martínez Maza

Abstract

Æthelthryth of Ely is portrayed in Bede's work with the virtues of a good Christian woman, in that any activity outside these ideals was reframed or suppressed. A thorough examination allows us to reconstruct this more worldly profile and the role of women like her in consolidating and stabilising the monarchy on the island.

Æthelthryth of Ely is one of the only two women given exceptional prominence in Bede's *Ecclesiastical History of the English People*.[1] The only other passages of similar length providing a detailed biographical account of a woman concern Hilda, Abbess of Whitby, who transformed her monastery into one of the greatest intellectual centres of her time and the cradle of the first generation of British-trained bishops.[2] References to other women who culminated their lives as abbesses are profusely scattered throughout Bede's *History*, but he generally limits himself to giving their names and status as the daughters, wives or mothers of the princes and kings of the incipient post-Roman kingdoms. Bede's portrait of Æthelthryth differs substantially from that of Hilda, who is described through a multitude of anecdotes as a wise woman, an adviser and the driving force behind intellectual activity at her monastery.[3] Nevertheless, the two chapters in Book IV devoted to Æthelthryth reflect the importance that Bede attributed to her life and example – especially given the small number of Anglo-Saxon saints included in his *History*[4] – and contain a sort of dual

---

* This work has been carried out within the framework of the Research Project PID2020-117597GB-100 funded by the Spanish Ministry of Science and Innovation.

1 Beda, *Historia eclesiástica del pueblo de los anglos*, J.L. Molarejo (ed.) Madrid 2013: Bed., Hist. 4.17–18.

2 P. Hunter Blair, *Whitby as a Centre of Learning in the Seventh Century*, in: M. Lapidge / H. Gneuss (eds.), *Learning and Literature in Anglo-Saxon England*, Cambridge 1985, 8–12. S. Foot, *Monastic Life in Anglo-Saxon England, c. 600–900*, Cambridge 2006, 82–85.

3 Bed., Hist. 4.23.

4 These Anglo-Saxon saints are St Augustine of Kent, Aidan, Oswald, Chad, Cuthbert and Hilda of Whitby. The abbesses Æbbe of Coldingham and Æthelthryth's half-sister, Æthelburh of

version of the life of the saint, which Bede himself calls *opus geminatum*.[5] The Abbess of Ely is depicted as having the customary feminine virtues typical of continental Christian hagiography, although each of the two chapters draws on different resources to emphasise and legitimise her sanctity, largely due to their different literary nature.

1   A Model Life of Sanctity

In keeping with its historiographical character, Chapter 17 maintains the prose style of the rest of the work, and, as we shall see below, it recounts the personal anecdotes necessary to establish her royal birth and extol her as a devout Christian of impeccable conduct. The following chapter, however, takes the form of a hymn in elegiac couplets that gives an idealised account foregrounding Æthelthryth's purity and thus further accentuating her sanctity.

Of among all her virtues, it is Æthelthryth's virginal nature that both versions underscore, which was one of the most highly valued qualities in Christian women, especially in those who had consecrated their lives to God.[6] The abbess's commitment is even more worthy since she maintained her chastity throughout two marriages. These were, therefore, personal circumstances deemed appropriate for inclusion in order to render her purity more admirable. Thus, the only two events described from the life of the abbess prior to taking the veil are her two marriages.

Bede briefly recounts her royal and Christian ancestry as the daughter of the Christian king of East Anglia, Anna (642–653). She also held royal status by marriage, her first being to Tondberht, a *subregulus* of her father who ruled the territory of the South Gyrwas, in the region of Norfolk. However, their union was short-lived due to his death, and she was married again, this time to Ecgfrith, King of Northumbria, enabling the Kingdom of the East Angles to unite with a powerful ally.[7] According to Bede, Æthelthryth was firmly committed to maintaining her virginity despite being married, thus contravening the fundamental goal of marriage and flouting her socially assigned duty and destiny as a king's wife, namely that of ensuring the continuation and stability of her husband's lineage and dynasty by providing him with heirs.

Faremoutiers-en-Brie, are also mentioned and some biographical anecdotes are given, but they never become the subject of such detailed attention.

5   W. Friesen, *The Opus Geminatum and Anglo-Saxon Literature*, in: Neophilologus 95 (2011), 124.

6   D. Watt, *Female Sanctity and the Relics of Early Women's Writing*, in: C.A. Lees (ed.), *The Cambridge History of Early Medieval English Literature*, Cambridge 2013, 368–369.

7   B. Yorke, *Kings and Kingdoms of Early Anglo-Saxon England*, London 1990, 70–71.

Although a devout Christian, Ecgfrith was displeased by Æthelthryth's desire to remain a virgin. Nevertheless, Bede conveys the image of a sensitive and compassionate king and husband who, as a good Christian, made no attempt to force his wife to fulfil her marital obligations. Ecgfrith's displeasure was probably related not so much to the spiritual reasons behind Æthelthryth's decision, but rather the consequent frustration of the social and political expectations inherent to a marriage negotiated between two kingdoms.[8] This would explain the King of Northumbria's persistent attempts to persuade his queen to fulfil her obligations, using all the resources at his disposal. He even turned to Bishop Wilfrid, who would have seemed the most promising mediator due to his close ties with both courts. Ecgfrith offered land and riches to the bishop if he could convince the queen to consummate their marriage, but his efforts were to no avail. The bishop's involvement enables Bede to cite him as a reliable, direct source of information on Æthelthryth's steadfast observance of celibacy during the twelve years of her marriage to Ecgfrith. Such chastity maintained in inconceivable circumstances renders it all the more admirable and worthy of emulation.

Ecgfrith finally acceded to his wife's wishes and allowed her to enter Coldingham,[9] a double monastery under royal patronage and governed by the king's aunt, the famous Abbess Æbbe.[10] There, Æthelthryth received the veil from Wilfrid himself and a year later she left Northumbria and founded a new double monastery on Ely, an island in her home region, where, according to Bede, "she built a monastery and became the virgin mother of many virgins consecrated to God, leading by her example of a devout life and her advice".[11]

Having decided to retire to the monastery, Æthelthryth gladly renounced a lifetime of wealth and comfort befitting her royal status, which is evoked as a counterfoil to her humility: she welcomed the tumour on her throat that eventually caused her death, considering it a penance for her vanity, which had led her to wear adornments such as necklaces, gold and pearls when younger. Now, the pain she endured in her neck served as atonement for having worn unnecessary jewellery. Her rejection of the privileges of worldly life was entirely in keeping with the renunciation that all ascetics made of their material goods in compliance with the Gospel.[12] The *paupertas* implicit in the ascetic life is also reflected in her eschewal of linen clothes in favour of wool, or her refusal to

---

8   Bed., Hist. 4.19; Yorke, 1990, 66–67.
9   Bed., Hist. 4.17.2.
10   On the dramatic end of Coldingham Monastery: Bed., Hist. 4.23.
11   Bed., Hist. 4.17.2.
12   Matt 1:21.

bathe in hot water except before such important festivals as Easter, Pentecost and Epiphany. Furthermore, she always bathed after the other sisters, whom she herself helped to wash, as if a servant, demonstrating a *humilitas* all the more admirable given her royal birth. In addition, she liked to fast every day and remained in the church, absorbed in prayer, from matins to dawn.

Nevertheless, these snippets of her life in community – which depict the abbess as an example of the ideal Christian – clearly indicate that class privileges were perpetuated within the monastery, and Bede himself hints at the presence of serving women who accompanied and waited on the queen in her retreat. Indeed, the abbess's royal status is one of the features that is persistently emphasised, even in the hymn dedicated to virginity that comprises the entire eighteenth chapter.

Thus, at the same time as Bede emphasises Æthelthryth's possession of the virtues of the ideal ascetic (humility, poverty, frugality, piety), he also highlights her lineage, not only to legitimise her election as the spiritual leader of her monastery, but also to further underscore the nature of her sanctity. Moreover, her ancestry served to demonstrate that it was not her birth – however noble – that had afforded her sanctity, but her rejection of an entitled life in favour of one that allowed her to serve Christ, the one true king. She renounced all the honours and privileges associated with her social position on earth, but she gained a far greater reward in return by becoming Christ's bride and queen. Her sanctity was exalted, in short, not because of her birth or marriages but because of her deeds, and this contrast between the earthly comforts renounced by royal women and the austerity of the monastic life they embraced with deep devotion became a common *topos* in hagiography to demonstrate that sanctity was the result not of status but of commitment to the monastic ideal.

In his *History*, Bede also evokes as admirable other royal women who, while fulfilling their traditional political and dynastic function, revealed themselves to be devout Christians that, after producing heirs to the throne, guided their husbands along the path of virtue. Such is the case of Eormenhild, who became regent on the death of her husband Wulfhere of Mercia, and who ended her days as abbess of the monastery of Ely, founded by Æthelthryth, her maternal aunt. Another similar example is given by Seaxburh, sister of Æthelthryth and mother of Eormenhild.[13] Both women demonstrate that celibacy in the cloister is the alternative proposed by hagiography to the virginity that these queens, wives and mothers had lost, and both culminate their lives as

---

13   Bed., Hist. 4.17.3.

abbesses.[14] Widowhood consecrated to God is thus portrayed as another avenue to sanctity, and as evidence of this, correspondence is established between the virtues of the virgin and the similar merits of the devout widow. The best illustration of this is provided by the two sisters Æthelthryth and Seaxburh, both abbesses, but one a virgin and the other a widow. Both are described in terms of their royal birth and their status as wives of Christ and both are venerated, one for her *virginitas* and the other for her *continentia*.

2   The Origin of the Veneration of Æthelthryth

Æthelthryth's preservation of her virginity throughout her married life was confirmed by a miracle that occurred several years after her death. Bede devotes almost the entire chapter to presenting the evidence for Æthelthryth's sanctity, and he does so by employing the canonical sequence of any hagiographic account, which always revolves around the appearance of a relic (*inventio*). In this case, Æthelthryth's mortal remains were located in their entirety in the monastery. Sixteen years had passed since her death (in 679) and her sister Seaxburh, now Abbess of Ely, had planned to wash the bones and transfer them to a new coffin, which would then be placed in a more prominent place inside the church. There would have been nothing extraordinary about this procedure, nor would the remains have had any other consideration than that of being those of the founding abbess, had not several miracles revealing Æthelthryth's sanctity occurred in rapid succession. The most remarkable of these was Seaxburh's astonishing discovery, when she opened the coffin in the presence of witnesses, that her sister's body remained incorrupt, a sign that was interpreted as incontrovertible proof that Æthelthryth had preserved her virginity until the end of her days, despite having had two husbands and having led fifteen years of married life.

To afford credibility to this finding, Bede presents himself as an objective observer[15] who prefers to transmit the testimony of other direct witnesses from outside the monastery, who were known to the deceased and were of unimpeachable reputation. Reference to authority figures who corroborate the

---

14   M. Deanesly, *The Pre-Conquest Church in England*, London 1961, 199–207; C. Neuman de Vegvar, *Saints and Companions to Saints: AngloSaxon Royal Women Monastics in Context*, in: P.E. Szarmach (ed.), *Holy Men and Holy Women Old English Prose Saints' Lives and Their Contexts*, Albany 1996, 52–53; S. Foot, *Veiled Women*, Aldershot 2000, chap. 2; ead., 2006, 150–152.

15   G.I. Berlin, *Bede's Miracle Stories: Notions of Evidence and Authority in Old English History*, in: NP 74 (1990), 440.

narrative was one of the literary techniques used in Christian historiography to invest *a priori* inconceivable events with historical verisimilitude and thus dispel any shadow of doubt.[16]

One of the figures Bede adduces is Wilfrid, appointed Bishop of Northumbria in 665 and one of the great ecclesiastical figures of the period who played an active role in the debates of the British Church,[17] including the synod of Whitby, where he managed to prevail over representatives of the Celtic Church and impose the Roman computation for the date of Easter.[18] Bede had also referenced him in an earlier passage to corroborate Æthelthryth's virginity throughout her marriages.

The other authoritative figure he cites is an expert, the physician Cynefrith, who had treated the abbess during her illness and had attended her in her dying days.[19] Bede quotes Cynefrith's words directly in order to provide the scene with greater veracity. Bishop and physician alike had both witnessed the abbess's intact body, seemingly asleep and without any trace of the tumour that had caused her death. Even the open wound caused by the incision that Cynefrith had made to remove the tumour from her jaw was now no more than a small scar, as if it had healed after death. The perfect state of preservation of the abbess's body is presented in this chapter as evidence of her purity of body and soul, while also reinforcing her role as a model par excellence and providing proof of her strength of spirit, capable of resisting her socially assigned destiny.

However, this is not the only miracle that Bede records as a consequence of the *inventio* of Æthelthryth's body. Touching the original wooden coffin had healed all those whose eyes were diseased or whose sight was failing, and the linen in which the corpse was wrapped had been used to heal the sick and perform exorcism.

A new miracle occurred during the subsequent stage that formed part of the usual process of consecrating relics, the *translatio*, performed to relocate Æthelthryth's body, and the consequent raising (*elevatio*) of her relics to display the holy abbess's body in the new sarcophagus and thus receive (*receptio*)

---

16   W.D. McCready, *Miracles and the Venerable Bede*, Toronto 1994, 232; A. Gransden, *Bede's Reputation as an Historian in Medieval England*, in: JEH 32 (2011), 399–403.

17   V. Blanton, *Signs of Devotion: The Cult of St. Æthelthryth in Medieval England, 695–1615*, Philadelphia 2007, 33–34; N.J. Higham, *Wilfrid and Bede's Historia*, in: N.J. Higham (ed.), *Wilfrid: Abbot, Bishop, Saint. Papers from the 1300th Anniversary Conferences*, Donington 2013, 55.

18   Bed., Hist. 3.25–26.

19   Bed., Hist. 4.19. The first reference to a physician in the island's history, according to N. Moore, *The Physician in English History*, Cambridge 2013, 9; S. Rubin, *The Medical Practitioner in Anglo-Saxon England*, in: Journal of the Royal College of General Practitioners 20 (1970), 63–71.

her remains in their final resting place inside the monastery church, where they would be venerated.

Æthelthryth's *translatio* has the added value of being the only one of a female saint that is documented in Britain during this period, although there are records of similar ceremonies for five other Anglo-Saxon male saints: Augustine at Canterbury, Aidan at Lindisfarne, Cedd at Lastingham, Chad at Lichfield and Cuthbert at Durham, although only the account of Cuthbert's *translatio* is recorded in comparable detail.[20] Bede relates that Chad's body was housed in a reliquary fashioned so as to be accessible to visiting pilgrims in a central location in St Peter's Church in Lichfield,[21] and that Cuthbert's remains were moved to a raised tomb containing both the original and the new coffin, located on the southern side of the church altar in Durham.[22] It is not unusual to find that such ceremonies shared common elements, but no relation can be deduced from such similarities, since they all correspond to archetypal models coined by hagiography, which were equally widespread in the continental Church.[23]

The miracle surrounding the transfer of the corpse is related to the task that Seaxburh entrusted to members of her community, namely to search for stone from which to make the new coffin. The quest was soon achieved through divine intervention, as a carved white marble sarcophagus was found at the foot of the walls encircling an abandoned city in the Cambridge area. The discovery of the sarcophagus is particularly interesting as a reflection of the historical context in which the story unfolds. It was located beside an abandoned city, Grantacaestir,[24] a vestige of the distant period of Roman rule and a testimony to the gradual decline of urban centres after the Romans departed. This decay did not affect Britain alone; from the third century onwards, there is evidence in the West of a widespread contraction in the urban fabric, an inability to maintain public spaces and the reoccupation of buildings for purposes other than their original ones. In Britain, the departure of the Romans, and with them, their administrative, political and cultural customs, was accompanied by the emergence of new forms of territorial control that gradually consolidated into

---

20   A. Thacker, *The Making of a Local Saint*, in: A. Thacker / R. Sharpe (eds.), *Local Saints and Local Churches in the Early Medieval West*, Oxford 2002, 46–47.

21   Bed., Hist. 4.3.

22   Vita Sancti Cuthberti in: B. Colgrave (ed.), *Two Lives of Saint Cuthbert: A Life by an Anonymous Monk of Lindisfarne and Bede's Prose Life*, Cambridge 1940, chap. XLII, 290–295.

23   J. Crook, *The Enshrinement of Local Saints in France and England*, in: Thacker / Sharpe, 2002, 206–207; Thacker, 2002, 59–60.

24   Now Grantchester.

the various Anglo-Saxon kingdoms.[25] The carved white marble sarcophagus found lying at the foot of the city walls appears a somewhat melancholic image that simultaneously evokes the Roman province of the past and a new political and religious landscape in which no symbolic weight was attached to the reuse of objects such as a tomb. Rather, this merely represented the use of very valuable material that would have been extremely difficult to acquire, so much so that to honour the memory of her sister and replace the wooden coffin in which her remains had been laid to rest, Seaxburh had intended to use virgin stone from the surrounding area, which would have been carved to size.

The discovery of the sarcophagus precedes the exhumation of the abbess, and it is only after recounting the discovery of her intact remains, the witness testimony of Cynefrith and anecdotes concerning the last days of Æthelthryth's life that Bede describes the transfer of her remains, and the miracle is completed with the revelation that the sarcophagus is exactly the right size for the abbess, even including the cavity for her head.

The over-riding importance of *virginitas* in Æthelthryth's portrayal would explain the inclusion of a hymn in her honour, which emphasises the preservation of her purity even within marriage, and her status as the bride of Christ. Thus, Chapter 17 presents the material evidence (forensic autopsy of the incorrupt body) and cites trustworthy witnesses of her virginity, while the hymn symbolically underscores her lifelong commitment by relating the miracle of her incorrupt body and drawing a parallel with the most outstanding virgin martyrs of early Christianity. In the order in which they are mentioned by Bede, the hymn names the following young virgins from privileged families who attained the crown of martyrdom through their profession of faith: St Agatha,[26] St Eulalia of Merida,[27] St Thecla,[28] St Euphemia,[29] St Agnes and St Cecilia.[30]

Including Æthelthryth in this list of holy virgins and martyrs, some of whom, such as Agatha and Agnes, had preserved their virginity in dire circumstances,[31] raised her beyond the status of a fervent Christian devotee to

---

25   N.J. Higham, *The Convert Kings: Power and Religious Affiliation in Early Anglo-Saxon England*, Manchester 1997; B. Yorke, *Kings and Kingship*, in: P. Stafford, A *Companion to the Early Middle Ages Britain and Ireland, c. 500–c. 1100*, Oxford 2009, 84–85; *ibid.*, P. Fouracre, *Britain, Ireland, and Europe, c.500–c.750*, 137–138.

26   Martyred at a young age in Catania (Sicily), during the Decian persecution in 250.

27   Even as a child, she demonstrated her courage and was martyred during Diocletian's persecution in 304.

28   One of the most popular virgins of the period, a follower of Paul the Apostle.

29   Martyred in Chalcedon during Diocletian's persecution in 304.

30   Both Roman virgins martyred in 304 and 230, respectively.

31   Both were condemned to a brothel.

erect her as a figure who fulfilled all the requirements for sainthood and veneration in East Anglia, Northumbria and even further afield, on the continent. Indeed, in Bede's martyrology, Æthelthryth is one of only two British saints (the other being St Alban), and 23 June is dedicated to her with a very simple entry describing her as: "Saint Æthelthryth, virgin and queen of Great Britain, whose body, buried for eleven years, was found intact".[32] This is one of the first textual references in which she is named as a saint, at a date very close to the *inventio* and *translatio* of her relics at her sister's behest, in the late seventh century.[33]

The veneration of Æthelthryth as a saint represents the culmination of a model life faithful to the principles of the Church, but also suggests a complementary reading that transcends Bede's idealistic reworking and sheds light on the role played by monasteries and their abbesses in the consolidation of Britain's emergent kingdoms.

3   New Forms of Political Positioning

The kingdoms of the Anglo-Saxon period deployed the usual strategies for consolidating royal power and ensuring dynastic continuity, but they also explored the additional options provided by Christianity as an ideological instrument in the service of the new state structures.[34]

There is no doubt that seeking political and social benefits through marriage alliances remained the primary and traditional goal of diplomatic endeavours,[35] and the marriages arranged within the East Anglian royal family are proof of this. King Anna married his daughters to influential leaders in neighbouring regions, creating connections that were all the more necessary given the threat to his rule posed by the reign of Penda, who sought to annex

---

32   *Martyrologium de Natalitiis Sanctorum*, in: J.A. Giles (ed.), *The Complete Works of the Venerable Bede in the Original Latin*, London 1843, 84.

33   The years 725–731 have been proposed as the date of writing; F. Lifshitz, *Bede, Martyrology*, in: T. Head (ed.), *Medieval Hagiography: An Anthology*, London 2000, 173.

34   C. Stancliffe, *Kings and Conversion: Some Comparisons between the Roman Mission to England and Patrick's to Ireland*, in: FMSt 14 (1980), 70–77; A. Angenendt, *The Conversion of the Anglo-Saxons, Considered against the Background of Early Medieval Mission*, in: Settimane 32 (1986), 747–766; P. Sims-Williams, *Religion and Literature in Western England, 600–800*, Cambridge 1990, 96; Yorke, 1990, 81–83; 136–142; ead., *The Conversion of Britain: Religion, Politics and Society in Britain, c.600–800*, Harlow 2006, 224–225.

35   T.S. Fenster / C.A. Lees (eds.), *Gender in Debate from the Middle Ages to the Renaissance*, New York 2002.

Middle Anglia to Mercia.[36] Æthelthryth's first marriage was to Tondberht, and her second and more influential marriage, to King Ecgfrith of Northumbria. Anna's second daughter, Seaxburh, was married to Eorcenberht of Kent for the same reason.[37]

However, two of his other descendants, his daughter Æthelburh and his stepdaughter Sæthryth, entered the Frankish monastery of Faremoutiers, in accordance with customary practice at a time when monasticism had not yet been established in Britain and the Frankish monasteries were held in high regard as intellectual centres.[38] After her husband's death, Seaxburh acted as regent and only took the veil once her sons, two of them the successive kings of Kent, had been raised.[39] She eventually assumed leadership of the monastery of Ely on Æthelthryth's death, after first leading the double monasteries of Milton Regis and Minster-in-Sheppey. Her daughter Eormenhild also served as abbess of the latter before becoming Abbess of Ely. In turn, the daughter of Eormenhild and King Wulfhere of Mercia, Werburgh, entered the monastery of Ely as a virgin and became its fourth abbess.[40]

This brief genealogical account of Æthelthryth's family illustrates the ubiquity of monasticism among the reigning dynasties as a parallel strategy to marriage alliances. Its popularity was not – or at least not entirely – due to religious motives, but should also be analysed from a political standpoint as an essential element in the expansion and consolidation of the nascent Anglo-Saxon kingdoms.[41] Thus, the foundation of monasteries represented an additional tool for royal houses or aristocratic groups with aspirations to rule, as monasteries afforded them stable influence over the surrounding region and population.[42] In addition, the retirement of women from the ruling houses to monasteries helped to bolster the stability of the various kingdoms by reducing the number of marriages and, consequently, the number of legitimate heirs with aspirations to rule; it also rid the court of widowed queens or those separated from their husbands when the latter wished to remarry.[43] Thus, the foundation of monasteries in which these women could then serve as abbesses gave the

---

36   The eastern part of what is now known as the Midlands: Yorke, 1990, 62–63, 70–71.

37   Lifshitz, 2000, 171–172.

38   Bed., Hist. 4.19; 25; Th. Pickles, *Church Organization and Pastoral Care*, in: Stafford, 2009, 161.

39   Eorcenberht died on 14 July 664; M.J. Swanton, *Anglo-Saxon Chronicle*, London 1998, 27. His sons were Ecgberht I of Kent (664–673) and Hlothhere of Kent (673–685).

40   G.S. Bertin, *The Hagiography of the Female Saints of Ely*, Oxford 2004.

41   Yorke, 1990, 81–83, 136–142; ead., 2006, 224–225.

42   Foot, 2006, 86–87.

43   K.J. Leyser, *Rule and Conflict in an Early Medieval Society: Ottoman Saxony*, London 1979, 64; M. Clunies, *Concubinage in Anglo-Saxon England*, in: PaP 108 (1985), 32–33.

latter continued public status, while their withdrawal from court ensured a peaceful dynastic succession.[44]

These motives would explain the East Anglian royal family's enthusiasm not only for founding monastic communities – to be led by its women – but also for encouraging veneration of King Anna's daughters, Æthelthryth, Seaxburh and Æthelburh, and his granddaughter Eorcongota (Seaxburh's daughter), all of whom were declared saints.[45]

The presence in the church of Ely of the incorrupt body of its first abbess as a relic was a symbol that the monastery capitalised on for centuries, and it became a centre of pilgrimage.[46] It was her sister Seaxburh who organised the memorable spectacle, including the attendance of prominent ecclesiastical and lay figures of the time, the ritual opening of the coffin, the miracles associated with the *inventio* and the transfer of the intact remains to a new sarcophagus located in a more accessible place inside the church. This helped preserve the memory of her family, since her father, King Anna, and her brother Jurmin, sole son and heir to the throne, had been killed in battle fighting against Penda.[47] The relationship between the monastery of Ely and the dynastic houses of Northumbria and Mercia must have encouraged the spread of the veneration of Æthelthryth beyond the territory of East Anglia, and her inclusion in Bede's martyrology is proof of the cult's popularity.[48]

In his *History*, Bede also included the *translatio* of the remains of Æthelthryth's sister, Æthelburh, also a saint, although she was connected with the Frankish monastery of Faremoutiers her entire life.[49] This reference is completely unrelated to the main motif of his *History*, but it provides additional support for Æthelthryth's virginity and may have served as an inspiration for the episode in the *inventio* of the first abbess of Ely.[50]

---

44   L. Eckenstein, *Women under Monasticism*, N. York 1963, 81; S. Hollis, *Anglo-Saxon Women and the Church: Sharing a Common Fate*, Woodbridge 1992, 80.

45   Bed., Hist. 3.8; When Eorcengota died, she exuded a sweet perfume, one of the usual manifestations of sanctity. *Vid.* Eckenstein, 1963, 79–80; D.W. Rollason, *Cults as an Instrument of Royal Policy c. 900–c. 1050*, in: Anglo-Saxon England 15 (1986), 92–98; Neuman, 1996, 52–53; Blanton, 2007, 11; *ead., Presenting the Sister Saints of Ely, or Using Kinship to Increase a Monastery's Status as a Cult Center*, in: Literature Compass 5 (2008), 755–771.

46   B. Nilson, *The Medieval Experience at the Shrine*, in: J. Stopford (ed.), *Pilgrimage Explored*, N. York 1999, 95–122.

47   Around 653 or 654 at the Battle of Bulcamp: Bed., Hist. 3.18.

48   Bishop Wilfrid unquestionably played a role in dissemination of the cult: N.J. Higham, *Preface*, in: Higham, 2013, xvi–xvii; ibid. C. Cubitt, *St Wilfrid: A Man for his Times*, 315–330.

49   Crook, 2002, 206–207.

50   Thacker, 2002, 59–60.

Æthelburh's virtue was beyond dispute, since she had entered the monastery
as a virgin and after her death was shown to have remained so all her life. Her
body had been buried on the site where she had intended to build a church, but
it was never finished. The exhumation of her body from her coffin and its subsequent transfer to a consecrated church demonstrated that her body was "so
well preserved that it was free from the corruption of carnal concupiscence".[51]
Her remains were washed and clothed in new garments before being buried in the church of St. Stephen the Martyr, where she was venerated every
7 July. Æthelburh's virginity, as demonstrated by the intact condition in which
her remains were found, automatically corroborated Æthelthryth's virginity some thirty years later, for if the conditions of the remains of both sisters
were the same and the virginity of Æthelburh was beyond doubt, then that of
Æthelthryth must have received the same consideration, even though she had
been twice married.

4   Æthelthryth's Worldly Profile and the Economic Management of
       Monasteries

As we have already seen, Bede's depiction of the Abbess of Ely adheres to the
canons established by Christian historiography. Her portrayal is not only consistent with those of other abbesses, but is also very close to those of her counterparts in continental hagiography. Like them, Æthelthryth is presented as
solely responsible for a life choice that would appear to be an exclusively individual decision, freely made to satisfy her innermost spiritual aspirations, and
her biography is adorned with qualities that confirm this choice as the only
option that accorded with her nature. Bede's idealised portrait also depicts
Æthelthryth as a pious, saintly abbess who conforms to the canons of feminine
conduct that prevailed in the monastic communities of Bede's own day, governed by the Benedictine rule and a rigorous observance of the cloister. In his
account, Bede omits any biographical details that are not consistent with this
model, which are precisely those that would have best reflected the character-
istic features of Anglo-Saxon monasticism in the seventh and eighth centuries.
     One aspect that is barely seen in Bede's *History* is the fundamental role
played by women connected with the reigning dynasties in the foundation
of monastic communities and thus in conversion to Christianity in Britain.[52]
Nevertheless, some indications of this particular feature of early Anglo-Saxon

---

51   Bed., Hist. 3.8.
52   B. Yorke, *Nunneries and the Anglo-Saxon Royal Houses*, London 2003, 17–46.

monasticism can be detected, and they suggest that the abbesses played a very active role in the religious sphere of their day and exercised a leadership that transcended the care of their congregations' souls. They appear as managers who were financially responsible for their communities and as administrators of the properties that they had contributed to the foundation. We know that kings and their entourages made donations to royal women when these founded a monastery, an essential concession when entering religious life but especially so when establishing a new community.[53] All foundations required gifts to guarantee the community's subsistence, and the properties granted by kings to female founders also served as a powerful incentive for future nuns to increase a monastery's initial wealth by donating their own goods.[54] Clearly, such donations had to be endorsed by a corresponding official document, a charter that recorded the granting of the property and which was intended as a guarantee for the monastery in receipt of the donation against possible claims by *subreguli* or the king's heirs, given the institution's status as the permanent and inalienable owner. These charters also served to record any privileges granted by the king, as the donation of land to monasteries was often accompanied by exemption from certain obligations such as the payment of particular taxes, or conversely, to record any obligations acquired by the monastery, such as the responsibility to provide sustenance to members of the royal household who were in transit.[55]

Few charters have been preserved concerning the estates granted in this period (seventh and eighth centuries) and none with an abbess as the direct beneficiary, but their existence can be deduced from Bede, especially when the abbesses he mentions were former queens, dowager queens, daughters of kings or women in a king's family, and despite the fact that he says

---

53   J. Tibbetts Schulenburg, *Female Sanctity: Public and Private Roles, ca. 500–1100*, in: M. Erler / M. Kowaleski (eds.), *Women and Power in the Middle Ages*, Athens 1988, 110; ead. *"Forgetful of Their Sex": Female Sanctity and Societies, ca. 500–1600*, Chicago 1998; Sims-Williams, 1990, 103–104.

54   F. Stenton, *The Latin Charters of the Anglo-Saxon Period*. Oxford 1955; P. Chaplais, *The Origins and Authenticity of the Royal Anglo-Saxon Diploma*, in: JSA 3 (1965–1969), 8–6; P. H. Sawyer, *Anglo-Saxon Charters: An Annotated List and Bibliography*, London 1968: www.esawyer.org.uk; D. Howlett, *Sealed from Within: Self-Authenticating Insular Charters*, Dublin 1999; M. Lupoi, *The Origins of the European Legal Order*, Cambridge 2000, 145–172; C. Lees / G.R. Overing, *Double Agents: Women and Clerical Culture in Anglo-Saxon England*, Cardiff 2009, 80–88; L. Oliver, *Legal Documentation and the Practice of English Law*, in: C.A. Lees (ed.), *The New Cambridge History of Early Medieval English Literature*, Cambridge 2013, 508–510.

55   Fouracre, 2009, 131–137.

no more about them than to mention their role as founders of a community.[56] In 679, Cyneburh, a relative of King Osric, founded Gloucester Abbey.[57]
Minster-in-Thanet is another of the double monasteries led by a woman and
founded under royal patronage;[58] Æthelthryth entered this monastery in the
time of its first abbess, Æbbe. After Æbbe, women of the royal house of Kent
assumed the leadership, starting with Æbbe's own daughter Mildred, who was
succeeded by Eadburh, probably also a member of the royal house of Kent
although her exact parentage is unknown.[59] Although Bede gives a brief biography of Æthelthryth, he does not mention any donations, but they can be
deduced from the foundation of Ely. Her sister Seaxburh had founded the
monastery of Milton Regis and then a second one, Minster-in-Sheppey, where
she was succeeded by her daughter Eormenhild.[60]

Documents do exist, however, concerning the gift of properties by a king to
other monastic communities, such as the double monastery of Wenlock led by
Mildburh, another of Æbbe's daughters and abbess at some point between 674
and 690. In this case, we know that her father, King Merewalh, endowed the
monastery with land.[61] The monastery at Barking led by Æthelburh received
estates from King Swithfrith of Essex, an East Saxon *subregulus* named
Œtheltred and her own brother Earconwald, perhaps a member of the East
Saxon royal family, who according to Bede founded another monastery that
he led before becoming Bishop of London in 675.[62] In the kingdom of Hwicce,
Æthelred also agreed to King Osric granting ten properties in Bath to Bertha "to
establish a monastery of virgin saints" in 675.[63]

A final example, also reported by Bede, is that of Ælfflæd, the future abbess
of Whitby, who entered the monastery of Hartlepool, bringing with her a substantial endowment. At the time, the monastery was led by the famous Hilda,
and when she founded the later renowned double monastery of Whitby, cradle
of the first generation of British-trained bishops, Ælfflæd accompanied her,
and was later appointed abbess after Hilda's death, first alongside her mother,

---

56   P. Stafford, *Queen Emma and Queen Edith: Queenship and Women's Power in Eleventh-
      Century England*, Oxford 1997, 63.
57   C. Lees / G.R. Overing, 2009, 81–82.
58   Sawyer, 1968, 13; S. Hollis, *The Minster-in-Thanet Foundation Story*, in: Anglo-Saxon
      England 27 (1998), 64.
59   D.W. Rollason, *The Mildrith Legend: A Study in Early Medieval Hagiography in England*,
      Leicester 1982.
60   Tibbetts Schulenburg, 1988, 110; ead., 1998.
61   Sawyer, 1968, 15 and 34; Boniface epist. X; H.P.R. Finberg, *The Early Charters of the West
      Midlands*, Leicester 1961, 201–206; Sims-Williams, 1990, 94.
62   Bed., Hist. 4.6.3; 4.9.1.
63   Sawyer, 1968, 51 and 1165.

and then as sole leader.[64] Bede relates that after Ælfflæd's father Oswiu had defeated Penda at the Battle of Winwæd in 655, he fulfilled his oath and consecrated her – at the tender age of one year old – as a perpetual virgin, granting her "twelve small estates" exempt from military obligations, one of the most frequent privileges included in an official land grant charter. The passage in question states that the donation was made so that these properties could support the community's constant devotion, to provide a place to exercise the heavenly militia and to pray for the eternal peace of the people.[65] This was not a rhetorical exhortation but one of the usual clauses in such documents. Six of the properties granted were in the territory of Deira and six in that of Bernicia, and each piece of land was worked by ten families, providing the community with a total of 120 families in its service. The grant thus concerned a substantial amount of land and labour and must therefore have been recorded in an official document, although this has not been preserved.

Even in those cases where records exist in the property registers of donations of land made to monasteries led by women, the abbesses remain completely invisible, despite being the direct and legitimate recipients and owners of the lands of a good number of monasteries in Britain, and consequently, directly responsible for the institution's financial resources and means of production.[66] This evidences a parallel omission in official administrative sources and ecclesiastical sources alike.

However, some aspects of the religious landscape of the time may nevertheless shed light on the worldly functions exercised by abbesses such as Æthelthryth. For example, the express prohibition issued at the Council of Hertford (the first council of the Anglo-Saxon Church held in 672–673) decreed that "no bishop may in any way interfere with the minsters dedicated to God or take from them by force any part of their property", endowing the abbesses with complete autonomy regarding the use they made of their monasteries' wealth.[67] The monasteries eventually lost this capacity for autonomous action,

---

64   P. Hunter Blair, *Whitby as a Centre of Learning in the Seventh Century*, in: M. Lapidge / H. Gneuss (eds.), *Learning and Literature in Anglo-Saxon England: Studies Presented to Peter Clemoes on the Occasion of his Sixty-fifth birthday*, Cambridge 1985, 8–12.

65   Bed., Hist. 3. 24; J. Eric, *Land Tenure in Early England: A Discussion of Some Problems*, Leicester 1964, 13–14; R.P. Abels, *Lordship and Military Obligation in Anglo-Saxon England*, Berkeley 1988, 49.

66   M.A. Meyer, *Land Charters and the Legal Position of Anglo-Saxon Women*, in: B. Kanner (ed.), *The Women of England: From Anglo- Saxon Times to the Present*, Hamden 1979, 70; C. Lees / G.R. Overing, 2009, 81–86.

67   Chap. 3: Bed., Hist. 4.5. Minster was the usual name at the time for the institutions referred to here, with reservations, as monasteries.

which was officially rescinded at the second Council of Clovesho held in 747,[68] when the bishops assumed control of the internal management of the monasteries. After this council, episcopal power continued to increase. Once again, there is a correlation between the monastic landscape that Bede depicts in his works and the ecclesiastical panorama of his own time, when the monasteries were completely subject to episcopal authority. Such intervention was justified as a measure to ensure proper religious observance in these communities, following reports of immoral practices in some monasteries. This same criticism also surfaces in Bede,[69] who even proposes an alternative form of episcopal control over such monasteries, suggesting to Abbot Ecgberht that these "innumerable places, which are known by the name of minster, but which in no way resemble a form of monastic life, should be constituted as an episcopal see so that close pastoral care could be provided."[70]

However, the abbesses not only had to administer their communities' wealth; they also had to tackle the economic hardships afflicting their monasteries as a result of scarce resources and heavy tax burdens. Although kings often granted monastic communities immunity from taxation, the fiscal advantages derived from these royal concessions were, in reality, no more than a declaration of goodwill. For example, the general privilege issued in 699 by Wihtred, King of Kent, granted all churches and monasteries in his realm exemption from taxation, but also noted the "honour and obedience" expected of them, which in practice implied considerable expense for the community.[71] At the very least, the *ius regium* to which monasteries were bound probably included an obligation to provide men for the army and labour for public works such as maintenance of bridges and walls (or instead to pay the costs), and may also have encompassed the provision of food. Consequently, the obedience that monasteries owed ultimately represented expenses that could bleed less prosperous

---

68   Chap. 5: A.W. Haddan / W. Stubbs (eds.), *Councils and Ecclesiastical Documents Relating to Great Britain and Ireland*, Oxford 1869–1878, 364; *The Councils of Clofesho*, Leicester 1994, 27.

69   Bede conveys a negative view of some double monasteries such as Coldhingam: Bed., Hist. 4.23.

70   Epist. ad Ecgbert of York (734): C. Plummer, (ed.), *Bede's Epistola ad Ecgbertum Episcopum*, Oxford 1896, vol. 1, 415; C. Cubitt, *Anglo-Saxon Church Councils C.650–C.850*, London, 1995, 100–101.

71   N. Brooks, *The Development of Military Obligations in Eighth and Ninth Century England*, in: P. Clemoes / K. Hughes (eds.), *England Before the Conquest: Studies in Primary Sources Presented to Dorothy Whitelock*, Cambridge 1971, 75–79; id., *The Early History of the Church of Canterbury: Christ Church from 397 to 1066*, Leicester 1984, 183–184; 192; H. Edwards, *Two Documents from Aldhelm's Malmesbury*, in: BIHR 59 (1986), 13–14.

communities dry.[72] These services implied a heavy burden for the monasteries, and their abbesses, who were also responsible for financial management, needed to administer their resources wisely if they were to meet their obligations. In a letter to Boniface, one abbess from Kent and her daughter describe the financial hardships assailing their monastery, not only because of the scarcity of resources in the barren land in which they lived, but also because of the *seruitium* owed to the king and his entourage.[73] Their testimony provides a clear illustration of the kind of responsibilities these abbesses assumed as community leaders and recipients of an endowment, and paints a picture of these women that transcends the idealistic model conveyed by Bede.

The silence on these facets of Æthelthryth's work, or that of other abbesses of early Anglo-Saxon monasticism, suggests a desire by the Church to preserve only those aspects of its history it considered necessary, appropriate and opportune. Evidently, all information that demonstrated the laity's leading role in founding monasteries and these institutions' full autonomy of action with respect to the fragile episcopal authority of the early days, as well as the monastic leadership exercised by the women of the royal family, their intervention in religious debates and their continuous interaction with the court, was erased or reworked according to the dictates of the Church in Bede's time; a Church that by then had at its disposal in Britain a better articulated episcopal structure and a network of monasteries whose control it aspired to monopolise. Besides compiling and disseminating the biographies of illustrious members of the Church as shining examples, hagiographic accounts such as that of Æthelthryth reveal those features of the canon that the Church wished to transmit to the faithful via its ecclesiastical structures.[74] In the autobiographical note with which he concludes his *History*, Bede states that his works were "for my own benefit and that of my brethren",[75] referring both to his brethren in the Wearmouth and Jarrow community and the wider ecclesiastical hierarchy of Northumbria.[76] Bede's portrait of Æthelthryth is a declaration of principles

---

72   Brooks, 1971, 69–84; R.P. Abels, *Lordship and Military Obligation in Anglo-Saxon England*, Berkeley 1988, 43–48; P.S. Williams, *Religion and Literature in Western England 600–800*, Cambridge 1990, 134–135.

73   Boniface epist. XIV.

74   M. Lapidge, *The Saintly Life in Anglo-Saxon England*, in: M. Godden / M. Lapidge (eds.), *The Cambridge Companion to Old English Literature*, Cambridge 1991, 243–263; P.A. Thompson, *St Æthelthryth: The Making of History from Hagiography*, in: M.J. Toswell / E.M. Tyler (eds.), *Studies in English Literature: "Doubt Wisely", Papers in Honour of E.G. Stanley*, London 1996, 476; N.J. Higham, *(Re-)Reading Bede: The Ecclesiastical History in Context*, London 2006, 62–63, 70.

75   Bed., Hist. 5. 24.2.

76   Higham, 2006, 41.

issued in response to what the episcopal hierarchy considered a perverse proliferation of monasteries promoted by and for the benefit of the aristocracy,
encouraged by base motives and interests. What was omitted, therefore, is as
informative as what was included, and it is necessary to investigate the vicis-
situdes of life that were silenced because they did not conform to the intended
message. These lacunas reflect a suppressed reality, and their study is revealing both of the historical scenario that was censored and of the reasons why
this was done. By unearthing the abbesses' role in all its facets, figures such as
Æthelthryth acquire a greater wealth of nuance and provide a more complex
reflection of Britain's religious landscape under Anglo-Saxon rule.

PART III

Iberia and the Mediterranean

Les très Puissantes Dames de Saint-Pierre

Premiers Jalons pour une Histoire de l'Abbaye Saint-Pierre de Lyon (VIᵉ–XVIᵉ s.)

Sylvie Duval

Abstract

This paper highlights first the fact that Saint-Pierre was founded in an area of the antique city of *Lugdunum* in which martyrial churches had been built. During the Carolingian period the abbey became one of the richest communities of Lyon, and the nuns, who were first called *puellae*, became *dominae*. Their powerful position however, was soon challenged by lay and religious authorities and then greatly diminished from the XIVth c. onwards.

A Lyon, le majestueux "Palais Saint-Pierre", aujourd'hui siège du Musée des Beaux-Arts, rivalise toujours, sur la place des Terreaux, avec l'Hôtel de ville, siège du pouvoir municipal depuis le XVIIᵉ siècle. L'expression "Palais Saint-Pierre", pour prestigieuse qu'elle soit, cache néanmoins aux Lyonnais qui l'utilisent traditionnellement la fonction première du bâtiment: ce "palais" n'est autre qu'une ancienne abbaye, une abbaye de femmes, dont l'existence est attestée au moins depuis le VIIIᵉ siècle, et qui constitua le premier noyau de l'urbanisation dans cette partie de la ville, aujourd'hui centrale. Le "palais" illustre la puissance des abbesses au XVIIᵉ siècle[1] et leur volonté de retrouver, à travers l'édification d'un immense bâtiment, leur antique pouvoir face à la récente (en comparaison de leur propre histoire) affirmation du pouvoir municipal lyonnais, et à son encore plus récente installation dans un "hôtel de ville" flambant neuf[2]. Aujourd'hui, l'hôtel de ville demeure, mais l'abbaye n'est plus, depuis la Révolution. Et il ne reste rien, ou si peu, dans la mémoire de la ville, de cette communauté qui fut puissante et dont l'histoire est, pour ainsi dire, consubstantielle à celle de la ville de Lyon.

---

1 La reconstruction de l'abbaye dans un style classique majestueux, œuvre de l'architecte François Royer de la Valfenière, a été décidée par l'abbesse Anne de Chaulnes, en 1659.

2 L'Hôtel de Ville de Lyon fut construit entre 1646 et 1674, sur les plans de l'architecte Simon Maupin. Il possède notamment une tour, symbole du pouvoir des échevins lyonnais.

© BRILL SCHÖNINGH, 2024 | DOI:10.30965/9783657791477_007

La question qui sous-tend le bref aperçu de l'histoire de l'abbaye qui va suivre est donc la suivante: comment la mémoire des "très puissantes dames" a-t-elle pu se perdre, et selon quel processus? Un premier indice peut être aisément trouvé: si l'on consulte aujourd'hui les pages internet, somme toute relativement nombreuses, qui sont dédiées à l'abbaye (ou au palais et au musée des Beaux-Arts qu'il abrite), on trouvera deux catégories d'informations. Tout d'abord, des descriptions des bâtiments eux-mêmes, dont l'étude a été relancée lors du classement à l'UNESCO des quartiers centraux de la ville de Lyon, en 1998; il ne sera pas question de cet aspect dans cet article. Quant aux autres informations, celles qui concernent l'abbaye elle-même et que l'on peut trouver tant sur les sites des journaux locaux que sur celui du Musée des Beaux-Arts, elles ne relatent bien souvent qu'une histoire faite de scandales, de "nonnes rebelles" et de spectres hantant, au XVIe siècle, les couloirs du palais[3]. Une "petite" histoire, anecdotique et parfois ridicule : c'est tout ce qui reste aujourd'hui, dans la mémoire collective des Lyonnais, des "très puissantes dames de saint Pierre".

Les archives disent bien autre chose. Elles racontent l'histoire d'une abbaye dont les "dames" (nous reviendrons sur l'importance des diverses appellations des moniales de Saint-Pierre) ont cumulé d'immenses richesses et d'importants pouvoirs. La longue histoire des "dames de Saint-Pierre" est faite de périodes de splendeur, de crises et de renaissances. Force est de constater, toutefois, que cette histoire a fait l'objet d'une véritable *damnatio memoriae*: on ne se souvient pas des "dames" comme des actrices de l'histoire de l'Église et de la ville de Lyon, mais comme des nonnains (l'appellation est dépréciative) à la vie dépravée – si tant est que l'on se souvienne de leur existence même. La bataille de la mémoire, et avant cela, de la réputation, a été perdue par les moniales. L'abbaye Saint-Pierre de Lyon représente un cas paradigmatique d'un phénomène que l'on retrouve ailleurs en Europe, de façon diffuse: à savoir la dépréciation des communautés religieuses féminines, et la négation – ou l'oubli – de leur rôle actif dans l'histoire, notamment au niveau des villes et des quartiers, mais aussi plus largement dans l'histoire culturelle et politique, en particulier médiévale[4]. Les religieuses sont aujourd'hui absentes de notre mémoire

---

3   Le "spectre" de la religieuse décadente Alice de Theizé aurait hanté l'abbaye au XVIe siècle. Quant à l'idée des "nonnes rebelles", elle naît d'une lecture univoque de la réforme radicale du début du XVIe siècle. Je reviens sur ces thèmes à la fin de l'article.

4   Heureusement, une forte historiographie se développe actuellement sur le thème des abbayes de femmes au haut Moyen Âge et au Moyen Âge central. On pourra se reporter avec profit au dossier thématique contenu dans Reti Medievali 20 (2019) et en particulier à l'introduction de V. West-Harling, qui fait le point sur le sujet: V. West-Harling, *Female Monasticism in Italy in the Early Middle Ages: New Questions, New Debates*, en ligne https://

collective, ou bien n'y sont-elles présentes que sous des aspects négatifs. Il s'agit d'un phénomène très marqué en France, dont l'histoire a été caractérisée par une forte laïcisation de la société dès le XVIIIe siècle, mais il est aussi très présent dans d'autres pays, en particulier de culture catholique, et remonte en réalité à des perceptions plus anciennes, que nous tenterons d'illustrer ici à travers l'exemple de l'abbaye Saint-Pierre.

Cet article se présente comme la première ébauche d'une recherche future, et fera seulement état de premières réflexions et de premiers repérages. L'objectif de la recherche, on l'aura compris, ne sera pas simplement de retracer l'histoire plus que millénaire de l'abbaye, mais aussi de comprendre les ressorts ayant conduit à cette *damnatio memoriae*, sur la longue durée de l'histoire de l'abbaye (VIe/VIIIe–XVIIIe siècle). Le fonds d'archives de l'abbaye Saint-Pierre, conservé aux Archives Départementales du Rhône à Lyon, est à la fois imposant et décevant: de nombreuses pertes et destructions lui ont donné sa physionomie actuelle. Le fonds, qui comporte 755 cotes, se compose en effet de documents se rapportant presque exclusivement à la gestion du patrimoine; ces documents, de plus, remontent essentiellement à la période s'étendant du XIIe au XVIIIe siècle (avec une nette augmentation du nombre de documents à partir du XIVe siècle). Les premiers siècles du Moyen Âge sont peu représentés: on ne possède que des copies tardives d'actes antérieurs au XIIe siècle – j'y reviendrai. Globalement, toutefois, la moisson est riche, en particulier dans le contexte français, où les fonds d'archives ont été notoirement décimés à la Révolution. En outre, on peut aussi compter sur la mention de l'abbaye dans le *Liber Memorialis* de l'abbaye Reichenau[5], rédigé en 824, qui comporte une longue liste de noms de moniales, ainsi que sur l'existence d'un obituaire remontant à la première moitié du XIIIe siècle dans le fonds Coste de la bibliothèque municipale de Lyon[6]. D'autres documents dispersés, notamment dans les fonds des chapitres de la cathédrale de Lyon et de l'église

---

doi.org/10.6092/1593–2214/6122. Sur la perception des communautés féminines, voir aussi S. Vanderputten, *Dismantling the Medieval: Early Modern Perceptions of Female Convent's Past*, Turnhout 2021. Sur l'importance du rôle politique des abbayes de femmes, voir A. Müller, *From the Cloister to the State: Fontevraud and the Making of Bourbon France, 1642–1100*, London 2021.

5   Voir *Monumenta Germaniae Historica, Necrologia Germaniae, Libri confraternitatum Sancti Galli, Augiensis, Fabariensis*, dans P. Piper (éd.), Hannover 1884, 259 et R. le Jan: Nomina viventium, nomina defunctorum: *les interactions entre vivants et morts dans les libri memoriales carolingiens*, dans: Société des historiens médiévistes de l'Enseignement supérieur public (éd.), *Les vivants et les morts dans les sociétés médiévales. XLVIIIe Congrès de la SHMESP, Jerusalem 2017*, Histoire ancienne et médiévale 158, Paris 2018, 121–134.

6   Fonds Coste de la Bibliothèque municipale de Lyon, ms. 1308.

Saint-Nizier[7], peuvent aussi être mis à profit. Nombreux sont, enfin, les textes hagiographiques ou littéraires qui mentionnent ou décrivent l'abbaye, depuis le haut Moyen Âge jusqu'au XIXe siècle.

Les historiens s'étant intéressés à l'abbaye sont peu nombreux – il fallait s'y attendre, au vu des premières constatations que nous venons d'effectuer. Aucun ouvrage récent n'a été consacré à l'histoire de Saint-Pierre, à l'exception d'un article publié par M. Rubellin[8]. Il faut, pour trouver des publications sur lesquelles nous pourrons efficacement nous appuyer, remonter au XIXe siècle, et aux recherches de l'archiviste paléographe Marie Claude Guigue, qui publia de très nombreux documents relatifs à l'histoire de Lyon, dont l'obituaire de l'abbaye Saint-Pierre en 1880[9]. A l'occasion de l'édition de ce document, Guigue revient sur la chronologie des abbesses de Saint-Pierre: il s'agit de la première critique historique moderne des sources de l'abbaye. Une cinquantaine d'années plus tard, l'historien Alfred Coville, dans ses *Recherches sur l'Histoire de Lyon du Ve au IXe siècle* (1928) revient sur l'histoire de l'abbaye, et en particulier sur les copies de documents anciens qui firent couler beaucoup d'encre[10]. Ce faisant, il intègre Saint–Pierre dans l'histoire de la ville, au sein d'un ouvrage qui repose sur une méthode rigoureuse et qui reste donc, par conséquent, l'un des éléments incontournables de l'historiographie concernant la ville de Lyon au haut Moyen Âge. Enfin, l'archiviste lyonnais Joseph Picot consacra sa thèse de doctorat à l'abbaye, sous la direction de Marcel Pacaut. L'ouvrage qu'il tira de sa thèse, publié en 1970, est très complet, et s'intéresse plus particulièrement aux domaines des dames et à leur gestion à la fin du Moyen Âge[11].

---

7   Le catalogue du fonds d'archives de l'abbaye Saint-Pierre, établi par René Lacour, est extrêmement détaillé et fournit également les références des pièces conservées dans d'autres fonds. Il est accessible sur le site des Archives départementales du Rhône (désormais AdR), https://archives.rhone.fr/media/ad469433–847a–4e1e–8195–92fe2c5b291b.pdf.

8   M. Rubellin, *Retour sur les origines du monastère Saint-Pierre de Lyon*, dans: J.F. Reynaud / F. Richard (éds.), *L'Abbaye d'Ainay des origines au XIIe siècle*, Lyon 2008, 73–90.

9   M.C. Guigue (éd.), *Obituaire de l'Abbaye de Saint–Pierre de Lyon du IXe au XVe siècle*, Lyon 1880.

10   A. Coville, *Recherches sur l'Histoire de Lyon du Ve au IXe siècle (450–800)*, Paris 1928. A. Coville et M.C. Guigue ont publié de nombreux articles sur l'histoire de l'abbaye. On sent chez eux une fascination pour ces religieuses, dont ils découvrent la puissance oubliée à travers les archives – je dois l'expression "les très puissantes dames" à M.C. Guigue (dans l'introduction à id. [éd.], l'*Obituaire de l'Abbaye de Saint-Pierre de Lyon du IXe au XVe siècle*, Lyon 1880), qui l'a forgée lui-même à partir des documents des XVIIe–XVIIIe, où les religieuses se décrivent elles-mêmes.

11   J. Picot, *L'Abbaye Saint-Pierre de Lyon*, Paris 1970.

1   **Les Brumes de la Fondation**

Les documents du fonds d'archives de Saint-Pierre figurent parmi les plus anciens du diocèse de Lyon, c'est pourquoi ils ont très tôt attiré l'attention des érudits[12]. Les discussions à leur propos se poursuivent depuis le XVIIᵉ siècle sans, pour lors, qu'on ne soit arrivé à une conclusion définitive[13]. Plutôt que de partir directement de ces documents ambigus, sur lesquels je reviendrai, il faut commencer par décrire l'importance et les particularités du site où l'abbaye est installée[14]. La géographie de Lyon est marquée par les deux fleuves (Saône et Rhône) qui traversent la ville, et par ses collines: celle de Fourvière, où la ville romaine avait son centre, et celle de la Croix-Rousse, au pied de laquelle se trouve aujourd'hui la place des Terreaux, bordée par le Palais-Saint-Pierre (l'abbaye) et l'Hôtel-de-Ville. Au temps où la ville romaine de Lyon était la capitale des Gaules, la colline de la Croix-Rousse abritait, sur son flanc sud, un complexe monumental de première importance: l'amphithéâtre et le sanctuaire des Trois-Gaules. Au pied de cette colline, au moins dès le IIᵉ siècle, s'était développée une zone urbanisée. Toutefois, dès le Vᵉ siècle, et pour toute la durée du Moyen Âge, l'emprise urbaine se réduisit très fortement, l'habitat se concentrant désormais sur une mince bande de terre située entre la colline de Fourvière et la Saône. La zone voisine de l'ancien amphithéâtre perdit la plupart de ses habitants mais elle ne fut pas pour autant abandonnée: elle abrita désormais des églises et basiliques martyriales[15]. Ces églises, dont il est difficile de savoir à quelle date exactement elles furent érigées, conservaient les cendres des martyrs lyonnais (ou du moins y étaient-ils vénérés[16]), et particulièrement

---

12   Voir les notes d'édition de M.C. Guigue dans le *Cartulaire Lyonnais. Documents inédits pour servir à l'histoire des anciennes provinces de Lyonnais, Forez, Beaujolais, Bresse et Bugey, comprises dans le Pagus Major Lugdunensis*, Lyon 1885, 2 tomes, en particulier tome 1 p. 1–4 (testament de saint Ennemond).

13   Pour une synthèse récente et complète, on pourra se reporter à Rubellin, 2008, 73–90.

14   Se référer à la carte publiée en annexe. On pourra aussi plus utilement se reporter, sur la question du site lyonnais et de ses aménagements successifs entre Antiquité et Moyen Âge, aux travaux de J.F. Reynaud, et notamment: J.F. Reynaud, *A la recherche d'un Lyon disparu. Vie et mort des édifices religieux du IVᵉ au XXᵉ siècle*, Lyon 2022.

15   Des pierres de l'amphithéâtre et du sanctuaire furent donc, comme c'était l'usage, remployées pour la construction des basiliques. Guillaume Paradin signale les inscriptions antiques qui lui sont connues et qui étaient visibles dans les murs de l'église Saint-Pierre au XVIᵉ siècle (*Mémoires de l'Histoire de Lyon*, Lyon, chez Antoine Gryphe, 1573, 422–425).

16   Eusèbe de Césarée dans son *Histoire ecclésiastique* (Eus., h.e. 5.62) précise en effet que les cendres des martyrs de 177 furent dispersées dans le Rhône. Ces cendres furent par la suite miraculeusement retrouvées, au cours du VIᵉ siècle, en un lieu dénommé *Athanaco*,

celles des Quarante-Huit martyrs de 177, suppliciés, pour la plupart d'entre eux, à l'amphithéâtre. Parmi ces martyrs, le vieil évêque Pothin et la vierge Blandine, dont l'histoire est contée dans la fameuse lettre citée par Eusèbe de Césarée, figurent parmi les saints les plus vénérés de l'Église de Lyon. Saint Irénée, qui succède à Pothin à la tête de l'Église lyonnaise, ne fut pas tué lors de cette persécution; il a néanmoins été "admis" parmi ces martyrs, notamment suite au récit de Grégoire de Tours[17]. Père de l'Église ayant laissé de nombreux écrits, il est d'ailleurs considéré, à bien, des égards, comme le véritable fondateur de l'Église de Lyon. Les sources semblent concorder pour identifier la principale de ces églises, c'est-à-dire la basilique dédiée aux Quarante-Huit Martyrs, à l'actuelle église Saint-Nizier. Celle-ci accueillit, dès le VIe siècle, la sépulture des évêques lyonnais, notamment saint Rustique (494–501), saint Sacerdos (549–552) et surtout saint Nizier (553–573), dont Grégoire de Tours, son parent, dresse le portrait hagiographique dans l'*Historia Francorum*[18]. Elle partageait dès le VIIe siècle, ce rôle avec une autre église proche, dédiée à Saint-Pierre qui, semble-t-il, accueillit la sépulture de saint Ennemond ou Chamond (654–658), reconnu comme martyr du fait de son meurtre par le maire du palais de Neustrie à Chalon-sur-Saône en 657–658, puis, pour quelques années seulement, celle de saint Bonnet (m. 710), évêque de Clermont. Cette église Saint-Pierre était-elle, à l'origine, l'église des Saints-Apôtres, dont les archéologues débattent encore aujourd'hui de la position exacte au haut Moyen Âge? Si tel est le cas, il faudrait considérer que la référence aux Saints-Apôtres aurait ensuite "glissé" à l'église voisine des Quarante–Huit Martyrs, ainsi que l'attestent les sources du IXe siècle[19]. L'intitulation au Prince des Apôtres est classiquement invoquée,

---

qui pourrait correspondre à Ainay. Les documents postérieurs au VIe siècle concordent toutefois vers l'identification de la basilique des Quarante–Huit Martyrs avec celle de Saint-Nizier. Voir notamment Reynaud, 2022, 50 *et sq.*

17   Greg. - T., Hist. 1.29.

18   Greg. - T., Hist. 4.36.

19   Adon, au IXe siècle, identifie implicitement la basilique des Saints-Apôtres à celle des Quarante–Huit Martyrs ([…] *apostolorum ecclesia, ubi cineres eorum conditi servantur*), et donc à Saint-Nizier. Y avait-il, à l'origine, deux basiliques, l'une dédiée aux Martyrs et l'autre aux Apôtres? Le souvenir de la dédicace aux Apôtres aurait pu "glisser" de Saint-Pierre, devenu une abbaye importante à l'époque où écrit Adon, à l'église voisine des Martyrs/Saint-Nizier. Mais on peut aussi envisager le contraire: un glissement de la titulature de l'église des Apôtres vers l'église des moniales (Saint-Pierre). Il est difficile de sortir du stade des conjectures, et ce d'autant plus que d'autres églises sont alors attestées dans la zone (Sainte–Marie, Saint–Saturnin) voir *infra*, en particulier n. 26. L'hypothèse de J.F. Reynaud selon laquelle la basilique des Saints-Apôtres pourrait être Saint-Pierre de Vaise ne correspond pas à ces textes. Ado Viennensis, *Martyrologium* (PL 123, 279).

aux VIe et VIIe siècle, pour les églises abritant des communautés féminines[20]. Cette église Saint-Pierre, qui accueillit la sépulture de certains évêques dès le haut Moyen Âge, est donc vraisemblablement celle de nos moniales, appelées dès les origines de leur communauté *puellae Sancti Petri*.

C'est dans le texte de la Vie de l'évêque saint Bonnet de Clermont, qui aurait été rédigée peu après la mort du saint, advenue en 710[21] que l'on trouve la pre-mière description détaillée[22] de l'abbaye des moniales ou vierges (*puellae*) de saint Pierre de Lyon, ayant alors à leur tête une abbesse nommée Dide. L'ense-velissement de saint Bonnet dans l'église des moniales suivait probablement une tradition déjà bien ancrée de sépulture des évêques dans les églises de cette zone de la ville de Lyon, ainsi que je l'ai évoqué plus haut, une habitude qui avait fait suite à la vénération des martyrs en ce même lieu[23]. Le texte de la *Vita Boniti* dit très clairement que deux églises se trouvaient alors côte-à-côte (*juxta*): l'église Saint-Pierre, celle des moniales, côtoyant une basilique

---

20   La dédicace des abbayes de femmes au Prince des Apôtres est attestée en plusieurs endroits, notamment à Tours (Saint-Pierre-le-Puellier) ou à Metz. Sur cette dernière abbaye, se référer à: G. Blennemann, *Die Metzer Benediktinerinnen im Mittelalter. Studien zu den Handlungsspielräumen geistlicher Frauen*, Husum 2011.

21   Elle fut éditée, par B. Krusch, dans les *Monumenta Germaniae Historica, Scriptores Rerum Merovingicarum* 6 (*Passiones Vitaeque sanctorum aevi merovingici*), Hannover 1913, 110–139.

22   A moins de considérer que le *monasterium lugdunense* cité par Grégoire de Tours dans son *Historia* soit cette même abbaye de saint Pierre (Greg. - T., Hist. 10.8). Il est difficile de trancher, sachant qu'un autre monastère féminin, Sainte–Eulalie, est attesté à l'époque de Grégoire.

23   Dans les basiliques du haut Moyen Âge, le culte des martyrs est fréquemment suivi par la coutume d'ensevelir les évêques locaux. Voir sur ce sujet, H. Noizet, *Les basiliques mar-tyriales au VIe et au début du VIIe siècle*, dans: Revue d'histoire de l'Église de France 87 (2001), 329–355. Le texte de la *Vita Boniti* est précis, il y a hélas une incertitude sur la dédi-cace de la basilique martyriale, probablement suite à l'erreur d'un copiste. La "basilique du saint martyr" est en effet décrite, quelques lignes plus haut, comme étant intitulée à Saint-Etienne (*beati Stephani*): il s'agit d'une proposition de l'éditeur, ainsi qu'il l'indique lui-même, suite à son refus d'accepter le nom porté par les manuscrits les plus anciens: *basilica beati Hieronymi*. Il est vrai qu'aucune église lyonnaise ne semble avoir été dédiée à saint Jérôme; la lecture proposée par B. Krusch est toutefois insatisfaisante à plusieurs titres. Premièrement, parce que le nom *Stephani* aurait difficilement pu être confondu avec *Hieronymi*. Ensuite parce que cette titulature est celle de la cathédrale d'alors, située non loin de l'actuelle cathédrale Saint-Jean. Or, l'hagiographe la mentionne plus haut dans le texte, qualifiant alors Etienne de "protomartyr", on voit mal pourquoi il ne le ferait plus par la suite. Une hypothèse pourrait être une erreur d'un copiste sur le nom originel de *beati Hirenei*, ce qui rendrait au texte une certaine cohérence puisque, nous le disions, Irénée était alors considérée comme un martyr, au même titre que les Quarante-Huit martyrs de 177, et comme le fondateur de l'Église de Lyon.

martyriale[24]. Les églises de Saint-Nizier (ancienne basilique des Martyrs) et de Saint-Pierre (aujourd'hui à l'intérieur du musée) sont bien, encore aujourd'hui, construites de manière parallèle, à une distance d'environ deux cent mètres l'une de l'autre. Bien des siècles plus tard, en 1305, à l'occasion d'une enquête ordonnée par l'archevêque de Lyon Louis de Villars, lui-même fondateur du chapitre de chanoines de Saint-Nizier, l'ancienne fonction sépulcrale et martyriale de ces très anciennes églises remonta à la surface – littéralement, puisque des fouilles furent effectuées dans les églises. Les conclusions de l'enquête, née d'un conflit entre les moniales de Saint-Pierre et les chanoines à propos de l'emplacement de la tombe de saint Ennemond sur lequel je reviendrai, sont d'une extrême importance. Les documents liés à cette longue procédure dressent en effet la liste des tombes qui furent alors retrouvées à Saint-Nizier: ce sont notamment celles des évêques Rustique, Sacerdos, Nizier. On ne retrouva néanmoins ni à Saint-Pierre ni à Saint-Nizier, la tombe disputée de l'évêque-martyr Ennemond. Le procès qui suivit, en 1307–1308, donna lieu à de nouvelles enquêtes. Parmi les notes relatives à cette procédure, on trouve une information concordante avec l'extrait de la vie de saint Bonnet cité plus haut: les procureurs de l'abbaye Saint-Pierre trouvèrent en effet, parmi la documentation liturgique disponible à la cathédrale, un *rotulum letaniarum antiquum*, où il était fait mention de la vénération d'Ennemond en l'église Saint-Pierre (et non en l'église de Saint-Nizier)[25]. Le document n'est pas précisément daté, mais l'église Saint-Nizier y est désignée sous le vocable d'"église des Apôtres et des Quarante–Huit Martyrs", ce qui supposerait une datation très ancienne, peut-être avant le IXe siècle – si l'on accepte, toutefois de se fier aux renseignements issus d'une recherche effectuée en faveur de l'abbaye Saint-Pierre. L'existence de deux églises martyriales, l'une dédiée aux Martyrs, l'autres à Saint-Pierre, dans le quartier situé au pied de l'ancien amphithéâtre, ne fait donc aucun doute, de même que celle d'une communauté de religieuses, rattachée à l'église Saint-Pierre, au moins depuis le début du VIIIe siècle.

La construction de l'église Saint-Pierre précéda-t-elle la fondation de la communauté des *puellae*, ou bien la communauté des religieuses fut-elle rattachée

---

24   ... *basilica beati martiris iuxta eandem beati Petri apostoli, in qua vir Domini quiescebat*, dans *Monumenta Germaniae Historica, Scriptores Rerum Merovingicarum* 6 (*Passiones Vitaeque sanctorum aevi merovingici*), Hannover 1913, 137.

25   AdR, Fonds Saint-Pierre, 27H33. [...] *Item continetur talia verba in quodam rotulo antiquo letaniarum civitatis Lugdunensi et dicte prefate maioris ecclesie Lugdunensi., ubi stationes consueverunt fieri in ecclesiis civitatis Lugdunensi, ubi dicuntur quod sequent: 'statio ad Sanctum Petrum. Sancte Amemunde s., sancte Petre s.', ad differentiam Ecclesie Sancti Nicetii, ubi dicitur: 'Statio ad ecclesiam Apostolorum et XLVIIIto martirium, dicendo verba qui sequntur: Sancte Nicetii s. Sancte Petre s.,' et tamen ibi nulla fit mentio de beato Amemundo.*

à l'église dès sa construction? Il est impossible, en l'état de nos connaissances, de répondre à cette question. L'existence de l'église, de son patrimoine foncier et de la communauté féminine dès le haut Moyen Âge sont indéniables: reste à savoir si les trois éléments ont, dès le départ, coïncidé. Il faut souligner le fait que l'abbaye de Saint-Pierre ne possède pas de récit de fondation. Lors de l'enquête de 1305, les procureurs, avant d'introduire les résultats de leurs recherches, ne manquèrent pas de rappeler aux juges que le culte rendu à Saint-Ennemond se tenait en l'église Saint-Pierre "depuis des temps immémoriaux", et que les processions du clergé lyonnais en l'honneur des saints s'y rendaient pour la fête du saint, en septembre, les reliques étaient alors exposées à la vénération populaire[26]. "Depuis des temps immémoriaux": cette expression se retrouve souvent dans les contestations et procès (et ils furent nombreux ...) qui opposèrent les religieuses à plusieurs de leurs voisins et à différentes autorités concurrentes. Cette absence de mémoire est donc, très paradoxalement, d'abord celle des religieuses elles-mêmes.

Revenons donc désormais aux documents anciens qui ont tant suscité la curiosité des érudits. Le caractère, manifestement composite, de leur contenu semble être une tentative de combler les vides laissés par cette mémoire perdue. En outre, on n'en possède que des copies tardives, qui jettent le doute sur leur authenticité. Ceux-ci nous ramènent tout d'abord à Ennemond, figure tutélaire de l'abbaye. Le "testament de saint Ennemond", formellement daté de 655, a longtemps été considéré comme le plus ancien document d'archive se référant à l'Église de Lyon. Ce document aurait été rédigé par l'évêque lui-même, qui y parle à la première personne[27]. Il s'agit en fait non pas d'un testament, mais d'un privilège de confirmation de donations antérieures. D'importants biens de l'abbaye, qui formèrent peut-être le premier noyau de son imposant patrimoine, y sont cités[28]. Il s'agit ici de combler un trou de

---

26   Ibid. Le mémoire procède par ordre. Les procureurs rappellent d'abord les usages "immémoriaux", contre lesquels les clercs de l'Église Saint-Nizier veulent attenter. Puis la possession par les moniales de reliques, probablement celles qui sont montrées lors de ces processions (un vêtement [*camisia*] et deux os). Enfin, un long passage où les procureurs relatent les résultats de leurs recherches dans les bibliothèques ecclésiastiques lyonnaises. Ce *rotulum* est le deuxième élément cité, après une ancienne *Vie* des Saints Côme et Damien, elle aussi conservée à la cathédrale, et qui situe explicitement la tombe d'Ennemond à Saint-Pierre. Dans le *rotulum* tel qu'il est ici cité, l'église Saint-Nizier est décrite comme étant dédiée aux Saints-Apôtres et aux Martyrs, comme dans le texte d'Adon. Voir *supra* note 19.

27   *Cartulaire lyonnais* 1, p. 1–4. La copie la plus ancienne de ce document ne remonte toutefois qu'à la fin du XVe siècle.

28   Notamment les possessions situées autour de Dolomieu, aujourd'hui dans le département de l'Isère.

mémoire bien embarrassant – celui de la provenance de ces biens – mais qui n'a toutefois pas directement trait à la fondation de l'abbaye. Or, sur ce sujet, le texte est maladroitement prolixe: il fait remonter l'existence du *monasterium Sancti Petri puellarum* au IIe ou au IIIe siècle, "peu après le martyr de saint Irénée". A cette époque, un *vir nobilissimus*, aurait donné la terre de Dolomieu à la communauté pour ses propres filles, *quas ibi sacrare fecit*. De même, un autre noble de la période, Julianus, aurait donné d'autres terres pour sa fille, ainsi que deux autres encore, Constantinus et Radulfus, toujours pour leurs propres filles. La mention du martyre de saint Irénée joue clairement ici le rôle d'un marqueur temporel sans réelle précision chronologique, servant à rattacher la fondation de la communauté aux premiers temps de l'Église de Lyon. Quant à l'attribution de cette confirmation de donations à saint Ennemond lui-même, elle relève probablement de la volonté de rattacher les possessions "immémoriales" à la figure tutélaire de l'abbaye. Il est important de noter que le texte, toutefois, n'attribue pas la fondation du monastère à l'évêque martyr, contrairement à des documents postérieurs (à partir du XIIIe siècle)[29]; ce qui permet de dater approximativement cette forgerie des XIe–XIIe siècles. Il n'est pas impossible que des éléments authentiques du haut Moyen Âge aient été fondus dans la version que nous possédons: il est difficile, néanmoins, en l'état de nos connaissances, de les faire émerger[30].

Un autre acte, erronément daté de 586 par un archiviste du XVIIIe siècle, fit lui aussi couler beaucoup d'encre. D'après une étude minutieuse d'Alfred Coville, cet acte remonte en réalité au Xe siècle[31]. Nous ne sommes pas ici, cependant, en présence d'un cas de forgerie similaire au testament d'Ennemond. Le document, si l'on admet la datation aux alentours de 990 proposée par Coville, est cohérent: c'est une donation d'une terre par deux parents, nobles bourguignons connus par ailleurs, à leur fille, vierge consacrée du monastère Saint-Pierre (le terme utilisé cette fois est *sponsa Jesu Christi benedicta*). Or, cette donation comporte une référence précise aux fondateurs de l'abbaye, un élément qui n'apparaît nulle part ailleurs. Celle-ci aurait été fondée par un couple royal, Gaudisellus (probablement Godégisile, m. 501) et sa pieuse épouse Theudelinde, rois des Burgondes. Godégisile affronta son frère Gondebaud en une violente guerre qui nous est racontée par Grégoire de Tours, dans les dernières années du Ve siècle. Quant à la reine Theudelinde, elle n'est mentionnée que dans un autre texte, remontant lui aussi au Xe siècle,

---

29   Voir *infra*, notamment n. 44.
30   Tel était l'avis de Mabillon. Voir *Cartulaire lyonnais* 1, p. 1–4.
31   A. Coville, *La prétendue charte mérovingienne de Saint-Pierre de Lyon*, dans: Le Moyen Âge. Revue d'histoire et de philologie 16 (1903), 169–184.

dont la fiabilité est contestée[32]. Il faut peut-être comprendre l'existence de cette mention dans l'optique d'une concurrence des mémoires liée à la fondation (ou à la refondation) de l'abbaye masculine d'Ainay, intervenue au IXe siècle[33]. Les moniales, de ce fait, perdirent leur position de seule abbaye présente dans la Presqu'île lyonnaise, c'est-à-dire dans la zone située entre Saône et Rhône[34]. Or, les moines d'Ainay pouvaient prétendre que leur abbaye avait été fondée par la reine Carétène, épouse catholique de Gondebaud (m.516)[35]. Ils s'appuyaient pour cela sur l'épitaphe de la reine, qui nous est justement connue par une inscription datée du IXe siècle longtemps conservée à Ainay[36]. Le texte, inspiré des écrits de Sidoine Apollinaire, décrit Carétène comme très pieuse, et atteste la fondation de la part de la reine d'une église à Ainay (non pas de l'abbaye, cependant, mais la basilique des Saints-Anges, devenue ensuite l'église paroissiale dédiée à Saint-Michel-Archange, toute proche de l'abbaye). Dans cette perspective, l'allusion à Godégisile et Theudelinde (*piissima*) apparaît parallèle aux fondateurs "voisins" d'Ainay, Gondebaud et sa pieuse épouse Carétène. Ceci pourrait expliquer le contexte de la citation: mais faut-il pour autant renoncer à la crédibilité de cette affirmation comme le fait Coville? Ainsi que l'a souligné R. Kaiser, la fondation d'établissements pieux par les reines catholiques, épouses de rois ariens, constituait un élément récurrent de la politique des rois burgondes permettant l'adhésion de leurs sujets catholiques[37]. Un autre document du VIIIe siècle, par ailleurs, pourrait

---

32   La reine Théodelinde est citée par E. Chevalley / J. Favrod, *Soleure dans le diocèse de Genève? Hypothèse sur l'origine du diocèse d'Avenches/Vinonissa*, dans: Revue d'Histoire Ecclésiastique Suisse 86 (1992), 47–68, repris par R. Kaiser, *L'entourage des rois du regnum Burgundiae aux époques burgonde et mérovingienne*, dans: J.L. Kupper / A. Marchandisse (éds.), *A l'ombre du pouvoir. Les entourages princiers au Moyen Âge*, Liège 2003, 77–95 et B. Dumézil, *La mixité religieuse chez les couples royaux burgondes*, dans: M. Aurell / T. Deswarte (éds.): *Famille, violence et christianisation au Moyen Âge: Mélanges Michel Rouche,* Paris 2005, 57– 66; Rubellin, 2008, 73–90) ne donne quant à lui pas crédit au texte.

33   Voir F. Richard / J.F. Reynaud (éds.), 2008.

34   Il n'y a pas, à ce moment-là, de religieux réguliers à Saint-Nizier, où le chapitre sera fondé au début du XIVe siècle, ni à Sainte-Marie-de-la-Platière, où les chanoines de Saint-Ruf arriveront au XIIe siècle.

35   Voir F. Prévot, *Saint-Michel d'Ainay d'après les sources antiques*, dans: Richard / Reynaud (éds.), 2008, 61–72.

36   R. Kaiser, *L'entourage des rois du regnum Burgundiae aux époques burgonde et mérovingienne*, dans: J.L. Kupper / A. Marchandisse (éds.), *A l'ombre du pouvoir. Les entourages princiers au Moyen Âge*, Liège 2003. L'article retrace par ailleurs de façon complète et efficace le contexte politique des VIe–VIIe siècle du royaume de Bourgogne, où gallo-romains et "barbares" cohabitent, et qui pourrait être celui de la fondation de la communauté des *puellae*.

37   Ibid.

conforter une telle hypothèse: il s'agit du testament d'Abbon, dernier patrice de Provence, daté de 739[38]. Ce proche de Charles Martel, issu d'une famille gallo-romaine, dota par l'intermédiaire de son testament l'abbaye, qu'il avait fondée, la Novalaise, d'un immense patrimoine foncier. Parmi les terres et biens mentionnés figurent les alpages du Mont-Cenis (*alpes in Cinisio*), qu'il avait obtenus par le biais d'un échange, dit-il, avec l'église Saint-Pierre de Lyon (*ecclesia Sancti Petri ... constructa Lugdunense*). Il ne s'agit pas là d'un simple échange de terres agro-pastorales: ainsi que l'a souligné L. Ripart[39], c'est par le col du Mont-Cenis, au pied duquel l'abbaye est stratégiquement placée que passe l'une des principales routes reliant le royaume des Lombards à la Gaule et à l'ancien royaume de Burgondes. Si l'on accepte l'idée d'une fondation de Saint-Pierre de Lyon par une reine burgonde de Genève (Theudelinde), la possession de ces terres alpines par les religieuses lyonnaises (ou du moins par l'*ecclesia Sancti Petri*), a priori incongrue, s'explique. L'hypothèse d'une fondation royale permet en outre de résoudre, au moins en principe, l'énigme de l'origine de l'imposant patrimoine de l'abbaye; elle permet de comprendre, enfin, le lien particulier d'Ennemond, évêque probablement issu d'une importante famille burgonde[40], avec la communauté. La citation du testament d'Abbon, toutefois, n'est pas sans poser problème[41], et je me limiterais pour l'instant à considérer l'idée d'une fondation royale burgonde comme une hypothèse à confirmer.

---

38 Sur le testament d'Abbon: G. Tabacco, *Dalla Novalesa a San Michele alla Chiusa*, dans: *Monasteri in alta Italia dopo le invasioni saracene e magiare, sec. X–XII.: Relazioni e comunicazioni presentate al XXXII Congresso storico subalpino [e al] III Convegno di storia della Chiesa in Italia. Pinerolo, 6–9 settembre 1964*, Torino 1966, 479–526 et E. Magnani, *Don aux églises et dons d'églises dans le sud-est de la Gaule: du testament d'Abbon (739) aux chartes du début du XIe siècle*, dans: F. Bougard / C. la Rocca / R. le Jan (éds.), *Sauver son âme et la perpétuer. Transmission du patrimoine et mémoire au Haut Moyen Âge*, Roma 2005, 379–400.

39 L. Ripart, *La Novalaise, les Alpes et la frontière (VIIIe–XIIe siècle)*, dans: F. Arneodo / P. Guglielmotti (éds.), *Attraverso le Alpi: S. Michele, Novalesa, S. Teofredo e altre reti monastiche*, Santo Spirito 2008, 95–114.

40 La loi Gombette cite un comte burgonde du nom d'Aunemundus. Voir R. Kaiser, *L'entourage des rois du regnum Burgundiae aux époques burgonde et mérovingienne*, dans: Kupper / Marchandisse (éds.), 2003.

41 *Galisiaca et alpes in Cinisio quem de ecclesia sancto Petro, de ipsa constructa Lugdunense, commutavimus*, dans L. Ripart, *La Novalaise, les Alpes et la frontière (VIIIe–XIIe siècle)*, dans Arneodo / Guglielmotti (éds.), 2008, 100; le manuscrit, BnF, lat. 13879 (Cartulaire de Saint-Hugues de Grenoble), est consultable en ligne sur le site https://gallica.bnf.fr/ark:/12148/bpt6k140097w.image on y trouvera la citation au f. 40v. La *Galisiaca* correspond à la Haute-Maurienne actuelle. Les *alpes* du Mont-Cenis forment l'ensemble des prairies naturelles permettant le passage de l'abbaye de Novalaise à la Maurienne.

Il nous reste donc à l'issue de ce parcours, assez peu de certitudes. Les contours de la fondation de la communauté des *puellae sancti Petri* demeurent brumeux, même si l'on peut pencher pour une fondation (au moins de l'église saint Pierre) au début du VIe siècle dans le contexte burgonde. Les documents apportent néanmoins une certitude: celle de l'importance acquise par l'abbaye Saint-Pierre dans le panorama lyonnais dès la première moitié du VIIIe siècle. Bien plus, Saint-Pierre fut probablement, aux VIIIe et IXe siècles[42], la seule abbaye féminine de la ville de Lyon, et très certainement l'une des plus puissantes communautés de la cité: seuls les chanoines de la cathédrale étaient supérieurs, en richesse et en pouvoir, aux *puellae Sancti Petri*. S'il est fort probable que la fondation réelle de la communauté des *puellae* fût en réalité plus ancienne, il s'agit néanmoins d'un moment que l'on peut qualifier de fondateur.

2   Des *Puellae* au *Dominae*: Richesse et Mode de Vie des Religieuses de Saint-Pierre

C'est dans la lettre de Leidrade, évêque de Lyon, à l'empereur Charlemagne, que la situation favorable de l'abbaye Saint-Pierre apparaît le plus clairement. Au IXe siècle, la renaissance carolingienne est une réalité pour l'ancienne capitale des Gaules. Leidrade, clerc originaire de Norique, est un proche de la cour impériale, et notamment d'Alcuin; il occupe le siège de Lyon de 798 à 814, date de sa renonciation et de sa retraite au monastère Saint-Médard de Soissons. Il faut donc dater du début du IXe siècle la lettre qu'il écrit à l'empereur pour lui rendre compte de la *renovatio* qu'il a accomplie dans le diocèse[43]. C'est dans les archives de l'abbaye Saint-Pierre qu'en est conservée la plus ancienne copie connue; la graphie permet de la dater de la fin du XIIe siècle ou du début du XIIIe siècle. Dans cette lettre, Leidrade informe l'empereur de ses travaux, y compris la restauration des établissements réguliers. Il y annonce notamment que:

> *Monasterium quoque puellarum in honorem Sancti Petri dedicatum ubi corpus Sancti Annemundi martiris humatum est. Ego, a fundamentis tam ecclesias quam*

---

42   Une autre abbaye de femmes, dédiée à sainte Eulalie, est mentionnée dans la lettre de l'évêque Leidrade à Charlemagne. Elle y est néanmoins décrite comme n'étant plus, à ce moment-là, une communauté existante. S'agit-il d'une communauté qui aurait précédé Saint-Pierre? C'est possible, en l'état des sources connues, rien ne permet de l'affirmer.

43   A. Coville, *Recherches sur l'Histoire de Lyon du Ve au IXe siècle (450–800)*, Paris 1928, 266 *et sq.*

domum restauravi cum sanctimoniales numero XXXII secundum institutionnem regularem viventes habitare videntur[44].

A l'extrait de la lettre présent dans les archives de Saint-Pierre, le copiste a ajouté un autre fragment de documentation carolingienne qu'il avait à sa disposition: il s'agit d'une liste des possessions des principales églises et abbayes lyonnaises – probablement celles qui étaient alors considérées comme royales. La structure de ce texte sans doute un peu postérieur à la lettre (années 820/30) correspond à celle d'autres brefs connus pour la même période, et qui répondaient probablement à la volonté de l'empereur de recenser les possessions des principales abbayes se trouvant sous son autorité[45]. D'après ce document, les possessions de Saint-Pierre sont, après celles des évêques et du chapitre cathédral, les plus importantes de la ville de Lyon. Seules trois abbayes de moines et de moniales sont citées dans ce bref (qui pourrait cependant avoir été tronqué par le copiste): outre Saint-Pierre, il s'agit des très anciennes abbayes de l'Ile-Barbe et de Saint-Rambert, toutes deux fondées au VIᵉ siècle. Leurs possessions sont toutefois moindres que celles des moniales. Or ces deux abbayes sont implantées loin, voire très loin, de la ville de Lyon[46]. Restent donc, à Lyon même, les "dames" sur la rive gauche de la Saône, et deux chapitres de chanoines, autour de l'archevêque, sur sa rive droite[47].

La prospérité et la puissance de l'abbaye ne se démentent pas par la suite. Ainsi, tandis que la lettre de Leidrade mentionne la présence de trente-deux moniales à Saint–Pierre, le *Liber* de Reichenau, rédigé vers 824, en nomme

---

44   Ibid. La partie *ubi ... humatum est* serait, selon Alfred Coville, un ajout postérieur, ce qui est tout à fait possible, puisque cette incise a rendu nécessaire l'usage du pronom *Ego*. Les manuscrits, toutefois, comportent tous la phrase suivante, plus longue: *... ubi corpus sancti Annemundi martyris humatum est, quod [monasterium] ipse sanctus martyr et episcopus instituit*. Il fait peu de doute que la partie *quod ... instituit* est une extrapolation, car il s'agit là encore d'une incise, mais aussi parce que la répétition du terme de *martyr* rend la phrase bancale. Il faut donc considérer que nous sommes face soit un ajout successif d'incises (la deuxième partie de l'extrapolation, concernant la fondation du monastère par Ennemond, ayant probablement été ajoutée lors de la rédaction de cette copie, soit à la fin du XIIᵉ–début du XIIIᵉ siècle), soit à une extrapolation qui ne concernerait que la seconde partie de l'incise (*quod ... instituit*) – ce qui ferait du témoignage de Leidrade sur la tombe d'Ennemond un élément capital.

45   Ainsi que le souligne Coville, *ibid.*

46   L'abbaye de l'Ile-Barbe, située sur une île de la Saône, se trouve à environ 6km de la ville historique. Quant à Saint-Rambert, s'il s'agit bien de l'abbaye de Saint-Rambert-en-Bugey, fondée au VIIᵉ siècle, elle se situe à une soixantaine de kilomètres de Lyon.

47   Reste à déterminer à quel moment l'abbaye d'Ainay fut fondée, d'emblée sous la protection du siège épiscopal, vraisemblablement au cours du IXᵉ siècle. Voir à ce sujet les contributions de l'ouvrage J.F. Reynaud / F. Richard (éds.), 2008.

une cinquantaine[48]. Il est intéressant de constater que l'abbaye lyonnaise y est citée en compagnie de celle de San Salvatore-Santa Giulia de Brescia, puissante abbaye de femmes fondée au milieu du VIIIe siècle par le roi lombard Desiderius. En 865, l'abbaye Saint-Pierre rénovée par Leidrade accueille la dépouille mortelle du roi Charles de Provence, ainsi que l'atteste un privilège donné par son frère Lothaire[49]. Ce privilège désigne l'abbaye comme le *monasterium quod est in veneratione beati Petri principis apostolorum inter ararum et Rhodanum situm, in burgo Lugdunensi.* Lothaire II y mentionne sa concubine Undrade, *amantissime coniugis nostrae Unadraddie,* ainsi que son frère Hugues[50]. Il donne à l'abbaye, où repose son frère Charles, des manses à Saint-Maximin[51]. Un autre privilège de la même époque, donné cette fois par Charles de Provence lui-même en faveur de l'abbaye des moines de l'Ile-Barbe est connu; toutefois, comme ce fut le cas deux siècles plus tôt avec l'évêque Bonnet, lui aussi en bons termes avec les moines de l'île, c'est l'abbaye des moniales qui est préférée pour sa sépulture[52].

Un seul acte, émis par Burchard, archevêque de Lyon, entre la fin du Xe et le début du XIe siècle, est connu pour illustrer cette période de la vie de l'abbaye. Il semble y être fait référence à la controverse qui opposa les moniales à la puissante abbaye d'hommes de Savigny[53]. La période suivante, celle des XIIe et XIIIe siècles, marque une sorte de nouvel apogée durant lequel la puissance des abbesses et des "dames" paraît incontestée, et où l'on voit que leur statut et leur mode de vie perdurent sans grand changement. Au cours du XIIe siècle,

---

48   Voir *supra* n. 5. On trouvera la page du document sur le site www.e-codices.unifr.ch. Les moniales sont citées au f. 61v. On trouve au f. 61r l'abbaye de l'Ile-Barbe, et au f. 62r celle de San Salvatore-Santa Giulia de Brescia.

49   Charles et Lothaire sont les frères de l'empereur Louis, mais aussi de Gisèle, abbesse de Brescia, voir T. Lazzari, *Una santa, una badessa, una principessa: Note di lettura sul capitello di santa Giulia nel museo di Brescia,* dans: Reti Medievali 20 (2019), 421–446.

50   AdR, 27H2. L'original n'est pas conservé.

51   Ce lieu n'a pas été identifié.

52   Il faut peut-être supposer l'existence d'un lien, au Haut Moyen Âge, entre l'Ile Barbe et Saint-Pierre. L'Ile Barbe est elle aussi mentionnée dans le *Liber Confraternitatum* à côté de l'abbaye Saint-Pierre; de plus, le parallèle entre saint Bonnet et Charles de Provence, tous deux lié à l'Ile Barbe de leur vivant mais enterrés à l'abbaye de femmes de Saint-Pierre, est intéressant. Enfin, l'obituaire du XIIIe siècle fait mémoire de Ponce, moine de l'Ile-Barbe qui devint prieur de Firmini (prieuré dépendant de l'abbaye de l'Ile-Barbe), *familiarus noster bone memorie* (M.C. Guigue [éd.], *Obituaire de l'Abbaye de Saint-Pierre de Lyon du IXe au XVe siècle,* Lyon 1880, 61). Aucune date n'est évidemment mentionnée; le manuscrit montre toutefois qu'il s'agit d'un ajout par rapport à la première rédaction (peut-être fin XIIIe siècle?).

53   *Cartulaire lyonnais* 1,14. Sur ce sujet, voir aussi J. Picot, *L'Abbaye Saint-Pierre de Lyon,* Paris 1970, 27.

l'abbesse Rolinde fait rebâtir l'église Saint-Pierre, dont il reste aujourd'hui un morceau de la façade[54]; on ne sait si la restauration de l'église paroissiale de Saint-Saturnin a lieu au même moment[55]. Le quartier est de plus en plus peuplé, et l'érection d'une nouvelle paroisse à côté de celle dont les moniales ont le patronage donne matière à un conflit arbitré par l'archevêque, dans les années 1130–1150. Il s'agit alors de donner les limites précises de la juridiction des moniales sur un quartier s'étendant au-delà des murs d'enceinte de la ville de Lyon, des pentes de la Croix-Rousse au nord aux rives du Rhône à l'est, mais non pas jusqu'à la Saône à l'ouest. La nouvelle paroisse limitrophe est confiée aux chanoines de Saint-Ruf, installés dans l'église Sainte-Marie, préexistante. Les documents liés à l'arbitrage nous montrent l'abbesse Oda et ses religieuses se rendant, en compagnie des chanoines, leurs opposants, et des représentants de l'archevêque, dans les rues du quartier pour effectuer les délimitations par le biais de témoignages d'habitants[56]. L'installation d'autres chanoines dans l'église (préexistante elle aussi, bien sûr) de Saint-Nizier en 1305 sera l'occasion d'un nouveau conflit dont nous avons déjà parlé: on voit bien ici que ce qui est en jeu à chaque fois, c'est l'influence et le pouvoir des communautés sur un quartier en plein essor aussi bien du point de vue de la population que des activités commerciales. La gestion de la paroisse de Saint-Pierre-et-Saint-Saturnin donnait lieu à la répartition des droits paroissiaux, notamment sur les sépultures, entre les moniales et l'abbesse, ainsi que l'atteste un document composite des premières années du XIVe siècle et dont la rédaction en franco-provençal suggère qu'il était à l'usage direct des moniales, et peut-être écrit par elles[57].

Outre les églises de Saint-Pierre (abbatiale) et Saint-Saturnin (paroissiale), d'autres chapelles et églises étaient rattachées à l'abbaye; toutes se trouvaient dans le nord de la Presqu'île (entre Saône et Rhône, aux pieds de la colline de la Croix-Rousse): la recluserie de Saint-Clair[58], dont les moniales nommaient l'occupant (reclus ou recluse) et le desservant; les chapelles de Saint-Côme-et-Damien et de Saint-Claude. Cet ensemble formait ainsi un réseau de sanctuaires qui, dans un même quartier, étaient tous rattachés aux Dames de Saint-Pierre. En outre, l'hôpital Sainte-Catherine, l'un des principaux

---

54   Actuelle rue Paul Chenavard (ancienne rue Saint-Pierre).

55   C'est l'avis de J. Picot (Picot, 1970, 30).

56   M. Rubellin, *Église et société chrétienne d'Agobard à Valdès*, Lyon 2003 (troisième partie, premier chapitre): l'auteur donne une traduction de ce précieux document.

57   AdR, 27H409. On trouvera une transcription de ce document dans *Obituaire*, Appendice, 83–91.

58   Celle de Saint-Clair, rattachée à l'église Saint-Irénée-du-Rhône, sur laquelle le fonds de Saint-Pierre aux AdR dispose d'une documentation abondante.

hôpitaux médiévaux de Lyon, est fondé en 1259 sur les terres de l'abbaye[59]. La description que l'historien Coville fait des nombreuses processions qui se déroulaient dans le quartier, ainsi que des célébrations où les religieuses étaient présentes, aussi bien dans l'église paroissiale de Saint-Saturnin que dans l'église abbatiale de Saint-Pierre, au milieu du peuple, est suggestive[60]. De même, la majesté que l'abbesse déployait dans ses apparitions publiques est attestée au moins depuis le XIIe siècle, date à laquelle l'archevêque de Lyon Jean de Bellesme lui accorda le droit d'avoir à son service personnel permanent quatre hommes (un prévôt, un cuisinier, un pontonnier et un homme d'armes)[61]; l'abbesse se déplaçait, ainsi que le confirment des descriptions du XVe siècle, en compagnie des hommes se trouvant à son service, crosse à la main.

Plus largement, la richesse des religieuses leur donnait une place stratégique au sein du réseau féodal des grandes familles de la région. Ainsi que l'attestent les documents, l'importance de leur patrimoine faisait d'elles non plus de simples *puellae*, mais bien des *dominae*. L'immense fonds d'archives de l'abbaye reste pour une bonne part à explorer; qu'il me soit permis, pour lors, d'en donner un aperçu rapide dans les lignes qui suivent, et de renvoyer le lecteur à la minutieuse étude de Joseph Picot sur la gestion de leur patrimoine par celles qui sont désormais, à partir du XIIe–XIIIe siècle, les "dames de Saint-Pierre". Les possessions urbaines de l'abbaye se composaient de maisons dans la zone des Terreaux, mais aussi de droits sur le pontonnage (traversées de la Saône et du Rhône) et de divers péages dans la zone, notamment sur les ports fluviaux. La puissance de l'abbesse reposait non seulement sur cette assise urbaine, mais aussi sur de vastes possessions dans la région qui, à partir du XIIe siècle, étaient gouvernées par l'intermédiaire d'un réseau d'une douzaine de prieurés dépendant de l'abbesse de Lyon, mais administrés *in loco* par des prieures. Celles-ci, tout en ayant voix au chapitre de l'abbaye, ne s'y rendaient guère, si l'on se fie aux descriptions liées à la réforme du XVIe siècle, et commandaient donc sur "leurs" terres de manière relativement indépendante – ce qui a pu, au cours de l'histoire de l'abbaye, occasionner des conflits entre les prieures et

---

59 J. Picot, *Moniales bénédictines et œuvres hospitalières. Les 'dames' de Saint–Pierre de Lyon et l'hôpital Sainte-Catherine*, dans P. Guichard / M.T. Lorcin / J.M. Poisson (éds.), *Papauté, monachisme et théories politiques*, Lyon 1994, 755–762.

60 A. Coville, *Une visite de l'abbaye de Saint-Pierre de Lyon en 1503*, Lyon 1912. Coville s'appuie, pour ses descriptions, principalement sur les rapports de visites effectuées au moment de la réforme de l'abbaye.

61 *Cartulaire Lyonnais*, tome 1, 84. Il s'agit en fait apparemment d'une confirmation d'un état de fait: l'archevêque accorde à l'abbesse la possibilité de nommer ces hommes et il leur accorde l'immunité.

l'abbesse[62]. Ce système permettait aux lignages aristocratiques du Lyonnais et des régions environnantes de placer leurs filles dans une situation qui n'était pas une simple alternative au mariage: il s'agissait d'une réelle source de pouvoir. Les religieuses professes n'ont, semble-t-il, jamais été très nombreuses avant la réforme de 1503; leur faible nombre renforçait leur pouvoir et surtout leur richesse. Outre l'abbesse et les prieures, les "simples" religieuses professes disposaient en effet de prébendes accordées par l'abbesse, dans l'entourage de laquelle elles se trouvaient placées, en attendant (pour les plus jeunes) de pouvoir prétendre à des prieurés, ou à des offices importants à Lyon même (sacristine, prieure claustrale). L'abbaye jouait donc peu ou prou le rôle d'un chapitre noble, tel qu'il en existait bien d'autres dans les terres d'Empire. Aux XIIe et XIIIe siècle, l'abbaye était liée en particulier aux familles des comtes de Forez puis des comtes de Savoie, dans le cadre d'une rivalité qui, en réalité, n'était que le reflet de la concurrence que ces deux familles se livraient pour la domination sur le Lyonnais. Le comte de Savoie, à partir du milieu du XIIIe siècle, rendait régulièrement et ostensiblement hommage à l'abbesse de Lyon pour le fief de La-Tour-du-Pin: les abbesses étaient alors pour la plupart issues de sa maison. L'un de ces hommages, d'ailleurs, eut lieu directement au château de Chillon, en 1279, où l'abbesse Agathe de Genève, cousine du comte, séjournait[63]. Il ne faut donc pas considérer que le rattachement de Lyon à la France en 1312 fut un épisode périphérique pour l'histoire de notre abbaye, alors si intimement liée à la famille de Savoie et au monde féodal local. De même, la création du pouvoir municipal (conseil des échevins) en 1320 marqua l'avènement définitif d'une nouvelle répartition des pouvoirs à Lyon, bouleversant l'ancien monde dont les dames faisaient partie. Le XIVe siècle marque donc le début de la parabole "descendante" de l'abbaye et de la contestation, non seulement de la puissance des "dames", mais aussi de leur mode de vie.

Les *puellae*, plus tard dénommées *dominae* suivaient-elles, au juste, la règle bénédictine? Au XIIIe siècle la puissance de l'abbesse et des dames est solide. La tenue de deux conciles œcuméniques à Lyon, en 1245 et en 1274, ainsi que la résidence du pape Innocent IV à Lyon entre 1244 et 1251 ne firent que confirmer cet état de fait. Les dames obtinrent en effet de la part du pape différents privilèges qui confirmèrent leur qualité d'abbaye exempte, et conférèrent à leurs biens la protection pontificale[64]. Il est un aspect, toutefois, qui ne manque pas d'attirer l'attention: dans chacune de ses bulles, le pontife rappelle l'appartenance des moniales à l'*ordo Sancti Benedicti*, et leur observance

---

62   Ibid. 193.
63   *Cartulaire Lyonnais* 1, 442.
64   *Cartulaire Lyonnais* 1, 493, 577, 580–582.

de la règle. C'est en soi une nouveauté: aucun document connu (pour lors) ne mentionne l'appartenance de l'abbaye à l'*ordo sancti Benedicti* avant cette période. Leidrade avait mentionné, dans sa lettre, vers 800, la restauration de la discipline régulière dans l'abbaye en même temps que celle des bâtiments: rien ne prouve, toutefois, à cette date reculée, que les moniales aient été bénédictines[65]. L'un des privilèges, donné par Innocent IV, en 1251, attire particulièrement l'attention: il interdit "que quiconque prétende changer l'habit de l'ordre (*religio*) dans lequel les religieuses ont fait profession, et l'état du monastère dans lequel elles vivent depuis des temps immémoriaux (*a tempore cujus memoria non existit*)". Le terme de *religio* semble ici se référer à la règle de Saint-Benoît. Or, si l'on considère qu'il n'existe justement aucune mémoire de l'obédience bénédictine des religieuses, auparavant décrites comme des *puellae*, et que celles-ci, au milieu du XIIIe siècle, vivaient ouvertement comme des chanoinesses (sans toutefois jamais se considérer comme telles), que signifie exactement ce privilège? Le pape protège-t-il les moniales, dans le mode de vie qu'elles mènent effectivement (à savoir un mode de vie qui ne prévoit ni la clôture ni la communauté de biens), ou bien s'agit-il d'une sorte de rappel à l'ordre, en un temps où la régularisation des monastères de femmes est l'une des grandes affaires de la papauté? Quoi qu'il en soit, il s'agit d'un rappel discret – Innocent IV ne pouvait guère, de toute façon, se permettre de froisser le comte de Savoie alors qu'il se trouvait à Lyon – le pape ayant par ailleurs garanti aux moniales une protection juridique et patrimoniale très étendue.

Ainsi, tandis que l'abbesse se comportait à tous égards comme une *domina*, disposant d'officiers à son service, tenant une cour de justice en son logis et se déplaçant en des voyages qui pouvaient la mener fort loin, au gré des besoins de la gestion de ses domaines et, peut-être, de son propre agrément, les prieures, nous l'avons dit, résidaient en leurs prieurés où, sans doute à une échelle moindre, mais selon les mêmes habitudes, elles menaient une vie de grandes dames. Point de communauté de biens, donc, ni de clôture. En ce qui concerne la clôture, aucun document médiéval n'en fait état, et le contraire, à vrai dire, eût été étonnant, puisque cette norme, au sens strict du terme, est une nouveauté du XIIIe siècle[66]. L'absence de communauté de biens, et même de communauté de vie, comme le démontrera la visite exécutée en 1503 (pas

---

65   Voir *supra*. Leidrade parle de *sanctimoniales*, ce qui ne permet pas de déterminer si elles suivaient ou non la règle de saint Benoît. Sur ce sujet, voir S. Vanderputten, *Dark Age Nunneries: The Ambiguous Identity of Female Monasticism*, Ithaca 2018.

66   La clôture bénédictine impose aux religieux de ne pas sortir de l'abbaye excepté pour certaines nécessités. La "stricte" clôture, qui interdit radicalement toute sortie et toute entrée et ne concerne que les femmes, change le sens de cette norme traditionnelle. Voir S. Duval, *Discourses on Religious Women's Enclosure: A Gendered Perspective (Thirteenth to Sixteenth*

de réfectoire ni de dortoir, mais des maisons individuelles), est bien plus problématique: cet état de fait a probablement suivi, néanmoins, des variations difficilement mesurables au cours du temps, en particulier suite aux évolutions dans la gestion de leur immense patrimoine de la part des moniales, mais aussi en réaction à la croissance urbaine dans les alentours immédiats de l'abbaye, et à la gestion des droits et revenus issus de ce quartier.

Les liens des moniales avec leur quartier sont intenses, et l'obituaire fait d'ailleurs état de nombreuses "possibilités" de se consacrer à Dieu au sein de l'abbaye: si les religieuses professes y sont fréquemment appelées, de manière révélatrice (la rédaction de l'obituaire se situe dans les mêmes années que la promulgation des bulles d'Innocent IV), *monachae* ou *moniales*, nombreuses sont aussi les mentions de *puellae* (terme utilisé depuis les origines du monastère). On trouve aussi de nombreuses mentions de *laichae* mais aussi, au masculin, de *laici*, ou encore de *conversae* et de *conversi* et, enfin, de quelques *deodicatae*. L'obituaire laisse ainsi transparaître non seulement la hiérarchie interne de la communauté, mais aussi ses interactions avec le quartier qui l'abritait. Il était en effet possible non seulement (pour les femmes issues de familles nobles) de devenir moniales, mais aussi, pour les femmes (et les hommes) des classes sociales modestes, de se consacrer à Dieu dans l'entourage des religieuses, telles les *deodicatae*, et peut-être certaines *puellae*, si l'on accepte l'idée que le terme ait pu changer de sens au XIIIe siècle[67]. L'obituaire rend aussi concrètement visible l'étendue des relations des moniales avec le monde laïc et avec d'autres communautés religieuses: on y trouve nommés, côte-à-côte, d'illustres représentants des familles comtales, de nombreux clercs lyonnais, mais aussi d'humbles habitants du quartier, dont le lien avec les religieuses (par une donation mais aussi du fait d'une existence passée à leur service) leur a valu de pouvoir figurer dans le livre des prières[68]. Les documents dont nous disposons ne nous permettent pas de supposer, en revanche, l'existence d'une participation active des moniales à la grande procession de la Fête des Merveilles, qui se tenait début juin, en l'honneur des martyrs lyonnais, et où les représentants des grandes églises de la ville défilaient en grand apparat, devant

---

Centuries), dans: C. Andenna / M. Standke-Hart (éds.): *Gendered Discourses in the Middle Ages* (en cours de publication).

67   Les *puellae* semblent alors être les novices. La question reste néanmoins ouverte.

68   Voici, pour exemple, le paragraphe correspondant au 9 des calendes de mai (23 avril): *Obiit Restabilia, puella, et Prisca, laica. Obiit Petrus, cocus bone memorie, anno Domini M°C-C°XXX°VII°. Obiit Arembergis, uxor Guigonis Artaudi; soror Alys, abbatisse et monacha Sancti Petri, que dedit pro anniversario suo conventui Sancti Petri X libras viennensium bone memorie.* Obituaire de l'abbaye Saint-Pierre, Fonds Coste de la Bibliothèque municipale de Lyon, ms. 1308, f. 4r. Et *Obituaire*, éd. M.C. Guigue, cit., 13.

la foule de fidèles, et se terminait à Saint-Nizier[69]. Les moniales, cependant – si tant est qu'elles n'y aient pas participé avant la mise par écrit de ces coutumes, qui décrivent seulement les usages de la deuxième moitié du XIVe siècle – se "rattrapaient" très probablement pour la fête de Saint-Ennemond, célébrée en septembre, devant la multitude du peuple. Un acte de 1255 la décrit: cette description correspond aux processions évoquées lors du procès qui opposera les religieuses aux chanoines de Saint-Nizier en 1307–1308 et que je citai plus haut, qui comprenaient aussi l'ostension des reliques au peuple[70]. En 1255, les moniales adressèrent une plainte aux clercs desservant l'église de Saint-Nizier qui, déjà, prétendaient que l'évêque Ennemond reposait dans leur église. Par l'intermédiaire de son procureur, l'abbesse de Saint-Pierre fit alors valoir au juge du tribunal ecclésiastique que ...

> ... quod cum corpus beati Augnemondi martiris, Lugdudensi quondam archiepis-copi, fundatoris dicti monasterii, in earumdem monasterio requiescat, publica fama ac communi opinione fortiter hoc etiam testimonium perhibente, et ad idem monasterium, ob reverenciam ejusdem martiris, confluere consueverit morbum caducum patientium et aliorum fidelium multitudo, in vigilia et festivitate dicti martiris annuatim, et ibidem oblationes facere consueverint [...].

Si cette affaire de 1255 ne semble pas avoir eu de suite, telle n'est pas le cas du procès de 1307–1308, auquel il a été fait référence plus haut. Celui-ci se prolon-gea en effet jusqu'au cœur du XVe siècle. Par la remise en question du culte d'Ennemond dans l'abbaye, ce procès entama durablement la réputation des religieuses, en touchant au cœur de leur relation avec leurs paroissiens et avec leur quartier, et aux origines mêmes de leur communauté, telles que les reli-gieuses les vantaient "depuis des temps immémoriaux". Cette attaque prépara le terrain pour l'offensive décisive des pouvoirs laïcs et séculiers qui aboutit au début du XVIe siècle à la réforme radicale de l'abbaye.

Au–delà de ce contexte local, le XIVe siècle est une période négative pour les abbayes et les communautés religieuses de femmes, aussi bien du fait de l'Église que de la société laïque. Le contexte politique, ainsi que je le disais plus haut, n'est alors pas favorables aux dames de Saint-Pierre, du fait de la perte d'influence de la famille de Savoie sur la ville de Lyon; notons d'ailleurs que non seulement Louis de Villars se montra plutôt favorable au rattachement de Lyon au royaume de France; mais qu'en outre, l'église Saint-Nizier, siège du chapitre faisant querelle aux moniales, était devenue depuis le XIIIe siècle un

---

69   Voir J. Rossiaud, *La Fête des Merveilles*, dans: J.F. Reynaud / F. Richard (*éds.*), *L'Abbaye d'Ai-nay des origines au XIIe siècle*, Lyon 2008, 33–50.

70   *Supra*, en particulier n. 26.

point de ralliement du pouvoir bourgeois naissant à Lyon[71]; un pouvoir qui ne pouvait considérer la puissance féodale des dames que de façon négative. Mais l'Église ne fut pas en reste. La décrétale *Periculoso*, promulguée par le pape Boniface VIII en 1298, établit définitivement l'obligation de la clôture pour toutes les religieuses professes. On a généralement sous-estimé la portée d'une telle mesure qui, de fait, équivalait à interdire la présence des religieuses dans l'espace public, en contradiction avec de nombreux usages traditionnels. Dans le cas des moniales de Saint-Pierre, cette norme s'opposait aussi bien à l'exercice de leur pouvoir féodal (hommages reçus, cour de justice, et plus généralement simple présence des dames sur leurs terre) qu'aux nombreux rites religieux locaux auxquels elles prenaient part dans leurs quartier (processions, prières avec le peuple dans les églises abbatiale et, paroissiale, etc.). A vrai dire, il ne semble pas que les religieuses de Saint-Pierre aient fondamentalement modifié leurs habitudes à la suite de la décrétale, comme du reste bon nombre d'abbayes au XIVe siècle[72]. Les événements postérieurs démontreront néanmoins qu'il ne s'agissait que d'un sursis: le mode de vie des moniales, qui tenait si peu compte de la clôture, était dès lors devenu une exception à la règle, et par conséquent susceptible à tout moment de tomber sous le coup d'une condamnation canonique ou simplement morale. L'enquête de 1305 sur la sépulture de saint Ennemond fait indirectement référence à cet état de fait: les religieuses, par l'intermédiaire de leur procurateur, s'y font en effet désigner avec constance par l'expression *coenobium puellarum*, en décalage visible avec l'utilisation traditionnelle, dans tous les documents jusqu'alors, du terme de *monasterium*, et avec une reprise ostensible du terme traditionnel de *puella* tandis que, nous l'avons vu, les documents du XIIIe siècle avaient introduit (bulles et obituaire) le terme de *monialis/monaca*. Il s'agit–là probablement d'une volonté de la part des religieuses de se distancier de la clôture imposée par la *Periculoso* qui assigne les *moniales* à la clôture: on retrouve des phénomènes similaires de résistance à la clôture dans d'autres régions au même moment[73].

---

71   M. Rubellin, *Église et société chrétienne d'Agobard à Valdès*, Lyon 2003 (troisième partie).

72   Sur ce sujet, voir E. Makowski, *Canon Law and Cloistered Women: Periculoso and its Commentators, 1298–1545*, Washington 1997.

73   Les premières années du XIVe siècle voient certaines archevêques répercuter efficacement dans leur diocèse les normes imposées par la *Periculoso*. C'est notamment le cas à Milan. Certaines religieuses refusent alors d'être appelées "moniales", voir N. Taglietti, Dicte priora et sorores non sint moniales nec earum monasterium appellatur. *La domus milanese delle Umiliate tra XII e XIV secolo*, dans: ASL 12 (1998–1999), 11–112; S. Duval, *Vierges et dames blanches. Communautés religieuses féminines à Milan, XIIe–XIVe siècles*, dans: Revue Mabillon.NS 31 (2020), 81–107.

Désormais, toutefois, la partie était perdue: aux transformations du contexte lyonnais, s'ajoutèrent comme partout les crises du XIVe siècle et, au–delà, la montée en puissance de l'Observance, auquel bien peu d'établissements réguliers purent échapper[74]. Au moment où la réforme, en 1503, frappa Saint–Pierre, la communauté possédait encore tous ses biens et, en apparence du moins, son antique puissance. Elle était toutefois désormais sous la coupe d'une seule famille noble, les Albon, qui n'eurent pas assez d'appuis pour résister à la volonté royale. La réforme, fut imposée "par le haut", par les rois et reines de France[75], ainsi que par l'archevêque François de Rohan. Pour reprendre les termes mélancoliques d'Alfred Coville à la fin du pittoresque opuscule qu'il consacra à cet événement, ce fut alors "la fin de l'ancienne et originale abbaye de Saint–Pierre". Les religieuses furent expulsées, et remplacées par d'autres femmes issues de monastères déjà réformés, mais aussi de familles bien moins puissantes et donc plus dociles.

C'est alors que le spectre de la jeune religieuse Alix de Theizé se mit à hanter l'abbaye. Alix était une religieuse plutôt libre de mœurs, qui n'accepta pas la réforme. Après une vie de souffrances qui fit suite à son expulsion de l'abbaye, elle revint, dit–on, hanter l'abbaye sous forme de spectre, jusqu'à que son corps fût enterré à l'intérieur de la clôture: les apparitions, dès lors, cessèrent. L'histoire ressemble fort à un *exemplum* destiné à appuyer le bien–fondé de la réforme érigée sur l'antique fondation de Saint–Pierre: Alix, représentante d'un mode de vie frappé d'infâmie, se soumit elle–même (mais après sa mort) à la vertueuse clôture, désormais garante d'une vie sage, vertueuse, mais aussi bien plus discrète. Les dames, néanmoins, n'avaient pas dit leur dernier mot et elles élevèrent, par un ultime acte d'orgueil qui devait leur survivre, l'actuel Palais-saint-Pierre, face à l'Hôtel-de-Ville.

---

74   Voir S. Duval / H. Morvan / L. Viallet, *Les Observances régulières: Historiographies. Introduction*, MEFRM 2018 (130–132): https://journals.openedition.org/mefrm/4182.

75   Le "problème" de l'abbaye Saint-Pierre paraît en effet être devenu une affaire d'Etat au début du XVIe siècle, puisque le roi a même recours à des arrêts du parlement de Paris. La reine Claude et la régente Louise de Savoie son citée dans la bulle de 1516 permettant la réforme; de même que la reine Anne de Bretagne. Voir *Obituaire*, p. XXVII–XXVIII.

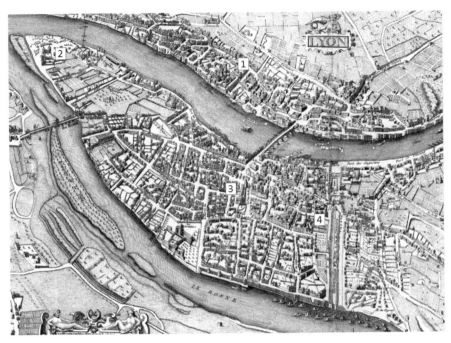

Fig. 6.1

Figure

Fig. 6.1 Lyon dans la première moitié du XVIe siècle, d'après le *Plan scéno-graphique de la ville de Lyon sous les règnes de François Ier et Henri II*, par M. Moithey, Paris, vers 1550 (ici plan réduit). 1. Le quartier de la cathédrale; 2. L'abbaye d'Ainay; 3. L'église Saint-Nizier; 4. L'abbaye Saint-Pierre.

The King Away from Court, the Queen in His Place
Castile, 12th–15th Centuries

Diana Pelaz Flores

Abstract

The king's obligations in his territories could lead the queen to assume functions not just of representation, but also of government. Although the institution of the lieutenancy is not formulated in the Crown of Castile, this paper will study the behaviour and political responsibility of the queen, through the moments in which the court dissociated itself from the king.

Introduction

The court is the "place where the king is, and his vassals and officials with him" according to the definition established by Alfonso X in *Las Partidas*.[1] Consequently, the court is presented as a constantly shifting stage around the monarch. This situation can affect the queen, because her movements often follow those of the sovereign. However, the queen also has her own court, made up of all the people who are in her service or those who come to petition her or meet with her.[2] The queen's court could be integrated into the king's court when the royal couple were in the same place.

Despite the words of Alfonso X, the displacement of the entire court was not always convenient. The king could be absent while hunting, on a pilgrimage, or at war. At such times it was preferable to establish the court in a place close to the royal figure or, at least, to the figure who represented the government of the kingdom. The queen could exercise these functions, particularly when the king's dedication to other matters was prolonged. This was

---

* This work was supported by "Espacios femeninos cortesanos: Ámbitos curiales, relaciones territoriales y prácticas políticas" [Lead Researcher: Diana Pelaz Flores, PGC2018-099205-A-C22], a research project funded by the Spanish Ministry of Science and Innovation, the Agencia Estatal de Investigación, and the European Regional Development Fund.

1 *Las Partidas del rey Alfonso X de Castilla*, Real Academia de la Historia (ed.), Madrid 1807, vol. II, Partida Segunda, Título IX, Ley XXVII, 82–83.
2 L. Ruiz Domingo, *El Tresor de la Reina. Recursos i gestió económica de les reines consorts a la Corona d'Aragó (segles XIV–XV)*, Barcelona 2022.

an effective division of roles in the social fabric of the Middle Ages, as conceptualised by Heide Wunder.[3] She defined the existence of a "working couple" in which the woman actively participated in the family business, in harmony and communication with her husband, a reality that can be extrapolated to different social strata and historical moments.[4] The representative and symbolic contribution provided by the queen stimulates the diversification of the image of the monarchy, whether due to the absence of the king, to political needs in distant places, or to the rhetorical connotation of the figure of the queen. The construction of the queen's image establishes her as a natural interlocutor with the monarch. She has sufficient capacity for action to be able to represent the interests of the monarchy and to act on its behalf: she is both a channel of communication and an authority in her own right in understanding the policy implications and making decisions that work for all parties.

This paper seeks to address the episodes that could have triggered a lieutenancy by the women of the Castilian royal family. The rhetorical formulas and some of the displacement patterns of the kings will be key elements of analysis. Not only will it consider the figure of the queen consort, but also her status as a mother and as a sister. This will deepen the knowledge of the bases of queenly power and the interweaving of a collective experience of female collaboration with the figure of the sovereign. It may not have been fully institutionalised, but it does have a solid customary basis, present in the memory of the kingdom and in the interpretation of the queenly political identity.

1   "[She] Walked the Land in the King's Stead"

The lieutenancy refers to an institution whereby the holder of a political and legal responsibility – the king, in our case – relinquishes his functions for a period of time, which is not always limited. The physical absence of the sovereign from his territories highlights the need to appoint a representative capable of continuing the political management and, moreover, the opportunity it represents for the queen. Although it is the king's prerogative, the lieutenancy cannot be entrusted to a person who is distant from the sovereign, neither in terms of family ties nor in terms of rank. There is no rule that the queen must assume the position of lieutenant, but it is a responsibility afforded to her at

---

3   H. Wunder, *He is the Sun, She is the Moon: Women in Early Modern Germany*, Cambridge 1998.
4   L. Oliván Santaliestra, *Por una historia diplomática de las mujeres en la Edad Moderna*, in: H. Gallego Franco / Mª del C. García Herrero (eds.), *Autoridad, poder e influencia: mujeres que hacen Historia*, Barcelona 2017, vol. 1, 61–77.

the king's pleasure. Other members of the royal family may eventually assume this position. However, the consistency of the bond they share through marriage favours the queen consort. Just as her itineraries are constructed in an interconnected manner and in clear dialogue, the queen helps the monarchy to diversify its presence in the kingdom.

The Mediterranean policy undertaken by the Crown of Aragon in the latter centuries of the Middle Ages encouraged the institutionalisation of the lieutenancy, and the leading role played by the queens in this respect. Eleanor of Sicily, r. 1349–1375,[5] Maria de Luna, r. 1372–1406,[6] and Maria of Castile, r. 1416–1458[7] demonstrated their skills in political management. Given the king's constant presence in the Castilian-Leonese territory during the medieval period, the lieutenancy does not seem to have been necessary. Only Alfonso X left the kingdom to attend the audiences with Pope Gregory X in Beaucaire, when he was preparing to assert the legitimacy of his rights to the imperial throne.[8] The possibility of having asserted the lieutenancy might not have led to the handing over of that responsibility to Violant of Aragon, but to the first-born, the *infante* Ferdinand.[9] However, it is worth considering the possibility that the lieutenancy could have been associated with specific undertakings or shorter periods of time.

The lieutenancy, understood as the responsibility that is assumed "in place of" another person in function of their office, must be understood in a more literal sense, according to which the king delegates his authority. The coincidence of the formula used in the Aragonese chancellery ("del qual tenim lloch") and its use in Castilian historiographical sources ("in the king's stead") suggests the existence of the same semantic interpretation, even if institutionalisation is only achieved in the first case. Francisco J. Hernández noted this circumstance in relation to the memory of the queen mother's actions, mentioned by

5   L. Ruiz Domingo, *Del qual tenim lloch. Leonor de Sicilia y el origen de la lugartenencia femenina en la Corona de Aragón*, in: Medievalismo. Boletín de la Sociedad Española de Estudios Medievales 27 (2017), 303–326.

6   J. Planas, *La paz de las plegarias: lecturas religiosas de la reina María de Luna*, in: e-Spania: Revue interdisciplinaire d'études hispaniques médiévales et modernes 20 (2015), (doi: https://doi.org/10.4000/e-spania.24155).

7   Mª del C. García Herrero, *María de Castilla, reina de Aragón (1416–1458)*: La mediación incansable, in: e-Spania. Revue interdisciplinaire d'études hispaniques médiévales et modernes 20 (2015), (https://doi.org/10.4000/e-spania.24120).

8   *Crónica de Alfonso X. Crónicas de los reyes de Castilla*, ed. Cayetano Rosell, Madrid 1875, ch. LIX, 47.

9   D. Pelaz Flores, *Reinas consortes. Las reinas de Castilla en la Edad Media*, Madrid 2017, 254–255.

Sancho IV years later.[10] Queen Violant's collaboration in the resolution of the conspiracy of the Cordoban nobles against Alfonso X, again acting on behalf of the king, insisted on this approach.

To travel the land "in place of the king" alludes to the reasons that justify the displacement of the sovereign. Since the queen's travels run parallel to those of her husband,[11] the substitution of the king refers to the tasks that he performs. Both the *Partidas*[12] and the *Cuadernos de Cortes*[13] link the usefulness of the royal journey to an awareness of the state of the kingdom.[14] The circumstances allude to the maintenance of royal jurisdiction and, consequently, to the act of dispensing justice.[15] However, the expression "in place of the king" can be linked to those moments when the sovereign hands over his authority to the queen to represent his interests. The queen becomes the king's interlocutor, but she is not a mere ambassador; queenly authority is used to obtain benefits or to quell revolts. When the monarch is part of the confrontation, it is necessary to find a figure with sufficient rhetorical backing and authority to intervene. Her attachment to the body politic of the monarchy places the queen at the epicentre of the action;[16] when the sovereign has to leave the daily business of

---

10 At the beginning of Sancho IV's reign: "el obispo [...] mostróme una sentencia [...] é por mandado del Rey, é de la Reyna mi madre, que andaba enton en logar del Rey por la tierra" (M. Risco, *España Sagrada. Tomo XXXV. Memorias de la Santa Iglesia esenta de León*, Madrid 1786, 454). According to the document, the king had to approach Leon after its proclamation and deliver the *Fuero Juzgo* ("después que yo fu Rey que llegué primeramente à León, fallé en verdad por D. Martin Fernandez, Obispo, é por el Cabillo [...] que los Reis que fueron ante de mí acostumbraron à dar el Libro Juzgo à una Persona, ò canónigo de la Iglesia de León"). F.J. Hernández, *La reina Violante de Aragón, Jofré de Loaysa y la Crónica de Alfonso X. Un gran fragmento cronístico del siglo XIII reutilizado en el XIV*, in: Journal of Medieval Iberian Studies 7 (2015), 99.

11 D. Pelaz Flores, *La lluna darrere el Sol? Ritmes de la itinerancia de les reines a la Corona de Castella (ca. 1252–1474)*, in: Recerques 81 (2022), 107–127.

12 *Las Partidas*, Partida Segunda, Título IX, Ley XXII, 77–78.

13 *Cortes de los antiguos reinos de León y de Castilla*, Real Academia de la Historia (ed.), Madrid 1883, vol. 1, 410.

14 A.I. Carrasco Manchado, *Desplazamientos e intentos de estabilización: la corte de los Trastámara*, in: e-Spania. Revue interdisciplinaire d'études hispaniques médiévales et modernes 8 (2009) (doi: https://doi.org/10.4000/e-spania.18876).

15 For example, Pedro de Ávila held these functions in the city of Ávila during the reign of the Catholic Monarchs: "Pedro de Ávila tiene ocupada la juredición de la dicha cibdad de Ávyla e su justicia en logar del rey e de la reyna" (VVAA, *Documentación medieval abulense en el Registro General del Sello: 31-I-1490 a 20-XII-1491*, Ávila 1993, 107).

16 T. Earenfight, *The King's Other Body: María of Castile and the Crown of Aragon*, Philadelphia 2010. D. Pelaz Flores *"Reynante(s) en vno". Fundamentación teórica del poder de la pareja regia en la Corona de Castilla durante la Baja Edad Media*, in: AEM 48 (2018), 845–869.

government to fight against the enemies of the Christian faith, she effectively becomes "the king's other body".

2 Duplicating the King's Body: on the Frontier and in His Kingdoms

Beyond the internal problems in the kingdom, the fight against Islam meant a distancing from political action, the nobility and the population. The preparation and maintenance of military campaigns resulted in the physical distancing of the king and his inability to "go about the kingdom doing justice". The queens Sancha of Leon, r. 1037–1067, and Berengaria of Castile, r. 1217–1246, supported the military ventures of their husband and son, respectively, and continued to manage the territory. Both are unique examples, being both queens consort, but also queens with undisputed rights to rule in their own name at the same time. Queen Sancha was heir to her father, King Alfonso V of Leon, after the death of her brother, King Bermudo III of Leon at the Battle of Tamarón (1037). In turn, Queen Berengaria renounced the government of the Crown of Castile to avoid the interference of King Alfonso IX of Leon, who had been her husband until the marriage was declared null and void due to the forbidden kinship between the spouses.[17]

The connection between the example of both queens and those of Maria de Molina and Catalina of Lancaster between the 13th and 14th centuries is worth examining. The responsibility assumed by both queens as regents on behalf of their children (and grandson, King Alfonso XI, in the case of Queen Maria) introduces an element of distinction from the queen consorts. These two queenly figures are distanced from each other by the maturity granted by their older age, and also by the role they play in relation to the king. On one hand, as mothers, they have an added authority towards the king, due to their kinship and affective bond with him.[18] These two traits are fundamental in assessing the power of the queen mother at court, supported by age, experience and institutional dignity.[19] Moreover, the queen consort is part of the king's body politic by virtue of her marriage, i.e. this link grants a greater degree of horizontality and proximity between the spouses. While the close presence of the queen consort to the king plays a key role in ceremonial terms in celebrating

17   M. Shadis, *Berenguela of Castile (1180–1246) and Political Women in the High Middle Ages*, New York 2009, 71–83.

18   F. Cosandey, *La Reine de France: Symbole et pouvoir. XVᵉ–XVIIIᵉ siècle*, Paris 2000.

19   L. Benz St. John, *Three Medieval Queens. Queenship and the Crown in Fourteenth-Century England*, New York 2012, 95–131.

military conquests and ratifying them through the showcasing of the royal couple, the queen mother offers other possibilities for the monarchy.

The journey of the king to the Muslim border led to the distribution of the royal image and government into two distinct spaces: "el real", the camp where the king established himself; and the court itself. This dissociation was not only restricted to the military sphere, but also to those occasions when the king decided to visit lands far from the spatial centrality of the monarchy in order to resolve conflicts with the nobility. For example, Sancho IV travelled to the Kingdoms of Leon and Galicia to pacify his nobles in what was known as the "cerca de Ronches" in 1287. The administration of Castile was not abandoned, but the count, together with the Bishop of Astorga and the Dean of Seville, the king's chief notary, were responsible for maintaining the functioning of the chancery and justice in the kingdom.[20] Unfortunately, neither the chronicle nor the archive documentation allows us to know where Queen Maria de Molina was and what her function was within this political situation.

The existence of a body politic that does not only affect the royal couple offers multiple possibilities for the female characters. Common patterns can be seen among the queens who played a more active role in the administration of the kingdom during the military campaigns against the Muslims. One of the most expressive testimonies refers to Berengaria of Castile. The chronicler Lucas de Tuy notes that Queen Berengaria "wisely stood in for the king" (*uices eius sapienter in regno Legionis et Castelle supplebat*)[21] both in Leon and Castile. Janna Bianchini has also noted the queen's performance as lieutenant.[22] Indeed, the king was on the southern border of his territory, even if the distance from the court was not as significant as it was for the kings of Aragon in the Mediterranean.

Berengaria's unified government of the Kingdoms of Leon and Castile had an impact on the single management of the lieutenancy, giving shape to a "general lieutenancy". Despite the separate identity of the kingdoms integrated into the Crowns of Leon and Castile, there is no evidence of the existence of a distinct lieutenancy, as may be the case in the Kingdom of Aragon. Thus, Maria de Luna was Lieutenant of the Kingdom of Valencia (1401–1406) and attempted to

---

20   C. Rosell (ed.), *Crónica de Sancho IV. Crónicas de los Reyes de Castilla*, Madrid 1875, ch. IV, 75–76.

21   The praise goes on: *regina Berengaria* [...] *in tanta securitate et pace utrumque regnum gaudebat, ut paruus uel magnus aliquis non auderet uilenter res alterius occupare* (L. Tudensis, *Chronicon Mundi*, E. Falque [ed.], Turnhout 2003, ch. XCIII, 340).

22   J. Bianchini, *The Queen's Hand: Power and Authority in the Reign of Berenguela of Castile*, Philadelphia 2012, 255.

appease the rebellious nobility,[23] Maria of Castile was Lieutenant of Catalonia (1420–1423/1432–1453) during the Mediterranean conflicts of Alfonso V; as was her successor, Queen Juana Enríquez, between 1461–1468, due to the armed conflict against John II.[24] The significant territorial extension of Leon and Castile, as well as the identities contained within them, did not pose a challenge to their governmental stability, at least in general terms. In fact, when the territory had to be divided after the death of Henry III, a north-south division was adopted. The king decided that his wife would rule the northern half, which included the main cities of Leon and Castile, while his brother, the *infante* Ferdinand of Castile, "el de Antequera", would rule from the south of the central system to Andalusia in order to continue military progress.[25]

Throughout the early and late Middle Ages, rivalries arose among the royal kinsmen who took advantage of the situation to take refuge in Leon or Galicia and claim sovereignty over these territories. These episodes were limited in time, but did not lead to a preventive reaction by the monarchy in the form of a lieutenancy. The centralisation of government in the figure of the sovereign from Castile underpinned a solid power. It resisted the delegation of its power to other institutional figures despite recurrent problems of legitimacy between the 13th and 15th centuries.[26] Furthermore, in most cases, these were challenges to royal authority coinciding with periods of regency. The *infantes* John of Castile, brother of Sancho IV, and Philip of Castile, son of Sancho IV and Maria de Molina, tried to become kings of Leon and Galicia, respectively. On both occasions Queen Maria de Molina was a key figure. Her resolute action in appeasing the kingdom and subduing them, both by word and by force,[27] managed to keep the kingdom united under the authority of the "child-king"

---

23   N. Silleras Fernández, *Power, Piety, and Patronage in Late Medieval Queenship: Maria de Luna*, New York 2008, 74–84.

24   N. Coll i Juliá, *Doña Juana Enríquez: lugarteniente real en Cataluña (1461–1468)*, Madrid 1953, vol. 1, 320–326.

25   P. Carceller Cerviño / Ó. Villarroel González, *Catalina de Lancaster. Una reina y el poder*, Madrid 2021, 167–170.

26   A. Rodríguez, *Sucesión regia y legitimidad política en Castilla en los siglos XII y XIII: algunas consideraciones sobre el relato de las crónicas latinas castellano-leonesas*, in: Mª I. Alfonso Antón / J. Escalona Monge / G. Martin (eds.), *Lucha política: condena y legitimidad en la España medieval*, Lyon 2004, 21–42; C. Valdaliso Casanova, *Discursos de legitimación de la dinastía Trastámara (1366–1388)*, in: F. Sabaté i Curull / M. Pedrol (eds.), *Ruptura i legitimació dinástica a l'Etat Mitjana*, Lleida 2015, 127–142.

27   "É la Reina quesiera que fueran cercar la cibdad de Leon, é ellos non lo tovieron por bien, é dijeron que querían ir á cercar á Paredes [...]. La postrimera semana de setiembre, é fueron cercar á Paredes estando dentro doña María, mujer del infante don Juan, que se llamaba reina de León, é un su fijo que decian don Lope con ella, é doña Juana, su madre, mujer del Conde. É la noble reina doña María punaba de acuciar á los de la hueste commo

Ferdinand IV.[28] Once again, an experienced woman, the king's mother who, on this occasion, occupied "the place of the king", as regent.

The titles of "queen regent" and "queen lieutenant" were clearly differentiated in the medieval period. Essentially, however, they share the importance of conferring, generally on a woman, a political significance with profound implications for the future of the monarchy. The king's absence, whether symbolic or physical, was used to test the solidity of the kingdom's administration through one of its most important assets.[29] The queen's connection, as a mother or as a wife, justifies her prominence.

However, the lieutenancy may have afforded the same relevance to other members of the royal family. During the final years of Alfonso X's reign, the *infante* Sancho served as lieutenant, taking advantage of his father's military campaigns against King Muhammad II of Granada.[30] Using the usual formula, it is indicated that Don Sancho, the heir to the kingdom, "travelled through the lands of Leon and Castile dispensing justice" (*"andaba en tierra de León y Castilla faziendo justicia"*) in 1279.[31] The queen consort, Violant of Aragon, neither acted nor was she questioned at the meeting of King Alfonso's sons, thanks to which the chronicler notes the activity carried out by the heir to the throne. Indeed, the future Sancho IV was only 21 years old, which could have been a way of bringing him closer to the workings of government. However, the queen's absence can be explained by her distancing herself from the king, even politically.

Despite the queen's active collaboration in Castilian politics, particularly visible in moments of tension with the nobility, Queen Violant left Castile after taking sides with the heirs of her first-born son, the *infante* Ferdinand de la Cerda.[32] The crisis in the royal marriage not only discouraged a female lieutenancy, but made it impossible. The same was not true of the *infante* Sancho. Although the queen had been a staunch defender of the rights of succession for the children of Ferdinand de la Cerda – her first-born son, who died in

---

combatiesen la villa" (*Crónica de Fernando IV. Crónicas de los Reyes de Castilla*, C. Rosell [ed.], Madrid 1875, ch. II, 105).

28   R. Morán Martín, *Niños reyes. La frágil fortaleza del pacto*, in: F. Foronda / A.I. Carrasco Manchado (eds.), *Du contrat d'alliance au contrat politique: cultures et sociétés politiques dans la Péninsule Ibérique de la fin du Moyen Âge*, Toulouse 2007, 139–184.

29   T. Earenfight, *Absent Kings: Queens as Political Partners in the Medieval Crown of Aragon*, in: T. Earenfight (ed.), *Queenship and Political Power in Medieval and Early Modern Spain: Women and Gender in the Early Modern World*, Burlington 2005, 33–54.

30   F.J. Hernández, *Los hombres del Rey y la transición de Alfonso X el Sabio a Sancho IV (1276–1286)*, Salamanca 2021, vol. I, 466–468.

31   *Crónica de Alfonso X* 1875, ch. LXXIII, 57.

32   M.ªJ. Fuente Pérez, *Violante de Aragón. Reina de Castilla*, Madrid 2017, 84–163.

1275 – Sancho sought reconciliation with his mother. So much so that he would not have been alone in his travels throughout the kingdom. At least in 1278, the *infante*, together with his mother, travelled through the Castilian cities "examining" the state of justice.[33]

The assertion of the figure of Queen Violant by the *infante* Sancho is truly interesting. The relationship between the *infante* and his father had become strained, initiating an estrangement that was irreparable until the death of Alfonso X, despite the search for reconciliation.[34] In contrast to his father, Sancho succeeded in bringing Queen Violant back from the Aragonese court. The *infante*'s desire to bring his mother back to him is much greater if we judge their joint display in the kingdom. Queen Violant made a unique contribution to Sancho's cause, even more so than the support of his uncle, the King of Aragon. The queen had become a political point of reference thanks to her conciliatory actions, years earlier, and therefore reinforced the position of the *infante* as heir to the throne in the face of discontent towards the king.[35] At the same time, the figure of the queen brought a feminine value to an incipient court in which there was not yet a queen consort. The queen mother offered the possibility of multiplying and disseminating the image of the monarchy and the unity of the new political project inaugurated by the *infante* Sancho. And, once again, the maternal figure connected to the lieutenancy.

A similar situation occurred during the reign of Ferdinand IV. Once her regency was over, the queen mother, Maria de Molina, continued to be a key component of King Ferdinand's government. Their good rapport is the main quality highlighted in the chronicles, and a simile is drawn with the Virgin Mary for her willingness to collaborate and provide support.[36] The queen's legacy is present beyond the institutional prominence granted by her role as guardian of Ferdinand IV. Queen Maria is presented as a figure of consensus and a synonym of good government, despite the ups and downs of her relationship with the king, due to the conspiracies against her by nobles and other members of the urban oligarchy. The campaigns against the Muslims would again be a key episode in testing the strength of the mother-son bond to ensure the stability of the kingdom. The chronicle leaves no room for doubt:

---

33   "*É la reina é el infante don Sancho andudieron por las villas de Castilla requeriendo la justicia*". *Crónica de Alfonso X* 1875, ch. LXXI, 55.

34   Hernández, 2021, vol. I, 150–180.

35   F. Arias Guillén, *The Triumph of and Accursed Lineage: Kingship in Castile from Alfonso X to Alfonso XI (1252–1350)*, London 2020.

36   P. Rochwert-Zuili, *La imagen de la madre, ¿un componente fundamental del Molinismo?*, in: F. Arias Guillén / C. Reglero de la Fuente (coords.), *María de Molina: gobernar en tiempos de crisis (1264–1321)*, Madrid 2022, 61–64.

"[King Ferdinand IV] agreed to set out towards the frontier, [...] and he begged the queen, his mother, to be left with the king's power in all his kingdoms to rule them while he was on the frontier. And he left her the seals so that her decisions would be respected in the same way as if the king himself had commanded it".[37]

The presentation of the seals gave the queen the power to validate governmental decisions of the most varied nature, as well as the staff of her chancellery at the request of her mistress. The management of her responsibilities as queen mother and the safeguarding of the interests of the kingdom coexisted in harmony through the symbolism of royal power.[38] The delivery of the royal seal signifies the transfer of the royal will to the queen, with the consequent legal recognition of any action undertaken by her and ratified by the seal.[39]

The frontier with the Moors and their harassment through the Crusades was the ideal situation for the lieutenancy. Military campaigns meant that the king was away for weeks or months at a time, while the business of government and administration had to continue. It is true that this procedure is not explicitly seen in all reigns. The reign of Alfonso XI, with important military campaigns against the Muslims, such as Teba, El Salado (1340) and the siege of Gibraltar (1349–1350), does not allow us to see the existence of a lieutenancy. The lack of affective and, to a large extent, political consideration for the queen consort Maria of Portugal made it difficult to choose her as lieutenant, despite her physical distance from the sovereign.[40] To all intents and purposes, it was the royal mistress, Eleanor de Guzman, who accompanied the king in the Andalusian campaigns, *de facto* occupying the space of power of the queen

---

37 "acordó de se yr su camino para la frontera, [...] é el rey rogó a la reyna su madre que fincase en todos sus reinos con su poder dél porque los rigese en quanto él estoviese en la frontera, é dexole los sellos que fisiesen por ella en todo asi como farian por su cuerpo mesmo". *Crónica de Fernando IV* 1875, ch. XVI, 162. See the same piece in: *Memorias del rey don Fernando IV de Castilla*, A. Benavides (ed.), Madrid 1860, vol. I, ch. IV, 216.

38 M. Serrano Coll, *Iconografía de género: los sellos de las reinas de Aragón en la Edad Media (siglos XII–XVI)*, in: Emblemata: Revista aragonesa de emblemática 12 (2006), 38–39.

39 Regarding the importance of the royal seal to demonstrate and/or claim royal power in favour of a third person, see the data provided by A.I. Carrasco Manchado (*Símbolos y ritos. El conflicto como representación*, in: J.M. Nieto Soria (dir.), *La monarquía como conflicto en la Corona castellano-leonesa [c. 1230–1504]*, Madrid 2006, 520–521). The author refers to the rivalries between the tutors of Ferdinand IV and Alfonso XI, as well as the making of royal seals by characters who claim their role as tutors of the king, such as don Juan Manuel.

40 J.P. Jardin, *La reina María de Portugal, entre padre, marido, hijo e hijastros: la mediación imposible*, in: e-Spania: Revue interdisciplinaire d'études hispaniques médiévales et modernes 20 (2015) (doi: https://doi.org/10.4000/e-spania.24140).

consort.[41] The palace buildings and infrastructures of Cordoba and Seville were able to provide shelter for the court and the kingdom's power brokers, whose presence was demanded by the king. In fact, the king awaited the arrival of nobles and representatives of the cities before besieging the fortress of Teba.[42]

However, during the regency of John II at the beginning of the 15th century, the situation was different. On this occasion, the presence of two tutors configured an alternative "royal couple" to the one formed only by mother and son. Queen Catherine of Lancaster and her brother-in-law, the *infante* Ferdinand, shared the regency of King John, following the indications of the will of Henry III of Castile. Both are characters with their own political agendas and the will to assert them: Queen Catherine describes the ideal of a queen mother looking after the interests of her son, while the *infante* Ferdinand seeks the reaffirmation of his political and military leadership in the kingdom. Proof of this are his military campaigns, waged from the beginning of his co-regency and rounded off by the capture of Antequera in 1410.[43] The chronicle describes the queen's desire to control the *infante* and to go to war with him in order to "command the provision of everything necessary for the royal camp".[44] This is a self-serving view, which responds to the chronicler's closeness to the *infante* Ferdinand to the detriment of Queen Catherine. However, the trip to Andalusia did not take place and it was agreed – once again the formula of consensus that goes beyond the kingly or queenly will – that the queen would remain in Segovia to tend to the administration of the kingdom.

It was then that the division of the territory into provinces came to fruition. The regents' interference in each other's territory was limited, although the *infante* did not give up the right to place people with similar interests in order to control the queen. Proof of this is the account in the chronicle of Perez de Guzman after the *infante*'s appointment as King of Aragon. In addition to leaving a commission of lay and ecclesiastical nobles "in place", Queen Catherine managed to place the Archbishop of Toledo, Sancho de Rojas, one of his main

---

41 A. Recuero Lista, *María de Portugal frente a Leonor de Guzmán: la lucha por el papel de reina durante el reinado de Alfonso XI de Castilla (1325–1350)*, in: M. García Fernández (coord.), *En la Europa medieval: mujeres con historia, mujeres de leyenda: siglos XIII–XVI*, Sevilla 2019, 80–92.

42 *Crónica de Alfonso XI. Crónicas de los Reyes de Castilla*, C. Rosell (ed.), Madrid 1875, ch. LXXXIII, 224.

43 V. Muñoz Gómez, *La guerra contra el Islam en el proyecto político de Fernando "el de Antequera", infante de Castilla y rey de Aragón (1380–1416)*, in: M. Ríos Saloma (ed.), *El mundo de los conquistadores*, Madrid 2015, 399–436.

44 C. Rosell (ed.), *Crónica de Juan II. Crónica de los reyes de Castilla*, Madrid 1875, 1408, ch. XVIII, 283.

supporters, in the queen's province.[45] Queen Catherine kept the Chancery and, therefore, the main judicial body in the kingdom. This institution had to be located wherever the king was, due to the intimate connection between the royal office and the administration of justice.

The model of co-regency and the division of the territory into provinces demonstrates the strength of the *infante* Ferdinand, even in the creation of the historiographical narrative. It also shows how the figure of the *infante*'s wife, Eleanor de Alburquerque, was used as a female representative of the Christian military triumph.[46] While Berengaria or Maria de Molina had a crucial weight in the chronological discourse, Queen Catherine appears subordinate to the political or military action of the *infante*. Neither did the death of the queen before John II came of age benefit the influence of the maternal figure as in previous reigns. Although Catherine of Lancaster had significant traits that enabled her to exercise power (maturity and experience, her own inheritance rights as heir of Peter I), her strength is not perceived in the same sense. On this occasion too, the crusade against the Muslims did not motivate a sole regency in her person or the lieutenancy over the *infante*'s province. The *infante*'s desire to maintain his autonomy and capacity for territorial management led other people to occupy these positions of representation and leadership. The kinship between the co-regents, as brothers-in-law, created a horizontal relationship that did not benefit the queen, despite her greater institutional dignity.[47]

3   In the Queen's Place? Representation, Negotiation, and Mediation from Another Perspective

The occasions on which medieval queens – not only Castilian or Iberian queens – intervened with their capacity for mediation are diverse and

---

45   The reason is the *infante*'s fear of the influence on the thought of the queen of other nobles contrary to his person, to the detriment of the common good of the kingdoms: "temiendo que algunos de los grandes despues de su partida quisiesen mover algunas cosas que no cumpliesen al bien de estos Reynos" (*Crónica de Juan II*, 1875, 1412, ch. X, 346).

46   J.M. Nieto Soria, *La ceremonialización de la vida política durante la regencia de Fernando de Antequera* (1406–1416), in: *Mundos Medievales: espacios, sociedades y poder. Homenaje al profesor José Ángel García de Cortázar y Ruiz de Aguirre*, Santander 2012, vol. 2, 1694–1695.

47   Ó. Villarroel González, *El alejamiento del poder de Catalina de Lancáster en 1408 y la propaganda del infante Fernando*, in: P. Díaz Sánchez / G. Franco Rubio / MªJ. Fuente Pérez (eds.), *Impulsando la historia desde la historia de las mujeres. La estela de Cristina Segura*, Huelva 2012, 380–386.

constitute a veritable leitmotif of the queenly condition. The political charac-
terisation of the queen is linked to her sex, offering the possibility of diversification and adaptation of the monarchical authority in order to condition the
negotiation setting for the benefit of the institution. The choice of the queen
as the king's interlocutor is influenced by several factors: the affinity and trust
between the spouses, the particularity or generality of political conflicts, the
extent to which the relationship between the king and the opposing actors is
strained, and/or the existence of the queen's kinship with the same actors. The
queen's institutional status is not enough; other personal factors encourage or
discourage her involvement.

However, the queen's actions are explained by the functions inherent to her
condition and status, by what she contributes to the monarchy from a rhetorical point of view. Her intervention does not respond solely to the interests
or will of the king, but to that of the royal council. The institutionalisation of
her political or diplomatic involvement through the governing bodies demonstrates their regard for the queen, both personally and institutionally.[48] The
queen brings her own networks of relationships (kinship, affinity, friendship)
with both external and internal agents in the kingdom and, on the other hand,
alludes to the characteristics of her status as *consors regni*.[49]

The queen's capacity for mediation is traced through rhetorical, symbolic
or juridical formulas, or under the cloak of institutional consensus. In the first
case, special mention should be made of the legal capacity demonstrated by
Juana Manuel de Villena as Henry II's procurator. King Peter IV of Aragon
requested a commitment from Juana Manuel, r. 1366/1369–1379, after she was
recognised as queen in 1366. Taking advantage of the queen's retinue pass-
ing through Zaragoza, Peter IV demanded the surrender of several frontier
towns in the Kingdom of Toledo, the bishopric of Cuenca and the Kingdom
of Murcia.[50] The queen acts as the "procurator" (*procuratrix*) of the new King
of Castile, with legal power to administer an oath.[51] In the second, Maria of
Aragon's role as intercessor before her brother,[52] the King of Aragon, acting "in

---

48   L. Ruiz Domingo, *Efectividad política y actividad diplomática: los embajadores al servicio
      de la reina María de Luna en el tránsito del siglo XIV al XV*, in: C. Villanueva Morte (ed.),
      Diplomacia y desarrollo del Estado en la Corona de Aragón (siglos XIV–XVI), Gijón 2020,
      165–185.

49   R. Le Jan, *Femmes, pouvoir et société dans le haut Moyen Âge*, Paris 2001, 39.

50   J. Zurita, *Los cinco libros postreros de la primera parte de los Anales de la Corona de Aragón*,
      Zaragoza 1668, vol. I, book IX, ch. LXIII, 26or.

51   ACA, RC, Reg. 1216, fol. 18r–v. 1366, December, 15. Barcelona.

52   Queen Maria of Aragon reigned as queen consort of Castile between 1420 and 1445.

place of the king", refers to the specific weight of the queen and her manipulation by the royal council depending on the political circumstances.[53]

In 1424, relations between John II of Castile and Alfonso V of Aragon had become strained due to the imprisonment of the brother of the King of Aragon and cousin of the King of Castile, the *infante* Henry. His leadership of the coup d'état of Tordesillas (1420) to take control of John II's court was the reason for his imprisonment.[54] The introduction of Queen Maria is for reasons of kinship, unlike other similar episodes in the past. In contrast to the example of Violant of Aragon and her intervention against the rebellious nobility, the aim was to strengthen the link between siblings as a source of understanding. The strategy is interesting for two reasons: first, the consideration of the queen as a political asset with her own potentiality. The queen could represent the interests of the Crown of Castile and lead diplomatic policy. The second was the presence of figures close to the side of the late Ferdinand de Antequera in the Castilian institutions.

It is precisely the divergence between the masculine and the feminine that is surprising when the roles of the two are reversed. The reception of the queen at her new court is a symptomatic example. The king was in charge of welcoming her, both ceremonially and as a gesture of courtesy towards the status of the woman who was to become his wife. However, neither Ferdinand III, Alfonso XI, or Peter I complied with this rule, delegating the action to Queen Berengaria of Castile (mother of the first), the *infanta* Eleanor of Castile (sister of the second), and Maria of Portugal (mother of the third). Although this action was not an act of the institution of the lieutenancy, the absence of the king and his replacement by women delegates of his authority is very revealing.

The use of the "place of the king" is either out of indifference towards the newcomer or, as in the first case, as a demonstration of authority by Queen Berengaria. The situation calls for a person close to and involved in the body politic of the monarchy to welcome the new member of the royal family. In this sense, the participation of the *infanta* Eleanor, Alfonso X's elder sister, as a delegate of the royal authority at the bride's reception fits perfectly with this representative purpose. Eleanor was the highest-ranking woman at court, after the disappearance of Constance of Portugal (queen mother) and Maria de Molina (queen grandmother). Her status as the king's sister gave her an

53   M. Lafuente, *Historia general de España*, Madrid 1861, vol. IV, part II, book III, 373.

54   J.M. de Flores (ed.), *Crónica de Álvaro de Luna, condestable de los reynos de Castilla y de León*, Madrid 1784, tit. XIII, 43.

authority that had its roots in the High Middle Ages.[55] It also reaffirms the indispensability of a woman belonging to the royal lineage to exercise leadership at court when there was no queen consort:[56] a strategy similar that seen in the case of Sancho IV, still an *infanta*, with his mother, Queen Violant, as previously noted.

Queens and *infantas* bring fundamental qualities to monarchical government. Although it cannot be dealt with here, the figure of the king's sister deserves to be studied in depth and from different perspectives. It is sufficient to examine the role of the *infanta* Eleanor of Castile in the Chronicle of Alfonso XI to appreciate the construction of a "lieutenancy of the queen". The kinship between siblings and, even more so, the role of the eldest sister, the first-born, is evidence of a special bond and trust by the king. This is corroborated by the examples of Urraca of Zamora (1033–1101), Sancha Raimúndez (1095/1099–1159), Berengaria of Castile (1179/1180–1246), Eleanor of Castile (1307–1359), and Maria of Castile (r. 1416–1458). In fact, Maria of Castile, Queen of Aragon, repeatedly claimed her status as the first-born *infanta* of Castile through her chancellery documentation, even after her marriage to Alfonso V of Aragon.[57]

The "place of the queen" has to be filled, even when there is no queen consort. Regardless of the existence of other members of the royal family, the king's older sister or his first-born daughter play a pivotal role as advisor and collaborator. Unlike other male siblings, they are not perceived as rivals to the throne. In addition, their age gives them greater experience and capacity for advice. The women of the royal lineage share a trajectory of mediation and representation, also in the creation of the historiographical narrative. Mothers, wives, sisters are three categories that the same woman could play and lead her to occupy "the place of the king". But, at the same time, these women, who, as part of the royal lineage, could receive the title of queens, as daughters of the king, could occupy "the place of the queen".

---

55   J.R. Lyon, *Princely Brothers and Sisters: The Sibling Bond in German Politics, 1100–1250*, Ithaca 2013.

56   M. Silva, *The Portuguese Household of an English Queen: Sources, Purposes, Social Meaning*, in: T. Earenfight (ed.), *Royal and Elite Households in Medieval and Early Modern Europe: More than Just a Castle*, Leiden 2018, 277.

57   For example, see the title used by Queen Maria of Castile: ACA, Cartas Reales, Alfonso IV [V], Serie General, 1375. 1421, Marc, 13. Tortosa.

4   Conclusions

The queen's representative capacity is one of the most common elements of female political agency during the Middle Ages, but the expression of the lieutenancy opens a new horizon of analysis. Her substitution of royal functions and authority at specific moments poses a new perspective, midway between the formal institutionalisation of these responsibilities for a longer period of time and the mere queenly representation through epistolary contact or travel. On the one hand, it is not a matter of collaboration or support, but instead of the power brokers' perception of the queen. In this sense, it shows the division of the monarchy's body politic according to the best option for the success of the royal family's interests. On the other hand, it reveals the queen's capacities as an institutional figure in her own right and the possibility of pursuing political action by taking advantage of her legal and jurisdictional status and status as the person closest to the king.[58]

In contrast to acting "in the king's name", using "the place of the king" has very clear implications. Whoever enjoys this position has the powers of the sovereign to dispense justice, settle disputes, visit places, organise space, and so on. She becomes his "alter nós" ("other we") in the words of Lledó Ruiz[59], because of her marital closeness, but also because of the queen's own skills and the recognition of other power brokers. Bodies such as the royal council actively participate in the spatial distribution of the image of the king and queen and in the distribution of duties. The institutions justify the queen's political involvement and encourage her involvement in conflict resolution, although the ultimate decision rests with the king.

However, the female lieutenancy in Castile did not achieve an institutional dimension comparable to that of the Crown of Aragon. Nor was it in the hands of the queen consort, but rather in her condition as a mother. Only the Empress Isabella of Portugal would receive this appointment on several occasions between 1528 and 1538. In the absence of Emperor Charles V, Isabella became regent of Castile, or lieutenant general.[60] Interestingly, very different dignities are alluded to, but with similar implications, both justified by the absence of the king. Whether due to the king's physical distance, or his death, the queen appears as the natural figure to replace him during a transitory period, which may have lasted for years. Because of the queen's relational capacity, capable

---

58   *Las Partidas*, Partida II, Título VI, Ley II, 42.

59   Ruiz Domingo, 2017, 311–312.

60   I. Jiménez Zamora, *La actuación política de la emperatriz Isabel (1528–1538)*, in: Espacio, Tiempo y Forma. Serie IV. Historia Moderna 29 (2016), 163–165.

of connecting intimately with the king, she becomes the ideal person to safe-guard the interests of the kingdom. She represents mediation, consensus, and understanding: virtues that she must emulate on a daily basis and which bring her figure, in institutional terms, closer to the Virgin in her capacity as a media-tor and sovereign of heaven. In the case of the queen, her status as a mother endows her with greater experience and, above all, a bond of loyalty to the king through her kinship. While the queen consort represents the present, the queen mother has greater authority, which is also present in her ability to influence the chronological apparatus; a fundamental feature when it comes to leaving evidence of her governmental support, even if only subtly.

Women, Trust and the Politics of Space in Thirteenth-Century Iberia

Antonella Liuzzo Scorpo

Abstract

Thirteenth-century Iberian sources reveal the multisensory practices of space and how they related to representations and manifestations of trust. Challenging the assumption that spatial and social boundaries were rigidly defined by sex, this study shows how women's access or exclusion from spheres of power and social communication also relied on trust.

As a foundation of most social exchanges involving individuals, communities and institutions, trust has been always viewed as an essential parameter in establishing different types of interpersonal relationships in both local and translocal contexts, within and beyond cultural boundaries. A cross-disciplinary and comparative framework of analysis, which focuses on cultural, political and women's history, offers fresh insights into the connections involving ideas and expressions of trust, gender, and the politics of space, and what they reveal about other important aspects of intersectionality, including social identity and legal status. Through a comparative examination of thirteenth-century Iberian chancery records and epistolary exchanges, alongside the literary and narrative production attributed to, and patronised by, Alfonso X of Castile (r. 1252–1284) and James I of Aragon (r. 1213–1276), this study examines the multisensory practices of space—as a physical, symbolic, and emotional construct—and their interactions with textual representations, customary practices and expected manifestations of trust. Particularly significant is the role that women—as historical agents—occupied in the networks and relationships that defined and characterised physical, yet symbolically charged, spaces and places of communication and negotiation. Challenging the assumption that the boundaries between 'public' and 'private' spaces were exclusively and rigidly defined by sex and gender-based expectations, this study argues that trust was one of the leading factors determining women's access or exclusion from spheres of power, authority and social communication.

© BRILL SCHÖNINGH, 2024 | DOI:10.30965/9783657791477_009

1 Definitions and Historiographical Approaches

1.1 *Trust*

Trust, as a relational framework, when examined in its historical, cultural and geographical contexts, reveals a multiplicity of meanings and values associated with its interpretations, uses and adaptations, which might vary when considering different socio-economic and cultural structures.[1] In the premodern world, trust was a fluid concept, negotiated within and between individuals and communities, as well as being rooted in widely recognised moral values and customary practices. As an adaptable construct, shaped by socio-cultural and intellectual parameters, pragmatic needs and historical contingencies, trust unfolded in a variety of communicative processes.[2] These included performative acts, such as rituals and ceremonies, and the negotiation of physical and symbolic spaces as part of those performances. Secondly, the use of a specific, yet adaptable, rhetoric and language (both oral and written) of trust.[3] Thirdly, the legitimisation and preservation of orally-sealed oaths and promises through their embodiment in the written word, hence through the creation of written documents. Finally, the expression and management of affective processes, alongside the multisensory experiences and perceptions of trust, which was believed to be closely connected to the senses.[4]

---

1 The historiography of trust is extremely broad and varied, especially when considering different disciplinary perspectives, including philosophy, sociology, anthropology, psychology, and behavioural sciences, among others. For an overview: R. Hardin, *Trust and Trustworthiness*, New York 2002; G. Möllering, *Cultivating the Field of Trust Research*, in: Journal of Trust Research 7 (2017), 107–114; S. Zmerli / T. van der Meer, (eds.), *Handbook on Political Trust*, Cheltenham 2017; R.H. Searle / A.M.I. Nienaber / S.B. Sitkin (eds.), *The Routledge Companion to Trust*, London 2018; E.M. Uslaner (ed.), The *Oxford Handbook of Social and Political Trust*, Oxford 2018. Among the numerous historical studies: S. Johnstone, *A History of Trust in Ancient Greece*, Chicago 2011; G. Hosking, *Trust: A History*, Oxford 2014; L. Kontler / M. Somos (eds.), *Trust and Happiness in the History of European Political Thought*, Leiden 2018; F. Granelli, *Trust, Politics and Revolution: A European History*, London 2020.

2 P. Schulte / M. Mostert / I. van Renswoude (eds.), *Strategies of Writing: Studies on Text and Trust in the Middle Ages. Papers from "Trust in Writing in the Middle Ages"* (*Utrecht, 28–29 November 2002*), Turnhout 2008; S. Enderwitz / R. Sauer (eds.), *Communication and Materiality: Written and Unwritten Communication in Premodern Societies*, Berlin 2015; A.J. Kunnel, *Trust and Communication. Foundations of Interconnectivity*, Berlin 2021.

3 J. Wubs-Mrozewicz, *The Concept of Language of Trust and Trustworthiness: (Why) History Matters*, in: Journal of Trust Research 10 (2020), 91–107.

4 J.R. Dunn / M.E. Schweitzer, *Feeling and Believing: The Influence of Emotion on Trust*, in: Journal of Personality and Social Psychology 88 (2005), 736–748; M. Williams, *In Whom We Trust: Social Group Membership as an Affective Context for Trust Development*, in: Academy of Management Review 26 (2001), 377–396; id., *Building Genuine Trust Through Interpersonal*

Trust characterised a broad range of personal and collective relationships: from agreements between merchants, neighbours, members of the same crafts and guilds, to vassalic bonds, fiefs, political and intellectual friendships, connections with religious and administrative institutions, and diplomatic exchanges, among others.[5] Trust often represented an essential tool in managing risks[6] and establishing connections based on reputation and information sharing.[7] As extensively studied by Ian Forrest for the English context between c.1200 and 1500, trust could also serve specific political interests, including those of the Church, that relied on, and deepened, inequalities within late medieval society, rooted on assumptions of trustworthiness. The latter were often structured around expectations of honour and worth related to wealth and social status, as well as sex.[8] Nonetheless, concepts, definitions and terminology associated with premodern trust varied when considering different sources and languages. The lack of a homogeneous definition reflects the complexity of trust as "an object of historical transformation".[9] For this reason, its plethora of definitions and expressions require careful assessment to avoid generalisations. As Justyna Wubs-Mrozewicz argued "Trust—as a concept, sentiment or action—needs to stand for something specific in order for it to be meaningful."[10] In her view, the study of the language of trust and trustworthiness, alongside its chronological developments and variations, offers a nuanced approach to examine the pragmatic needs and the social expectations of those involved. In other words, it provides a window into what contemporaries expected from a relationship based on trust.

Examining trust in its historical contexts and from cross-disciplinary perspectives helps advance knowledge by revealing the multi-layered and intersectional nature of its meanings and adaptations. Recent historiographical developments point towards new approaches to this complex subject by

---

Emotion Management: A Threat Regulation Model of Trust and Collaboration Across Boundaries, in: Academy of Management Review 32 (2007), 595–621.

5   D. Weltecke, *Trust: Some Methodological Reflections*, in: P. Schulte et al. (eds.), *Strategies of Writing*, 2008, 379–392 (386–389).

6   N. Luhmann, *Trust: A Mechanism for the Reduction of Social Complexity*, in: id., *Trust and Power: Two Works by Niklas Luhmann*, New York 1979, 1–103; S. Aslanian, *Social Capital, 'Trust' and the Role of Networks in Julfan Trade. Informal and Semiformal Institutions at Work*, in: Journal of Global History 1 (2006), 383–402.

7   M. Jucker, *Trust and Mistrust in Letters: Late Medieval Diplomacy and its Communication Practices*, in: P. Schulte et al. (eds.), *Strategies of Writing*, 2008, 213–236.

8   I. Forrest, *Trustworthy Men: How Inequality and Faith Made the Medieval Church*, Princeton 2018.

9   D. Weltecke, *Trust*, 2008, 384.

10 J. Wubs-Mrozewicz, *The Concept of Language*, 2020, 91.

promoting a perspective of the History of Experience, which embraces both the History of Emotions and the History of the Senses.[11] Integrating the body and the senses within the same paradigm of analysis helps focus on the human-side of historical subjects, who lived in and experienced a world shaped by individual agency, actions and reactions, but also conceived and understood as part of superimposed socio-cultural and political frameworks. If the study of the body and the senses is so central for a more holistic understanding of human experience in history, then the physical and symbolic places occupied and created by such 'bodied-individuals' must be, too.

1.2 *Space and Place*

The significance of space,[12] along with its changing historical meanings and interpretations, have been at the core of the so-called *spatial turn* in historical research, especially since Lefebvre's seminal work *The Production of Space*.[13] The *spatial turn* has also inspired new approaches in Medieval Studies, lead-ing to interesting cross-disciplinary developments, which have been enriched through the perspectives of Gender Studies and Women's History.[14] The politics of space have never been homogeneous, but in flux. They have been determined by historical attitudes, contingencies and agents, and framed by the source register through which they have materialised and evolved.[15] Scholarly debates also abound regarding the spatial practices created by the

11   M. Eyice, *When Feelings Grow Cold. What to Do Next in the History of Emotions?* in: Lychnos. Årsbok för idé- och lärdomshistoria, 2021, 295–307, available online: https://tidskriften-lychnos.se/article/view/22773/21436 (last accessed 21/11/2023); W. Leidhold, *The History of Experience. A Study in Experiential Turns and Cultural Dynamics from the Paleolithic to the Present Day*, Abingdon 2023.

12   For an overview of spatial reflections in three of the most influential French critical think-ers, R. West-Pavlov, *Space in Theory. Kristeva, Foucault, Deleuze*, Leiden 2009.

13   H. Lefebvre, *La production de l'espace*, Paris 1974; D. Wallace, *Premodern Places*, Oxford 2004; B. Warf / S. Arias (eds.), *The Spatial Turn: Interdisciplinary Perspectives*, Abingdon 2009; M. Cassidy-Welch, *Space and Place in Medieval Contexts*, in: Parergon 27 (2010), 1–12; J. Weiss / S. Salih (eds.), *Locating the Middle Ages: The Spaces and Places of Medieval Culture*, Woodbridge 2012.

14   A. Flather, *Gender and Space in Early Modern England*, Woodbridge 2007; K. Beebe / A. Davis (eds.), *Space, Place and Gendered Identities: Feminist History and the Spatial Turn*, Abingdon 2017; B. Zibell / D. Damyanovic / U. Sturm (eds.), *Gendered Approaches to Spatial Development in Europe: Perspectives, Similarities, Differences*, Abingdon 2019; E. Jimenez Rayado (ed.), *Espacios de la mujer en la Península Ibérica medieval*, Madrid 2023.

15   L. Howes (ed.), *Place, Space and Landscape in Medieval Narrative*, Knoxville 2007; E. Gertsman / J. Stevenson (eds.), *Thresholds of Medieval Visual Culture: Liminal Spaces*, Woodbridge 2012; V. Blud / D. Heath / E. Klafter (eds.), *Gender in Medieval Places, Spaces and Thresholds*, London 2019.

superstructures of power and how individual agency—in the past as well as in the present—could challenge or break such customary practices, as well as confirming them.[16]

Assessing the terminologies of space and place, alongside relevant historiographical perspectives and their implications, is essential to avoid theoretical and historical misunderstandings, especially when considering premodern versus modern contexts (a problematic periodisation that informs rigid, and often inaccurate, compartmentalisations).[17] Montserrat Piera discussed these points effectively in her study of medieval Iberian women's textual spaces and cultural practices, reminding us that medieval philosophical discussions dealt with *loci*/places (rather than space, as a modern, abstract construct), the meanings of which were semantically charged, and varied in time, often from one individual and community to another.[18] Mindful of these historical distinctions, in this study I will use the term 'place' when referring to physically-identifiable spatial entities with their semantic and symbolic meanings; and 'space' to indicate broader historiographical frameworks and social intersections, with both medieval and post-medieval connotations.

Similarly fluid for the premodern period were the concepts of 'public' and 'private'.[19] The tendency to rigidly define their boundaries along a sex axis (public spaces dominated by, and often limited to, men; and private spaces as the remit of women) is problematic and might reveal more about the social constructions, anxieties and trajectories of later generations approaching a distant past than about the actions and views of individuals who experienced a complex and nuanced medieval world, within which some of what are regarded today as unambiguous boundaries were much more fluid than we might assume.

1.3   *Female Spaces and Places of Trust*

Among the plethora of social relationships based on trust, friendship—with its multiple definitions, expressions and meanings—has occupied a central position across different historical, socio-cultural and geographical settings.

---

16   B.A. Hanawalt / M. Kobialka (eds.), *Medieval Practices of Space*, Minneapolis 2000.

17   K. Davis and M. Puett, *Periodization and "The Medieval Globe": A Conversation*, in: The Medieval Globe 2 (2016), 1–14. Available online at Project MUSE muse.jhu.edu/article/758522 (last accessed 22/11/2023).

18   M. Piera, *Women Readers and Writers in Medieval Iberia*, Leiden 2019, 8–9.

19   G. Duby (ed.), *Revelations of the Medieval World*, A. Goldhammer (trans.), vol. 2 of *A History of Private Life*, Cambridge, Mass., 1988; F. Riddy, *Looking Closely: Authority and Intimacy in the Late Medieval Urban Home*, in: M.C. Erler / M. Kowaleski (eds.), *Gendering the Master Narrative: Women and Power in the Middle Ages*, Ithaca 2003, 212–228 (214–215); S. McSheffrey, *Place, Space, and Situation: Public and Private in the Making of Marriage in Late-Medieval London*, in: Speculum 79 (2004), 960–990.

Friendship was generated and strengthened by loyalty, mutual affection and support, respect of a friend's secrets, and other parameters influenced by, and adapted to, the socio-cultural standards of reception through which previous philosophical, religious and even legal models and ideas of *amicitia* were filtered.[20] As discussed in my previous work, social status, reputation, honour and family ties were among the main factors determining whether women could be trusted as friends and loyal companions.[21] Age, religious and ethnic categorisations, alongside their marital status (married, unmarried, widowed, and so on), were also central parameters in defining women's legal status and their perceived trustworthiness. In particular, it was women's moral stature (which included the abovementioned core virtues required of friendship, most of which proceeded from the Greek Classical tradition)[22] that gave them access to spheres of trust, especially in interactions with men. Significantly, in the historical, legal and literary production patronised and supervised by King Alfonso X of Castile, which I examined in my previous work (the legal code Las *Siete Partidas*, the illuminated and musically annotated Marian collection of miracle stories *Cantigas de Santa Maria*, and the chronicles *General Estoria* and *Estoria de Espanna*), the space of trust was restricted to mothers, sisters and sometimes wives, as their familiar and legal ties with the men close to them should have limited, at least in principle, the lustful and sinful actions associated with female temptation.[23] The didactic message promoted through the works produced in the Castilian royal *scriptorium* seems to reflect Alfonso X's own conceptual and discursive space of trust, especially concerning women and their impact on his political and private life.[24] Women who featured in Alfonso's X work and entourage, informing his political actions and legacy, were his mother, Beatriz of Swabia (r. 1219–1235) and grandmother,

---

20   The studies on friendship are numerous and cover a broad range of disciplinary perspectives. For an overview focusing on the medieval period: B.P. McGuire, *Friendship and Community: The Monastic Experience, 350–1250*, Ithaca 1988; R. Hyatte, *The Arts of Friendship: The Idealization of Friendship in Medieval and Early Renaissance Literature*, Leiden 1994; A. Classen / M. Sandidge (eds.), *Friendship in the Middle Ages and Early Modern Age: Explorations of a Fundamental Ethical Discourse*, Berlin 2010; S. Stern-Gillet / G.M. Gurtler SJ (eds.), *Ancient and Medieval Concepts of Friendship*, New York 2014; L. Hermanson, *Friendship, Love, and Brotherhood in Medieval Northern Europe, c. 1000– 1200*, A. Crozier (trans.), Leiden 2019; R.J. McDonie, *Friendship and Rhetoric in the Middle Ages: The Linguistic Performance of Intimacy from Cicero to Aelred*, Abingdon 2020.
21   A. Liuzzo Scorpo, *Friendship in Medieval Iberia. Historical, Legal and Literary Perspectives*, Farnham 2014, 177–198.
22   D. Konstan, *Friendship in the Classical World*, Cambridge 1997.
23   A. Liuzzo Scorpo, *Friendship*, 2014, 177–198.
24   M.ª P. Rábade Obradó, *Aproximación al entorno femenino de Alfonso X*, in: e-Spania 39 (2021), 1–28. Available online: https://journals.openedition.org/e-spania/40874#bibliography (last accessed 21/11/23).

Berenguela (r. 1217–1246), whose memory and genealogy respectively contributed to legitimise his imperial and Castilian-Leonese claims. His only legitimate wife, Yolant of Aragon (r. 1246–1301), daughter of James I of Aragon and Violant of Hungary (r. 1235–1251), also occupied a significant space of mediation, as she frequently interceded in Alfonso's peninsular politics and especially in the unstable relationship with his father-in-law.[25] Less dominant, but still surfacing from the surviving records, are Alfonso X's stepmother, Juana of Ponthieu (who married Ferdinand III after the death of Beatriz of Swabia, ruling as queen consort between 1237 and 1252),[26] some of his daughters, sisters and concubines—among the latter, the most renowned was Mayor Guillén de Guzmán.[27]

Similarly, an examination of the sources concerning King James I of Aragon offers an overview of the women who contributed to establishing his authority and legitimacy (his mother, Marie of Montpellier), enhancing his power through marital diplomacy (his first wife, Eleanor of Castile) and political agreements (Aurembiaix, Countess of Urgell), and who occupied prominent spaces of mediation and trust (his second wife Violant of Hungary, and his daughter—later queen consort of Castile—Yolant).[28] Particularly revealing is James I's *Llibre del fets* (*Book of Deeds*, henceforth *LDF*), regarded as the first vernacular autobiography attributed to a Western Christian king, whose deeds and emotions are narrated from a first-person perspective.[29] Perhaps not surprisingly, in a work of royal self-construction such as the *LDF*, James I's

---

25   M.ªJ. Fuente Pérez, *Violante de Aragón, reina de Castilla*, Madrid 2017; id. *Las cartas visibles e "invisibles" de una mujer política. Violante de Aragón (1236–1300), reina y madre*, in: J.P. Jardin / J.M. Nieto Soria / P. Rochwert-Zuili / H. Thieulin-Pardo (eds.), *Cartas de mujeres en la Europa medieval: España, Francia, Italia, Portugal (siglos XI–XV)*, Madrid 2018, 17–33.

26   A. Sánchez de Mora, *Doña Juana de Ponthieu, reina de Castilla y señora de Marchena*, in: J.L. Carriazo Rubio / R. Ramos Alfonso (eds.), *Actas de las XI Jornadas sobre historia de Marchena: la mujer en la historia de Marchena. Marchena, del 4 al 7 de octubre de 2005*, Marchena 2007, 11–24; A. Cobos Rodríguez, *Intereses políticos. La diplomacia en el enlace de Juana de Danmartín o Ponthieu*, in: J.M. Nieto Soria / O. Villarroel González (eds.), *Diplomacia y cultura política en la Península Ibérica (siglos XI al XV)*, Madrid 2021, 243–256.

27   P. Martín Prieto, *Las Guzmán alfonsinas. Una dinastía femenina en la Castilla de los siglos XIII y XIV*, in: Mirabilia 17 (2013), 251–272.

28   M.ª Carme Roca, *Les Dones de Jaume I*, Barcelona 2008.

29   *Llibre dels feits del rei En Jaume*, in: F. Soldevila (ed.), *Les quatre grans Cròniques*, vol 1, Barcelona 2007. For an English translation D.J. Smith / H. Buffery (eds.), *The Book of Deeds of James I of Aragon: A Translation of the Medieval Catalan Llibre dels Fets*, Farnham 2003. I will reference only chapters (rather than page numbers) for quotations from the *LDF*, as they coincide across both the Catalan edition and its English translation.

numerous lovers and concubines (with the exception of Aurembiaix, although the nature of their relationship is ambiguous, as will be discussed later) were purposefully omitted.

Before examining the place and space of trust in relationships between men and women, it is important to analyse whether and to what extent norms, expectations and interpretations of trust applied to relationships established by, between and among women. To what extent did the cultural politics of space affect and influence the consolidation of female networks of trust or mistrust? Turning once again to the works patronised by Alfonso X of Castile, there are references to female *compannas* (companies/groups) within different settings (monastic, courtly and urban, among others), often gathering separately from men, with a few exceptions, among which are travel and pilgrimage. When women's customary spatial boundaries—the household, the nunnery and so forth—were broken, even if temporarily, different types of relationships could take place, as they were accepted and legitimised, at least within specific contexts. The *Cantigas de Santa Maria* (henceforth *CSM*), a collection of 427 Marian poems and miracles stories and two prologues (numbered following Mettmann's 1986–89 edition),[30] composed in Galician-Portuguese, helps reflect upon the interplay between sex, 'spiritual trust' (in this case towards the Virgin Mary), and the female experience of sacred places.[31] The *CSM* offer multiple examples of women travelling to visit holy shrines to ask for miraculous interventions. Often, but not always, these women were accompanied by their husbands and male relatives, but there are instances in which they feature alone or with female companions. *CSM* 383 narrates the story of a woman from Sigüenza, who travelled as far as Acre and other holy places, assisted only by her daughter.[32] Other miracles emphasise the role of public spaces and sacred intervention to mediate and resolve situations of conflict among women. *CSM* 68, for example, describes the Virgin Mary's intervention to reconcile a legitimate wife with her rival in love. When the two women met in the street, according to *CSM* 68, thanks to the miraculous intervention of the

---

30 Alfonso X, el Sabio, *Cantigas de Santa María*, W. Mettmann (ed.), 3 vols, Madrid 1986–1989. For an English translation: *Songs of Holy Mary of Alfonso X, the Wise: A Translation of the Cantigas de Santa María*, C.L. Scarborough (ed.), K. Kulp-Hill (trans.), Tempe 2000. I will reference volume and page numbers from Meetmann's edition. The number of the *cantigas* coincide in the English translation.

31 L.A. Craig, *Wandering Women and Holy Matrons: Women as Pilgrims in the Later Middle Ages*, Leiden 2009; A.E. Bailey, *Modern and Medieval Approaches to Pilgrimage, Gender and Sacred Space*, in: History and Anthropology 24 (2013), 493–512; M. González Vázquez, *Women and Pilgrimage in Medieval Galicia*, in: C.A. González Paz (ed.), *Women and Pilgrimage in Medieval Galicia*, Farnham 2015, 27–50.

32 *CSM* 383, lines 22–23, Mettmann, vol 3, 1989, 279.

Virgin, the adulterous woman publicly repented, promising not to pursue her sinful behaviour in the future.[33]

These physical places of miraculous mediation, often public and dominated by the presence of witnesses, became core spaces of trust for women. On the one hand, devotion, faith, piety, pain, sadness and desperation (which prompted the women protagonists of these stories to ask for miraculous cures and redemption) generated itinerant "emotional communities" (to adopt Rosenwein's definition)[34] with fewer of the spatial and physical boundaries that in other contexts (urban, monastic and courtly) would have determined more rigid social, sex- and gender-based segregations. On the other hand, the female presence par excellence—that of the Virgin Mary—appearing on site, created a multisensory experience of trust that acted as a supernatural confirmation of 'truth'.[35] Seeing, hearing, feeling and experiencing—in this case the supernatural wonders of the Virgin Mary, in other (as we'll see later) women's presence and voices in circumstances that required their intervention and mediation—constituted what Jucker defined as "plurimedial occurrences" for establishing and strengthening trust.[36] Such plurimedial and multisensory experiences, and their embodiment in a written text with visual and musical components, contributed to legitimising the role of women in shaping the devotional, emotional, and political landscape around them. For its musical, visual and poetic contents, the *CSM* epitomise such multisensory dimensions, while reflecting broader socio-cultural and political dynamics. By the thirteenth century, when the Marian cult had become popular across Western Europe, the image of the Virgin Mary (often humanised and womanised in the *CSM*) was pragmatically and symbolically adopted by Alfonso X to legitimise his own politics of space, which might have been devotionally inspired, while being also led by pragmatic goals. Most of these miracle stories sought to channel pilgrims towards Marian shrines, some of which were located in newly conquered territories under Christian control, so they would have served both to promote Christian devotional practices, and encourage the protection of those sacred and strategic places. This is evident when examining the 24 miracle stories referring to Santa María del Puerto (Jerez), a particularly unstable

---

33　　*CSM* 68, Mettmann, vol 1, 1986, 229–230.

34　　B. Rosenwein, *Emotional Communities in the Early Middle Ages*, Ithaca 2006.

35　　L.K. Twomey, *The Sacred Space of the Virgin Mary in Medieval Hispanic Literature*, Woodbridge 2019.

36　　M. Jucker refers specifically to diplomatic communication and letters, but there is scope to use this framework of analysis more broadly. M. Jucker, *Trust and Mistrust in Letters: Late Medieval Diplomacy and Its Communication Practices*, in: P. Schulte et al. (eds.), *Strategies of Writing*, 2008, 213–238 (227–235).

area for its geographical position, and for the related risks of a possible Muslim counteroffensive.[37]

As a window into the thirteenth-century Iberian devotional and cultural landscape, the *CSM* present different types of interactions with and between women that in some instances challenged established customary practices by breaking rigid spatial boundaries. Some of the descriptions concerning imperial and royal courts offer relevant examples. *CSM* 136 describes a miracle that allegedly occurred in Foggia, when a German woman "a gambler and a fool" at the court of King Conrad IV (r. 1250–1254), son of the Emperor Fredrick II, offended the Virgin Mary by throwing a stone against her statue, in anger because she had lost a game of dice. As a punishment for her gesture, the Emperor ordered that the woman should be "dragged through all the streets of the town", as humiliation and physical penance were parts of public displays of justice.[38] What is particularly relevant in this story is its context: "Men and women of his [scil. Conrad IV's] company were playing dice before the holy statue, as is their custom."[39] This image of men and women gathering together to play dice echoes other courtly settings, including those described and visually depicted in another Alfonsine work, the *Libro de Ajedrez, dados y tablas* (*The Book of Chess, Dice and Other Games*):

> "E como quiere que todos estos iuegos son muy buenos cadaunos en el tiempo e en el logar o conuienen; pero por que estos iuegos que se fazen seyendo son cutianos, e se fazen tan bien de noche como de dia; e por que las mugieres que non caualgan e estan encerradas an a usar desto; e otrossi los omnes que son uieios e flacos, o los que han sabor de auer sus plazeres apartadamientre por que non reciban en ellos enoio nin pesar; o los que son en poder ageno assi como en prision o en catiuerio o que uan sobre mar. E comunalmientre todos e aquellos que han fuerte tiempo; por que non pueden caualgar nin yr a caça ni a otra parte; e han por fuerça de fincar en las casas & buscar algunas maneras de iuegos con que hayan plazer e se conorten e no esten baldios".[40]

---

37   X.R. Pena Sánchez, *De Alcanate a Santa María do Porto. Arredor dun 'cancioneiro' integrado ñas Cantigas de Santa Maria*, in: Anuario de Estudios Literarios Galegos (2001), 187–199.

38   D. Lord Smail, *The Consumption of Justice: Emotions, Publicity, and Legal Culture in Marseille, 1264–1423*, Ithaca 2003; Massimo Vallerani, *Medieval Public Justice*, S. Rubin Blanshei (trans.), Washington 2012.

39   *CSM* 136, lines 20–21, "de ssa companna jogavan ant' a Majestade/dados omees e molleres, com'é usança", Mettmann, vol 2, 107.

40   R. Calvo, *El Libro de los juegos de Alfonso X el Sabio*, in: Alfonso X el Sabio, *Libros de Ajedrez, dados y tablas*, Madrid and Valencia 1987, 1r–1v, 127–135.

These forms of entertainment allowed women, as well as captives, elderly and ill people, and those who could not engage in physically demanding activities, such as martial games, to find enjoyment, while avoiding inertia and apathy that could lead to sin. Whether this description reflects actual courtly practices, or Alfonso's idealised image for his own old age, is open to debate. What is noteworthy is that some of the illuminations of this manuscript give spatial prominence to women playing games at court. Some scholars have argued that some of these illuminations portrayed Mayor Guillén de Guzmán (Alfonso X's lover and mother of his daughter Beatriz, who would later become Queen of Portugal), and his only legitimate wife, Yolant of Aragon.[41] Whether or not these illuminations are accurate portraits of these women, their presence, and the symbolic place they occupied in both the discursive narratives and the visual depictions of courtly life that appear across different types of sources offer an insight into ideal types of social interactions, which must have been recognised and recognisable among different audiences. Exclusion based on mere sex-based boundaries did not appear to be so prominent. Other factors, including trust, could instead determine whether and how women shaped and constructed the physical and discursive spaces between and around them.

1.4   *Political and Diplomatic Spaces of Trust*
Secrecy and confined spheres of trust were often pivotal in the establishment and consolidation of interpersonal relationships, and even more so in determining the outcomes of diplomatic negotiations and political encounters. 'Private' spaces favoured direct access to sources of information, allowing those involved to express their emotions freely, rather than conforming to what Reddy defined as "emotional regimes", that is to say established, and often performative, emotional norms of behaviour shaped by, and recognised as part of, contemporary theological and legal views.[42] King James I of Aragon's *LDF* provides numerous examples of the space and place of secrecy in diplomatic exchanges. On the one hand, the chronicle-autobiography shows an explicit concern with defining both a physical and emotional space of trust in preliminary negotiations, different to the public and ritualised display that might have instead accompanied later formal agreements. On the other hand,

---

41   M. Golladay, *Los Libros de Acedrex Dados e Tablas: Historical, Artistic and Metaphysical Dimensions of Alfonso X's Book of Games*, Doctoral thesis, University of Arizona 2007.

42   W. Reddy, *The Navigation of Feeling. A Framework for the History of Emotions*, Cambridge 2001.

there is a clear dissonance between the secrecy of these informal political and diplomatic negotiations, and the fact that they were recorded in writing (in the same *LDF*), prompting questions about authorial agendas and purposes.[43] Initial 'secret' negotiations often occurred through letters, although the contents of such messages were often transmitted orally, entrusted to loyal mediators, translators and ambassadors, and were not always recorded in the body of those letters. If the outcomes of such earlier private interactions were successful, they were followed by the stipulation of formal written agreements, which embodied the legitimisation of personal trust.[44]

Political and diplomatic negotiations were mostly, but not always, led by men. It is not unusual to find queens and noblewomen managing and leading some of these processes.[45] However, despite their physical presence in contexts of negotiation, such as courts, chambers, and even military sieges, their voices on the written page were frequently (although not always, as recent discoveries have demonstrated) mediated by male scribes and notaries.[46] The example of Queen Violant of Hungary, James I of Aragon's second wife, the only known daughter of Andres II of Hungary (who held the title of Latin Emperor of Constantinople from 1216 to 1217) and Yolanda of Courtenay, daughter of Peter II of Courtenay and Yolanda of Flanders (the latter ruled as Empress of the Latin Empire in Constantinople as wife of Peter II first, and as regent until 1219) offers important points of reflection. According to both the *LDF* and other records preserved in the Archive of the Crown of Aragon (a chancery tradition that started as early as 1218, of which James I is regarded as the initiator),

---

43   A. Liuzzo Scorpo, *Emotional Memory and Medieval Autobiography: King James I of Aragon* (*r. 1213–1276*)'s *Llibre dels fets*, in: Journal of Medieval Iberian Studies, 10 (2018), 1–25.

44   M. Mostert / P.S. Barnwell (eds.), *Medieval Legal Process: Physical, Spoken and Written Performance in the Middle Ages*, Turnhout 2011. A. Liuzzo Scorpo, *'Emotional Diplomacy': Trust and Political Communication in Thirteenth-Century Iberia*, in: id. (ed.), *A Plural Peninsula: Studies in Honour of Professor Simon Barton*, Leiden 2023, 95–122.

45   T. Earenfight (ed.), *Queenship and Political Power in Medieval and Early Modern Spain*, Abingdon, 2005; L. Wilkinson and S.J. Wolfson, *Introduction: Premodern Queenship and Diplomacy*, in: Women's History Review 30 (2021), 713–722.

46   Research is in progress about premodern female scribes and their work. This includes the projects *Repertorium of Manuscripts Illuminated by Women in Religious Communities of the Middle Ages*, available online: http://www.agfem-art.com/introduction.html (last accessed 21/11/2023) and *All She Wrote: Female Scribes Before 1500 AD*, available online: https://femalescribes.blogspot.com/2021/03/databases-of-pre-modern-female-scribes.html (last accessed 21/11/2023). The most recent discovery, confirmed in February 2023, by PhD student Jessica Hodgson, was that of an eighth-century signature by a female scribe ('Eadburg') on a manuscript now preserved in the Bodleian Libraries' special collections, MS Selden Supra 30.

Violant acted as James I's outstanding partner in power and trustworthy coun-
sellor.[47] On 13 September 1238, Zayyān (Zaèn in Catalan), governor of Valencia
(r. 1229–1238), asked James I for a safe-conduct for his envoy, Alí Albaca (who
must himself have been a trustworthy messenger, as he appears as a negotiator
in another embassy two years earlier).[48] LDF 271 narrates that James I decided
to keep this embassy and Zayyān's message secret from his men, sharing this
information only with Queen Violant and the appointed messenger, who also
acted as translator (as a complex act of linguistic and cultural transfer, translation requires and generates trust):[49]

> "So we went to see the queen and we told her the words that Alí Albaca had said
> to us and we communicated our thoughts to her, to see if it seemed good to her.
> And we asked her and we ordered her that none of the army should know about
> it, but only we and she, and the messenger, who was the interpreter".[50]

In the episode concerning the negotiations with Zayyān, Violant "[...] considered it a good idea that nobody else participate in the agreement, so that
nobody might oppose it in any way."[51] She also remarked upon the need to keep
these negotiations secret until Valencia was taken, as "she had already seen in
other places" that some of the knights and nobles acted out of self-interest
rather than loyalty.[52] The secrecy of these negotiations between Zayyān and
James I continued for a while, and so did James I's remarks about the need

---

47   M. van Landingham, *Royal Portraits: Representations of Queenship in the Thirteenth-Century
      Catalan Chronicles*, in: Earenfight (ed.), *Queenship and Political Power*, 2005, 109–119.

48   *LDF* 242.

49   R. Salicrú i Lluch, *Más allá de la mediación de la palabra: negociación con los infieles y
      mediación cultural en la Baja Edad Media*, in: CSIC (ed.), *Negociar en la Edad Media: actas
      del coloquio celebrado en Barcelona los días 14, 15 y 16 de octubre de 2004*, Barcelona 2005,
      409–439; id., *Mercaders, diplomàtics, torsimanys: els perfectes mediadors en els contactes
      de la Corona d' Aragó amb l'Islam occidental?* in: R. Salicrú i Lluch / M.M. Viladrich /
      L. Cifuentes Comamala (eds.), *Els catalans a la Mediterrània medieval: noves fonts, recer-
      ques i perspectives*, Roma 2015, 405–424; id., *Between Trust and Truth: Oral and Written
      Ephemeral Diplomatic Translations between the Crown of Aragon and Western Islam in
      the Late Middle Ages*, in: M.M. Hamilton / N. Silleras-Fernandez (eds.), *Iberian Babel:
      Translation and Multilingualism in the Medieval and the Early Modern Mediterranean*,
      Leiden 2022, 124–146.

50   *LDF* 271, "E entram a la reina e dixem-li aquelles paraules que Alí Albaca nos havia dites
      e que aixi era nostre pensament, si a ella bo li semblava, e que la pregàvem e li manàvem
      que a null hom de la host no ho sabés, sinó tan solament nós e ella e el missatge, que era
      trujamà."

51   *LDF* 271, "E que tenia per bo que null hom no cabés en aquestes paraules, per tal que negú
      no hi pogués re destorbar."

52   *LDF* 271, "car ella havia ja vists d'altres llocs."

for the queen and the messenger/translator to be the only people aware of any private consultations.[53] *LDF* 277 confirms the centrality of secret spaces of trust in the description of the events that followed, when James I sent for the queen and once she arrived "we ordered all the women who had come with her and all the others to leave, and from them on, she alone remained with us."[54] Violant's advice regarding these negotiations was directly solicited by James I, who also felt the need to present his own point of view in the *LDF*, emphasising the worth of his own contribution to enhance and improve Violant's already good, yet somehow incomplete (or so it is presented), piece of advice. This narrative intervention might be explained by the fact that the *LDF*, in all likelihood conceived as a didactic work addressed to James I's successors (as suggested by the use of the vernacular Catalan in its original version, and only later translated into Latin), emphasises the importance of advice and trust as supportive and complementary aspects of kingship, aimed at enhancing royal wisdom and decision-making abilities.

The physical presence of the queen in places conquered by James I, or the surrender of which was under negotiation, was particularly important as a tool to engender trust. *LDF* 237, for instance, narrates how in 1238, following the military campaign to take El Puig, James I was determined (by honour, according to *LDF* 234) to continue his territorial advance, despite dissent from most of his knights. Forced by their threat to withdraw support if he had left (even if temporarily), James I promised his host to support them and to confirm his commitment:

> "And we shall send for the queen, and our daughter (who is now Queen of Castile), for them to come, so that you may appreciate the great determination we have to remain here and to conquer this kingdom [scil. Valencia], in the service of God".[55]

The queen was halted at Ulldecona, on her way to Peñíscola, because of bad weather (so the *LDF* 239 tells us), so James I had to meet her on the way. During

---

53 *LDF* 276.

54 *LDF* 277, "faem-ne partir totes les dones que ab ella eren vengudes e tots los altres, e no romàs ab nós d'elles sinó ella sola."

55 *LDF* 237, "E enviarem per la regina nostra muller e per nostra filla, que és ara regina de Castella, que vinguen, per ço que entenats que major volentat hinc havem d'aturar e de conquerre aquest regne, que sia a servici de Déus." The reference to James I's daughter, Yolant, as Queen of Castile is inaccurate, as she only married Alfonso X in 1249 and became queen once Ferdinand III died in 1252. This might suggest that this part of the chronicle was written after 1252, as suggested by Soldevila.

their 'private' consultation the queen was not alone.[56] With her, there was Don Ferdinand, who was King Peter II of Aragon's brother, hence James I's uncle. He must have been regarded as a trustworthy presence alongside the queen, even if this had not always been the case. Don Ferdinand had sided against James I during his minority, claiming the throne for himself, and was originally very sceptical about the conquest of Valencia, which he only fully supported at a later stage. This example is relevant to reflect upon several aspects. First, the fluid, and sometimes even itinerant, nature of 'private' spaces of trust, which brought together individuals linked among themselves and to each other through bonds of different types, strengths and duration. Second, relationships based on interpersonal, social and institutional trust were neither static nor immutable. Trust could be placed in different individuals at different times, and could easily be threatened, especially in moments of crisis, power vacuum, rebellion and social unrest.

When considering all these factors, the long-term stability (even if not without difficult moments) of the relationship of trust between James I and Violant appears even more remarkable. For example, James I entrusted her with the long and problematic negotiations with the warlord Abū 'Abd Allāh Muḥammad b. Hudhayl, known as Al-Azraq, who posed an ongoing threat to the stability of the Valencian territories. Earlier peace agreements (including the bilingual Castilian-Arabic treaty between Al-Azraq and Alfonso, James I and Eleanor of Castile's son, in 1244 or 1245) were followed by a ten-year war of rebellion (or rather a counter-crusade, according to Burns' interpretation) with alternated truces between 1247 and 1276.[57] A letter from 1250 sent by Al-Azraq and addressed to Queen Violant sheds further light on these events. The letter does not specify what the content of the message was, as this was disclosed orally by Al-Azraq's envoy. Yet, it must have reached Violant, as the letter survives in the royal chancery.[58]

---

56   *LDF* 240.
57   The vernacular document is dated 16 April 1244, but its Arabic correspondent shows a different date: 14 April 1245. This has generated several interpretations and debates. See for example M.ªC. Barceló Torres, *Documentos Árabes de Al-Azrāq (1245–1250)*, in: Saitabi 32 (1982), 27–41; R.I. Burns SJ and P.E. Chevedden, *El tractat de rendició d'al-Azraq amb Jaume I i l'Infant Alfons en 1245: el text arab i el context valencia*, in: Homenatge al Professor Manuel Sanchis Guamer, Espill, XVII–XVIII (1983), 242–257; R.I. Burns SJ, *The Crusade Against Al-Azraq: A Thirteenth-Century Mudejar Revolt in International Perspective*, in: AHR 93 (1988), 80–106.
58   Archive of the Crown of Aragon (henceforth ACA), *Carta árabes*, n. 154, in: M.ªC. Barceló Torres, *Documentos Árabes*, 1982, 40–41.

The document includes the following passage:

> "I have instructed our confident, the commander Abū I-Qāsim, to take your hand in our stead and kiss it. We have instructed him with what he tells you verbally, so trust in him, for I speak through him, and what he says to you I say to you".[59]

The plurimedial components of trust are here on full display, as it was articulated verbally, in written form (through this letter) and in gestures, here conforming to the Christian custom of performing vassalic homage embodied by the kissing of the queen's hand. A question remains: why was this letter addressed directly to Violant?

One of the possible answers lies in the space of mediation and arbitration that Violant—in line with contemporary models of queenship[60]—occupied, and for which she was renowned. In 1249, she acted as arbiter in the dispute between James I and Peter of Portugal (1187–1258), son of Sancho I of Portugal and Dulce of Aragon, and Count of Urgell from 1229 and 1231. Their dispute followed James I's decree to expel the Muslim population of some areas north of Valencia who had rebelled in 1247, under Al-Azraq's leadership.[61] Some of those territories (Segorbe, Almenara, Murviedro, and Castellón) were under Peter's *vitalicio*, so the expulsion of their inhabitants, who paid taxes to him, would have had an impact on his finances. The *LDF* confirms and emphasises the key role of Violant in these negotiations with Peter of Portugal, and in several others where familial, political and diplomatic boundaries were blurred. The wavering relationship between James I and Alfonso X, which I discussed in a previous study, is one such compelling example.[62] Both Violant and her daughter, Yoland, who married Alfonso X in 1249, exercised significant functions of mediation, supported by their communication skills, positions and the familiarity and trust that they engendered. The *LDF* mentions letters written

---

59   Ibid.
60   Á. Muñoz Fernández, *Semper pacis amica. Mediación y práctica política* (*siglos VI–XIV*), in: Arenal 5 (1998), 263–276; M.ªC. García Herrero, *El entorno femenino de los Reyes de Aragón*, in: J.Á. Sesma Muñoz (ed.), *La Corona de Aragón en el centro de su Historia, 1208–1458*, Zaragoza 2010, 327–350.
61   ACA, *Cancelleria. Pergamins de Jaume I*, n° 1146. Available at https://www.jaumeprimer.uji.es/cgi-bin/arxiu.php?noriginal=000941 (last accessed: 22/11/2023). See also A. Huici Miranda / M.ªD. Cabanes Pecourt (eds.), *Documentos de Jaime I de Aragón*, 5 vols, Valencia, 1976; J. Torró, Guerra, repartiment i colonització al regne de València, 1248–1249, in: E. Guinot / J. Torró (eds.), *Repartiments a la Corona d'Aragó* (*segles XII–XIII*), Valencia, 2007, 201–276 (218).
62   A. Liuzzo Scorpo, *"El mellor amigo que nos avemos": Friendship and Political Communication in Thirteenth-Century Iberia*, in: Cahiers d'études hispaniques médiévales 42 (2019), 107–122.

by Yolant to her father, James I, interceding for her husband, although often in the name of her family ties with James I and for the protection of her rights, and those of her children.[63] According to the chronicle-autobiography, Yolant contributed to rescuing several of the tense exchanges prompted by the clash of ambitions of both her husband, Alfonso X and father, James I. Her skills recall those of her mother, Violant, whose actions and experience as a political mediator emerge prominently from contemporary sources. Violant's fame as a political mediator might have preceded her, explaining why Al-Azraq might have addressed his letter to the queen directly. Al-Azraq had been in contact with the infant Alfonso of Aragon (with whom he had signed a peace agreement in 1245, previously mentioned) and through him with the Castilian court, and with Alfonso X. He must have been also aware of the situation of Peter of Portugal, so Violant's fame and her successful interventions in the political arena might have reached the Muslim warlord before his letter was sent to her. Trust relied on reputation, honour and 'fame', alongside values, merits and reliability, which were broadly recognised by individuals and communities, even when their authenticity was not experienced first-hand. By the same token, James I's exploits of *ira regia* (some of which are described in his chronicle-autobiography with a range of physical, as well as emotional details) might have been also known beyond his close circles, and might have therefore informed the choice of a different interlocutor to establish a channel of communication with the sovereign and his court.[64]

1.5   *Women and Trust in Uncustomary Spaces*

> "Cuenta la estoria que acabo el día de tres dias despues que el çid fue finado arribo el Rey Bucar de Tunez al puerto de Valencia et sallio a terrenno et traye consigo tan grant poder que era marauilla. Et vinien con el treynta e seys Reyes de moros et traye consigo vna mora negra que traye trezientas moras negras consigo. Et todas eran tras quiladas sinon sennas vedijas que trayen ençima delas cabeças. Et esto era en razon de commo que vinien en romeria et commo a perdon. Et todas muy bien armadas de lorigones et de arcos torquis. Et el Rey bucar mando fincar las tiendas derredor de Valencia. [...] Et el Rey Bucar mando aquella mora negra que posasse mas çerca dela villa con todas sus conpannas. Et ella fue la prima que los cristianos mataron en la fazienda assy commo oyredes adelante".[65]

---

63   M.ªJ. Fuente Pérez, *Tres Violantes. Las mujeres de una familia en el poder a lo largo del siglo XIII*, in: Anuario de estudios medievales 46 (2016), 137–165; id., *Las cartas visibles*, 2018, 17–33.

64   A. Liuzzo Scorpo, *Emotional Memory*, 2018, 11–16.

65   Alfonso X, *Estoria de Espanna*, best known to modern readers through Ramón Menéndez Pidal's edition, originally published in 1906 and reprinted in 1955 and 1977, bearing the title *Primera Crónica General*. EE 955, 636, a43–b14.

This is how the Alfonsine chronicle *Estoria de Espanna* (henceforth *EE*, c. early 1270s, regarded as the first vernacular history of Spain, from its legendary origins up to the death of Ferdinand III, Alfonso's father, in 1252)[66] described the intervention of a company of 300 black Muslim female archers, leading the Almoravid siege of Valencia.[67] The military-spatial choices here are key for the narrative, as the 300 female archers were sent to camp the closest to Valencia, ahead of the male part of their army. This might have been justified by a shared trust in their martial skills, or because they were regarded as expendable human resources. Or because, despite the fact that their territorial advance was viewed "like a pilgrimage"—in all likelihood referring to the vow of celibacy sworn in those circumstances, which should have protected both men and women from licentious behaviour—it would have been safer and customary practice to keep a physical separation between male and female combatants. Significantly, as Elena Lourie demonstrated, this narrative disappeared from later Arabic chronicles, and it was subsequently misinterpreted by European scholars who considered it a Christian invention embedded in the *EE*, although this is unlikely considering that the event was depicted as a Christian victory by deceit and one against women. As Lourie suggested, this narrative reveals the anxiety of later historians, who faced unexpected and converging conceptions of femininity belonging to different cultures and spaces, normally separated by vast geographical and chronological distances, more than contemporary (Almoravid and Christian) views of female involvement in military spheres.[68]

The *EE* describes another example of female companionship in arms, this time in a Christian context. *EE* 1054 narrates that, during the nobleman Álvar Pérez de Castro's (c. 1196–1239) absence from his territories, his unnamed wife (only mentioned in the *EE* as 'the Countess') defended the castle of Martos—one of the two castles recently surrendered by the Muslim lord of Baeza to Castile, that Álvar had received from Ferdinand III in 1225, once he returned as Ferdinand's vassal, after having served in Al-Andalus under several

---

66 More recently, the *Estoria de Espanna Digital* project has developed transcriptions of five complete manuscripts, developing the crowdsourcing of other witnesses: https://blog. bham.ac.uk/estoriadigital/the-estoria-de-espanna-digital-about-this-edition/#What-is-the-Estoria-de-Espanna (last accessed 21/11/2023).

67 *EE* 956.

68 E. Lourie, *Black Women Warriors in the Muslim Army Besieging Valencia and The Cid's Victory. A Problem of Interpretation*, in: Traditio 55 (2000), 181–209. On women's involvement in the battlefield, see also M.ªC. Marín Pina, *Amazonas y doncellas guerreras, virgines bellatrices*, in: Páginas de sueños. Estudios sobre los libros de caballerías castellanos, Zaragoza 2011, 239–263.

taifas.[69] According to the *EE*, in 1228 Ibn Ahmar[70] (King of Arjona and later of Granada) threatened the Countess in Martos, but she reacted heroically, gathering all the women at her service and asking them to abandon their female customs to embrace arms: "the Countess ordered them to separate and stand up, and to embrace the weapons, and to position themselves in the walkways; and so they did".[71]

The identity of the Countess is not made explicit in the *EE*, and some of the most popular biographical overviews of Álvar Pérez de Castro only mention his second marriage with Mencía López de Haro, daughter of Lope Díaz de Haro II, and Urraca Alfonso, hence granddaughter of Alfonso IX de León, who had grown up at the court of Ferdinand III, close to Beatriz of Swabia and Alfonso X.[72] Who was, therefore, his first wife? The Countess mentioned in the *EE* was Aurembiaix of Urgell (c. 1203–1231), daughter of Count Ermengol VIII of Urgell and Elvira de Subirats (Elvira Núñez de Lara), but their marriage was annulled in 1228 because of consanguinity.[73] Cross-referencing our sources from thirteenth-century Castile and Aragon provides additional information. Mentions of Aurembiaix and her early marriage with the Castilian *ricohombre* appear in the *LDF*, although what is omitted from James I's chronicle-autobiography is any reference to her military defence of Martos.

The *LDF* tells us that Aurembiaix asked for James I's support to legally reclaim her rights over several territories which had been controlled until then by her cousin Guerau de Cabrera, de facto Count of Urgell (1217–1227), who had been supported by James I on condition that he return those rights to Aurembiaix whenever she reclaimed them. The 1228 agreement between Aurembiaix and James I has been frequently cited as an example of a concubinage contract, as scholars often linked it to the fact that Aurembiaix's widowed mother, Elvira de Subirats, had signed an agreement with James I's father, Peter II of Aragon, in 1210 promising her daughter to James. This agreement was meant to protect the inheritance of the County of Urgell that belonged by right to Aurembiaix, but which was challenged by her uncle Ponç Guerau de Cabrera.[74]

---

69   B. Vázquez Campos, *Sobre el origen del cargo de Adelantado de la Frontera*, in: M. González Jiménez (ed.), *Sevilla 1248. Congreso Internacional Conmemorativo del 750 Aniversario de la Conquista de la Ciudad de Sevilla por Fernando III* [...], Madrid, 2000, 813–820.

70   https://dbe.rah.es/biografias/6494/muhammad-i (last accessed 14/08/23).

71   *EE* 1054, "La Condesa mando asus duennas que se des tocasen e se parasen en cabellos e que e tomasen armas en las manos e que se parassen en el andamio e ellas fezi eron lo así."

72   Real Academia de la Historia: https://dbe.rah.es/biografias/14111/alvar-perez-de-castro (last accessed 22/02/2023).

73   After Álvaro Pérez de Castro, she married Peter of Portugal, Sancho I of Portugal's son.

74   F. Soldevila, *Fou Aurembiaix d'Urgell amistançada de Jaume I?* in: Revista de Catalunya 28 (1926), 399–410; D. Domingo, *A la recerca d'Aurembiaix d'Urgell*, Lleida 2007.

Nonetheless, as Miriam Shadis convincingly argued, the 1228 agreement was more likely a type of *conveniencia*, which "does not necessarily eliminate sex, but allows us to reinterpret its gendered elements as not being solely about sexual submission", but rather as a way of negotiating feudal relationships.[75] The events that preceded and surrounded the signing of this agreement (of which one charter survives)[76] are also described in the *LDF*, which dedicates a total of nine chapters to Aurembiaix, mentioning a broad range of skills and values attributed to her, making her choice to request James I's support even more significant. According to *LDF* 34, in July/August 1228, Aurembiaix went to see James I in Lleida. Following established procedures aimed at generating spaces of trust (similar to what occurred during other meetings, when negotiations did not start on the first day): "We [scil. James I] made her welcome, after she had been there for two days, we went to see her."[77] At the meeting, her guardian and stepfather, Guillem de Cervera, was present and despite her asking him to intervene on her behalf, Guillem encouraged her to use her own voice instead: "Lady, you should say it, as you know better than I how to explain it and say it."[78]

Trust, as a multisensory experience, included all the aspects that Aurembiaix was required to embody and show here, as her physical presence and her own voice acquired both pragmatic and symbolic meanings. *LDF* 42 confirms this theory through the description of how Aurembiaix's physical presence was requested by her vassals in the castles, cities and territories that she was reclaiming as a natural lady. Aurembiaix was certainly an expert communicator (as her words recorded in the chronicle and the entitlement by her councillor suggest) and, according to the Castilian chronicle *EE*, even a martial leader when needed. Yet, when she arrived at Balaguer, the chronicle-autobiography tells us: "[...] one of the knights said in her name: 'Are the men of Balaguer here?' However, they remained silent and did not respond the first time [...] A knight said: 'The countess requests that you listen to her a little, for she is a woman and is unable to shout.'"[79] The emphasis on 'expectedly' feminine characteristics, such as a feeble voice, might have served a specific authorial agenda: let's not forget that the *LDF* was James I's self-portrait aimed at

---

75   M. Shadis, *"Received as a woman": Rethinking the Concubinage of Aurembiaix of Urgell*, in: Journal of Medieval Iberian Studies 8 (2016), 38–54 (52).

76   ACA, *Cancelleria. Pergamins de Jaume I*, n° 389.

77   *LDF* 34, "E nós acollim-la bé e, quan venc que hac estat dos dies, anam-la ver."

78   *LDF* 34, "–Dona, mostrats-la vós, que mills la sabrets vós mostrar e dir que jo."

79   *LDF* 42, "–Sots aquí los de Balaguer? E ells callaren e no responeren la primera vegada [...] E dix un cavaller: –Prega-us la comtessa que l'escoltets un poc, que dona és e no pot alt parlar."

aggrandising his chivalrous behaviour, which included the support and rescue of women (including powerful women) in need of his help.[80]

Two important points emerge from these examples of women acting at the crossroads of political and martial spheres. First, the pragmatic duties associated with the defence of a place (and the subsequent threatening of human lives) could generate strong bonds of loyalty and trust, which included female friendships in arms. Although not prominent in the sources, it was not impossible for noblewomen and those at their orders, in Iberia and beyond, to inhabit—even if temporarily—spaces, places and roles that were culturally and ordinarily conceived as male spheres of action, including that of military leadership.[81] Second, the meagre number of explicit references in the sources to women acting in 'uncustomary' places, such as military sieges, should not prevent us from considering the relevance of these narratives of sex, gender, and space, and what they suggest about their context of production and reception, alongside the customary and symbolic value of the multisensory presence of women in such places of trust.

2   Conclusion

Spaces and places of trust, as physical, pragmatic and symbolic constructs had both public and private connotations. With their presence or absence, women—as historical agents—played a substantial role in shaping practices and experiences related to spheres of communication and interaction. This brief overview of different types of narrative, literary and documentary evidence from thirteenth-century Castile and Aragon, offers a critical reassessment of the communication strategies, which included the rhetoric and spaces of trust, deployed in different types of social exchanges and political negotiations. The study of women's roles and place in devotional, military, social, political and diplomatic networks has shed further light on the symbolic and pragmatic politics of space, and the role of trust (rather than sex exclusively) in shaping, promoting and legitimising different types of social agreements and communication.

---

80   S.M. Cingolani, *Jaume I: Història i mite d'un Rei*, Barcelona 2007.

81   J.F. Verbruggen, *Women in Medieval Armies*, in: Journal of Medieval Military History 8 (2006), 119–136; S. Harwood, *Medieval Women and War: Female Roles in the Old French Tradition*, London 2022. H.J. Nicholson, *Women and the Crusades*, Oxford 2023.

Despite female voices often being mediated by male authors, scribes and notaries in the surviving written records, their place on the written page is highly significant, as it helps understand how converging or distinct politics of space were reflected in written narratives, and how they contributed to shaping historical and cultural memories associated with them. Cross-referencing different types of sources from both Castile and Aragon has been fruitful from different perspectives. First, it has revealed how trust and space were parts of an entangled and dynamic process, which would benefit from shared interests, beliefs, social belonging and values, including loyalty and honour. Although essential, such characteristics did not always guarantee the longevity and stability of relationships based on trust. Some of them might have reflected the temporary nature of the settings and conditions defining those connections (for example, in the case of pilgrimages); others might have been influenced by changing attitudes and choices dictated by pragmatic circumstances and external factors. Second, this study has demonstrated that women across the social spectrum occupied a central place in converging dynamics of trust involving men, but also other women. The examples under scrutiny suggest that trust was not strictly gendered, as women were not excluded from networks of trust merely because of their sex. However, the parameters to define trustworthiness sometimes conflicted with customs informed by theological, medical and cultural views that reflected gender-based attitudes. The example of Aurembiaix of Urgell, who appears in both Castilian and Aragonese sources, is revealing. She is described in both cases as a strong and powerful woman, but in the Alfonsine chronicle she remains without an individual identity (other than "the Countess", Álvar Pérez de Castro's wife) despite her being explicitly depicted as a military leader. In James I's autobiography, by contrast, she occupies a significant portion of narrative space, she is described as a determined and authoritative woman (recognised as such by her subjects), but there is no mention of her military skills, while the emphasis is on her 'feminine' characteristics, such as her beauty, gentle voice and her own trust in the men who would help her, including James I. Rather than contradictions, our sources reflect the complexity of converging views and perspectives in which historiographical writing, personal experiences and authorial agendas merged and were filtered through a male gaze. Finally, this study has focused on the pragmatic and symbolic value of the multisensory politics of space, especially those concerning women. Female presence (physical or mystical, as in the case of the miraculous apparitions of the Virgin Mary), their voices, words and actions in both customary and uncustomary places (including military sieges and contexts of conflict) generated trust, affecting the establishment, development and strengthening of bonds of solidarity and support for themselves and those in their closest family and kinship networks.

This study has only scratched the surface of what a broader interdisciplinary approach to the study of women and trust in the premodern world could reveal about the entangled dimensions of family, politics, networks of solidarity, law, community and society. This is an open call to embark on new collaborative and cross-disciplinary research to reassess socio-political dynamics of broader cultural impact (including modes of interpersonal communication and exchanges within and across ethnic and religious communities) through the lens of trust as "a set of values, a suite of emotions, a conversation involving speech-acts and physical performance, and a way of negotiating the spaces in which relationships were conducted."[82]

---

82   I. Forrest, *Trust in Long-Distance Relationships, 1000–1600*, in: Past and Present 238 (2018), 190–213 (193).

María de Quesada's Leadership during the Castilian Crisis and the Different Factions of the Fajardo Clan (Kingdom of Murcia, Mid-15th Century)

María Martínez Martínez

Abstract

María de Quesada carried out the functions of viceregality – representing the king in the kingdom of Murcia – on behalf of her son, a minor, Pedro Fajardo. She led a faction in the war between the Fajardo clan, at the same time as the Castilian political crisis taking place between Juan II and his favourites, the infantes of Aragon and the Nasrid emirate. This article recovers her political role as acting "vicereine".

1   Women in Politics and War

The women of Western Christianity participated in the political, economic and social cultures that characterised late medieval Europe, as well as in the disturbances, crises and wars that devastated it, forming or leading the construction of societies. Historiography has recovered women from the exclusively private, domestic and family sphere, and retrieved the real female history.[1] Their mouths were not always silenced,[2] their minds not always closed and their hands not always tied to their 'predestined' role. Research has shown that females were not excluded from public life – or from politics – because of their feminine role in marriage and procreation. After a long process initiated in Spain during the 1980s, the history of women has been given the recognition of their rightful historiographic trends: A history of women;[3] Gender and History,

---

1   B.S. Anderson / J.P. Zinsser, *Historia de las mujeres: una historia propia* 1, Barcelona 1991; G. Duby / M. Perrot (dirs.), *Historia de las mujeres 2. La Edad Media*, Madrid ²2000 (1ª ed. 1990); P. Ariés / G. Duby (dirs.), *Historia de la vida privada*, Madrid 1987.
2   S. Ferrer, *Mujeres silenciadas en la Edad Media*, Madrid 2022 (2º ed.).
3   D. Pelaz Flores / Mªl. del Val Valdivieso, *La Historia de las mujeres en el siglo XXI a través del estudio de la reginalidad medieval*, in: RevHisto 22 (2014), 101–127; C. Segura Graíño, *Las mujeres medievales. Perspectivas historiográficas*, in: Mªl. del Val Valdivieso / J.F. Jiménez Alcázar (coords.), *Las mujeres en la Edad Media*, Lorca 2013, 33–54; F. Fuster García, *La Historia de las mujeres en la historiografía española: propuestas metodológicas desde la Historia Medieval*, in: EMRH 10 (2009), 247–273.

© BRILL SCHÖNINGH, 2024 | DOI:10.30965/9783657791477_010

and more recently the concept of "reginality" or *Queenship*,[4] associated to the terms of *Kingship* or *partnership*.[5]

Queens, aristocrats, ladies and common women acted in public and private, urban and rural spaces, used the resources at their disposal and established vital relationships of all kinds in their specific, personal and political contexts.[6] The female presence in written testimonies allows us to recover the forgotten power of María de Quesada – a noblewoman related to the Fajardo lineage – and her role in the biggest advances made by the kingdom of Murcia since the end of the 14th century. Wife and mother of the viceroy, she was the consort of the highest representative of the kingdom, and gained her own recognition when, as a widow, she carried out that role while her son Pedro Fajardo was still a minor. She used her authority and influence in political conflicts, championing one side of the warring factions for the viceregality, disputed by other members of the Fajardo clan. Her activity was seen during the Castilian crises of Juan II, when the kingdom of Murcia was drawn into the war between factions of the Fajardo lineage. From 1444 until 1450 – for six years following the death of her husband – she firmly defended the legitimacy of her young son's position; the Castilian monarch had appointed him viceroy of the kingdom of Murcia. She intervened in diplomatic pacts and negotiations leading to peace, which did not come until much later, when the viceroy came of age, and after eighteen years of conflict with his paternal cousin Alonso Fajardo, governor of Lorca. María, as she signs, is a good example of the active participation of noblewomen in political and military life. She was considered head of a faction in the – very masculinised – world of war, materialised in the response given by the infantes of Aragon to the Castilian monarchy of Juan II and his private Álvaro de Luna.

In this dual warlike context, she carried out her role against battle-hardened relatives: Alonso Fajardo and Mosén Diego Fajardo, her nephews-in-law. Due to her historical importance, this woman's public space was registered in official

---

4   T. Earenfight (ed.), *Queenship and Political Power in Medieval and Early Modern Spain*, Aldershot 2005.

5   D. Pelaz Flores, *Teoría y práctica del ejercicio del poder en la baja edad media castellana*, in *Las mujeres en la Edad Media*, in: MªI. del Val Valdivieso / J.F. Jiménez Alcázar (coords.), 2013, 277–287; D. Pelaz Flores, *Poder y representación de la reina en la Corona de Castilla (1418–1496)*, Ávila 2017.

6   J. Jasperse, *Medieval Women, Material Culture, and Power: Matilda Plantagenet and her Sisters*, Amsterdam 2020; W. Mark Ormrod, *Women and Parliament in Later Medieval England*, London 2020; H.J. Tanner (ed.), *Medieval Elite Women and the Exercise of Power, 1100–1400: Moving beyond the Exceptionalist Debate*, London 2019; S. Broomhall, *Women and Power at the French Court, 1483–1563*, Amsterdam 2018; T. Evergates (ed.), *Aristocratic Women in Medieval France*, Philadelphia 1999.

written records. Within the broad female universe, María adds to the practice of political power exercised by queens, aristocrats and ladies, making female leadership visible in war, where current historiography continues to recover the active role of women.

Individual female identities and/or those representing the group reflect a wide range of relationships and activities, complaints, mediations, agreements, violence of female power in medieval times and spaces, with the geopolitical singularity of applying them to Castilian Murcia, capital of a kingdom that bordered the Nasrid emirate of Granada from the mid-13th century to the end of the 15th.[7] From their social position and economic level, these women took refuge in the laws and resources within their reach to defend or maintain "what is theirs" or that of their lineage. A visible power, influence and authority that could be seen in María de Quesada's acts, another woman who "made history".[8] Obviously, the noble female elite had a more institutional role that came from her belonging to families that monopolised political, territorial and municipal, urban and rural power. There were powerful women who were represented and whose public acts were more passive, but many – in addition to their representation – exercised real power, beyond the usual queens.[9] Ladies who carried out the functions of government and administration, politics, war and diplomacy of royalty[10] within their social scale. A female elite made up of the Fajardos, mothers, daughters, wives or widows of Murcian viceroys, and especially María de Quesada, due to the political and war circumstances she had to address. Widow of the viceroy, between 1444–1450 she supervised the Murcia viceregality while Pedro Fajardo was still a minor. And she did so as

---

7   M.ª Martínez, *Vivir en la frontera murciano-granadina en los tiempos bajomedievales,* in: Fundación Sánchez Albornoz (ed.), *Cristianos y musulmanes en la Península Ibérica: la guerra, la frontera, la convivencia. XI Congreso de Estudios Medievales, León, del 23 al 26 de octubre de 2007,* Ávila 2009, 611–631.

8   H. Gallego Franco / M.C. García Herrero (eds.), *Autoridad, poder e influencia. Mujeres que hacen historia,* Barcelona 2017; C. Segura Graíño / A.I. Cerrada Jiménez (coords.), *Las mujeres y el poder. Representaciones y prácticas de vida,* Madrid 2000; V. Márquez de la Plaza, *El poder de las mujeres en la Historia de España,* Madrid 2022, 99–146.

9   G. Martin (dir.), *Femmes et gouvernement. Gouverner en Castille au Moyen Âge: la part des femmes,* in: e-Spania 30 (2006); M. García-Fernández / S. Cernadas Martínez (coords.), *Regina Iberiae. El poder regio femenino en los reinos medievales peninsulares,* Santiago de Compostela 2015; D. Pelaz Flores, *Poder y representación de la reina en la Corona de Castilla (1418–1496),* Ávila 2017; D. Pelaz, *Reinas consortes. Las reinas de Castilla entre los siglos IX–XV,* Madrid 2017.

10   M.ªI. del Val Valdivieso / C. Segura Graíño (coords.), *La participación de las mujeres en lo político. Mediación, representación y toma de decisiones,* Madrid 2011.

acting vicereine, representing her son and performing as legitimiser and transmitter of the succession, recognised by Juan II.

The role of powerful women in the culture of war and peace has been researched in many studies carried out over the last two decades.[11] María de Quesada is aligned with this public sphere of power, and more specifically, the war between noble factions and the monarchy. Consort queens and proprietor queens of Castile and ladies of the nobility acted in the politics of factions and diplomacy. They assumed the prevailing value system in the warrior mentality, a masculine role par excellence, and deployed networks of marriages, alliances, friendships, solidarities, patronage and vassalage in the private and public space. These facts are recorded with words that indicate charisma in the exercise of feminine power, of regality or *Queenship*, and *Ladyship*.[12] Traditional historiography relegated women and their participation in politics and war, because their inclusion had a supplementary character in the absence of men, as regents or widows; while modern research shows that when they exercised government or political, military and diplomatic power, they showed leadership capacity, institutional authority, social influence and decision-making capabilities equal to those of men, and without losing their identity.

Many examples of "medieval women warriors" have been compiled within the framework of female experience in wars,[13] showing they were knowledgeable about military strategy, as is the case of the Castilian queens (Urraca, 12th Century; Berenguela, 13th Century; María de Molina, 14th Century; Isabel I, 15th Century), and women who defended towns and castles from Muslim sieges in the absence of their husbands and townsmen, or participated anonymously in revolts and riots. This was necessary in the colonisation and organisation

---

11   G. Martín, *Mujeres y poderes en la España Medieval: cinco estudios*, Alcalá de Henares 2011; E. Pardo de Guevara, *Mujeres con poder en la Galicia Medieval (ss. XIII–XV)*, Santiago de Compostela 2017; J. Castrillo: *Poder, autoridad e influencia de las mujeres de la nobleza y las élites urbanas en las provincias vascas a finales de la Edad Media*, in: EEM 45 (2022), 237–259; A.J. Barbarín López, *Juana Núñez de Lara, mediadora entre el linaje y la monarquía*, in: M.ªP. Carceller Cerviño / J.M. Nieto (coords.), *La nobleza y la cultura política de la negociación en la Baja Edad Media*, Madrid 2020, 139–161; A. Arranz Guzmán / M.ªP. Rábade / O. Villaroel González (coords.), *Guerra y paz en la Edad Media*, Madrid 2013; C. Trillo (ed.), *Mujeres, familia y linaje en la Edad Media*, Granada 2004; A.M. Aguado (ed.), *Mujeres, regulación de conflictos sociales y cultura de la paz*, Valencia 1999.

12   A. Muñoz Fernández, *Los estudios sobre las mujeres medievales. Agencia femenina y poder: claves y problemas en un momento de consolidación historiográfica*, in: E. López Ojeda (coord.), *Las mujeres en la Edad Media*, Logroño 2021, 327–366.

13   Y. Guerrero Navarrete, *Las mujeres y la guerra en la edad media: mitos y realidades*, in: JFGWS 3 (2016), 3–10; T. Vinyoles Vidal, *Actitudes femeninas ante las guerras feudales*, in: M.D. Molas Font (ed.), *De las mujeres, el poder y la guerra*, Barcelona 2012, 61–80.

of societies and towns that bordered al-Andalus, as they were victims of captivity and considered qualified booty, resulting in sexual violence being a common threat. In addition to these aggressions they had to suffer the loss of husbands and children in border wars. A disturbing emotional world that links women, directly or indirectly, with war. This follows from the political actions and inherent feelings (fear, aggressiveness, suspicion, revenge, fear, damage, enmity, resentment, hatred, conciliation, forgiveness, etc.) that encompass the sides, pacts, alliances, partialities, confederations, clienteles and leagues in the hierarchies of power and government of the kingdoms and cities of late medieval Castile. We must continue to recover – precisely because they are not well known – the functions women have carried out in war (leading armies; organising struggles and resistance in their territories; accompanying the troops to conflict zones, etc.) throughout history.[14] Female groups have always been perceived as weak and unprotected in the collective imagination.

In the Middle Ages, queens and ladies, educated to govern their houses and manors, participated as representatives or actively in politics and wars,[15] in the direct intervention of marriage alliances and in the diplomatic mediation of truces, agreements, consensus and peace as political subjects and objects linked to lineages. Royal and aristocratic women were present, either visibly or invisibly, in war together with their husbands in places close to where war was carried out against al-Andalus (in the case of Isabel I) or by leading fights between kingdoms or noble factions, but not directly in the line of combat, with the exception of Queen Toda of Navarre, Juana Manuel and Maria de Aragon. Warrior women who, apart from myths, formed the medieval scene[16] by representing a legendary anonymous group that, on certain occasions, crossdressed as men to repel attacks and desist the Muslim enemy, or by participating in war strategies and the defence of fortresses and estates in the absence of their husbands. They were also used as hostages, or sent away from the conflict, as the bellicose Alonso Fajardo did with his wife and daughter, who he sent to the Nasrid court in 1457.[17] Or the case of princesses, future queens and ladies who were trained in military art and horsemanship as potential strategists against the Andalusian enemy or the nobility.

---

14   M. Nash / S. Tavera (eds.), *Las mujeres y las guerras: el papel de las mujeres en las guerras de la Edad Antigua a la Contemporánea*, Barcelona 2003.

15   B. Bolton / Ch. Meek (eds.), *Aspects of Power and Authority in the Middle Ages*, Turnhout 2007.

16   Y. Guerrero Navarrete, *Las mujeres y la guerra en la edad media: mitos y realidades*, in: JFGWS 3 (2016), 3–10 (6–8).

17   J. Torres Fontes, *Don Pedro Fajardo, adelantado mayor del reino de Murcia*, Madrid 1953, 78.

Feminine power was more present when there was dialogue and mediation for the resolution of armed conflicts between kingdoms, in civil wars and factions. Does this mean that these powerful ladies are the example or the exception? P. L'Hermitte-Leclerq believes that the political role of feudal ladies was almost always "precarious, adventitious or interim and contingent: women "can" be called to public affairs, to take the place of a man".[18] This being so, when she replaces or represents a man because of her role of consort, regency or guardian, her interventions are not abstract but personalised in each case, since she transcends political-institutional representation and assumes the expected virtues of virility. In the final centuries of the Middle Ages, queens, princesses and ladies carried out public functions in political strategies, wars and conflicts between the nobility. It was not a question of the political power of women, spread by historiography,[19] but of how they exercised it, whether there are differences compared to men, and the historical reality in which they had to live, nuanced by their personality.

The role in war that corresponded to knights in feudal theory was exercised by royal and noble women. María de Quesada is an example of a woman who directly participated in the crisis of the Crown of Castile, related to the kingdom of Murcia, towards the middle of the 15th century. A powerful, active woman and defender of the rights of her son Pedro Fajardo, heir to the viceregality. Like her male opponents, she maintained authority, power, and influence in the upper echelons of royal and council power and led an armed faction against her enemies. She capitalised on war with the tactics, mediation, resistance, solidarity, patronage, violence, coercion, information and practices of the time. It was not a literal participation with sword in hand and on a horse at the head of the troops (albeit plausible) but in the deciding of peaceful and violent strategies according to the development of the conflict, in diplomatically recruiting support to participating in the direction and consequences of the events resulting from the conflict between factions. As the daughter of a

---

18   P. l'Hermitte-Leclercq, *Las mujeres en el orden feudal (siglos XI y XII)*, in: G. Duby / M. Perrot (dirs.), *Historia de las mujeres 2. La Edad Media*, Madrid 1991, 247–300.

19   M.H. da Cruz Coelho, *O protagonismo da mulher na política da dinastía de Avis*, in: M.ªI. del Val Valdivieso / J.F. Jiménez Alcázar (coords.), *Las mujeres en la Edad Media*, Lorca 2013, 243–257; C. Barquero Goñi, *Las mujeres de la Orden de San Juan en la Península Ibérica durante los siglos XII y XIII*, in: del Val Valdivieso / Jiménez Alcázar (coords.), 2013, 259–265; C. Benítez Guerrero, *María de Molina, reina madre entre la Literatura y la Historia*, in: del Val Valdivieso / Jiménez Alcázar (coords.), 2013, 267–275; D. Pelaz Flores, *Queenship: teoría y práctica del ejercicio del poder en la Baja Edad Media castellana*, in: del Val Valdivieso / Jiménez Alcázar (coords.), 2013, 277–287; P. Romero Portilla, *Doña Mencía o un matrimonio que no logró separar un reino*, in: del Val Valdivieso / Jiménez Alcázar (coords.), 2013, 289–296.

nobleman and married to the person who held the highest power in the kingdom, Viceroy Alfonso Yáñez Fajardo II, María de Quesada used her political resources and showed her accumulated experience. Experience and advice that she passed on to her son, who in turn was influenced by a mother who was well-versed in the internal politics of the kingdom and the external politics of the Castilian monarchy, aligned with Constable Álvaro de Luna and Juan II. A noble woman educated to share and represent the government of the kingdom with her husband, and ensure her institutional behaviour established a binding relationship that was appropriate to a monarchical couple.

The feminisation of the power of the viceregality was a reality for María during her marriage and widowhood, in a representative manner as the consort of the viceroy and a practical manner in the functions she carried out for the contested position she kept for her son. She used the institutional role of wife and mother of viceroys – the separation of male and female public roles was blurred during the guardianship – in addition to her strong political personality. Aware of her legitimate authority and how to use it for the benefit of her son, she was not daunted: she led and adapted her actions to the political suitability of each circumstance during the Castilian and Fajardo war.

2   María de Quesada in the War for the Viceregality (1444–1450)

The territorialisation of the viceregality of Murcia,[20] a kingdom of Castile bordering Islam, began with the Trastámara monarchy and Alfonso Yáñez Fajardo I (1383–1395),[21] appointed viceroy by Juan I. The second holder of the lineage, Alfonso Yáñez Fajardo II (1424–1444), remarried María de Quesada, whose issue were Pedro, María and Catalina.[22] Commanderies, estates or royal towns were governed by Fajardos.[23] The power of this lineage ran parallel to their accumulation of wealth. The rich stately heritage was bequeathed by the

---

20   M. Martínez, *La territorialización del poder: los adelantados mayores de Murcia (ss. XIII–XV)*, in: AEM 25 (1995), 545–569.

21   J. Torres Fontes, *Los Fajardo en los siglos XIV y XV*, in: MMM 4 (1978), 107–178; J. Torres Fontes, *Linaje y poder en el reino de Murcia (siglos XIIII–XV)*, in: M. González Jiménez (ed.) / I.M. Romero-Camacho / A.C. García Martínez (coords.), *La Península Ibérica en la Era de los Descubrimientos (1391–1492), actas III Jornadas Hispano-Portuguesas de Historia Medieval* 2, Sevilla 1997, 901–928 (924–925); J. Bernal Peña, *Alfonso Yáñez Fajardo I. Historia de una ambición*, Murcia 2009; M. Rodríguez Llopis, *Poder y parentesco en la nobleza santiaguista del siglo XV*, in: NHA 12 (1996), 55–90.

22   Torres Fontes, 1997, 901–928 (926–928).

23   Ibid. 901–928 (916–917).

marriage in 1438 to the eldest son via majorat[24] together with appointment of the position, while his two sisters received 25,000 maravedís per year for rent from butcher stalls in the city of Murcia.[25] Pedro was the third Fajardo viceroy,[26] represented between 1444–1450 by his mother María de Quesada, who, from her estate in Molina, for six years defended her eldest son's right to office at all costs until his recognition in the capital and in the kingdom after a long conflict. The hegemony of power and social rise achieved by Pedro Fajardo,[27] who became a great man in Castilian noble households, would not have been possible without his mother's previous struggle to maintain his ownership of the viceregality. Beyond the specifics and factual, the exercise of power by women like María responds to political contexts that transcend a mere territorial framework.

The cohesion of lineage was undone with the death of the viceroy Alfonso Yáñez Fajardo II, a fact that alerted Juan II, since it coincided with the war fought in Castile by the infantrymen of Aragon against the valid and constable Álvaro de Luna. The fear of a vacuum of power, the foreseeable reactions against the offences committed by the deceased viceroy and the entry into Murcian lands of the infantes, were well-founded reasons that were known by the king.[28] The conflict between the Fajardos over the viceregality continued from 1444 to 1461; however this article focuses on the six years of María de Quesada's guardianship-regency during the time her son was a minor. In 1444, taking advantage of the crisis in the monarchy and that the ownership of the viceregality fell to a child, two members of the lineage, Mosén Diego Fajardo and, especially, Alonso Fajardo, disputed with their paternal cousin Pedro Fajardo about the position of viceroy inherited from his father. It was not theoretically a hereditary position, but Juan II confirmed it as such, according to established practice.

Perhaps the adversaries, paternal cousins of the child, had not adequately measured the strength of their aunt-in-law, and began a conflict that would last a long time and alter the normal political, social and economic development

24   A. de los Reyes, *Molina de Segura en la Edad Media murciana*, Murcia 2008, 424–427. Lords of Librilla, Alhama and Molina, plus the territorial conquests on the border of the Nasrid kingdom (Vélez Rubio, Vélez Blanco, Albox, Arboleas, Cantoria, Xiquena and Tirieza, with the exception of these last two, the rest would be lost) in Torres Fontes, 1997, 901–928 (916).

25   A. de los Reyes, *El señorío de Molina Seca, hoy de Segura*, Murcia 1996, 245.

26   J. Torres Fontes, *Don Pedro Fajardo, adelantado mayor del reino de Murcia*, Madrid 1953.

27   The matrimonial strategies associated him with the more distinguished families of the kingdom, Torres Fontes, 1997, 901–928 (926–928).

28   J. Abellán Pérez (ed.), *Documentos de Juan II*, Murcia 1984, 581 and 584.

of the kingdom, especially in the places where the supporters were located: two royal cities, Murcia, capital of the kingdom, divided between the Fajardista factions; and Lorca, a military base on the border with Granada, where Alonso Fajardo was governor; and Molina, the town of María de Quesada and Pedro Fajardo, near the border with Aragon.[29] An internal war of factions-lineage, of variable alliances, complicated and turned into factions-biases in the Castilian political crisis and the border conflicts with the Nasrid emirate. In these over-lapping power struggles, the figure of María powerfully emerges, a strong participant in the political game between monarchy and private feuds, the infantes of Aragon and the divided alignments of the Fajardos that fractured the whole of Murcian society. The Fajardo House represented the most power-ful lineage that, emerging from the new Trastamara nobility, rose to the top of Castilian nobility during the mid-15th century.

In these circumstances of armed conflict, María was aware of her respon-sibility, transmitted by birth and marriage. The daughter of Pedro Diaz de Quesada,[30] knight from Santiago and third lord of Garcíez and Santo Tomé and of Juana Fernández de Cárcamo and Argote, and second wife of Alfonso Yáñez Fajardo II, became depositary and guardian of the viceregality. Her responsibilities included personalising her son as the legitimate head of the lineage and exercising the functions inherent to the inherited position that she protected and defended: that of viceroy and representative of the monarchy in the kingdom. Wife and mother of the viceroy, her role is comparable, at a social scale, to that of a queen mother, queen consort or Castilian regent, such as María de Molina or Catherine of Lancaster.[31] And like them, who were able to reign and govern, the rich "vicereines" consorts in this case actually carried out political and military actions, in addition to institutional representation, exemplified by María de Quesada. She was considered and performed as acting viceroy, substituting her first-born son. And when that power was contested, she joined the forces of her estates, the capital of the kingdom, the nobles and the king to face her opponents.

Shortly after the death of Alfonso Yáñez Fajardo II in March 1444, on 23 April 1444, the Murcian council appointed two of its governors (Sancho González de Arróniz and Sancho Dávalos) to pay the new viceroy Pedro Fajardo,

---

29 Fajardo had his main strength and support in Lorca, Albudeite, Albanilla, Caravaca and Cehegín; María and her son in Molina, Cartagena, Alhama, Librilla, Mula, Ricote, Lorquí and Pliego.

30 M.ªA. Carmona Ruiz, *Los Quesada, señores de Garcíez y Santo Tomé (Jaén) durante la dinastía Trastámara*, in: ETFHM 28 (2015), 159–199.

31 M.ªP. Carceller Cerviño / O. Villaroel González, *Catalina de Lancaster. Una reina y el poder*, Madrid 2021.

a minor, the homage he was due, together with the two governors (Pedro de Soto and Pedro González de Arróniz) presented by the widow María. These "four older relatives" would act together (with a majority of three votes) as representatives of the viceregality while Pedro Fajardo was a minor.[32] But this acting commissioned delegation was not effective because it coincided with the Castilian political crisis and the war declared by the Fajardos who had immediately disputed his inheritance of the viceregality, as Alonso Fajardo believed he had more rights to it than his cousin Pedro. María tried to stay in power in the capital of the kingdom and ensure her son's rights, but the faction of the Fajardo cousins, Diego and Alonso, led a popular uprising against her, forcing her to take refuge in the capital's fortress. Finally, with the war unleashed, she had to abandon the fortress and retreat with her son and collaborators to Molina Seca (currently Segura),[33] approximately 11 km north of Murcia, making the estate there the "de facto" political capital of the kingdom.

The viceregality was disputed between three Fajardo cousins, which in the end became two, Pedro and Alonso, who were supported by and aligned with the biases that existed in the Castilian monarchy crisis: María and her son Pedro Fajardo together with the constable Álvaro de Luna (Private of Juan II); Alonso Fajardo, mayor of Lorca, next to the infante Enrique, master of Santiago; and Diego Fajardo, Governor of Murcia, on behalf of the Infante Juan, King of Navarre. In addition María initially obtained the support of Rodrigo Manrique (father of the writer Jorge Manrique), commander of Segura from Santiago, with whom, on 4 May 1444, she arranged the marriage of his daughter, Leonor Manrique, with her son, the minor Pedro Fajardo.[34] Above all, María positioned herself loyally alongside the Castilian monarch and against the infantes of Aragon.

Once war was declared between the Fajardo cousins, the infante of Aragon and master of Santiago, Enrique, received complaints from María about the declaration of war from Alonso and Diego Fajardo, which forced her to leave Murcia "together with certain relatives and servants and public officials of the viceroy".[35] A truce in the newly launched Fajardista war was arranged by the Murcian council on 14 May 1444, and signed on 27 May.[36] On 12 June, the infante-master of Santiago sent Rodrigo Manrique (future in-law of María) to

---

32   Torres Fontes, 1997, 901–928 (919).
33   The chief merino of the deceased viceroy, Andrés de Montergull, accused of perpetrating all kinds of misdeeds with his gang, moved with them: J. Torres Fontes, *Nuevas estampas medievales*, Murcia 1997, 25.
34   A. de los Reyes, *El señorío de Molina Seca, hoy de Segura*, Murcia 1996, 245–251.
35   J. Torres Fontes, *Fajardo el Bravo*, Murcia 2001, 142.
36   De los Reyes, 1996, 246.

sign the agreement between her and her nephews-in-law and put an end to "the debates that have taken place these days in that city". The master urged her to sign the agreement, specifying that María and her supporters could return to their homes in Murcia and "all that was theirs and the alcazar could be restored, and taken and received as acting viceroy for the said Pedro Fajardo, since the king, my lord and my cousin, granted him the mercy of [...], because they are friends and between them there is harmony and peace".[37] But it was not possible.

The strategy of the side opposed to María and her son was to occupy the fortresses in the kingdom to isolate them and plunder their estate lands. Violent actions and counter-reactions that the leaders denounced to the capital council: María claimed theft of cattle and the debt owed to her late husband; Alonso Fajardo, after writing "many times to the said towns and to the said Maria", requested the return of the stolen mares, and the master of Santiago complained about extortions carried out by the Molina Seca Fajardista factions.[38] The mediation of the commander from Santiago (related to María) in the truce raised doubts in the Murcian council about whether the position of "vicereine" was in favour of the infante-master of Santiago or the king. Juan II allayed fears when he confirmed to the council of Murcia on 10 April 1445 María and the viceroy's monarchical loyalty:

> "I ask you to know that it is said that there is a certain suspicion put on Maria de Quesada and the viceroy Pedro Fajardo, her son, saying they are not at my service, of which I am amazed at those who have said this or say this, because I am certain that Maria and the aforementioned viceroy are at my service with complete loyalty and enthusiasm [...], that I would give orders and the said Maria and the aforementioned viceroy as my servants would act within their reason [...]".[39]

---

37 Torres Fontes, 2001, 142–143.
38 Ibid. 144; de los Reyes, 1996, 248.
39 "Fago vos saber que a mi es fecha relación que entre vosotros se dize o pone alguna sospecha en doña Maria de Quesada e en el adelantado Pero Fajardo, su fijo, diciendo ellos no ser a mi seruiçio, de lo qual sy asi es yo soy mucho marauillado de los que lo tal lo han dicho o dicen, por cuanto yo soy cierto que la dicha doña Maria e el dicho adelantado son a mi seruiçio con toda lealtad e buen animo [...], que dedes orden que lo tales dezires çesen e vos tractedes con la dicha Maria e con el dicho adelantado como seruidores mios e los honrredes e acatedes con esta en razón [...]": J. Abellán Pérez (ed.), *Documentos de Juan II*, Murcia 1984, 593. The translation of the original Spanish text into English was done by the autor.

The mediation of María de Aragon,[40] wife of Alfonso V, in pursuit of the failed truce ("deal or dismissal") in the conflict between her brother Juan II of Castile and his brothers-in-law the "infantes", is well known:

> "I let you know [...] that through the queen Maria of Aragon, my very beautiful and very beloved sister [...] moved with good zeal to the aforementioned, but because I am certain and it has been certified that the aforementioned has been procured and is procured by the infante and by those of his worth with intent and purpose of good time and place for better and more harmless to him and his places to do certain things to my great disappointment and to the detriment of my relatives and even to the dismay of my love and of all of you [...]".[41]

The queen had been informed by her brother-in-law, the infante-master of Santiago, Enrique, of the situation of Murcia in the double monarchy-favourite-viceroy (María de Quesada) war against the infantes of Aragon and the Fajardo cousins clan. On 4 February 1445, Enrique wrote to his sister-in-law "the excellent lady" from his commandery Blanca (Murcia), informing her of the grievances (damage, evil, theft, force, seizure, insult, offences, oppression) suffered by "her people" from the cities of Murcia, Cartagena, Jumilla and from estates and the viceroy's serfs and his mother, María de Quesada. And he asked the queen that María, in her name and in that of her son, respect the truce agreed between him and the Fajardista bloc of Mosén Diego and Alonso Fajardo, and cease hostilities.[42] But an agreement did not come: Juan II did not accept the ceasefire proposed to his sister the queen of Aragon, as he believed it was a deceptive strategy by the master of Santiago to gain time.

Before the victory of Olmedo in 1445, on 15 October 1444, the king ordered the kingdom of Murcia to act against the "infantes", and prohibited the sale of food, weapons and horses to it. After the death of the infante-master Enrique

---

40   Mediator for peace or truce in the war between the infantes of Aragon, her brothers-in-law (Juan II, King of Navarre, Pedro and Enrique) and her brother Juan II of Castile and Constable Álvaro de Luna, stood in the field of battle, determined to avoid the conflict of 1429 in the vicinity of Cogolludo: V. Márquez de la Plaza, *El poder de las mujeres en la Historia de España*, Madrid 2022, 305–306.

41   "Fago vos saber [...] que mediante la reyna doña Maria de Aragon, mi muy cara e muy amada hermana [...] se mouio con buen zelo a lo sobredicho, pero porque yo soy cierto e çertificado que los sobredichos se procuro e procura por el dicho ynfante e por los de su valia con entençion e proposyto de auer tienpo e lugar para mejor e mas syn dapño suyo e de sus lugares fazer algunas cosas en gran deseruiçio mio e dapño de mis regnos e aun desa mi çibdad e de todos vosotros [...]: J. Abellán Pérez (ed.), *Documentos de Juan II*, Murcia 1984, 588–589 (13 February 1445). The translation of the original Spanish text into English was done by the autor.

42   J. Torres Fontes, *Fajardo el Bravo*, Murcia 2001, 145–148.

de Trastámara (15 June 1445),[43] as a result of injuries sustained on the battle-field, and the consequential triumph of Juan II in Olmedo (19 May 1445), nego-tiations and repositionings began. The commander from Santiago, Rodrigo Manrique, proclaimed himself master of Santiago following the death of Enrique and fell out with the monarch and the constable, thus aligning himself with the infantes. On 21 June 1445, the council of Murcia wrote to Lorca's coun-cil to negotiate and sign the truce between the factions of María de Quesada and Alonso Fajardo. To that end, they elected their respective representa-tives and the capital council elected theirs to agree on harmony and resolve grievances:

> "[...] being at the table with what your messenger said [...] of the dates given by Maria and by other people, to these we respond that our understanding and will is to be good and to keep the stability and security granted by the Infante, may God forgive, and by this city, through the interaction of the Lady Queen of Aragon, as well as the said Infante. And for this we say that you are asked to choose a person from among you, and the said Donna Maria will choose another for herself, and we will choose another for this city, to whom is given enough power by all the said parties so that all three together can debate and question [...]".[44]

Prior to the meeting to negotiate the truce, Alonso Fajardo assured the Murcian representatives through a letter written on 6 August 1445 that they will travel to Lorca and promised that while the negotiation lasted, no violence would be committed on the estate properties of his aunt and cousin. The mayor of Lorca proclaimed the cessation of hostilities and consequently that "any attack was invalid [...], by one party to the other or the other to the other".[45]

The agreed truce deteriorated due to the border Muslims joining the conflict, with whom Alonso Fajardo maintained good relations. The Nasrids attacked castles in the Almanzora valley (Vélez Blanco and Albox), the domain of María and her cousin. Nothing about the border war against the Nasrid emirate was recorded in the agreement signed between the fajardista factions. This was condemned by Alonso Fajardo on 26 August 1445 to the council of Murcia, informing them that he wrote to the Muslims to return the loot captured in

---

43 When the master died, on 23 August 1445, he ratified that the council of Murcia should not help the Navarrese monarch in their incursion into Murcian territory: J. Abellán Pérez (ed.), *Documentos de Juan II*, Murcia 1984, 599.

44 Torres Fontes, 2001, 151–152. The translation of the original Spanish text into English was done by the autor.

45 María is mentioned first: "that as long as these events between you and me are discussed, that no troubles will be made in the places of the said Donna Maria and her son": Torres Fontes, 2001, 153–154.

the Christian border territories. He maintained in this regard that "the Moors never responded to me", which meant – he continued arguing – that his influence in Granada politics was nil: "That I cannot pressure such a great Kingdom as that one". The Fajardista conflict was taken advantage of by the Nasrids and was complicated by moving the war to the south-eastern border of the kingdom. There was a succession of replies and counter-replies, looting and captivity on both sides: Almogavars from Vélez Blanco and Albox (Almería) assaulted neighbouring Muslim territories and arrested Alonso Fajardo's squire, Diego Mellado.[46]

On 22 September, in another letter to the council of Murcia, the brave Fajardo condemned the attacks of the Christians of Vélez Blanco and justified those of the Muslims of Vera (Almería). However, he set himself up as a mediator for the exchange of captives: "that the Christians and Moors, from one part as from the other, be exchanged for each other without any delay". And he warned that the Muslim leaders were preparing an attack with 600 men to assault the capital of the kingdom, the town of Mula and other of his aunt and cousin's territories. Alonso Fajardo predicted the defeat of the Murcians by the powerful Nasrid army. At the end of his letter he addressed María seriously and expressly:

> "And my lady, aunt Maria de Quesada, I write this letter to you, believe that all of them would come upon me in this city, and that I be one of those defeated and destroyed, that I will defeat as well, that the defeat and destruction will turn into tears".[47]

Despite this, a few days later, on 10 October 1445, he informed the council of Murcia of the release of 30 of María's captive serfs: [...] for what more honour Maria has to satisfy of our decrease, I have freed thirty of your captives from Albox [...].[48]

The war included Castile, Aragon and Granada, but the most serious was the Murcian border because of the Fajardo conflict. The viceroy Pedro Fajardo's

---

46   Torres Fontes, 2001, 154–155; F. Veas Arteseros, *La prisión de Diego Mellado en Vélez Blanco*, in: RV 3 (1984), 21–35.

47   "E mi señora tia donna Maria de Quesada aya esta letra por suya e crea, que todos quantos ellas querria e espera vengan sobre mi e esta cibdad, lo qual ella desea e yo sea dellos vencido e destroydo, que yo me vencere tanbien, que el vencimiento e destruycion se les tornara en llanto": Torres Fontes, 2001, 156–158. The translation of the original Spanish text into English was done by the autor.

48   "[...] he por que mas onrra aya donna Maria de sastifazer nuestra mengua, yo he sacado los suyos de Albox treinta cautivos [...]": J. Torres Fontes, *Fajardo el Bravo*, Murcia 2001 (2ª ed.), 159. The translation of the original Spanish text into English was done by the autor.

Vélez Blanco villa was in the line of fire and attacked by the Nasrids at the end of 1445 and although besieged, the castle resisted. Its mayor Pedro Iñíguez informed María of the situation. The "vicereine" requested military assistance from the council of Murcia, Prince Enrique (future Enrique IV) and his enemy Alonso Fajardo, according to the letter issued from Molina on 27 November 1445 to the council of Murcia:[49]

> "Very honourable gentlemen. I received your letter that you sent me with Garcia Platero and read it, God knows the pain and labour there was in my heart on hearing this news, for which gentlemen, I ask you to please in the name of most people of that city to go to the aid of that town, and as powerful as they can be, almost that place is lost, well you will see in how much work is put into the places that are your neighbours. And gentlemen, I wanted to know from Mayor Pedro Ynniguez how he left the castle, and he said, that he left the new squires, well dressed and handsome, and twenty free men on foot, also fair, and four Jews, and flour in barrels and in urns so that they can eat for three months, and more than five hundred bushels of wheat, and mills for seven or eight to grind by hand, and wine to drink for one year, and in a cistern that is very large, more than half of water, a very lot of wood, nine or ten cabbages, coarse, and well stocked and well equipped and dressed with falling buffes, and the castle all raked. I truly believe that the castle cannot be taken, and about this, gentlemen, I am writing to my nephew Alfonso Fajardo, asking him to help this town, which I believe he will do so with great diligence. And gentlemen, please answer me later and do what you are pleased to do, because the viceroy's territories are ready to join you. May our Lord God always keep you.
>
> De Molina, 28 November. Likewise, he wrote to our lord the Prince on this date.
>
> Maria".

Faced with the attacks by Muhammad X – the truce with Castile was broken – the Fajardista factions joined against it, who had previously counted on Nasrid military support in their fratricidal war. Alonso Fajardo prepared to defend the Granada incursion, Juan II sent war captains to Murcia, Mosén Diego Fajardo commanded the council militia and María in her role, prepared for the Muslim onslaught.[50] Being on the border, not only was his Lordship in danger, but the

---

49   Torres Fontes, 2001, 160–161: Representative letter of the direct intervention of queens and nobles in politics and war; J.P. Jardin / J.M. Nieto Soria / P. Rochwert-Zuili / H. Thieulin-Pardo (coords.), *Cartas de mujeres en la Europa medieval. España, Francia, Italia, Portugal (ss. XI–XV)*, Madrid 2018. The translation of the original Spanish text into English was done by the autor.

50   The collaboration of the council militia recruited by Diego Fajardo and that of Alonso Fajardo did not come to fruition because when they went to help Vélez Blanco at the beginning of 1446, the castle had capitulated: J. Torres Fontes, *Don Pedro Fajardo, adelantado mayor del reino de Murcia*, Madrid 1953, 33.

entire kingdom. Thus, the Fajardista war was briefly regulated to second priority to the armed force of Granada, whose looting of Cieza in 1448 was noteworthy. However, between 1446–1449 the side of María de Quesada and the viceroy, allied with Juan II-Álvaro de Luna, the bishop of Cartagena and the magistrate of Murcia, was besieged in the town of Molina by Alonso Fajardo and the Murcian governor Diego Fajardo, supported by the "infantes" King Juan II of Navarre and his brother King Alfonso V of Aragon, plus the master of Santiago Rodrigo Manrique, the fickle prince Enrique and the king of Granada.

The recognition of the leadership of María de Quesada by her opponents is revealing of her political strength;[51] she was considered a great ally of Juan II of Castile, who donated the town of Jumilla to her in 1447. The Murcian supporters of María and the viceroy, expelled from the capital, reinforced the troops who were armed and surrounded in Molina de Segura, which could not be taken despite several attempts. With the Aragonese neighbour Orihuela, who supported the Infante-King of Navarre and whose people were affected by the violence, María granted a truce of 30 days while the city consulted.[52] Negotiations undertaken simultaneously with various sides achieved a temporary cessation of war. On 21 December 1449, María wrote to the council of Murcia informing them of the peace concluded with Alonso Fajardo, whom she refers to as "my friend, whom I had instead of a son":

> "Honourable gentlemen and friends. God keep you. You already know how my lord nephew Alfonso Fajardo came here to negotiate peace with me and with the viceroy my son for the good peace of the land. And by the grace of God he is my friend and I his, whom I took instead of my son, his cousin, the friendship that we had with him. We swear to the city and to my lord nephew Mosen Diego Fajardo, we ask that you gracefully not remember past things and with good will receive us as a friend, for we will do only good deeds and give what is ours to any neighbours of that city, as other people have received from us and from now on with good and joyful will we forgive any neighbours of that city for all the damages that to our land or to us and ours have been done. And because it is reason that this city is honoured by all of us and in the facts it is important, it has been agreed between my lord nephew Alfonso Fajardo and us that the city order peace between it and all of us and we want to keep that and our reason and service to the king our lord, of whom we are very certain, and we wish to always serve, and

51   On 30 January 1449, when the prosecutor for the King of Aragon urged the city of Orihuela to lend its support to the master of Santiago, Rodrigo Manrique, the role of María de Quesada as the great enemy is noteworthy, who divided the political passions of the people of Orihuela among her supporters, those of the master of Santiago, Rodrigo Manrique and those of the city of Murcia: M. Rodríguez Llopis (ed.), *Documentos de los siglos XIV y XV. Señoríos de la Orden de Santiago*, Murcia 1991, 93.

52   A. de los Reyes, *Molina de Segura en la Edad Media murciana*, Murcia 2008, 316–317: the author includes fragments of two letters from María.

we want the king our lord to thank the city for this great good of the earth and the service of God. And it pleases you that my son and I will never leave your ordinance and that my son asks for the services that he has done to the king and his father, may God, he did, and my nephews, Diego Fajardo and Alfonso Fajardo, and we are satisfied with them. And we all ask the Lord King for the frankness of that city for the evils and damages it has suffered. I know not what else to write, but we will do whatever it pleases. In Molina, twenty-first of December. Maria."[53]

The Murcian regiment, still divided between the Fajardista factions, signed the agreement or "friendship contract" and sealed it with the seals of the council, the viceroy, the bishop, María and Mosén Diego Fajardo[54]. Harmony between the Fajardos and Alonso Fajardo's agreement of Castilian sovereignty was ensured by the fact that Prince Enrique – in opposition to his father – offered the kingdom of Murcia to Aragon, and also because of the Muslim attacks on the Granada border. After that, María and her son returned to Murcia, coinciding with the coming of age of the viceroy.[55] The peace lasted only two years, as at the beginning of 1453 the family war between the cousins, the viceroy, already of legal age, and the mayor of Lorca resumed, until 1461, with the distance of the viceroy's kingdom, the educated and defiant Fajardo. After 18 years of intermittent conflict – and after granting a royal pardon to the mayor's side in 1458 – the viceroy finally triumphed; María de Quesada had ensured, with weapons, the legitimacy of the viceroy Pedro Fajardo, disaffected by the new monarch, Enrique IV.

The entrenching of the sides was projected on the people of their territories, who were subject to reprisals, threats, coercion, robbery and death. In 1454 Alonso Fajardo denounced that a young farmer from Lorca had been assaulted near Molina by a servant of María, and the Murcian Pedro de Cisneros informed the king of:

"The hate and animosity that the viceroy Pedro Fajardo, my servant, and Maria de Quesada, his mother, and Pero Veles de Gueuara and his squires, and free men, and servants, and other relatives, and friends receive [...], we feared and

---

53   De los Reyes, 2008, 427–428. The translation of the original Spanish text into English was done by the autor.

54   De los Reyes, 2008, 428–431. Half a year later, on 13 June 1450, the conditions of the pact that ensured social peace for two years were recorded: ibid. 431–435. English translation is my own.

55   When his father Pedro Fajardo died, he was aged between eight and ten years old, so his coming of age in the mid-15th century would have been between 14–16 years old. De los Reyes, 2008, 333.

fear they want to inflict, kill, cripple, steal, or do other evil or damage or disorder to people and property".[56]

Once Juan II was informed, he granted the accuser a letter of assurance.[57]

María's influence continued and was recognised after the coming of age of her son to the role of the viceregality. His energy was noted in the political culture of the mid-15th century. As Torres Fontes said:

> "A seasoned woman who struggled and sacrificed, she knew how to resist the impetuous attacks of her nephew Alonso Fajardo to the real and necessary maximum; when all the fortresses of the viceregality were lost, she became strong in the last place she had left, the town of Molina Seca, and not only resisted Alfonsino's push, but also knew how to turn it into a base of operations from which her son reconquered the lost fortresses and would later continue his triumphal march until he definitively expelled his indomitable rival".[58]

While for A. de los Reyes:

> "Maria Quesada was not a dazzling lady but deserves a unique history and should be included in the long list of those who have carried out heroic or notable deeds. She was, simply, a woman on whom the responsibility of the Murcian government fell for a few years".[59]

María de Quesada's personality was key for Pedro Fajardo who inherited the role of the viceregality and consolidated such absolute power that he was considered almost a ruler during the reign of Enrique IV. And he rose to the heights of the great nobles of Castile when he submitted to the Catholic Monarchs. Documentary records of María were lost at the beginning of this reign, when she was over sixty years old.[60] Away from the capital, her old age was spent in Molina, a town that her son bequeathed to her, in addition to other income, such as that from the salt mines, which allowed her to live according to her stately status.[61]

---

56   Torres Fontes, 2001, 190. The translation of the original Spanish text into English was done by the autor.

57   J. Abellán Pérez (ed.), *Documentos de Juan II*, Murcia 1984, 695–696. The translation of the original Spanish text into English was done by the autor.

58   J. Torres Fontes, *Don Pedro Fajardo, adelantado mayor del reino de Murcia*, Madrid 1953, 33. English translation is my own.

59   De los Reyes, 2008, 333. The translation of the original Spanish text into English was done by the autor.

60   A. Moratalla Collado (ed.), *Documentos de los Reyes Católicos (1475–1491)*, Murcia 2003, 151, where "Molina de doña Maria" is cited.

61   De los Reyes, 2008, 334–335.

3 Powerful Women

The history of women is intertwined with the public sphere, and their role in the exercise of power[62] is noteworthy, especially when, like María de Quesada, they were widowed. Territorial ladies and ladies of the urban oligarchy were necessary parts of the power relations between monarchy, nobility and councils and in the consolidation of noble lineages. Female political leadership is a field that has recently been opened by new historiography showing women acting in masculinised war,[63] behaving like men in the fight for their rights and those of their descendants. Like queens, noble women were politically connected with men in the institutional sphere, and the action of each influenced that of the other and the institution they represented. Powerful women administered estates and patrimony, ran monasteries and abbeys, reigned and ruled, and engaged in war and diplomacy as kings and lords.

María de Quesada faced the Fajardo men in a war for the viceregality of Murcia. She successfully carried out the political duty that circumstances required of her. Bold and expert, respected and with recognised power, her personal worth is of interest: being a "widow of" or a "mother of" guaranteed the successful exercise of power that she maintained as acting viceroy. She represented and executed power in the first person, and she could have done it well or badly, just like any man. Lineage, wealth and authority made her distinction: "in honour and contemplation of Maria de Molina".[64] Due to her social and institutional standing, she received gifts: after having just married, she arrived in Murcia in July 1430, where the council "because of her lineage and the wife of the aforementioned viceroy" welcomed her with a calf, thirty pairs of chickens, six rams and a jar of good wine.[65]

---

62   C. Segura Graíño / M.ªI. del Val Valdivieso, *Las mujeres y el poder*, in: P. Pérez-Fuentes Hernández, (coord.), *Las mujeres en la Historia de España y América Latina*, Barcelona 2012, 223–238.

63   D. Pelaz Flores / M.ªI. del Val Valdivieso, *La Historia de las Mujeres en el siglo XXI a través del estudio de la Reginalidad medieval*, in: RevHisto 22 (2014), 101–127 (123); B. Majo Tomé, *Las leonas de Castilla: revisión historiográfica y planteamiento para el estudio de la participación de las mujeres de las ciudades castellanas en la Guerra de las Comunidades*, in: B. Arizaga Bolumburu / J.A. Solórzano Telechea / A. Aguiar Andrade (eds.), *Ser mujer en la ciudad medieval europea*, Logroño 2013, 329–348.

64   C. Veas Arteseros, *Fiscalidad concejil en la Murcia de fines del Medievo*, Murcia 1991, 164.

65   J. Torres Fontes, *Los Fajardo en los siglos XIV y XV*, in: MMM 4 (1978), 107–178 (138). The wife of Pedro López Dávalos and daughter of the master of Santiago received a similar gift in 1418: L. Rubio García / L. Rubio Hernández, *La mujer murciana en la Baja Edad Media*, Murcia 2000, 199.

Raised to the highest position in the kingdom, the powerful "vicereine" women were respected and distinguished as representatives of shared power and as ladies of villas and fortresses. María de Quesada had the opportunity to show her direct and active political action. Her role reproduces that of some queens who reigned and ruled at a time when Christine de Pizan's claims were sounding; or also that of Juana Pimentel, "the sad countess", wife of Álvaro de Luna, who, in 1459, led a noble confederation against Juan Pacheco and Enrique IV with the Marquis of Santillana.[66]

Women acting like men, queens like kings, vicereines like viceroys, ladies like lords. María adopted the behaviour, bellicosity and political resources of power. Widow and mother of the viceroy, she sought support and obtained alliances to maintain the viceregality, executing the functions of the position with authority over her serfs and with war strategies against the faction that disputed that authority. And she carried out the role reserved for the men of the family. Did her opponents believe that the fight for the viceregality would be favourable to them because it was being protected by a widowed woman? What María showed was that she knew the rules of politics and did not succumb to masculine power because she was a woman. Her individuality as a leader in the Fajardista war was acknowledged by the participants. She maintained relations with the king, great men and oligarchs, safeguarding the viceregality for her son. She was able to successfully assume her public role and political responsibility. And being a woman did not affect her job of protecting that institution.

---

66   A. Lafuente Urién / A. Sierra López (coords.), *Mujer, nobleza y poder: documentos escogidos para la historia de las damas nobles en el Archivo de la Nobleza*, Madrid 2021, 170.

PART IV

Islam in the West

El Poder en la Sombra

Las Sultanas y el Harén en la Corte Nazarí de Granada (siglos XIII–XV)

María Mercedes Delgado Pérez

Abstract

In Islam, and in the elites' main female space, the harem, women actively contributed to the exercise of power established by men. In Nasrid Granada it was a determining factor from the beginning of the dynasty's establishment, and continued to be so until its end. Here, we analyse that of the last great sultana, Fāṭima, and her enormous and significant role, narrated mainly through three contemporary chronicles.

1 Mujer y Poder en el Islam

La escritora marroquí Fátima Mernissi aborda en *Sultanes oubliées*[1], de forma pionera, un aspecto fundamental en la comprensión del papel en la Historia de la mujer musulmana, que hasta entonces se había limitado casi exclusivamente a ser estudiada desde el punto de vista de la religión y el derecho islámicos (y preislámicos, en consecuencia)[2], con una atención especial al matrimonio y a la descendencia.[3] Esta nueva perspectiva es su relación con el ejercicio activo del poder.

En el terreno estrictamente profano se había enfocado el estudio de la mujer, especialmente, desde la óptica de la literatura (de nuevo con referencias al período preislámico)[4] y del erotismo (sobre todo por la imagen sicalíptica occidental sobre el harén).[5] Pero la comprensión de la mujer en el islam como sujeto histórico ha ido avanzando progresivamente y ha abarcado un número más amplio y diverso de facetas: desde las diferencias sociales a las diferentes etapas de su vida; el hecho de ser musulmana o perteneciente a la *dimma* (cristianas y judías); vivir en el campo o en la ciudad; su procedencia étnica (aborigen, árabe, beréber, magrebí, eslava, etc.); su estado (soltera,

---

1 Hemos manejado la edición en inglés *The Forgotten Queens of Islam*, Minneapolis 2006.
2 Véase E. Mercier, *La condition de la femme musulmane dans l'Afrique septentrionale*, Alger 1895.
3 Véase, por ejemplo, G.H. Stern, *Marriage in Early Islam*, London 1939.
4 Así, en N. Perron, *Femmes arabes. Avant et depuis l'Islamisme*, Paris 1858.
5 Véase A.Ch. Bolognese, *Vera relatione della gran città di Costantinopoli et in particolare del serraglio del Gran Turco*, Bracciano 1621.

casada, viuda, separada); su posición económica; su maternidad; su formación; su espiritualidad, etc.[6]

En el caso específico de al-Andalus, el historiador argelino Ṣalāḥ Khāliṣ realizó en 1966 una doble distinción esencial en la mujer andalusí: la del vulgo (ᶜāmma) y la de las élites (jāṣṣa), y la mujer libre y la esclava[7]. Es evidente que existió una enorme diferencia en la condición de la mujer andalusí dependiendo de su estatus social y que la mujer que tuvo acceso al ejercicio del poder fue la que se encontraba en la cúspide social[8].

Por fin, otro aspecto que afecta de forma significativa a la comprensión del mundo femenino, esta vez específicamente andalusí, es la conformación del tejido social, que fue estudiado por Pierre Guichard en su tesis de 1972[9]. Guichard presenta los rasgos de la sociedad andalusí como un típico patriarcado de base esencialmente agnaticia, que establece una estricta transmisión patrilineal del linaje, con fuerte carácter endogámico, lo que ha sido discutido posteriormente[10].

Aparte las consideraciones sociales hay que tener en cuenta, también, las diferentes situaciones contextuales que afectaron la vida de la mujer andalusí: desde los momentos más o menos rigoristas en la aplicación de las prescripciones e inhibiciones religiosas y jurídicas, a los períodos de crisis económicas o demográficas, lo que repercutía, por ejemplo, en la realización de los matrimonios por el aumento o escasez de candidatos dependiendo de cada coyuntura histórica[11]. Así, un descenso de la natalidad provocaba la lógica disminución de candidatos, lo que afectaba de forma especial a las familias de la élite, pues se veían forzadas a realizar matrimonios que les permitieran conservar una posición social honorable y mantener la obligación (kāfa') de que la mujer no superase el estatus social de su marido.

A todo lo expuesto podemos añadir cierto orgullo de clase entre las mujeres andalusíes, si consideramos válido el testimonio del cronista judío de la primera mitad del siglo XVI, Rabí Eliyahu Capsali, que se hace eco de la negativa

---

6   Todas estas diferencias en: M. Marín, *Vidas de mujeres andalusíes*, Málaga 2006, 17–31.

7   Ṣ. Khāliṣ, *La vie littéraire à Séville au XIᵉ siècle*, Alger, 1966, 38–43.

8   Estas mujeres en las élites y en relación con el poder fueron estudiadas más detenidamente en: M.ªJ. Viguera (coord.), *La mujer en al-Andalus: Reflejos históricos de su actividad y categorías sociales*, Sevilla 1989.

9   Se publicó en España como *Al-Andalus: Estructura antropológica de una sociedad islámica en Occidente*, Barcelona 1976.

10   M.ªJ. Rubiera, *El vínculo cognático en al-Andalus*, en: *Andalucía medieval: Actas del I Congreso de Historia de Andalucía, diciembre de 1976*, Córdoba 1978, v. 1, 121–124.

11   Marín, 2006, 34–35.

de ᶜĀ'išā[12], la hermana del último sultán nazarí, Abū ᶜAbd Allāh Muḥammad XI b. ᶜAlī (Boabdil) (1482–1492 EC), de contraer matrimonio con el sultán de Fez, Muḥammad al-Šayj, ciudad en la que se encontraba refugiada con su familia y su hermano el sultán desde finales de 1493:

> "los reyes de Granada eran de elevadísimo linaje entre los ismaelitas, procedentes de los antiguos reyes de Damasco, que desde siempre fueron de prosapia; y es creencia de los ismaelitas guardar y honrar especialmente su linaje y su raíz. No le deshonrarían para que se mantuviera a sus hijos y a sus hijas en el lugar más idóneo del mundo. A la descendencia de esa monarquía y a la familia de los gobernadores de Granada se les llamaba Aben Alahmar [scil. Ibn al-Aḥmar]. No hubo linaje entre todos los reyes de Ismael, próximos o lejanos, más grande que aquél.
> Después de venir el rey Chiquito [scil. Muḥammad XI] con su madre y su hermana, el rey de Fez *envió a hacer indagación acerca de la mujer*, para desposarse con la hija de Alī Muleik Alhacén [scil. Abū l-Ḥasan ᶜAlī] hermana del mencionado rey Chiquito. Lo escuchó la hija del rey, *pero no le pareció bien* porque el rey de Fez no era del linaje de Ismael. Insultó y maldijo a la mujer que negociaba la boda y la hizo volver al rey de Fez [...] El rey de Fez oyó esto y le pareció mal porque vio que los hijos de Alí no le tenían en consideración ni le concedían rango real a pesar de ser el rey de Fez".[13]

Esto parece indicar un fenómeno característico de la sociedad nazarí señalado por Rubiera, en contradicción a las tesis de Guichard: la trasmisión de la calidad del linaje a las generaciones sucesivas a través de las mujeres. Esta investigadora explica que el debilitamiento de la solidaridad agnaticia (ᶜaṣa-bīya), característica de la sociedad árabe-beduina, supuso que se impusiese un modelo "bilateral", en el que tenían igual fuerza los vínculos familiares agnaticios y cognaticios.[14] Y esto quizá fue debido al influjo de una sucesión matri-lineal dominante en la sociedad hispana anterior a la llegada de los árabes,[15] peculiaridad que compartiría con otras sociedades de la periferia de la Dār al-Islām, como la turca o las de algunos territorios de África del Sur.[16]

---

12   Su nombre se desvela en L. Seco de Lucena, *La sultana madre de Boabdil*, en: al-Andalus 12 (1947), 359–390, (370 y 382–390).

13   E. Capsali, *El judaísmo hispano según la crónica hebrea de Rabí Eliyahu Capsali: Traducción y estudio del Seder Eliyahu Zutá (capítulos 40–70)*, Granada 2005, 174–175. Las cursivas son de la editora y señalan las inserciones literales de textos bíblicos, una característica del estilo literario de Capsali.

14   Rubiera, 1978, 121–124.

15   Ead., 124.

16   L.M. Jreis, *Brujas, prostitutas, esclavas o peregrinas: Estereotipos femeninos en los relatos de viajeros musulmanes del Medievo*, en: Miscelánea de Estudios Árabes y Hebraicos. Sección Árabe-Islam 63 (2014), 119–142 (139).

Por tanto, las mujeres en la Granada nazarí transmitían a sus descendientes el honor y la nobleza de su familia. Esto se dio desde el principio de la dinastía, pues los dos linajes asociados al trono del primer sultán, los Banū Ašqilūla y los Banū l-Mawl, tenían vínculos cognaticios con Muḥammad I Ibn al-Aḥmar (1232–1273 EC). Ambos muestran, igualmente, el mismo título honorífico característico de los miembros de la dinastía Banū Naṣr, arraeces (al-rāʾis), es decir, "*chief, leader* of a recognisable group (political, religious, juridical, tribal, or other*", lo que, generalmente, se refería a "the head of a village, a city or a city-region".[17] En Granada se aplicó a los "parientes del primer sultán" y de los posteriores[18].

Como indica Rubiera, las Banāt Naṣr (mujeres de la dinastía nazarí) podían transmitir su alcurnia a sus descendientes, por lo que realizaban matrimonios desiguales con hombres de inferior estatus social, lo que contradecía la costumbre y el derecho islámico, que establecía que el hombre debía desposar a una mujer de igual condición social.[19] De este modo, dos sultanes se elevaron al trono por vía femenina: el primero, Abū l-Walīd Ismāʿīl I (1314–1325 EC) que, aunque era nieto de un hermano de Abū ʿAbd Allāh Muḥammad I, Ibn al-Aḥmar (1232–1273 EC) y, por tanto, miembro colateral de la dinastía, fue elegido por ser hijo de Fāṭima, una hija del sultán Muḥammad II al-Faqīh (1273–1302 EC); el segundo fue Yūsuf IV b. al-Mawl (1432 EC), que contaba únicamente con sucesivos vínculos cognaticios con los Banū Naṣr desde los inicios de la dinastía, pues era nieto de Abū ʿAbd Allāh Muḥammad VI (1360–1362 EC).[20]

Ana Echevarría y Roser Salicrú, al analizar este proceso, dan tres causas fundamentales para explicar la complicada genealogía de los nazaríes a lo largo del siglo XV:

> "the Islamic tradition of marrying the paternal cousin or uncle; parity between spouses, established by maliki tradition that is, the need for a father to marry a daughter with a husband of the same social and economic status; and, finally, the extraordinary situation of Granada, almost isolated from other Islamic lands, which increased the need to establish alliances through marriage (*musahara*) with clans and lineages within the emirate, or else, though only rarely, with other neighbouring sultanates".[21]

---

17   Cl. E. Bosworth / S. Soucek, "raʾīs", en: Cl.E. Bosworth / E. Donzel / W.P. Heinrichs / G. Lecomte (eds.), *The Encyclopaedia of Islam* 8, Leiden 1995, 402–403.

18   F. Vidal, *Historia política*, en: M.ªJ. Viguera (coord.), *El reino nazarí de Granada (1232–1492): Política, instituciones, espacio y economía*, Granada 2000, 47–248 (223, nota 181).

19   Rubiera, 1978, 123.

20   Ead., 123–124.

21   A. Echevarría / R. Salicrú i Lluch, *The 'Honourable Ladies' of Nasrid Granada: Female Power and Agency in the Alhambra (1400–1450)*, en: E. Woodacre (ed.), *A Companion to Global Queenship*, Amsterdam 2018, 255–270 (256).

2   Espacios Femeninos de Poder

En 1906 Gonzalvo exploró un cambio conceptual sobre uno de los estereotipos recurrentes en Occidente sobre la cultura islámica: la presencia del harén (*ḥarīm*), que se percibe como una expresión máxima del sometimiento de la mujer y de la voluptuosidad concupiscente de la mentalidad masculina en esa sociedad.[22]Pese a las consideraciones negativas de este espacio femenino, que en primera instancia se presenta como un lugar de reclusión y apartamiento, una barrera que la aleja y oculta del espacio público, este autor aprecia también la posibilidad de ser un ámbito discreto específico para la intervención directa de determinadas mujeres en la vida pública y, especialmente, en las tramas del poder.[23]

En un tiempo y ambiente cultural en el que la mujer tenía por horizonte vital el matrimonio, que era lo que "definía" su historia personal[24], el ámbito doméstico era su lugar de acción, su medio natural de expresión, "the territory of women" para Mernissi.[25] Esto afectó, lógicamente, al ejercicio del poder por parte de las mujeres que, según Rubiera,[26] tenían tres únicas posibilidades de actuar políticamente: ante la ausencia de una figura masculina y, por tanto, supliendo a los varones; en el marco de lo que denomina "politics of the harem",[27] esto es, "entre concubinas y eunucos", lo que transformaba el espacio privado en verdadero "campo de batalla" que trascendía al espacio público; y, por último, el caso excepcional de alguna figura femenina concreta que sobresalía por méritos propios pese a verse rodeada de fuertes personalidades masculinas y, por tanto y en principio, dominantes.

Leila Ahmed ha visto en el harén un lugar de relación entre mujeres, tanto verticales, cruzando las *class lines*, como horizontales.[28] Allí pueden compartir

---

22   Esta visión estereotipada y de tono etnocentrista, por ejemplo, en: E. Lott, *Harem Life in Egypt and Constantinople*, London 1867. Otras versiones más realistas y transmitidas desde el interior de estos espacios: M.-H. Malik-Khanam, *Thirty Years in the Harem: or the Authobiography of Melek-Hanum, Wife of H.H. Kibrizli-Mehemet-Pasha*, London 1872.

23   L. Gonzalvo, *La mujer musulmana en España*, Madrid 1906, 16–17. Este cambio de percepción se ha ido imponiendo con el tiempo, por ejemplo: N.M. Penzer, *The Ḥarēm: An Account of the Institution as It Existed in the Palace of the Turkish Sultans with a History of the Grand Seraglio from Its Foundation to the Present Time*, Philadelphia 1935.

24   M. Marín, *Vidas de mujeres andalusíes*, Málaga 2006, 31–38.

25   Mernissi, 2006, 50.

26   M.ªJ. Rubiera, *La princesa Fāṭima Bint al-Aḥmar, la 'María de Molina' de la dinastía nazarí de Granada*, en: Medievalismo. Boletín de la Sociedad Española de Estudios Medievales 6 (1996), 183–189 (189).

27   Expresión que también utiliza Mernissi, 2006, 92.

28   L. Ahmed, *Western Ethnocentrism and Perceptions of the Harem*, en: Feminist Studies 8 (1982), 521–534.

su vida, pero también su espacio vital, intercambiar experiencias e información e, incluso, realizar un análisis crítico, a menudo desenfadado, del mundo masculino. Por otro lado, para Schick[29] el harén es, sobre todo, una *representation* y no tanto una *social institution*, con múltiples, diversos y contradictorios significados. Por un lado: "its portrayal ranging from a microcosm of Oriental despotism and the locus of phallocratic oppression"; pero es visto, también, como: "a space of female autonomy in wich Muslim women are able to engage in social, economic, and even political activities unhindered by male domination".

En todo caso, el harén es un fenómeno característico de las élites del mundo islámico que abarca múltiples aspectos: la esclavitud, la vida sexual, el matrimonio, la propiedad, las creencias tradicionales, la intimidad y privacidad, la expresión cultural (por ejemplo, el canto) y, desde luego, a la mujer en su conjunto.[30] Pero no era el único espacio reservado a la mujer en las élites del mundo islámico, pues en los primeros siglos del islam las mujeres podían tener sus propias casas y palacios particulares,[31] lo que se repitió siglos después en la dinastía nazarí, por ejemplo, con la Dār al-Ḥurra (actual Santa Isabel la Real), situada en la Alcazaba Qadīma de Granada, y que perteneció a Fāṭima,[32] esposa de Abū l-Ḥasan ᶜAlī y madre de Muḥammad XI (Boabdil).[33]

Schick aplica al concepto de harén dos términos procedentes de la misma raíz de la lengua árabe.[34] En primer lugar, *ḥarīm*, que define como una zona de la vivienda "whose use is forbidden to all but the rightful owner". En segundo lugar, *ḥurma*, que se refiere a "something held sacred and inviolable, something which it is one's duty to honor and defend, and only in this specific sense to a man's wives and family". Esta división característica de las edificaciones

---

29   I.C. Schick, *The Harem as Gendered Space and the Spatial Reproduction of Gender*, en: M. Booth (ed.), *Harem Histories: Envisioning Palces and Living Spaces*, Durham, 2010, 69–84 (81).

30   S.n. "Ḥarīm", en: B. Lewis / V.L. Ménage / Ch. Pellat / J. Schacht (eds.), *The Encyclopaedia of Islam* 3, Leiden 1986, 209.

31   H. Kennedy, *La corte de los califas*, Barcelona 2008, 211, 215–216.

32   Este es, y no ᶜĀᵗišà, el nombre correcto de la sultana madre de Boabdil. Sobre esta cuestión, véase especialmente: R. Peinado Santaella, *Una propiedad latifundista en el Reino de Granada: la hacienda del corregidor Andrés Calderón (1492–1500)*, en: Chronica Nova 22 (1995), 303–355 (325–326, nota 92).

33   M.ªE. Díez, *El espacio doméstico: Lo femenino y lo masculino en la ciudad palatina de la Alhambra*, en: Cuadernos de la Alhambra 38 (2002), 155–181 (166); W. Hoenerbach, *¿Qué nos queda de la Granada árabe?*, en: Miscelánea de Estudios Árabes y Hebraicos: Sección Árabe-Islam 36 (1987), 251–288 (279–280).

34   I. C. Schick, *Space: Harem*, en: J. Suad (ed.), *Encyclopedia of Women & Islamic Cultures* 4: *Economics, Education, Mobility and Space*, Leiden 2007, 544–548 (544).

palaciegas islámicas se encuentra, también, en la Alhambra de Granada (ss. XIII–XV), donde hay un recinto palatino perfectamente delimitado: un espacio público y de ceremonia, el Palacio de Comares (*Qaṣr al-Sulṭān*) y otro para la vida privada del sultán y su familia, el Palacio de los Leones o El Jardín Feliz (*Qaṣr al-Riyāḍ*). Aunque en ambos palacios se identifican hoy día estructuras en los pisos altos que parecen haber tenido esta función de harén, el más conocido es el situado sobre la Sala de Abencerrajes.[35] Esta distribución sirvió como modelo e inspiración en la arquitectura palaciega posterior en el Occidente musulmán.[36] Según Díez, no existía una separación radical entre los espacios públicos y privados de la Alhambra, sino una estrecha conexión entre ellos que se producía, eso sí, mediante corredores, acodos y celosías que permitían guardar la privacidad, compartiendo intimidad con aquellos otros espacios masculinos de uso público pero jerarquizados en cuanto a su accesibilidad, como el Salón del Trono en el *Qaṣr al-Sulṭān*.[37]

Desde el punto de vista de la dicotomía público-privado, se creaba un ámbito sagrado del hogar, tanto para hombres como para mujeres, de igual forma que se construía un ámbito de recepción y de esparcimiento para ambos.[38] Por ejemplo, la escritora y activista turca Halidé Edib, todavía a comienzos del siglo XX, cuenta cómo durante la celebración de la ruptura del ramadán (*ifṭār*), el abuelo de la casa presidía el *selamlik*, mientras que la abuela lo hacía en el harén, mostrando dos ejes de autoridad en cada uno de los dos espacios domésticos diferentes.[39]

3   Poder Efectivo

El rol de soberana se ha asociado, por lo general, con el limitado papel de esposa y madre, una estrecha visión que hoy día se está rectificando por otra más amplia de la participación de la mujer en las altas esferas del poder en tiempos históricos, lo que se engloba en el concepto ya consolidado de *queenship*, "a cluster of customs, practices, and political theory that focuses on who queens were and what they did; how they were perceived by their peers; and how they were vital to family, culture, religion, and economics in the European Middle Ages".[40]

---

35   Díez, 2002, 165–166.
36   Mernissi, 2006, 47.
37   Díez, 2002, 166–167.
38   Schick, 2010, 77.
39   H. Edib, *Memoirs of Halidé Edib*, Londres 1926, 74.
40   Th. Earenfight, *Medieval Queenship*, en: History Compass 15 (2017), e12372.

Este campo de visión eurocéntrico se ha ido ampliando y extendiendo, y ahora se analiza el papel de las soberanas en otros tiempos y geografías con el objetivo de ofrecer una perspectiva de género en los estudios de estas mujeres, observando su papel en la historia, pero no necesariamente vinculado al rol de los varones, "queenly patronage, political agency, household dynamics, reputation and representation, and, more recently, diplomatic activity".[41] De igual modo, el ejercicio de la potestad soberana se contempla desde una perspectiva dinámica, cambiante en función del desarrollo de las experiencias vitales de estas mujeres en el poder, lo que Woodacre denomina "full cycle of queenship" y ejemplifica mediante el añadido de diferentes adjetivos a la función soberana: "regnant"; "regent"; "dowager"; and "consort".[42] En cada una de estas etapas y funciones el grado de poder efectivo que podían ejercer estas soberanas dependía de las circunstancias de tiempo y lugar, ofreciendo una amplia gama de posibilidades: desde una regencia con amplios poderes durante la minoría de edad de un futuro gobernante, por ejemplo, su hijo, hasta un limitado ejercicio del poder de una reina "regnant" que debía compartir y equilibrar su soberanía con su consorte masculino. En todo caso, lo realmente importante del nuevo punto de vista es la posibilidad de observar a las soberanas con su propia y característica capacidad política: "no matter what societal framework they operated under, women could be equally effective administrators, patrons, and leaders as their male counterparts or consorts".[43]

Para el caso específico del mundo islámico, Mernissi explica que las dos palabras que, en lengua árabe, encarnan el concepto de poder, es decir, califa e imán, excluyen su posible aplicación a las mujeres. Para ella, la razón reside en que ambas,

> "replace the Prophet in his mission, which is to make it possible for the group to live according to religious laws that guarantee a harmonious life on earth and a happy one in Paradise. Not just anyone can claim to be a caliph; access to this privilege is subject to strict criteria [...] The secret of the exclusion of women lies in the criteria of eligibility to be a caliph".[44]

Estos criterios son ocho: poseer libertad (ḥurrīya) para ser dueño de sí y poder ejercer la autoridad sobre los demás; ser varón (ḏukūra), por la advertencia del ḥadīṯ sobre que ningún pueblo que tiene al frente una mujer puede llegar

---

41   E. Woodacre, *Introduction: Placing Queenship into a Global Context*, en: E. Woodacre (ed.), *A Companion to Global Queenship*, Amsterdam 2018, 1–7 (1).
42   Ead., 6.
43   Ead., 7.
44   Mernissi, 2006, 4–12.

a prosperar; tener plena capacidad jurídica (*taklīf*) y, por tanto, ser púber y cuerdo; presentar integridad física (*salāmat al-aᶜḍāʼ*), lo que incluye cualquier imperfección corporal que produzca un impedimento para actuar de forma inmediata y con energía; el conocimiento de la ley divina (*ᶜilm*); juicio y coraje para tutelar la comunidad de forma correcta, tanto en la paz como en la guerra; vida moral (*ᶜadāla*), esto es, una "conducta irreprensible desde el punto de vista de la ley y de la ética musulmana"; y, por último, pertenecer a la descendencia (*nasab*) de la tribu del Profeta, Qurayš.[45]

Como señala Mernissi, ello no impidió que las mujeres ejercieran otras altas dignidades del estado musulmán que no implicaban un sentido de elección divina, tales como las representadas por los títulos de sultana (*sulṭāna*) o de reina (*mālika*), u otros menos usuales: *sitt* (dama), término que aparece en la dinastía fatimí de Egipto y parece referirse a mujeres de especial talento; *šarīfa*, referido a capacidades de liderazgo, tanto espiritual como temporal (militar); princesa (*amīra*), jefa del ejército; y, en el islam asiático, el de *khatūm*, sobre todo en las dinastías turcas y mogolas.[46] A estos apelativos propios del ejercicio de la soberanía política para el caso específico de las mujeres pueden añadirse otros, como *al-ḥurra*, en sentido literal "free woman",[47] concepto que describe, especialmente en el contexto del harén: "the legal wife, often of aristocratic descent"; lo que se opone a la idea de *jarya*, es decir, la esclava adquirida en un mercado. Pero, históricamente, el término *ḥurr*, libre, se asocia al de noble, de igual manera que el concepto de aristocracia (*sayyīd/sayyīda*, señor, señora) se opone al de esclavitud o esclavo (*ᶜabd*): "*Hurr*, then, is a concept intrinsically linked to *sharaf*, the aristocracy, the elite, the superior group".

Echevarría y Salicrú explican, a través de la documentación diplomática entre Granada y la Corona de Aragón, que el título de reina (*mālika*) no se empleaba entre las mujeres asociadas al trono en la Granada nazarí, y el de sultana tampoco era nada corriente, sino que se empleaba con asiduidad el término "honourable lady" (*sayyīdat al-ḥurra*):

> "further than nobility, *al-ḥurra* referred to the legal capacities accorded to free women in Islamic law, among them education and, especially, the capacity to act – *i.e.* the individual's effective ability to carry out juridical acts, to exercise rights, and to assume obligations".[48]

45   D. Santillana, *Istituzioni di diritto musulmano malichita con riguardo anche al sistema scia-fiita*, Roma 1925, v. 1, 18–19.

46   Mernissi, 2006, 12–13, 20–21.

47   Sigo, en todo este párrafo, y en los entrecomillados, a: ead., 14–15.

48   Echevarría / Salicrú, 2018, 260.

Las mujeres de la dinastía nazarí que ostentaron estas distinciones son un ejemplo claro de la importancia histórica de la participación femenina en las esferas de poder, asumiendo un rol más pasivo o más activo según las circunstancias y posibilidades que, en cada caso, se les brindó: "The influence of Nasrid princesses within courtly circles came from their origin, from their fortune, and from their role as regents during minorities".[49] La dinastía utilizó en varias ocasiones las alianzas matrimoniales para consolidarse en el poder desde sus remotos orígenes en Arjona. De este modo, la madre del primer sultán nazarí, Muḥammad I, llamada Fāṭima bint Ašqīlūla, era miembro de una poderosa familia local y su hijo, el sultán, se preocupó por estrechar fuertes lazos familiares con ellos, de modo que casó a dos de sus hijas, Mū'mina y Šams, con dos hijos de ᶜAlī b. Ašqīlūla.[50] Boloix apunta, incluso, a la posibilidad de que estas dos mujeres fueran hijas de un segundo matrimonio del sultán con otra pariente de los Banū Ašqīlūla, lo que reforzó enormemente los lazos endogámicos trazados por el iniciador de la dinastía,[51] algo que fue predominante en la sucesión de los nazaríes, especialmente en relación con las primas paternas (*bint al-ᶜamm*).[52]

La consanguinidad fue una constante en los matrimonios de la dinastía, hasta el punto de que Echevarría y Salicrú comentan que, durante el mandato de Saᶜd, abuelo de Muḥammad XI Boabdil, "the involvement of the Nasrids with these families was so strong that most of the important families in the emirate, including the dynasty, were relatives".[53]

El ofrecimiento de las mujeres de la familia para reforzar alianzas políticas es una buena muestra del destacado papel que cumplieron. Además, fueron usadas como prenda en las tramas de poder, por ejemplo, en la huida de la Alhambra del sultán Muḥammad IX al-Aysar, en 1431 EC, quien, acosado por sus rivales, se llevó consigo los instrumentos de poder que podían asegurarle mantener abierta su causa política, esto es, el tesoro regio y tres valiosos rehenes: dos hijos del antiguo sultán Muḥammad VIII el Pequeño, al que había hecho asesinar, y una sobrina que era hermana de Yūsuf V el Cojo, es decir, familiares cercanos con los que había rivalizado por el trono y que habían

---

49   Ead., 257.

50   Vidal, 2000, 79 y 91; R. Arié, *L'Espagne musulmane au temps des Naṣrides (1232–1492)*, Paris 1973, 66, nota 3.

51   B. Boloix, *Beyond the Ḥaram: Ibn Al-Khaṭīb and His Privileged Knowledge of Royal Nasrid Women*, en: Medieval Encounters 20 (2013), 384–403 (390).

52   B. Boloix, *Las sultanas de la Alhambra: Las grandes desconocidas del reino nazarí de Granada (siglos XIII–XV)*, Granada 2013, 49–50. Como ejemplo, cabe destacar que la primera mujer de Muḥammad I, ᶜĀ'išà, era hija de su tío paterno Muḥammad b. Muḥammad.

53   Echevarría / Salicrú, 2018, 257.

constituido en el sultanato sus propias facciones políticas con las que podían hacerle sombra.[54] Destacan, también, algunos enlaces por vía matrilineal, como ya habíamos mencionado a través del estudio de Rubiera, aunque Echevarría y Salicrú insisten en la vía patrilineal de sucesión como la más habitual, mientras que la vía materna se explicaría, según estas autoras, en momentos puntuales de inestabilidad política.[55]

Podemos medir la importancia de la capacidad política de la mujer en el periodo nazarí a través de figuras femeninas fuertes como, por ejemplo, la sultana al-Ḥurra Umm al-Fatḥ, viuda de Yūsuf III y madre de Muḥammad VIII el Pequeño que, en 1427, ocupó el papel de "reina madre" y "se erigió en interlocutora válida de la política internacional del sultanato y, por consiguiente, de algún modo, en actora de la vida política interna granadina".[56] Llegó a tratar asuntos de Estado con Alfonso V el Magnánimo, rey de Aragón, aunque de forma indirecta, a través de la reina aragonesa María de Castilla. Con ello, recurriendo a lo que Salicrú llama "complicidad de género", consiguió salvar los obstáculos formales que impedían el trato personal de una sultana con un rey cristiano.[57]

4   Fāṭima bint Muḥammad IX

Tanto en la literatura cristiana como en la musulmana que se refiere a la decadencia del reino de Granada se atribuye el origen y desencadenante de su caída a la disensión interna vivida durante toda la decimoquinta centuria en el sultanato, especialmente la facilidad en derrocar a sus gobernantes y las intrigas desatadas entre sus élites, en las que ambiciosas mujeres habrían tenido un papel muy destacado.

Hay dos relatos históricos acerca de los últimos cincuenta años de existencia de la Granada nazarí, uno musulmán y otro cristiano, que contribuyeron a la extensión de esta idea, por la enorme influencia que tuvieron en narraciones posteriores,[58] las *Ajbār al-ᶜaṣr fī inqiḍā' dawlat Banī Naṣr* (*Noticias históricas sobre el fin de la dinastía nazarí*), escritas en 1540 EC en el norte de África por

---

54   Ead., 165, 217, nota 90; Boloix, 2013, 90.

55   Echevarría / Salicrú, 2018, 257–258.

56   R. Salicrú, *Sultanas emergentes: visualización de la mujer musulmana en las fuentes cristianas*, en: *VIII Estudios de Frontera. Mujeres y fronteras*, Jaén 2011, 447–483, 478.

57   Salicrú, 2011, 481–482.

58   La bibliografía generada sobre la llamada Guerra de Granada (1482–1492) es especialmente abrumadora y podría decirse que es el acontecimiento histórico más influyente y destacado de la Historia de España.

un autor anónimo (probablemente un militar granadino perteneciente a la élite del sultanato),[59] y trasladadas con correcciones y adiciones años después, en el siglo XVII, bajo el título *Nubḏat al-ʿaṣr fī aḫbār mulūk Banī Naṣr* (*Breve narración sobre la historia de los reyes nazaríes*);[60] y, por otro lado, la *Historia de los reyes moros de Granada* de Hernando de Baeza, escrita *ca.* 1516 por el trujamán de Muḥammad XI (Boabdil) con los Reyes Católicos, testigo de vista o de oído de mucho de lo que cuenta, incluidos diferentes personajes de la Granada islámica, como los elches (cristianos conversos al islam), el propio sultán y, de manera excepcional, las mujeres de la corte.[61] A estas dos fuentes debemos añadir, en el ámbito de la cultura hebrea, el testimonio de Rabí Eliyahu Capsali, de 1523–1524, elaborado en parte con relatos de testigos presenciales: sefardíes huidos a Creta tras el decreto de Expulsión de los judíos de España en 1492.[62]

Estas tres fuentes prestan especial atención al reinado de los tres últimos sultanes nazaríes (Abū l-Ḥasan ʿAlī, su hijo Muḥammad XI, Boabdil, y su hermano Muḥammad XII al-Zagal) y a sus luchas de poder, y siguen un mismo patrón argumental para explicar la situación política del momento: tras un período inicial de estabilidad interna y fortaleza frente al enemigo cristiano

---

59 Se estudia en: Á.C. López / F.N. Velázquez, *Ajbār al-ʿaṣr*, en: J. Lirola / J.M. Puerta (dirs.), *Biblioteca de al-Andalus* 1: *De al-ʿAbbādīya a Ibn Abyaḍ*, Almería 2012, 55–57. Editado por: M.J. Müller, *Ajbār al-ʿaṣr fī inqiḍāʾ dawlat Banī Naṣr=Erzählugen der Epoche betreffend das Aufhören der Dynastie der Naçriden*, en: id. (ed.), *Die letzten Zeiten von Granada*, München 1863, 1–56 (texto árabe), 103–159 (texto alemán).

60 Se estudia en: Á.C. López / F.N. Velázquez, *Nubḏat al-ʿaṣr*, en: J. Lirola (dir. y ed.), *Biblioteca de al-Andalus* 6: *De Ibn al-Ŷabbāb a Nubḏat al-ʿaṣr*, Almería 2009, 621–622. Editado en: A. Bustani (ed. y pról.), C. Quirós (trad.), *Fragmento de la época sobre noticias de los Reyes Nazaritas o Capitulación de Granada y Emigración de los andaluces a Marruecos*, Larache 1940. Cito siguiendo esta edición.

61 Editado parcialmente en: M.J. Müller (ed.), *Cosas de Granada*, en: id. (ed.), *Die letzen Zeiten von Granada*, München 1863, 57–99; y en: E. Lafuente, *Últimos sucesos del Reino de Granada*, en: *Relaciones de algunos sucesos de los últimos tiempos del Reino de Granada*, Madrid 1868, 1–44. La edición del final de la crónica con la copia descubierta en el mss. Escalante-Portilla, en: M.ªM. Delgado Pérez, *A newly Discovered Manuscript of the 'Historia de los Reyes Moros de Granada' by Hernando de Baeza*, en: Manuscript Studies: A Journal of the Schoenberg Institute for Manuscript Studies 2 (2017), 540–567; y con los finales del mss. de la Real Biblioteca y de la Heinecke de Yale, en: M.ªM. Delgado Pérez, *Certezas e hipótesis sobre el final de la crónica granadina de Hernando de Baeza*, en: Anaquel de Estudios Árabes 29 (2018), 33–62.

62 La parte dedicada a la historia española, en: Y. Moreno (ed.), *El judaísmo hispano según la crónica hebrea de Rabí Eliyahu Capsali. Traducción y Estudio del Seder Eliyahu Zutá (capítulos 40–70)*, Granada 2005. Una versión anterior, en: Y. Moreno, *La conquista de Granada y la expulsión de Sefarad, según las crónicas hispanohebreas*, en: *Andalucía medieval. Actas del I Congreso de Historia de Andalucía. Diciembre de 1976*, Córdoba 1978, v. 2, 329–338.

durante el gobierno de Abū l-Ḥasan ᶜAlī (primer mandato, 1464–1482), se vivió
un segundo ciclo verdaderamente caótico (entre 1483–1485), que se explica
por tres causas fundamentales: la asfixiante presión fiscal sobre los súbditos,
motivada por la recuperación de los bienes particulares de la dinastía (*bayt
al-jāṣṣ*)[63] enajenados en épocas anteriores en favor de particulares; la repre-
sión violenta que llevó a cabo contra la élite disidente del sultanato, especialmente los agrupados bajo el nombre de Abencerrajes; y, de forma muy
especial, su comportamiento marital, que lo llevó a ser infiel a su esposa legal
(*zawiŷa*), Fāṭima, y repudiarla para elevar a la dignidad de sultana a su concubina (*jariya*) favorita, Ṯurayyā, lo que ponía en riesgo los derechos de sucesión
al trono de la descendencia nazarí.

El autor de las *Ajbār al-ᶜaṣr* dice: "El rey se dedicó a los placeres, se entregó
a sus pasiones y se dió a divertirse con cantoras y danzaderas. Sumido en el
mayor ocio y descuido, destrozó el ejército del cual suprimió gran número de
esforzados caballeros".[64] Baeza, por su parte, se explaya aún más y afirma que
el sultán se encontraba "metido en sus vicios",[65] que expone con harta elo-
cuencia al relatar la historia de Ṯurayyā: "estando pues ella en casa del rrey,
como todos los rreyes moros por la mayor parte fuesen muy dados á la luxuria,
especialmente este que tenia por prosupuesto lleuar todas las donzellas de su
casa por un rrasero, emboluióse con esta".[66] Y Capsali, a su vez, señala: "poco
a poco los ancianos de Ismael le iban abandonando, porque dijeron: '¿Acaso
serviremos a un hombre como este, que tomó por mujer a su prisionera, una
goy (*gentil*), y repudió a su bellísima esposa?'".[67]

Las tres crónicas coinciden en resaltar la enorme importancia que tuvo en
el curso de los acontecimientos posteriores y en la propia caída del sultanato
el enfrentamiento entre Abū l-Ḥasan ᶜAlī y su esposa legal, Fāṭima, debido a
los manejos de Ṯurayyā, a la vez que destacan las intrigas tejidas por la mujer
repudiada en favor de sus hijos varones (Muḥammad XI, Abū l-Ḥaŷŷāŷ Yūsuf
y un tercero, al que llaman Algazir)[68]. Las *Ajbār al-ᶜaṣr* relatan: "Llegó a tanto

63   Tesoro real, diferente al tesoro público (*bayt al-māl*), aunque en la Granada nazarí la dis-
     tinción no era muy clara: L. Seco de Lucena Paredes, *La administración central de los naza-
     ríes*, en: Cuadernos de la Alhambra 10/11 (1974/1975), 21–26.
64   *Nubḏat al-ᶜaṣr*, 1940, 7.
65   Müller, 1863, 65.
66   Id., 64.
67   Capsali, 2005, 157. Interpretamos *goy* como *gentil*, del latín *ethnicus* según traducción
     latina de Paul Fagius en el diccionario llamado *Tishbi* de Elijah Levita, editado en Isny (Ale-
     mania) en 1541. Ver: I. Broydé, *Levita, Elijah*, en: I. Singer (ed.), *The Jewish Encyclopedia* 8:
     Leon-Moravia, New York 1906, 46–49.
68   Baeza (Müller, 1863, 74) y Capsali (2005, 154) son las únicas fuentes para conocer a este
     tercer hijo varón, aunque solo el segundo menciona su nombre.

el desenfreno del emir, que dió preferencia sobre su esposa a una cristiana llamada Zoraya, abandonando a su prima y a los hijos habidos en ella".[69] De ello surgieron los celos, "que en tales ocasiones suelen concebir las mujeres respecto a sus esposos" y las "disensiones" en el matrimonio, en las que los hijos de Fāṭima se pusieron a favor de la madre, que temió por sus vidas dado el "natural colérico e impetuoso" del padre.

Ṭurayyā (en árabe, Las Pléyades;[70] Toraya o Zoraya en las fuentes castellanas),[71] la Romía (*al-rūmīya*), según Baeza, es decir, "persona que fué subjeta al señorío rromano [*i.e.* de la Iglesia católica]",[72] era una pastora cristiana que, en edad infantil, fue capturada por los nazaríes en el término de Aguilar, Córdoba, durante una algara, y acabó en la Alhambra como esclava cautiva[73].

Según López de Coca, su captura debió suceder en los primeros años de la década de 1470, pues hay cierta referencia documental de una propiedad legada a ella por el sultán en diciembre de 1476[74]. Aquí aparece con los atributos de la grandeza: "honesta, libre, limpia y noble", lo que quiere decir que ya había nacido su primogénito y se había convertido en "madre de un hijo varón" o "concubina madre" (*umm al-walad*), momento a partir del cual destacó del resto de concubinas y pasó a ser "esclava *sultanizada*".[75] Efectivamente, eso debió suceder así, ya que en 1470 Abū l-Ḥasan ʿAlī firmaba una carta desde el "alcázar feliz", es decir, el Palacio de los Leones[76], lo que indica que aún vivía allí con Fāṭima pues, como refiere Baeza, tras el enfrentamiento con Ṭurayyā,

---

69   *Nubḏat al-ʿaṣr*, 1940, 7.

70   *Nubḏat al-ʿaṣr*, 1940, 7. La traducción del vocablo árabe, en: J. Aguadé / F. Corriente / Á. Vicente / M. Meouak (eds.), *Estudios de dialectología norteafricana y andalusí*, Zaragoza 2006, 125–126. Capsali traduce este nombre como "lámpara" (155), lo que puede tener cierta validez en relación con la voz "açoraya/e", recogida en: Corriente, 2006, 125.

71   La primera forma en: M. Garrido (ed.), *Las capitulaciones para la entrega de Granada*, Granada 1910, 184. La segunda en: AGS, CCA, CED, 1, 78, 1, *Bienes 'de la reyna Çoraya, mora' en la ciudad de Granada*, 1494/07/24, Segovia; AGS, CCA, CED, 1, 88, 2, *Orden a Andrés de Medina, receptor de los bienes confiscados por la Inquisición del obispado de Córdoba, para que pague 'a la reyna Çoraya, mora, que está en esta çibdad de Córdova', la cantidad anual que tiene asignada para su mantenimiento y que no le ha sido entregada en el último año*, 1494/08/08, Segovia.

72   Müller, 1863, 65.

73   Id., 63–64.

74   J.E. López de Coca, *The Making of Isabel de Solís*, en: R. Collins / A. Goodman (eds.), *Medieval Spain: Culture, Conflict and Coexistence*, Londres 2002, 225–241 (228).

75   En palabras de Boloix, 2013, 184–187, 191–196.

76   E. Lafuente, *Documentos relativos al desafío de d. Alonso de Aguilar y d. Diego Fernández de Córdoba*, en: H. de Baeza (ed.), *Relaciones de algunos sucesos de los últimos tiempos del Reino de Granada*, Madrid 1868, 71–143, (80–83).

el sultán recluyó en esta zona de la Alhambra a su esposa legal para pasar a habitar el de Comares con su concubina.

Fāṭima fue, por tanto, su mujer legítima (*zawiŷa*)[77], *sunniya* y *al-ḥurra*, término que insiste en su condición de mujer libre, que nunca ha sido esclava, "horro de servidumbre", como recoge el vocabulario de árabe granadino de Pedro de Alcalá[78]. Era de sangre noble, prima de su marido, como afirman las *Ajbār al-ʿaṣr*,[79] ya que fue hija de la primera mujer del sultán Muḥammad IX al-Aysar (el Izquierdo), Umm al-Fatḥ, y hermana de ʿĀʾišà, de donde, quizá, haya podido venir la confusión de su nombre.

Capsali da protagonismo en el primer enfrentamiento entre ambas esposas a la hija de Fāṭima, ʿĀʾišà, a quien considera "perversa", y de quien llega a decir: "por medio de ella y por su causa se perdió el reino de la dinastía".[80] Según su versión, "maquinó hacer palidecer el rostro de su padre públicamente, avergonzarle ante los ancianos de su pueblo y ante Ismael".[81] De modo que hizo pública la infidelidad de su padre y maltrató físicamente a la concubina.[82] Baeza da una versión parecida, pero sin mencionar a ʿĀʾišà, e implica en la agresión y el escándalo a todas las mujeres del harén.[83]

Tras esta dura escena se produjo el repudio de Fāṭima por Abū l-Ḥasan ʿAlī y la consecuente legalización del concubinato, lo que se materializó públicamente en un acto de homenaje realizado por las mujeres de Granada a Ṯurayyà durante la celebración de la fiesta del *ʿīd al-aḍḥà*.[84] Esto provocó una división de la corte en dos facciones enfrentadas, una verdadera "guerra civil" según las *Ajbār al-ʿaṣr*,[85] lo que Baeza confirma: "visto el desconcierto de su persona [el sultán], leuantáronse ciertos caualleros en el rreyno, así criados de la rreyna como de el rrey su padre de ella, y alçaronla obediencia del rrey, y hiziéronle cruda guerra, entre los cuales fueron ciertos de los que dezian aben çarrajes".[86]

Las *Ajbār al-ʿaṣr* dan a entender que Fāṭima y sus hijos fueron instrumentalizados por el grupo de opositores de Abū l-Ḥasan ʿAlī, pero Baeza cuenta con bastante más precisión cómo fueron las luchas que se produjeron en el interior del harén entre ambas esposas. Como vimos anteriormente y tras estallar su

---

77 Garrido (ed.), 1910, 33.
78 P. de Alcalá, *Vocabulista arávigo en letra castellana*, Granada 1505, s. p. [303].
79 *Nubḏat al-ʿaṣr*, 1940, 7.
80 Capsali, 2005, 154.
81 Id., 155.
82 Id., 155–156.
83 Müller, 1863, 64.
84 Id., 65.
85 *Nubḏat al-ʿaṣr*, 1940, 13.
86 Müller, 1863, 65.

enemistad, el Palacio de Comares, centro del poder real y donde se ubicaba el Salón del Trono, pasó a ser residencia del sultán, Ṭurayyā y sus dos hijos, Saʿd y Naṣr, mientras que el Palacio de los Leones quedó como residencia de Fāṭima y sus hijos, que vivían prácticamente recluidos.[87] Tras el fallecimiento de Algazir,[88] el hijo menor de Fāṭima, toda la familia se trasladó a otras dependencias, más alejadas aún del entorno regio, parece que en el Partal.[89] Desde allí la sultana Fāṭima urdió un plan de fuga por el que, en 1482, sus hijos varones, Muḥammad y Yūsuf, lograron descolgarse con sogas por los muros de la Alhambra y huir a Guadix con sus partidarios,[90] con quienes hicieron la guerra al sultán, su padre, y a su tío, Saʿd.

Baeza parece estar en lo cierto al referirse a la enorme importancia de Fāṭima en la vida política granadina ya que, tras la captura de Muḥammad XI por los cristianos en abril de 1483 en la Batalla de Lucena, dirigió una embajada al rey Fernando el Católico para negociar su liberación:

> "Estando el rey en la ciudad de Córdova, vinieron a él mensajeros de la madre de Mulehi Bahadeli de Granada, que estava preso en poder del conde de Cabra, y de parte de otros cavalleros y cabeceras del reyno de Granada que estavan a su obediencia le suplicaron que le pluguiesse ponerlo en su libertad y reduzirlo a su reyno".[91]

La rivalidad entre estas dos mujeres llegó a su punto culminante en febrero o marzo de 1484, con la más que probable participación directa de Ṭurayyā en la muerte, por orden de su propio padre, del segundo hijo de Fāṭima, Yūsuf, en Almería, donde estaba refugiado con su hermana y su madre. Baeza cuenta este terrible episodio con los detalles más dramáticos.[92] La ejecución del infante significó el final político para Abū l-Ḥasan ʿAlī, que perdió el juicio arrepentido por la crueldad del acto,[93] y fue Saʿd quien, durante el verano de 1485, se hizo con el trono como Muḥammad XII de Granada y tomó a Ṭurayyā y a sus hijos como rehenes, esperando, según Baeza, obtener el sustancioso

---

87   Id., 65.

88   Baeza dice que de pestilencia: Müller, 1863, 74. Capsali retrasa el hecho y habla de una caída del caballo durante su huida con su madre y hermanos de Granada en 1483, tras la captura de su hermano Muḥammad XI Boabdil en Lucena y el regreso a la capital de su padre: 2005, 163.

89   L. Torres Balbás, *Crónica arqueológica de la España musulmana XXIV*, en: Al-Andalus 14 (1949), 175–210 (187).

90   Müller, 1863, 75; *Nubḏat al-ʿaṣr*, 1940, 13.

91   F. de Pulgar, *Chrónica de los muy altos y esclarecidos Reyes Cathólicos don Fernando y doña Ysabel, de gloriosa memoria*, Valladolid 1565, 175v.

92   Müller, 1863, 82–84.

93   Id., 84–86. Según Baeza (Müller, 1863, 82–86) y Capsali (2005, 164–166), fue el encargado de cumplir la sentencia de muerte del infante Yūsuf.

tesoro de su hermano.[94] Algunas fuentes sugieren que Ṯurayyā trató de que el mayor de sus hijos fuese encumbrado al trono de Granada, pero su plan se frustró.[95]

Durante todo este periodo como esposa, pero también durante los dos reinados de su hijo Muḥammad XI (1482–1483 y 1487–1492 EC), Baeza situó a Fāṭima como protagonista de la acción y, por primera y única vez en todas las fuentes contemporáneas a los hechos, da voz a una sultana madre, distinguiéndose así de las crónicas musulmanas, que silencian a sus mujeres.[96] Baeza describe en ella todos los rasgos de una personalidad fuerte, preocupada por su hijo, por su familia, por su casa y por el fututo de Granada y sus habitantes.[97] En los momentos finales del sultanato, días antes de la capitulación de 25 de noviembre de 1491, Fāṭima estallaba en lágrimas junto a su hija ʿĀʾišá, su nuera Maryam (esposa de Muḥammad XI) y el resto del harén al ver salir a su hijo, el que sería el último sultán de Granada, hacia el campo de batalla, en un encuentro bélico decisivo con las huestes cristianas; le recrimina:

> "Pues, hijo, [¿]á quién encomendais vuestra triste madre, y muger, y hijos y hermana, parientes, y criados, y toda esta cibdad, y los otros pueblos que os son encomendados? [¿]qué cuenta dareis á Dios dellos, poniendo en ellos tan mal rrecaudo, como poneis, dándola horden que dais, para que todos muramos á espada, y los que quedaren sean captiuos? mirá bien lo que hazeis, que en las grandes tribulaciones an de ser los grandes consejos".[98]

Para Mernissi, Fāṭima fue testigo y protagonista del final de al-Andalus y es el mejor ejemplo de la emergencia de la mujer en momentos críticos para el islam.[99] Según ella:

> "The fall of Granada propelled other women on to the political scene, women of the elite who would otherwise have led a somnolent life in the harem and whom the debacle pitched into the political melee, obliging them to assume responsibility and participate in the momentous events shaking the community and with it the western Mediterranean. Freed from the iron grip of tradition that immobilized them in domestic space and despite their inexperience, women showed themselves to be clever strategists, at least as resourceful as men".[100]

---

94   Müller, 1863, 86.
95   J.E. López de Coca, *La conquista de Granada: El testimonio de los vencidos*, en: Norba. Revista de Historia 18 (2005), 35–50 (42).
96   M. Marín, *Una vida de mujer: Ṣubḥ*, en: M.ª L. Ávila / M. Marín (eds.), *Biografías y género biográfico en el occidente islámico*, Madrid, 1997, 425–445 (441).
97   Müller, 1863, 94–95.
98   Ibid.
99   Mernissi, 1993, 16.
100 Id., 18.

5   Conclusión

En el sultanato nazarí de Granada la mujer no solo ocupaba los roles que se le
asignaban por las normas jurídico-religiosas o por la tradición, sino que, además, durante los periodos de crisis política, ciertas personalidades femeninas
especialmente fuertes tuvieron un inusual protagonismo en la escena pública y
un significativo liderazgo, especialmente en el entorno cortesano más próximo
al trono. Podemos concluir, por tanto, que existió una verdadera política de
harén, que podría definirse como la traslación de las tramas de poder e iniciativas de gobierno desde los espacios privados palatinos a la vida pública y a las
decisiones gubernativas.

Naṣrid Women Inside and Outside Madīna Garnāṭa
Wealth and Influence

Carmen Trillo San José

Abstract

This study analyses the Naṣrid women who lived inside and outside the city of Granada from the perspective of wealth and influence, based on new recently published 15th century Romanised Arabic sources. We will explore two areas: women of the royal family and other women, sometimes associated with government elites, who had properties in Vega de Granada.

Introduction[1]

The study of women in al-Andalus is of interest to historians and Arab scholars, as their position in society sheds light on their degree of Islamisation. For Sánchez Albornoz, women living in Muslim Spain enjoyed freedom.[2] Conversely, for Guichard, after the Muslim conquest, there was a confrontation between Western kinship, whose characteristics prioritised couples, exogamy and bilinearity, and Eastern kinship, defined by the extensive family group, endogamy and patrilineality, which ended in al-Andalus with the triumph of the East.[3] This also implies the existence of Arab and Berber tribal structures, clans and tribes, and that woman were hidden and family honour resided in them.

---

1 This study has been carried out within the framework of the research project *The peri-urban area of an Islamic city: la Vega de Granada (14th–16th centuries)* P18-RT-3588, financed by the Ministry of Universities, Research and Innovation of the Junta de Andalucía and FEDER funds.

2 C. Sánchez-Albornoz, *El Islam de España y el Occidente*, in: *L'occidente e l'Islam nell'Alto Medioevo, 2–8 aprile 1964: XII settimana di studio organizzata per il Centro Italiano di Studi sull'Alto Medioevo* 1, in: Settimane di Studio del Centro Italiano di Studi sull'Alto Medioevo 12, Spoleto 1965, 149–308.

3 P. Guichard, *Los árabes sí que invadieron España. Las estructuras sociales de la España musulmana*, in: id., *Estudios sobre Historia Medieval*, Valencia 1987, 27–71 (43–68).

© BRILL SCHÖNINGH, 2024 | DOI:10.30965/9783657791477_012

This issue has been subject to continuous historiographical debate.[4] Manzano does not believe that a tribal organisation existed, but that it is mentioned in the written sources metaphorically, as an expression of a social ideal that has been lost. Conversely, he also affirms that the elite group of the Arab conquerors integrated with the indigenous ruling classes through marriage,[5] which implied an acquisition of land and workers from them.

We did not find a tribal society during the Naṣrid period either, although it is probable that more or less recognisable traces of an extended family have remained. Seco de Lucena has already pointed out that people from Granada identified more with their village (*alquería*) of origin than their tribe.[6] Acién noted the lack of coherence between the *nasab* or even the *nisba* tribal and gentile place names.[7] Drawing from Ibn Khaldún, Guichard suggests that what was defined for other eras in terms of the existence of tribal structures in *al-Andalus* would not necessarily be valid for Naṣrid society.[8] We believe that a strong urbanisation in the Naṣrid period – having initially started in the Taifa period – would have contributed to a weakening of extensive kinship ties; although this does not mean they were absent. We must also consider the war, payments of *parias* [tributes] to Castile and, therefore, the fiscal pressure on the people of Granada.

Authors such as Manuela Marín have studied women in al-Andalus and emphasise the importance of gender separation and the concealment of women from public life, especially in urban areas. Christine Mazzoli-Guintard reflects on the spaces in the city where women can or cannot be.[9] They are mandatory in domestic areas, prohibited in military areas, disapproved of in cemeteries, souks and on the street, and controversial in mosques. Women in the Alhambra have been studied by Boloix.[10] We know that, during the Naṣrid

4   M. Acién Almansa, *Entre el feudalismo y el Islam. 'Umar Ibn Hafsun en los historiadores, en las fuentes y en la historia*, Jaén 1994.

5   E. Manzano Moreno, *Conquistadores, emires y califas. Los omeyas y la formación de al-Andalus*, Barcelona 2006, 115.

6   L. Seco de Lucena Paredes, *Documentos arábigogranadinos*, Madrid 1961, XLI.

7   M. Acién Almansa, *Reino de Granada*, in: Miquel Barceló (ed.), *Historia de los Pueblos de España*, Barcelona 1984, 47–55 (49).

8   P. Guichard, *Introduction. The Naṣrid Kingdom in the History of al-Andalus*, in: A. Fábregas García (ed.), *The Naṣrid Kingdom of Granada between East and West (Thirteenth to Fifteenth Centuries)*, Leiden 2020, 1–36.

9   Ch. Mazzoli-Guintard, *¿Dónde las mujeres podían estar o no en las ciudades andalusíes? Los lugares para mujeres según las cinco calificaciones religiosas (Córdoba, ss. VIII–XIII)*, in: HAL Id: hal-03668304 https://hal.science/hal-03668304.

10   B. Boloix Gallardo, *Las sultanas de la Alhambra. Las grandes desconocidas del reino nazarí de Granada (siglos XIII–XV)*, Granada 2013.

period, women played a key role in the Arab notarial documents from the 15th century.[11] Zomeño believes it was a society in which dominant factors included the nuclear family, tactics to benefit daughters and avoid inheritance laws, and exogamy.[12] Naṣrid society was unequal, progressively more urbanised and a place where the conjugal family and women were increasingly important.

We have analysed the final period of the Naṣrid emirate (13th–15th centuries) and its nearby territory, a plain known as Vega de Granada, where the River Genil runs through its 1,362 km² from east to west. The documentation we analysed for this study, especially Romanised Arabic texts from the 15th century, allowed us to better understand their socio-economic situation at the end of the Naṣrid period. In this sense, we can confirm that in this area close to the capital of the Naṣrid emirate there was a significant presence of royal patrimony, sometimes in the hands of the women from the ruling family. Similarly, there is mention of a class of public officials, in which governors stand out, with purchasing power to buy land from the royal treasury and land in the surroundings areas of Madīna Garnāṭa, especially during the second half of the 15th century. The presence of women is also of note in this Romanised Arabic documentation, often belonging to the social class of state public officials, who own property and exercise rights over it, which will be further looked at below.

1   Women of the Alhambra: Wealth and Power

We have already pointed out the importance of the role of women in defining Andalusian society. Guichard was one of the first authors to study these aspects, which basically placed women within an Islamic kinship structure, characterised by the aforementioned endogamy and patrilineality. Rubiera notes that the Naṣrid lineages, and particularly the ruling dynasty, the Banū Naṣr, did not base their solidarity on agnatism but on bilateral kinship. Thus

---

11   M. Shatzmiller, *Her Day in Court: Women's Property Rights in Fifteenth-Century Granada*, Cambridge 2007; A. Zomeño Rodríguez, *Siete historias de mujeres: sobre la transmisión de la propiedad en la Granada nazarí*, in: M.I. Calero Secall (coord.), *Mujeres y sociedad islámica: una visión plural*, Málaga 2006, 175–197; A. Zomeño Rodríguez, *Families and Family Ties in Naṣrid Granada*, in: A. Fábregas García (ed.), *The Naṣrid Kingdom of Granada between East and West (Thirteenth to Fifteenth Centuries)*, Leiden 2020, 195–215; M.D. Rodríguez Gómez, *Fāṭima bint Muḥammad vende una finca de regadío. Sobre mujeres nazaríes y propiedades en la Granada del siglo XV*, in: F. Toro Ceballos / J. Rodríguez Molina (eds.), *Mujeres y frontera: homenaje a Cristina Segura Graíño. VIII Congreso Internacional Estudios de Frontera celebrado en Alcalá la Real (Jaén, 19–20 November 2010)*, Jaén 2011, 415–430.

12   Zomeño Rodríguez, 2020, 195–215.

the women of the royal family would have been transmitters of their nobility to less important lineages. In fact, there were several marriages with the Banū Ašqīlūla and the Banū Mawl that allowed the Banū Naṣr stay in power. In addition, there were several Naṣrid kings that arrived through the maternal line. This is the case of Ismāᶜīl I, son of Abū Saᶜīd Faraŷ, who in turn was the son of a brother of Muḥammad I (1238–1273). Although the people of Granada offered the throne to Abū Saᶜīd during the reign of Naṣr (1309–1314), son of Muḥammad II, Abū Saᶜīd suggested it pass to his son, who became Ismāᶜīl I, as he had Banū Naṣr blood through his maternal line: his mother, Fatima, was also the daughter of Muḥammad II (1273–1302).

There are many cases of how the women of the Naṣrid royal family transmit the right to the throne[13]. Muḥammad VI, "The Red One" (1360–1362), great-grandson of Abū Saᶜīd Faraŷ, who married a daughter of Yūsuf I, with the intention of ennobling his membership into the royal family.[14] A daughter of this marriage would subsequently marry a member of the Banū Mawl and from this union, the issue of the emir Yūsuf IV Ibn Mawl (1431–1432), who rose to power through the influence of his maternal line.

Rubiera[15] thus notes the existence of cognatic alliances, as well as agnatic ones, and questions what Guichard stated about the predominance of Eastern or patrilineal kinship over the bilateral ones typical of the West in al-Andalus.[16] On this the author has more recently indicated that the Banū Naṣr family functioned as a large endogamous block in which marriages took place between its members, including the collateral branches of other lineages such as those mentioned, thus he does not consider them to be exogamous.[17] For Echevarría and Salicrú,[18] this situation of female empowerment might have been accentuated when the rivalry between candidates for the throne grew and intervention by the Kingdom of Castile increased, such that matrimony with a Naṣrid princess could be the difference between the aspirants and serving to reinforce their legitimacy.[19]

---

13   Boloix Gallardo, 2013, 82–83.
14   M.J. Rubiera Mata, *El vínculo cognático en al-Andalus*, in: *Actas del I Congreso de Historia de Andalucía. Andalucía Medieval*, Córdoba 1978, 121–124 (123); Boloix Gallardo, 2013, 82.
15   Rubiera Mata, 1978, 121–124.
16   Guichard, 1987, 27–71; J. Zenka, *The Great Ruling Family of the 14th Century: Musahara in the Age of Ibn al-Khatib*, in: ME 20 (2014), 306–339.
17   Guichard, 2020, 5–6.
18   A. Echevarría / R. Salicrú, *The "Honourable Ladies" of Naṣrid Granada*, in E. Woodacre (ed.), *A Companion to Global Queenship*, Leeds 2018, 255–270.
19   Echevarría / Salicrú, 2018, 257–258.

In addition to the matrilineal influence over accession to the Naṣrid throne, some women in the royal family played a more important role than might appear at first glance. This is the known case of Fatima bint al-Aḥmar,[20] daughter of Muḥammad II, who played an important political role in the emirate throughout her long life, dying at the age of over 90. She was the wife of her father's paternal cousin, Abū Saᶜīd Faraŷ Ibn al-Aḥmar, who was a prominent political figure and an adviser to the emir on economic aspects associated with the growth of the royal patrimony.[21] Abu Saᶜīd was appointed governor of Malaga after the rebellion of Banū Ašqīlūla, cognate allies of Banū Naṣr.

Fatima was also very present during the following reigns, that of her uterine brother, Muḥammad III (1302–1309), who was rumoured to have been associated with the death of his father, and later to her half-brother Naṣr, who came to power by a conspiracy in 1309. In a new rebellion the usurpers put forward Abū Saᶜīd Faraŷ for the throne. Despite being a legitimate candidate, a Banū Naṣr, Muḥammad II's first cousin, after his return to Malaga, he changed his mind and proposed his son Ismāᶜīl. This shows the influence of the maternal lines to the throne: he was a grandson of Muḥammad II through his mother, Fatima, which leads us to ponder her role in such a decision.[22]

It was likely that Ismāᶜīl's mother would have accompanied him during his rule (1314–1325), since his father, who had betrayed him, was imprisoned until his death (1320).[23] Ismāᶜīl was assassinated and subsequently succeeded by his son Muḥammad IV (1325–1333), at the age of 10, who was tutored by his grandmother Fatima and by the vizier Riḍwān. The supervision of her grandson affected the political context, as exemplified by the fact that his vizier, Muḥammad b. Aḥmad al-Maḥrūq (The Burned One), was assassinated at Fatima's palace while visiting.[24]

When Muḥammad died in 1333, assassinated by his paternal cousin, *arráez* of Algeciras, his brother Yūsuf I (1333–1354) ascended the throne at the age of 15; he also had to be supervised by his father's mother, Fátima bt. Muḥammad, and by the vizier Riḍwān. He was one of the main emirs of Granada, and

---

20   M.J. Rubiera Mata, *La princesa Fāṭima Bint al-Aḥmar, la "María Molina" de la dinastía nazarí de Granada*, in: Medievalismo 6 (1996), 183–189; B. Boloix Gallardo, *Mujer y poder en el reino nazarí de Granada: Fāṭima Bint al-Aḥmar. La perla central del collar de la dinastía* (*siglo XIV*), in: AEM 46 (2016), 269–300.

21   M.J. Rubiera Mata, *El arráez Abū Saᶜīd Faraŷ B. Ismāᶜīl B. Naṣr, gobernador de Málaga y epónimo de la segunda dinastía naṣrí de Granada*, in: BAEO 11 (1975), 127–133 (128); Boloix Gallardo, 2016, 283.

22   Rubiera Mata, 1996, 187.

23   Ibid. 187–188.

24   Ibid. 188; Boloix Gallardo, 2013, 252.

dedicated himself to the construction of the Madrassa, the new grain market (Alhóndiga Nueva), and in the Alhambra, the Palace of Comares, the Gates of Justice and the Seven Floors. Fatima was praised at her death as an exceptional woman by Ibn al-Jaṭīb, not often done for women of her time, and she was buried in the royal cemetery of the Alhambra.

Women did not always play such a visible role in the political context, but not an intangible one either. They had access to enough goods and wealth to allow them to exercise influence over the domestic sphere, as well as over political, social and cultural relations. In fact, it can be said that the women of the royal family seem to be associated with the ownership of a considerable number of goods of all kinds – often the urban or peri-urban area, such as water mills, fulling mills, inns, baths, shops, houses, farms, orchards, etc. These assets generally belonged to the royal treasury and other private ones, however, as we will explore below, the line that separated that was blurred and the difference was sometimes invaluable.

Indeed, we know that there was, on one hand, the royal patrimony, which passed from one king to another and that it was, theoretically, inalienable.[25] However, on one occasion Muley Hacén (1464–1482) claimed the assets of the royal crown that had been transferred by his predecessors. On the other hand, in the surrender signed by the Catholic Monarchs with the King of Granada, a distinction was made between the private assets of Boabdil and those of the royal treasury "those that the Kings of Granada had and possessed as Kings".[26]

The royal patrimony had been formed by the legacy of other dynasties, such as the Almohad, by the inheritance of the deceased without agnatic heir, by the revitalisation of dead lands (mawāt), by purchases and confiscations. It was made up of the best land, almost always close to the city, farms, orchards, meadows, salt mines and urban buildings, among other assets.[27] They could be sold under certain conditions, so that the buyer was obliged, in addition to paying the sale price, to provide the census with half the property.[28] The

---

25   AGS, Consejo Real, leg. 651–659, in: R.G. Peinado Santaella, *El patrimonio real nazarí y la exquisitez defraudadora de los principales castellanos*, in: id. (ed.), *Aristócratas nazaríes y principales castellanos*, Málaga 2008, 211–230 (215).

26   *Capitulación ajustada entre los Reyes Católicos y el último Rey de Granada Baaudili*, *CODOIN*, VIII, Madrid 1846, 411–420 (415–416).

27   A. Galán Sánchez / R.G. Peinado Santaella, *De la madīna musulmana al concejo mudéjar. Fiscalidad regia y fiscalidad concejil en la ciudad de Granada tras la conquista castellana*, in: D. Menjot / M. Sánchez Martínez (eds.), *Fiscalidad de Estado y fiscalidad municipal en los reinos hispánicos medievales*, Madrid 2006, 197–223.

28   AGS, Consejo Real, leg. 651–659.

transaction was recorded in the royal accounting books, so that these assets could be claimed by the principle of the inalienability of royal patrimony.

The main function of the royal treasury (*amlāk al-ŷānib, mustajlaṣ,* etc.)[29] was to ensure that the king had wealth independent of the treasury of taxes (*bayt al-māl*) and the treasury of *aḥbās* (*bayt al-māl al-muslimīn*). Despite these different financial entities being clearly well defined and managed, they were sometimes permeable. This means that, especially in times of crisis, the king could take assets from these other treasuries, and could also finance wars or pay public officials with the royal patrimony.[30]

With this wealth, the king did various things, all of them to keep him in power or to facilitate a possible escape from the throne and settle elsewhere in the event of an uprising. The royal treasury also helped him to win supporters in moments of crisis. Another function of this institution was to finance public offices that were sometimes also in the king's domestic service. This was not the usual way of subsidising state public officials, but possible, as they normally received part of the taxes they collected in their area as salary.[31] This is the case of the governors, who in addition to working in criminal justice, military activity and tax collection, also managed the royal properties, such that they are sometimes called butlers or servants, also as *nadir* (from Arabic *nāẓir*, supervisor).

Another essential objective of the royal treasury was to maintain the royal family and especially women, since they were continuously present as owners or possessors of these assets. Why are females often listed as the owners of real estate, some of which belonged to the royal house?

On one hand, these properties might have rightly corresponded to them as inheritance and dowry. However, the delivery of real estate to the women of the ruling family could also be a way of protecting them, raising their status, and thus facilitating marriage at a higher social level. We must remember that the dowry provided by the husband (*acidaque*), essential for the legality of the nuptial union, depended on the wife's social and personal characteristics.[32] On

---

29   E. Molina López, *El Mustajlaṣ andalusí (I) (s. VIII–XI)*, in: Revista del Centro de Estudios Histórico de Granada y su Reino 13/14 (1999/2000), 99–189; E. Molina López, *Más sobre el Mustajlaṣ nazarí*, in: C. Castillo Castillo / I. Cortés Peña / J.P. Monferrer Sala (eds.), *Estudios árabes dedicados a D. Luis Seco de Lucena (En el XXXV Aniversario de su muerte)*, Granada 1999, 107–118.

30   L. Seco de Lucena, *La administración central de los nazaríes*, in: Cuadernos de la Alhambra 10/11 (1974/1975), 21–26.

31   C. Trillo San José, *Agentes del Estado y mezquitas en el reino nazarí*, in: Historia, Instituciones, Documentos 34 (2007), 279–291.

32   A. Zomeño Rodríguez, *Donaciones matrimoniales y transmisión de propiedades inmuebles: estudio del contenido de la siyāqa y la nihla en al-Andalus*, in: M. Fierro / J.P. van Estaëvel /

the other hand, providing single women with income throughout their lives was a way of safeguarding their future. However, the king himself might have benefited from the dispersal of royal patrimony assets into female hands.

Women also fought to put their candidate on the throne and made use of their wealth during this campaign. An example is given by Ibn al-Jaṭīb about the government of Muḥammad V (1354–1359/1362–1391). This emir locked his paternal brother, Ismāᶜīl, mother and sisters up in the Alhambra and provided them with abundant income. This did not prevent that woman from motivating her son to take the throne, for which she used the wealth from the royal treasury that she had taken after the death of Yūsuf I and which was kept in her chamber. This allowed her to convince her son-in-law, the future Muḥammad VI, and a group of a hundred men to help her enthrone her scion as Ismāᶜīl II (1339–1360). So it appears in *al-Lamḥa*:

> "It happened that, when power came to him, he forced his brother Ismāᶜīl to remain in one of his father's palaces that were close to his, in a luxurious life and with abundant income. He made the mother of Ismāᶜīl live in it too, and his uterine sisters; on the same day of his father's death [Sultan Yūsuf] said lady seized the vast wealth, belonging to the royal treasury, which was deposited in her chamber, and found, with it, the way to intrigue in favour of her son Ismāᶜīl".[33]

The fact that the women received assets did not imply a loss for the royal treasury, since it was inalienable and the king could always recover it, although perhaps that was something exceptional. In addition, and due to the inheritance law, there was a circulation of assets within the royal family that sometimes benefited the emirs themselves. Thus, for example, from his sister Haxa and his homonymous aunt, Muley Hacén received several properties that they had in Otura and Arenales farm property, which he later passed to his children the Infantes of Granada, whom he had with Soraya.[34]

We also know that the manner in which these assets reached women was through purchases. Sometimes it was the king himself who would sell a princess some land or farms that had belonged to the royal patrimony. One questions whether these sales were a way of transferring assets from the royal

P. Cressier, *L'urbanisme dans l'occident musulman au moyen âge: aspects juridiques*, Madrid 2000, 75–100.

33 Ibn al-Jaṭīb, *Historia de los Reyes de la Alhambra. El resplandor de la luna llena (Al-Lamḥa al-badriyya)*. J.M. Casciaro (trans.), Granada 1988, 135.

34 AGS., Casas y Sitios Reales, leg. 10, fol. 200. J.E. López de Coca Castañer, *Granada en el siglo XV: las postrimerías nazaríes a la luz de la probanza de los infantes don Fernando y don Juan*, in: E. Cabrera (ed.), *Andalucía entre Oriente y Occidente (1236–1492). Actas del V Coloquio Internacional de Historia Medieval de Andalucía*, Córdoba 1988, 599–642.

treasury into the private hands of members of the ruling family itself. It was not, therefore, the usufruct of an asset but an authentic ownership through a sale. Curiously, to carry out this transaction, permission from the emir, as guarantor of the royal treasury, was required. These operations would make distinguishing the dynastic family's private assets from those that belonged to the royal patrimony and had been sold to private purchasers difficult.

An example of this is the Huete farmhouse, which belonged to the royal house.[35] In 1370, during the second reign of Muḥammad V (1354–1359/1362– 1391), the farmhouse is bought from the royal treasury by the emir's wife, Meriem, to be donated to her daughter Omalfata; the king gave his consent to both processes, the sale and the donation. Later, in 1492, King Boabdil authorised Princess Omalfata's sale of the Huete farmhouse to the mayor Juan de Haro, with everything belonging to the royal house. Despite the fact that the formality of referring to the real estate asset as officially royal patrimony is maintained, in practice, the transactions are carried out are completely private.

Another example is Nublo (Dār al-Nubluh), which existed within the royal patrimony during the reign of Yūsuf III (1408–1417); it was sold by Muley Hacén in the middle of raŷab 869 (1465) to the children he had with his first wife ʿĀʾiša, Abu Avdali Mahomad (Boabdil) and Avu Jajid (Abū Ḥaŷŷāŷ Yūsuf).[36]

There are more purchases of bazaar stores belonging to the royal crown by Muley Hacén for the children from his first marriage, Habil Hagix Yuçaf and Abdili Mahomad. It is then stated that the purchase price would be used by the king for the service of Muslims, which seems simply to be an excuse to mollify the consequences of the sale on the royal treasury. Similarly, Soraya, the second wife of Muley Hacén, buys part of the rights to an inheritance that belonged to the royal crown, and it is noted that she does this with her own money.[37]

According to the witnesses of the *Probanza de los Infantes de Granada* (1506) investigation, an audit that was carried out of the goods that could belong to them, that this emir handed over royal patrimony properties to both Soraya and

---

35   M. Espinar Moreno, *La alquería de Huete: desde Juan de Haro a Fernando de Zafra*, in: Estudios sobre Patrimonio, Cultura y Ciencias Medievales 23 (2021), 143–198.

36   C. Trillo San José, *El nublo, una propiedad de los infantes de Granada*, in: *Homenaje al profesor Fórneas Besteiro* 2, Granada 1994, 867–879 (877). We agree with this identification made by J.E. López de Coca Castañer, *Los infantes de Granada y sus descendientes (1492– 1605). La reivindicación de una herencia*, in: Baética 41 (2021), 13–48 (21).

37   A. Malpica Cuello / C. Trillo San José, *Los Infantes de Granada. Documentos árabes romanceados*, in: Revista del Centro de Estudios Históricos de Granada y su reino 6 (1992), 361–422 (382, 384, 391).

the children he had with her, Ṣaᶜd and Naṣr.[38] Once again, the line that separates the public from the private – the royal treasury from the private assets of the royal family – is extremely blurred. A witness, Hernando de Fez, who was a servant of Muley Hacén, in no uncertain terms states the problem between Muley Hacén and his brother El Zagal (1485–1486): "The cause of discord that occurred between the kings extended from how much the king inherited and gave to the said queen Lady Ysabel and to the said infantes, her children".[39] It is also said that Queen Soraya enjoyed these properties while her husband was alive, but that, when he died, her brother-in-law seized her and took possession of them. It seems that the claim they made on behalf of the king for them, was based on the idea that they had belonged to the royal treasury, and that it was legitimate to take them and return them.[40]

The women of the royal family appear as owners of land that they sell to third parties. It is probably land from the royal patrimony, but the transactions carried out with it transfer it to the buyers, so it loses that distinction. This is the case of infantas Haxa, Enamaxcoa and Omalfata, sisters of King Ṣaᶜd (1454–1455/1455–1462/1463–1464), who sold and bartered five irrigated plots in Daragedid, today Casanueva, about 20 km northwest of the capital, between 1460 and 1468.[41] Later, a Romanised Arabic document from 1477 states that these plots belong to the Royal House. At that time, *Daragedid*, or a part of it, was already in the hands of the governor Abulxaxe Yucaf Vencomixa, and it was exchanged for another possible royal estate, Huécar, which belonged to the merchant Abuljafar Amette, son of Farax Adamasquí.[42] Another piece of information that suggests a link between *Daragedid* and royal patrimony is that the *Falconer's Chronicle* mentions it belongs to the King and his family, along with other "villages",[43] although nothing is specifically said of Daralichet (*Daragedid*). In three purchases by these princesses, in 1460, the estates adjoin another royal property, Balaumín, and on one occasion with other land belonging to them. Balaumín (Varromín) is described as a "village that was very good, that belonged to the prince Abraham Almahul"[44] in the campaign against the

---

38   AGS, Casas y Sitios Reales, leg. 10, fol. 200.

39   Ibid.

40   Ibid.

41   C. Trillo San José, *La Vega de Granada a partir de documentación árabe romanceada inédita (1475–1494). Estudio, edición e índices*, Helsinki 2020, documents no. 5.12, no. 7.1, no. 7.2, no. 7.3 and no. 7.4.

42   C. Trillo San José, 2020, document 15.1.

43   In the future it will be necessary to specify whether it was the property of authentic villages (*alquerías*-village), *caseríos* (alquerías-estate) or *almunias* (recreational houses).

44   P. Carrillo de Huete, *Crónica del Halconero de Juan II*, J. de Mata Carriazo / R. Beltrán (eds.), Madrid 1946, 100.

Vega of 1431. It is quoted in the *Iḥāṭa* as an orchard and farmhouse (*ḥušš Būmal wa qaryat Balūmāl*).[45] Finally, in one of the sisters' deeds of sale, the King gives his consent, which would make more sense if it were royal treasury properties.

The sales and bartering that these princesses – sisters of Ṣaᶜd – carry out with these assets results in them becoming privately owned, not by members of the ruling family, especially since original purchasers then resell them. In all three deeds from 1460, the buyer is the Jew Muse Ben Alí Bendanén. In 1466, this same Jew bartered 244 marshes in payment for Vnque Alamel, in addition to 94 in Rachel, in exchange for 441 jugs of oil belonging to Abuzacaría Yahía, son of Habraén Alnayar. This means that much of the land this Jew acquired from the princesses ended up in the hands of Yahía Alnayar, grandson of Yūsuf IV Ibn al-Mawl. It also means that this relative of the governing dynasty was dedicated to the agricultural exploitation of olive groves and the commercialisation of oil. This is not surprising, as we know that the emirate royal family often exploited various means of production which used to belong to the royal patrimony, such as mills, oil mills, fulling mills, baths, shops, bakeries, etc., which in reality was part of the *hagüela*. In addition, the kings were interested in commercial activities, as well as market-oriented agricultural production, etc.[46]

On another occasion, a farmhouse property was a concession from the King who, once purchased, gave it to a woman in his family: Yūsuf I gave this Escóznar farmhouse to his sister Meriem in 1439.[47] The queens owned several villages, among many other assets. For example, the villages of Ánzola and Zujaira belonged to Zahr al-Riyāḍ, wife of Muḥammad IX the Left Handed;[48] the Huete farmhouse belonged to Omalfata, Boabdil's wife, the Beas farmhouse to the Moorish queens,[49] and the Arenales farmhouse to Abulhacén Ali's aunt, Onmalfata, among others.

Favouring women in the enjoyment and ownership of royal treasury assets could have been a strategy by the emirs to ensure they had access to resources that could help them remain in power or have a more comfortable and safe

45   Ibn al-Jaṭīb, *Al-Iḥāṭa fī ajbār Garnāṭa*, 'Inān (ed.), El Cairo 1973, 136; M.C. Jiménez Mata, *La Granada islámica. Contribución a su estudio geográfico-político-administrativo a través de la toponimia*, Granada 1990, 323.

46   A. Fábregas García, *La actividad comercial de los reyes nazaríes y su implicación con los representantes del gran comercio occidental a finales de la Edad Media*, in: Studia Histórica. Historia Medieval 25 (2007), 171–190.

47   A. Malpica Cuello, *Sobre el mundo agrícola nazarí: la alquería de Escóznar en el siglo XIV*, in: M. Reglero de la Fuente (ed.), *Poder y Sociedad en la Baja Edad Media Hispánica: estudios en homenaje al profesor Luis Vicente Díaz Martín* 2, Valladolid 2002, 1007–1024.

48   Carrillo Huete, 1946, 100.

49   AGS, Consejo Real, leg. 651–659.

exile. But, we must remember that the royal patrimony also served to support the family, as it had since Emiral and Caliphate times. Several witnesses of the aforementioned Probanza de los Infantes de Granada stated that Muley Hacén gave assets to his young children, those he had with Soraya, because they were poor. In addition, when Boabdil left, other deponents of the aforementioned evidence explained that, at the time of his departure, he showed concern for his half-siblings, Saʿd and Naṣr, and considered the possibility of leaving them assets not only to get them out of poverty them but also so that they could maintain their status as part of the royal family to which they belonged: "that the will of the king was to leave assets to the aforementioned, his brothers, so that they would no longer need and could maintain their honours".[50] Regardless of the veracity of these testimonies, it was clear that the deponents believed the members of the royal family were entitled to the royal patrimony.[51]

2   Women in Vega de Granada: Ownership and Autonomy

Thanks to the significant volume of recently published 15th century Romanised Arabic documents[52] we can shed light with new data on women and their properties in the peri-urban area of Granada. According to Shatzmiller, a woman could access various properties throughout her life, either as a dowry or inheritance. This legal right was sometimes hampered by family practices that effectively prevented women from disposing of their property, giving control to a male member of the family or her husband. However, the overwhelming presence of women in the Arabic and Romanised Arabic notarial documents from the Kingdom of Granada analysed also indicates that they had a fairly active economic and social role. We could even speculate that their right to own property allowed them certain independence within their marriage.[53] Also of note is that in most cases this Arabic and Romanised Arabic documentation is from the last century of the emirate, and is almost always referred to urban and peri-urban classes, which often form part of a public officials and economic elite.

---

50   AGS, Casas y Sitios Reales, leg. 10, fol. 200.
51   Ibid.
52   Trillo San José, 2020; C. Trillo San José / M. Espinar Moreno, *Hernando de Zafra, secretario de los Reyes Católicos: sus propiedades en Cubillas (Granada), según documentos árabes romanceados (1413–1493)*, Granada 2022.
53   Shatzmiller, 2007.

In the Arabic documentation published by Seco de Lucena, certain aspects can be appreciated in relation to the Naṣrid family and women[54] throughout the 15th century. The family might have been essentially nuclear, but this did not mean the extended family group was ignored. Polygamy was not detected, which would have been restricted to the court, but some examples of bigamy were. Endogamy was only identified in only a small part of the verified marriages. Divorce is documented on a single occasion, but it is symptomatic of an Islamic society, since it did not exist in the Christian one, or when it did it was repudiated. When their purpose is family, the assets from the *aḥbās* or foundations seemed to be mainly for women, perhaps with the aim of ensuring their upkeep or improving what they received as an inheritance. Woman appeared more as owners of urban personal property and real estate (houses, storage areas, orchards, etc.) than rural property, although the Arab documentation analysed is mainly focused on Madīna Garnāṭa and the surrounding areas.

As for the two collections of recently published Romanised Arabic documents to which we refer: they deal with the properties of Don Álvaro de Bazán in Vega de Granada, and with the assets of Hernando de Zafra and his family in the Cubillas River. The first text corpus,[55] that of Bazán, is made up of 22 documents, in which there are 80 texts, of which 65 are in Romanised Arabic, dating from 1457 to 1494. They were translated by Miçer Ambrosio Xarafí, notary public from Granada between 1508 and 1509.

The second collection of Romanised Arabic documents, that of Cubillas,[56] is made up of 43 documents, totalling 82 texts. Of these, 40 are in Romanised Arabic, and are dated between 1413 and 1493, while the Spanish documents date from 1495 to 1605. Some of them were translated into Spanish by Messer Ambrosio Xarafí and his son Bernaldino in the early years of the 16th century (1508, 1510 and 1512, etc.), but most were done by Alonso del Castillo in 1564, all of them public notaries.

Regarding the analysis of the first corpus, that of Bazán, we found that there were 65 Romanised Arabic deeds, 61 of which reflect different legal actions: 42 sales (68.85% of the total actions), 10 declarations of property ownership or inheritance (16.39%), eight barters (13.11%) and one guardianship (1.63%).

Regarding the family and social structure observed in these texts: the first point to note is that the names of the individuals almost always appear with

---

54 Seco de Lucena, 1961; L. Seco de Lucena, *Escrituras árabes de la Universidad de Granada*, in: Al-Andalus 35 (1970), 315–353; C. Trillo San José, *La familia en el reino nazarí de Granada (siglos XIII–XV)*, in: F.J. Lorenzo Pinar (ed.), *La familia en la historia*, Salamanca 2009, 41–62.

55 Trillo San José, 2020.

56 Trillo San José / Espinar Moreno, 2022.

nasab, and that there are almost no *nisba*-s depicting geographic location. This could be interpreted as kinship ties being given priority over other types of ties; it could also be a sign of low social mobility. However, it is not a definitive explanation, since in the Castilian documentation that dates from immediately after the conquest of Granada, a greater number of *nisba*-s depicting geographic location is detected, which could indicate an increase in migrations at the end of the emirate.

It also seems that the family is conjugal or nuclear, almost always made up of parents and three to five children, and the figure of the paternal grandmother sometimes appears. Some data suggest that in certain cases there is a relationship with collateral family members, such as uncles and nephews who have undivided land, perhaps the result of inheritance, and also two cousins who buy land together.

Other data show that endogamous marriages with the daughter of the paternal uncle (a female cousin or *bint al-ᶜamm*) from the traditional Islamic society is barely present. There are 12 marriages in the 61 texts analysed, of which only one is clearly endogamous. Thus, we see it in the case of an inheritance, on 14 Raŷab 899 (20 April 1494) in which the deceased person, the governor Abulcazín, son of Abdallá Venzalamón, left his three children, Maamar, Abdallà and Hamette, and his wife, who had the same *nasab*, Menibebiz, daughter of Mahomar Venzalamón as his heirs.[57]

This endogamy is probable on two other occasions: although the *nasab* of the husband and wife do not match exactly, we could conclude that they are similar, perhaps resulting from the Romanised translation. This is what occurred on 25 rabīᶜaṭ-ṭānī 897 (25 February 1492): the young man Aboadily Mahomad, son of Zead Ayar Zity, acted in a sale on behalf of his wife Axa, daughter of Aly Axinxity.[58] We saw something similar on 27 ŷumāda al-awwal 897 (27 March 1492) when Mahomar, son of Mizad Alchameque, who sold an asset to Don Álvaro de Bazán on behalf of his relatives and his mother, Haxa, daughter of Abrahén Venaxamén.[59]

Within this endogamy, one case of levirate has been identified, when after the male spouse died, a second marriage took place between the widow and the brother-in-law. Thus, the children of the first marriage become stepchildren to their paternal uncle, while the children of the second union are maternal brothers while simultaneously being paternal first cousins of the children from the first marriage. On 18 ŷumāda al-awwal 874 (25 November 1469) Zead

---

57   Trillo San José, 2020, document 18.2.
58   Trillo San José, 2020, document 17.3.
59   Trillo San José, 2020, document 20.5.

Velmuza passed away and his heirs were: his wife, Fatima, daughter of Amette Alandanjy, his mother, Axa, daughter of Axid Ven Farax, and his five brothers, who were sons of his uncle, Mahomar, brother of the deceased person's father.[60]

With the exception of these marriages, the rest of those verified, that is, 9 out of 12, were exogamous. However, although an exogamy of kinship was detected, there did exist endogamy in terms of social class. Thus, the matrimonial union of families with positions in the governing administration, such as governors and cadis [judges], and often also public scribes, is frequent. There are even some cases of matrimonial union between these public officials and the merchant classes. As an example, Talía Acood, daughter of the governor Amy Alax Guerit, marries the merchant Abulazín Aly Alaciaque.[61] This depicts the link between elites of different origin, one political and the other economic, which favours the consolidation of both classes.

Of the total of these aforementioned 61 Romanised Arabic documents by Bazán, women appear in just under a third (20, that is, 32.78%), which indicates a significant presence. Of these 20 deeds, on six occasions (30%) women acted as members of a family, while on 14 (70%) they are the principal actors of the transactions that are carried out. From this number we would have to remove the five deeds already mentioned in which the sisters of King Ṣaᶜd sell and barter their properties, through their servant and guardian, as they are royal family, making those deeds an exceptional situation. We will therefore analyse the remaining nine examples, where females act alone in the transaction. Of these nine cases, three of them are sales of women's assets, where the husband has given his consent. In two of those three cases, it is explicitly stated that it is because they are minors. The other six cases are documents: confirming the females' properties; where the females appear as guardians or representatives of family members who are minors, such as nieces; or where the females act alone, such as with an elderly woman who wants to sell.

The second corpus, the one referring to the River Cubillas, contains 40 Romanised Arabic texts, and in more than half, specifically 22, there are women. Of these 22, they appear with men to whom they are related or as part of a family group in three cases; while in the remaining 19, they are the principal actor, almost always sole actor, although sometimes accompanied by other women in the family.

Four of these deeds are about the partition of a house on the farmhouse property of Cubillas between mother and daughter, including the delimitation

---

60   Trillo San José, 2020, document 5.8.
61   Trillo San José, 2020, document 7.6.

of the houses, the provisional and final partition and its implementation.[62] This sheds light on the need to live in different houses – even though they are adjacent – in adulthood.

Two other texts deal with the same transaction. They refer to a transfer of a piece of land in Cubillas made by a woman in favour of her son. And the final two also refer to the same activity, which is the sale that a woman makes of an orchard to her niece, the daughter of her brother in the same locality.

As in the previous case of Don Álvaro de Bazán's documents, those of Cubillas largely refer to a public official elite, generally governors and marshals and their families. One aspect that we note is that there is significant endogamy between these actors, on three levels. First, there is an inheritance of the role within the family, such that the governor's sons usually take the same position when their father passes away. Sometimes there is no correspondence between the same position from parents to children, so that one might be a marshal and the other a governor, but they all usually belong to the group of State public officials. On the second level, there is a matrimonial endogamy within this public official elite. And the third level is that economic transactions, i.e., sales, donations, etc. take place within this social class.

A very clear example of this matrimonial endogamy among the civil servant class can be seen in the family of Fátima Abengarrón. Fátima was the daughter of the governor Abilhageg Yuçuf, son of Abdi Alrrahmén Avengarrón, who was married to her mother, Meriem, daughter of the marshal Abilhacén, daughter of Oveyt el Vacar. Fátima Avengarrón contracted a first marriage with the also governor Abu Abdelehí Mohamad, son of Mohamad Aventahir, and they had a daughter Haxa and son, who was the governor Abu Abdelehí Mohamad. In her second marriage, Fátima Avengarrón married the governor Abu Abdilehí Mohamad, son of Zeminín, who was also named a marshal. The first husband of Fátima Avengarrón, the governor Aben Tahir, married Fátima, daughter of Hazén Benobeid and had another child, with the same name as the one already mentioned as his and Fátima Abengarrón's son, who was the marshal Abi Abdilehí Muhamad, son of Muhamad Abentaher. Fátima Avengarrón's mother was from the Benobeid family.

Finally, of the 19 transactions carried out by single women, of which we can identify 14 different operations, all of them, except in one case, occur within this social class of emirate administration positions. They were transfers to children, sales, dowries and inheritances.

Of these, a dowry that Umalfathe receives from her father, the governor Abdiabdilehí Tahir in Cubillas, is of note. It is a house, land, cultivated and

---

62   Trillo San José / Espinar Moreno, 2022, documents 28, 29, 31.2, 31.4.

calm lands and other similar unspecified things. It was possibly this same dowry that the protagonist sells to Ms Leonor de Torres, in 1492, for 90 ducats of silver.[63]

The second relevant example is that of the aforementioned Fatima, daughter of the governor Avengarrón,[64] symptomatic of the autonomy of some women of this social class and is also very detailed in that we know their assets and how they were disposed. Thus there is a first document of the constitution of a legacy for the poor in general and for various women around them, among some other maids. We also found a valuation of their assets, which include five irrigated farms, 2/7ths of some land, a house in Cubillas, as well as another house in the old Alcazaba of Granada, household items, jewellery and a black slave. Thirdly, there is a distribution of properties among her relatives, who are her parents, her children and her husband, following the Māliki rules of inheritance.[65] As for the type of property, her house in the Alcazaba neighbourhood of Granada is worth more than twice as much as the rural properties in the Cubillas farmhouse. Furthermore, movable property, jewellery and slaves have a value (37,386 osorí silver ducats[66]) that is much higher than real estate (27,120 osorí silver ducats). This is not strange, since they include, in addition to gold jewellery and belongings often made of noble materials (silks, wool, leather, etc.), a slave and what the woman contributed at the time as a dowry. The total value of Fátima's estate is 64,506 osorí silver ducats.

In addition to owning this set of valuable real estate and assets, as well as a slave and several maids, we must note that Fatima was probably able to dispose of them with certain autonomy. This is seen in the creation of a habiz for the benefit of the poor in general and other collateral for their servants, a female slave and relatives, thereby showing some sensitivity to the situation of the women around them. Finally, her inheritance is divided between her parents and her son and daughter, following the Māliki rules of inheritance, which we know privilege males over females in the same degree of kinship. Even in later times, in the Mudejar stage, inheritances are governed by Māliki

---

63 Trillo San José / Espinar Moreno, documents 17.1 and 17.2.

64 C. Trillo San José, *Fátima, hija del alcaide Avengarrón: sus propiedades en Cubillas y Granada, según documentos árabes romanceados inéditos (1465–1466)*, in: Espacio, Tiempo y Forma, serie III, Historia Medieval 35 (2022), 651–678.

65 D. Santillana, *Istituzioni di diritto musulmano malichita con riguardo anche al sistema sciafiita* 2, Roma 1938, 514–522.

66 M. Gaspar Remiro, *Escrituras árabes de Granada*, Granada 1907, 9; Trillo San José / Espinar Moreno, 2022, document 27.

rules, as we know what happened in the bishopric of Malaga (1497).[67] In such a legal context, when there are agnates, that is, men through the male line, up to the third degree of kinship, the King does not receive anything, while he does have the right to inheritance when there are daughters or mother's brothers. Likewise, men can get twice as much as women in the same degree of kinship, as occurs for the son compared to the daughter, and the widower with respect to the widow.

From all this we can conclude that there is significant information about the elites of the Naṣrid emirate in the recently published Arabic and Romanised Arabic documentation that has been preserved from the ancient kingdom of Granada. Within these documentary sources, women have quite a presence, sometimes carrying out economic activities as part of a family group, but more often acting alone. There does seem to be marital control of these economic activities when they are young, but we find many cases where they act on their own, which could be associated with greater maturity and autonomy.

The endogamy that is recorded refers to several areas. Thus, there is a tendency to retain the position or a certain position in the family group, so that almost all children inherit it from their parents. A marriage exogamy is documented from a kinship perspective, but a socio-economic class endogamy prevails. Thus, nuptial links are generated among this elite, which could mean that the clan society, strong in other times in al-Andalus, is weak towards the end of the Naṣrid emirate, or which is equivalent to assuming that the economic differences are notable. This makes marriage between equals more desirable than that traditionally performed with paternal relatives. Lastly, this elite tends to exchange goods through purchase, barter, donation or inheritance, such that this social class is the main actor in the Romanised Arabic documents analysed.

---

67   M.A. Ladero Quesada, *El duro fisco de los emires*, in: Cuadernos de Historia 3 (1969), 321–334 (331–333).

List of Contributors

Mattia C. Chiriatti

PhD (2016, University of Barcelona). He is a Lecturer in Ancient History at the University of Granada. In 2019, he was awarded the ISHR prize for his project "Los *basilikoí lógoi* de Gregorio de Nisa". He specialises in the study of the Late imperial speeches, the history of Late Antiquity and Early Byzantium and the evolution of female power during this time. Recently he has edited the following volumes on this topic: M.C. Chiriatti / M. Vallejo Girvés (eds.), *Riflessi di porpora. Declinazioni di potere femminile tra Roma, Bisanzio e l'Occidente Medievale*, Spoleto 2023; M.C. Chiriatti, *Female Power and its Propaganda*, in: M. Vinzent / M.C. Chiriatti / D. Olkinuora (eds.), *Studia Patristica. Vol. CXXX – Papers presented at the Eighteenth International Conference on Patristic Studies held in Oxford 2019, volume 27: From the Fifth Century Onwards (Latin Writers)*; *Female Power and its Propaganda; Theologizing Performance in the Byzantine Tradition; Nachleben*, Leuven / Paris / Bristol (CT) 2021; M.C. Chiriatti / R. Villegas Marín (eds.), *Mujeres imperiales, mujeres reales. Representaciones públicas y representaciones del poder en la Antigüedad tardía y Bizancio*, Paderborn 2021.

María Mercedes Delgado Pérez

PhD (2011, University of Seville). She is a Senior Lecturer in Arabic Language and Literature at the University of Seville. In 2003, she was awarded the Ciudad de Sevilla 2003 research prize for her work *Hernando Colón: decurso histórico de un hombre y su biblioteca*. She specialises in the study and editing of an unpublished and complete manuscript of the *Historia de los reyes moros de Granada*, by the chronicler and interpreter of Muhammad XI, sultan of Grenade, Hernando de Baeza. The discovery has been published, under the title "A Newly Discovered Manuscript of the *Historia de los reyes moros de Granada* by Hernando de Baeza", *Manuscript Studies*, 2/2, 2017, 540–567. She discovered another complete and unpublished manuscript of this chronicle in an erroneously catalogued codex of the Royal Library of Madrid, which she made public in the article "Certezas e hipótesis sobre el final de la *crónica granadina* de Hernando de Baeza" *Anaquel de Estudios Árabes* 29 (2018), 33–62). She is a member of the International Research Project: *HI(s)POCRENE: The horse and the interpreter in Iberian and Hispanic literatures* (LR: Professor Marie-Eugénie Kaufmant, University of Caen, ERLIS, France) and Lead Researcher of the HUM-1093 group (*History, Civilisation and Arab-Islamic Culture*), in the Arabic and Islamic Studies Department, Faculty of Language and Literature, University of Seville.

Sylvie Duval

PhD (2012, Universities of Lyon and Florence). She is an Associate Professor of Medieval History at the *Alma Mater* University of Bologna. She specialises in the history of religious women (non-cloistered nuns: beguines, penitents, beatas) and female juridical and economical agency in medieval societies, pragmatic literacy. This research project was funded by the European Union with an MSCA Individual Fellowship (Heinrich-Heine-University Düsseldorf, 2021–2022). In parallel, she is co-director of the *Sorores* project on the history of non-cloistered nuns. In this, she researches the place of female religious communities in medieval urban societies, from the 9th to the 15th century, specifically through the example of the cities of Lyon and Clermont. Among her publications: *Comme des anges sur terre. Les moniales dominicaines*, 1385–1461 (Rome, 2015).

Álvaro Ibáñez Chacón

PhD (2014, University of Malaga). He is a Senior Lecturer in Greek Language and Literature at the University of Granada. His research focuses on Graeco-Roman and Byzantine literature, especially on mythography, paradoxography and hagiography, with a particular interest in the transmission of the texts and the Photian milieu. His most recent publications on these topics are: *Parallela minora Graeco-Byzantina. Las traducciones de Guarino de Verona y Constantino Láscaris* (Granada, Centro de Estudios Bizantinos, Neogriegos y Chipriotas, 2019); "Uno σχεδάριον, due rielaborazioni: Fozio *Epist.* 94 e *Bibl.* 186, 131b.32–40", *Jahrbuch der Österreichischen Byzantinistik* 71 (2021), 259–268; "Un escolio en el Vat. Gr. 1340 y la transmisión de la Καινὴ ἱστορία de Tolomeo Queno", *Revue d'Histoire des Textes* 17 (2022), 145–170; "Rumores (in)fundados en torno a la emperatriz Procopia", in M.C. Chiriatti – M. Vallejo-Girvés (eds.), *Riflessi di porpora. Declinazioni di potere femminile tra Roma, Bisanzio e l'Occidente Medievale*, (Spoleto, CISAM, 2023, pp. 205–213).

Antonella Liuzzo Scorpo

PhD (2009, University of Exeter). She is an Associate Professor of Medieval History at the University of Lincoln (UK), the President of the Society for the Medieval Mediterranean and a Fellow of the Royal Historical Society. She specialises in medieval Iberian social and cultural history, with a particular focus on 13th century Castile and Aragon. Her areas of research include the study of medieval friendship; social communication, and cultural networks; trust and diplomacy; transcultural collaborations; and the History of Emotions. Her publications include the monograph *Friendship in Medieval Iberia: Historical,*

Legal and Literary Perspectives (Ashgate 2014, paperback Routledge 2020) and the edited volume *A Plural Peninsula: Studies in Honour of Prof. Simon Barton* (Brill, 2023).

María Martínez Martínez

She is a Professor of Medieval History at the University of Murcia. Her research contributions encompass over a dozen books and a hundred articles, and her research topics include clothing and fashion, women and border societies, the culture of water, the daily life of Andalusian Murcia, the representation of power and the Ordinances of cultivated land and rural areas. She has taught courses and master's degrees classes at various Universities (Oviedo, Granada, Tetouan, Bologna and Mexico). She has recently published "Entre la historia y la novela: *Sidi*, de Arturo Pérez-Reverte" (Castellón, 2021).

Clelia Martínez Maza

She is a Professor of Ancient History at the University of Malaga. Her main research lines are: Religions in Late Antiquity with a particular interest in the relationship between Christianity and pre-Christian religions, Christianisation of the Roman Empire, and Women's Religious Life in Antiquity. She has published more than 100 papers in national and international publishers of recognised impact. From the beginning of her researcher activity, she has led and/ or participated in many competitive research projects. Furthermore, she is the Lead Researcher of the DINORAMA (Dynamism and Religious Innovation in the Ancient World) investigation group. She is currently working on the Christianisation of rural areas focusing on its own idiosyncrasy, the importance of space morphology, and the variety of agents who dynamically interact in rural landscapes.

Diana Pelaz Flores

PhD (2015, University of Valladolid). She is a Senior Lecturer in Medieval History at the University of Santiago de Compostela. She specialises in queenship and royal studies, having publishing extensively in this area, particularly related to the Castilian context within the Iberian Peninsula (14th–15th centuries). She is the author of four monographies related to the Queen's Household in the Late Middle Ages (*La Casa de la reina en la Corona de Castilla* [*1418–1496*], 2017), the Queen Lands and the female agency (*Poder y Representación de la Reina en la Corona de Castilla* [*1418–1496*], 2017 and *Reinas Consortes. Las reinas de Castilla en la Edad Media, ss.* XI–XV, 2017), and the symbolic use of water in the courtly space (*Rituales Líquidos. El significado del agua en el ceremonial de la corte de*

Castilla (*ss. XIV–XV*), 2017). She is currently the Lead Researcher of a project focused on the cultural, politics, and economic exchanges between Iberian and European courts through royal women and Comparative History. She is also editing a new volume about the Queens'Lands in the Iberian Peninsula from a comparative perspective (2024).

Pablo Poveda Arias

PhD (2018, University of Salamanca). He is a Lecturer in Ancient History at the University of Valladolid. His research interests focus on Late Antique Iberia and Gaul. His research is mainly devoted to the study of the dynamics of power in the Merovingian and Visigothic kingdoms, both in the secular and ecclesiastical contexts. Likewise, in relation to the latter, his studies have also led him to approach the religious dynamics that took place particularly in Visigothic Iberia.

Jordina Sales-Carbonell

PhD (2011, University of Barcelona). She is a Reader in Medieval History at the University of Barcelona, where she is also a researcher. Awarded with the *Josep Barberà i Farràs* 2011 prize (*Societat Catalana d'Arqueologia*), she specialises History and Archaeology of Late Antiquity, with a special focus on the implementation of the first Christianity in the Western part of the Empire, as well as the genesis and role of Christian constructions within the framework of Roman entertainment buildings. She has developed interpretive models to locate and identify primitive monasteries (*In unum estis congregati: arqueologia del primer monacat cristià*, Barcelona 2018) and Christian buildings in Hispania (*Las construcciones cristianas de la Tarraconensis durante la Antigüedad Tardía: Topografía, arqueología e Historia*, Barcelona 2012).

Marta Sancho i Planas

She is a Professor of Medieval History and Medieval Archaeology at the University of Barcelona and member of the Institute for Research in Medieval Cultures (IRCVM). She specialises in archaeological sources for the study of Medieval History, with a special focus on productive technology: mining and steel, the exploitation of forest resources, water uses, livestock and agriculture in mountain areas. She researches the transition centuries between Late Antiquity and the Early and Late Middle Ages, especially in mountain areas and in aspects such as the construction of the mountain landscape, forms of habitat and occupation of the territory, communication routes, early mountain monasticism, power structures and fortresses prior to the 11th century.

Elena Tinas Uceda

MA in History (University of Granada 2023), MA in Teacher Training and Education (University of Granada 2023), she specialises in the studies of the evolution of the female power and its main protagonists in Late Antiquity and Byzantium. She is also the author of "Irene of Athens: the first basileus" (*Estudios Bizantinos* 12, in press).

Carmen Trillo San José

Carmen Trillo San José is a Professor of Medieval History at the University of Granada. Her specialisation lies in the late period of Islamic rule and the Castilian changes following the conquest of the Kingdom of Granada during the 15th and 16th centuries. Within this time frame, she has addressed topics such as territorial organisation, political landscape, and water management. She has edited and studied many Romance Arabic documents from the late 15th century, including: *La Vega de Granada from unreleased Romance Arabic documentation (1457–1494)* (2020), and *Hernando de Zafra, secretary of the Catholic Monarchs: his properties in Cubillas, according to Romance Arabic documents (1413–1493)* (2022, with Manuel Espinar). She has also focused her research on the study of elites, women, and family life during the Nasrid era: *Almunias, the estates of the elites in the Islamic West* (2018, with Julio Navarro), *Women, family and lineage in the Middle Ages* (2004), and more recently, "The Nasrid princesses, sisters of King Sad" (2023).